LAST MAN

2

The Royal Cup

Balak + Sanlauille + Uiuès

:01
First Second
New York

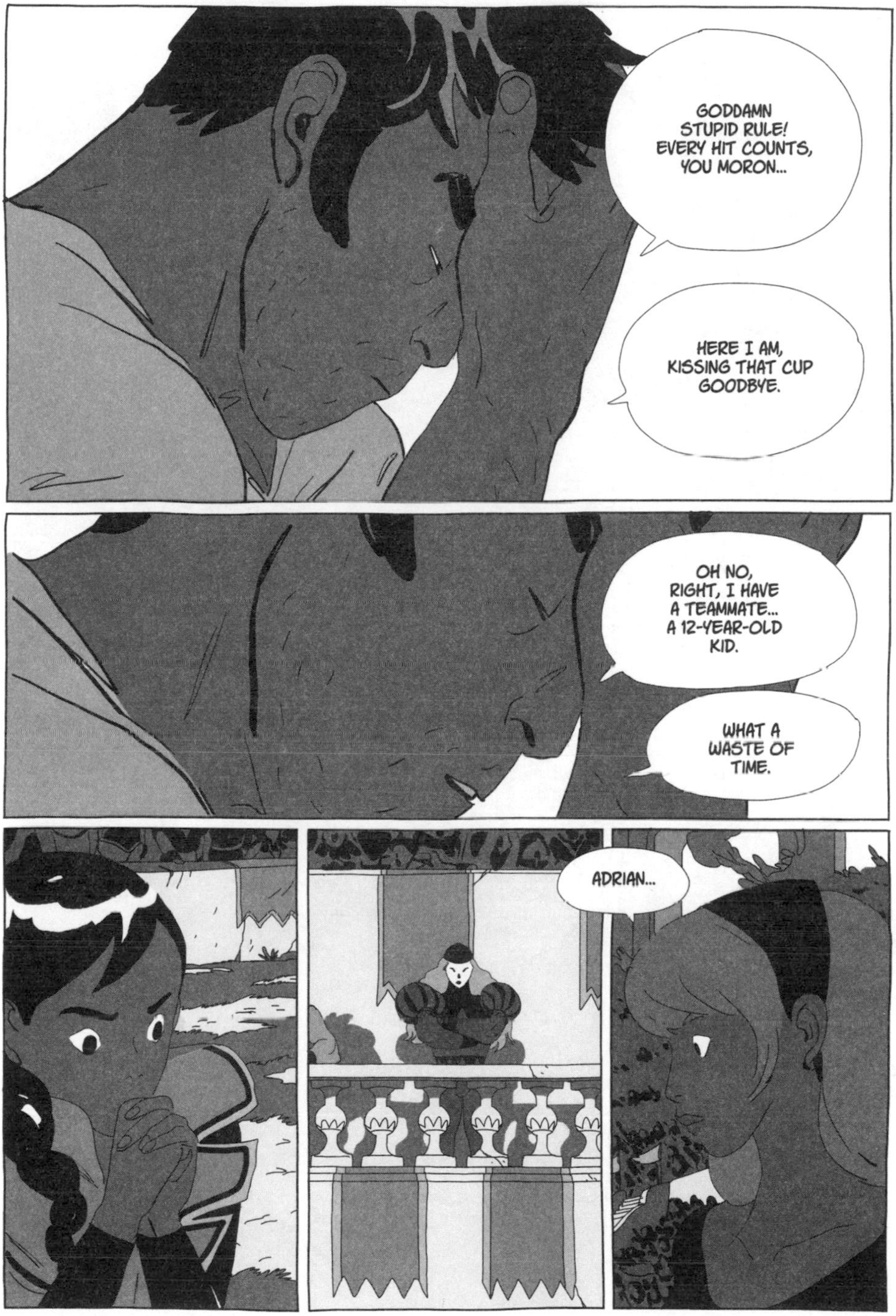
GODDAMN STUPID RULE! EVERY HIT COUNTS, YOU MORON...
HERE I AM, KISSING THAT CUP GOODBYE.
OH NO, RIGHT, I HAVE A TEAMMATE... A 12-YEAR-OLD KID.
WHAT A WASTE OF TIME.
ADRIAN...

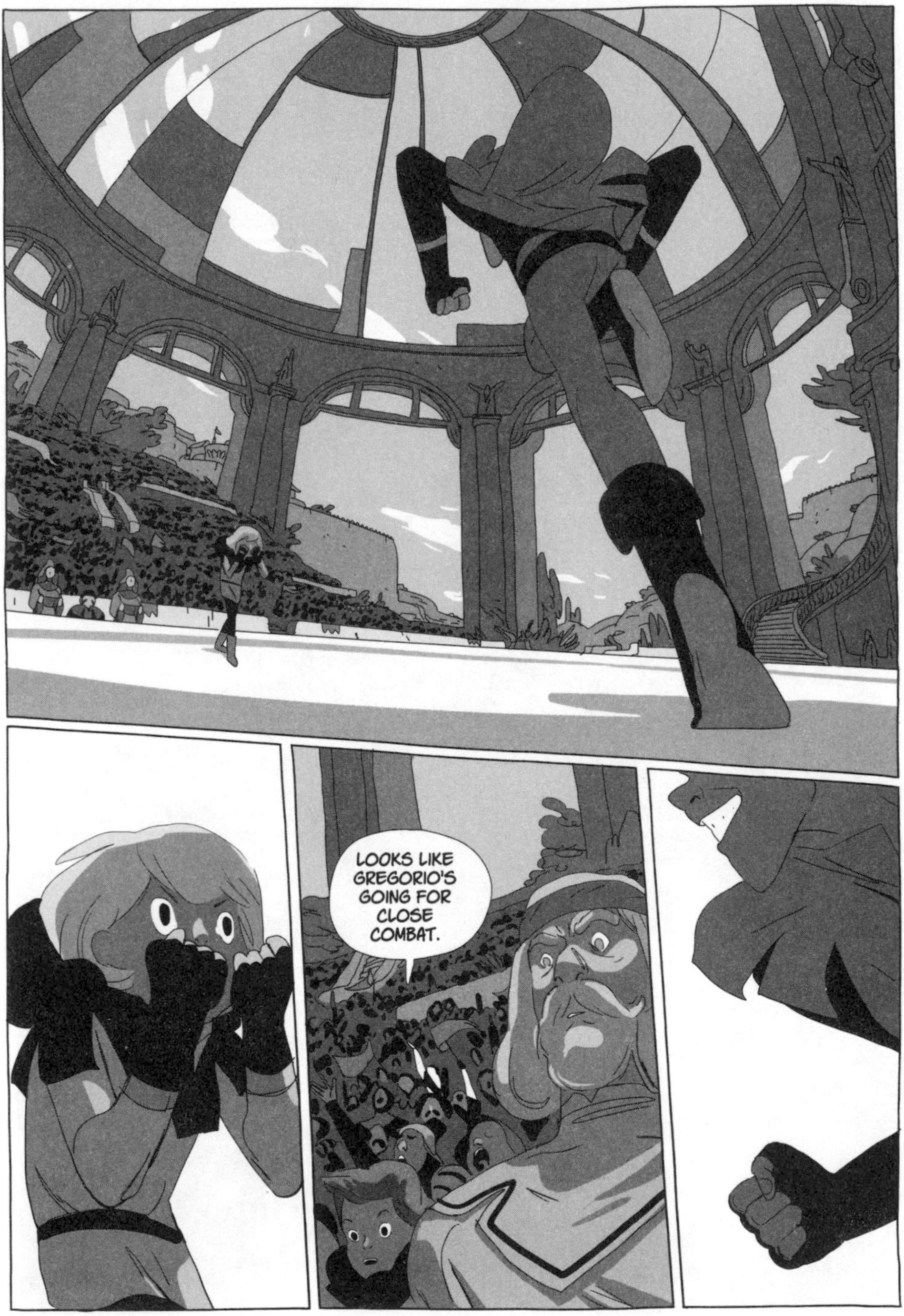
LOOKS LIKE GREGORIO'S GOING FOR CLOSE COMBAT.

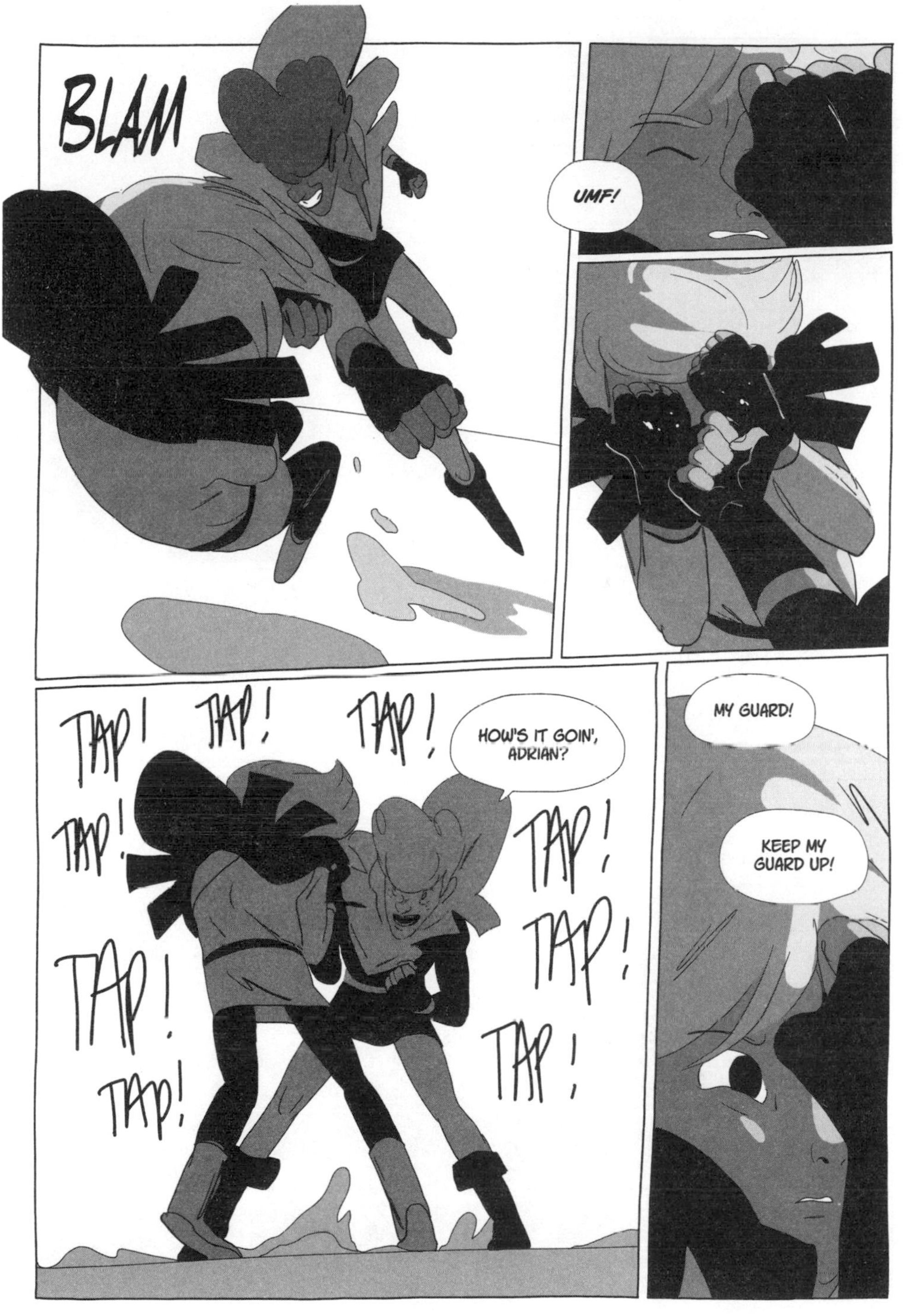
BLAM
UMF!
TAP! TAP! TAP!
TAP!
TAP!
TAP!
HOW'S IT GOIN', ADRIAN?
TAP!
TAP!
TAP!
MY GUARD!
KEEP MY GUARD UP!

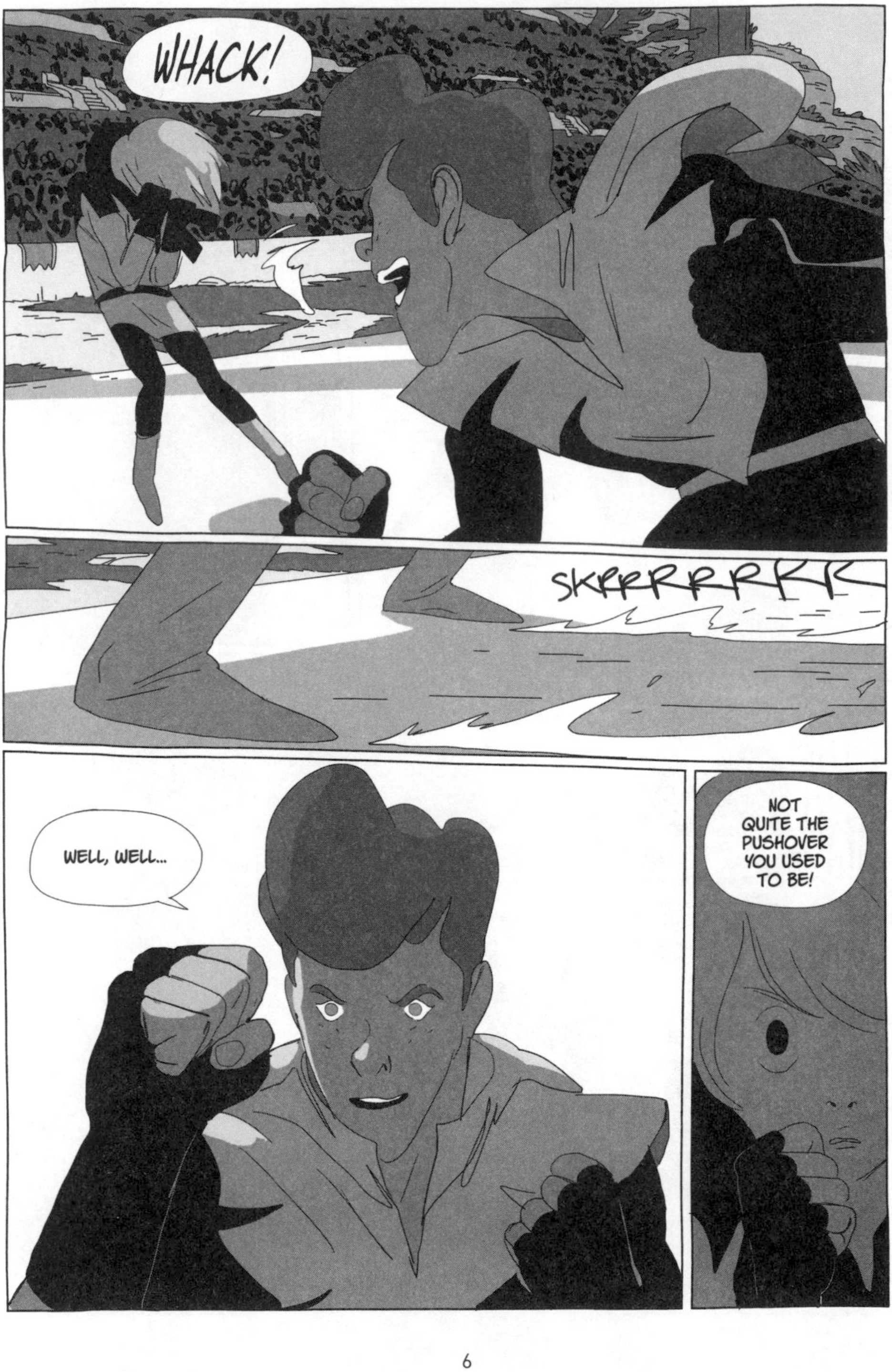
WHACK!
SKRRRRRRRK
WELL, WELL...
NOT QUITE THE PUSHOVER YOU USED TO BE!

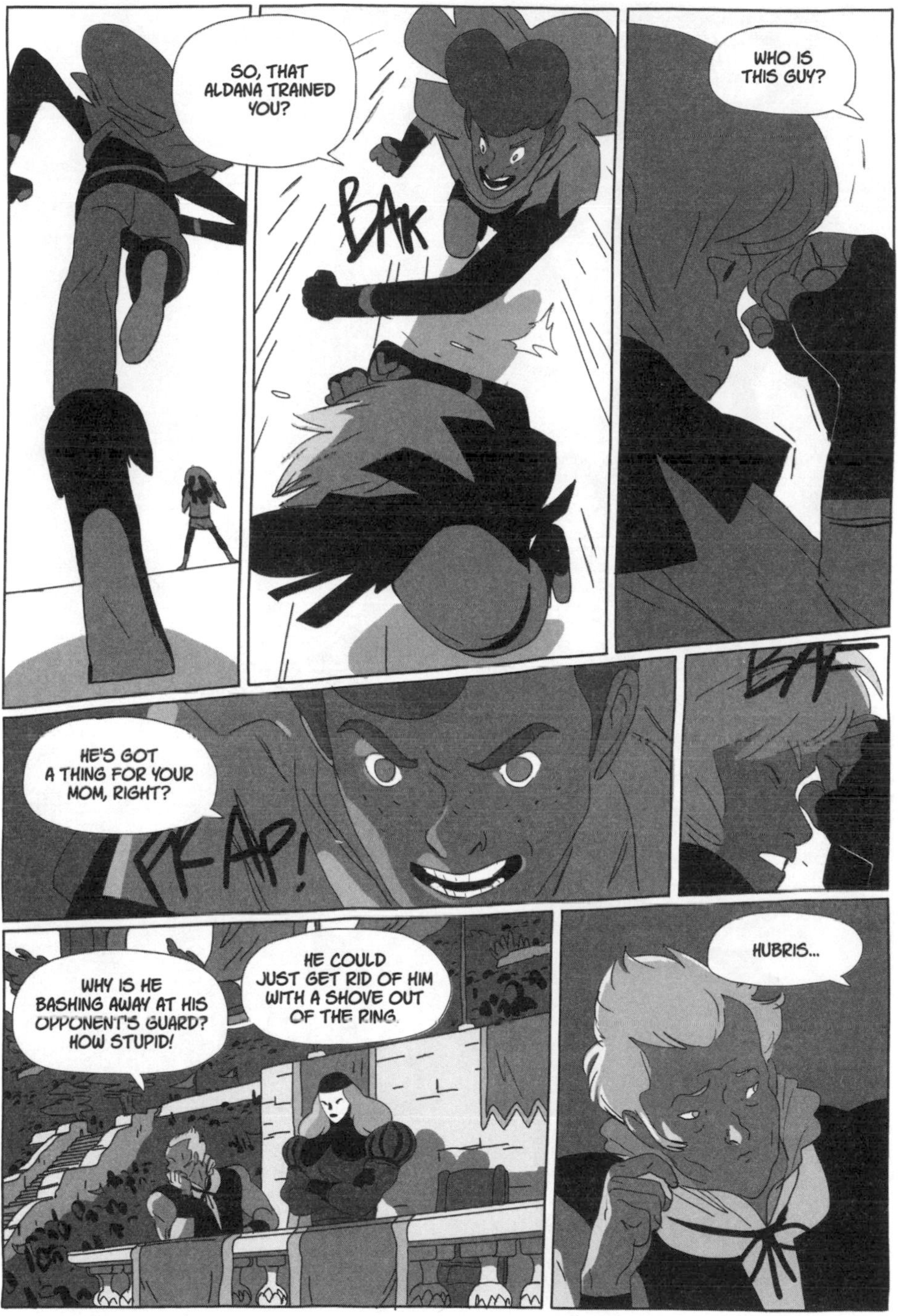
SO, THAT ALDANA TRAINED YOU?
BAK
WHO IS THIS GUY?
HE'S GOT A THING FOR YOUR MOM, RIGHT?
KRAP!
WHY IS HE BASHING AWAY AT HIS OPPONENT'S GUARD? HOW STUPID!
HE COULD JUST GET RID OF HIM WITH A SHOVE OUT OF THE RING.
HUBRIS...

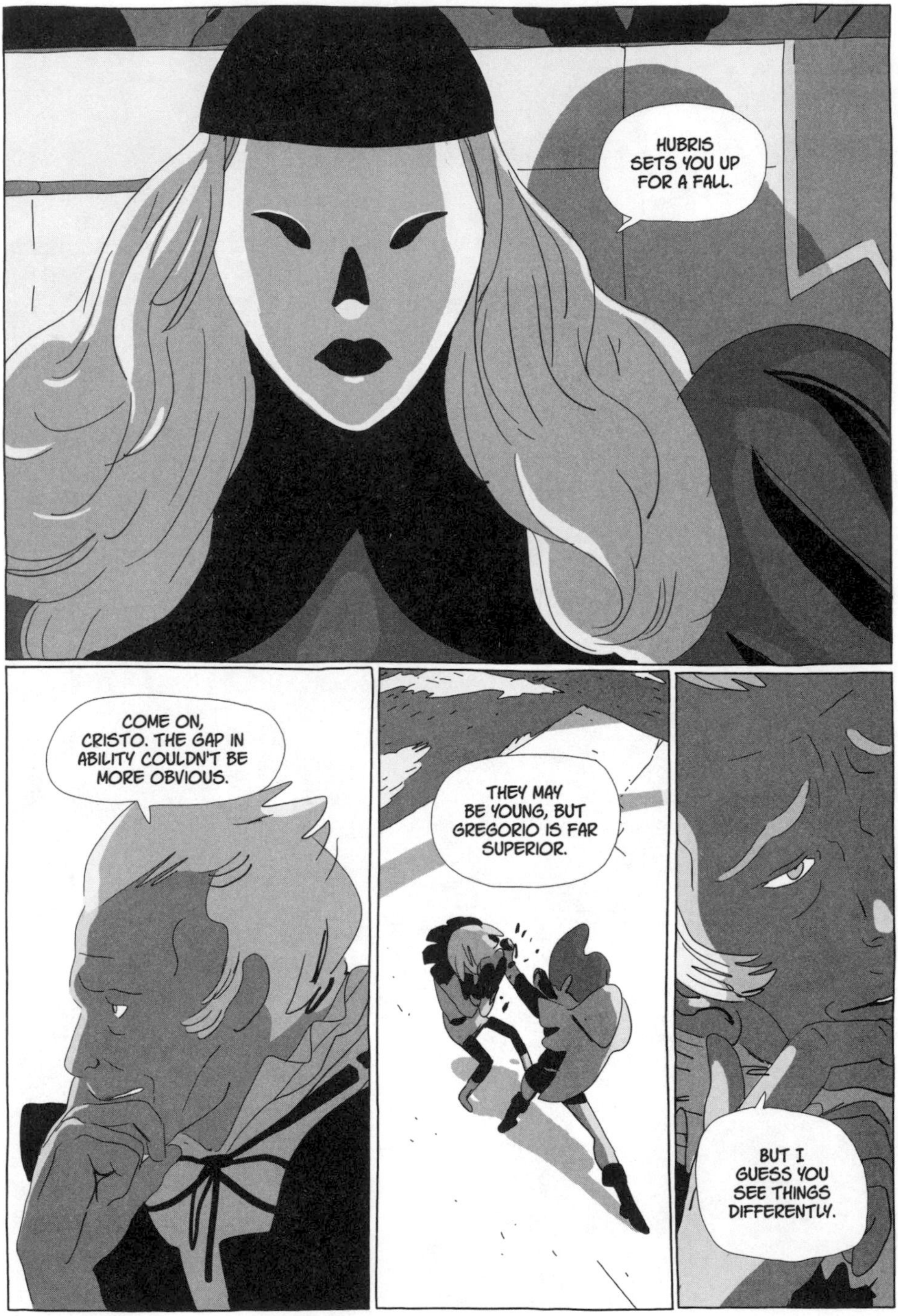
HUBRIS SETS YOU UP FOR A FALL.
COME ON, CRISTO. THE GAP IN ABILITY COULDN'T BE MORE OBVIOUS.
THEY MAY BE YOUNG, BUT GREGORIO IS FAR SUPERIOR.
BUT I GUESS YOU SEE THINGS DIFFERENTLY.

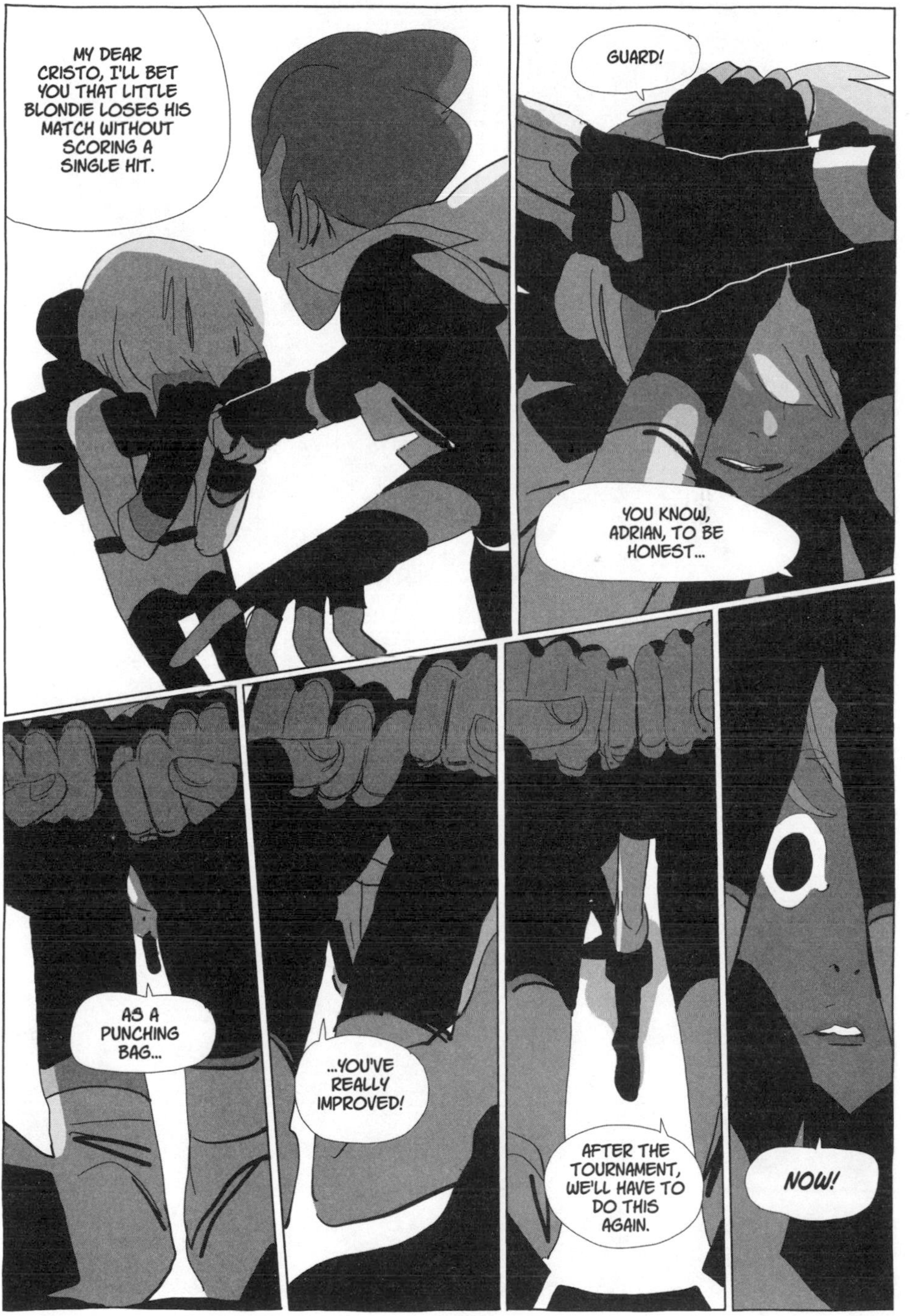
MY DEAR CRISTO, I'LL BET YOU THAT LITTLE BLONDIE LOSES HIS MATCH WITHOUT SCORING A SINGLE HIT.
GUARD!
YOU KNOW, ADRIAN, TO BE HONEST...
AS A PUNCHING BAG...
...YOU'VE REALLY IMPROVED!
AFTER THE TOURNAMENT, WE'LL HAVE TO DO THIS AGAIN.
NOW!

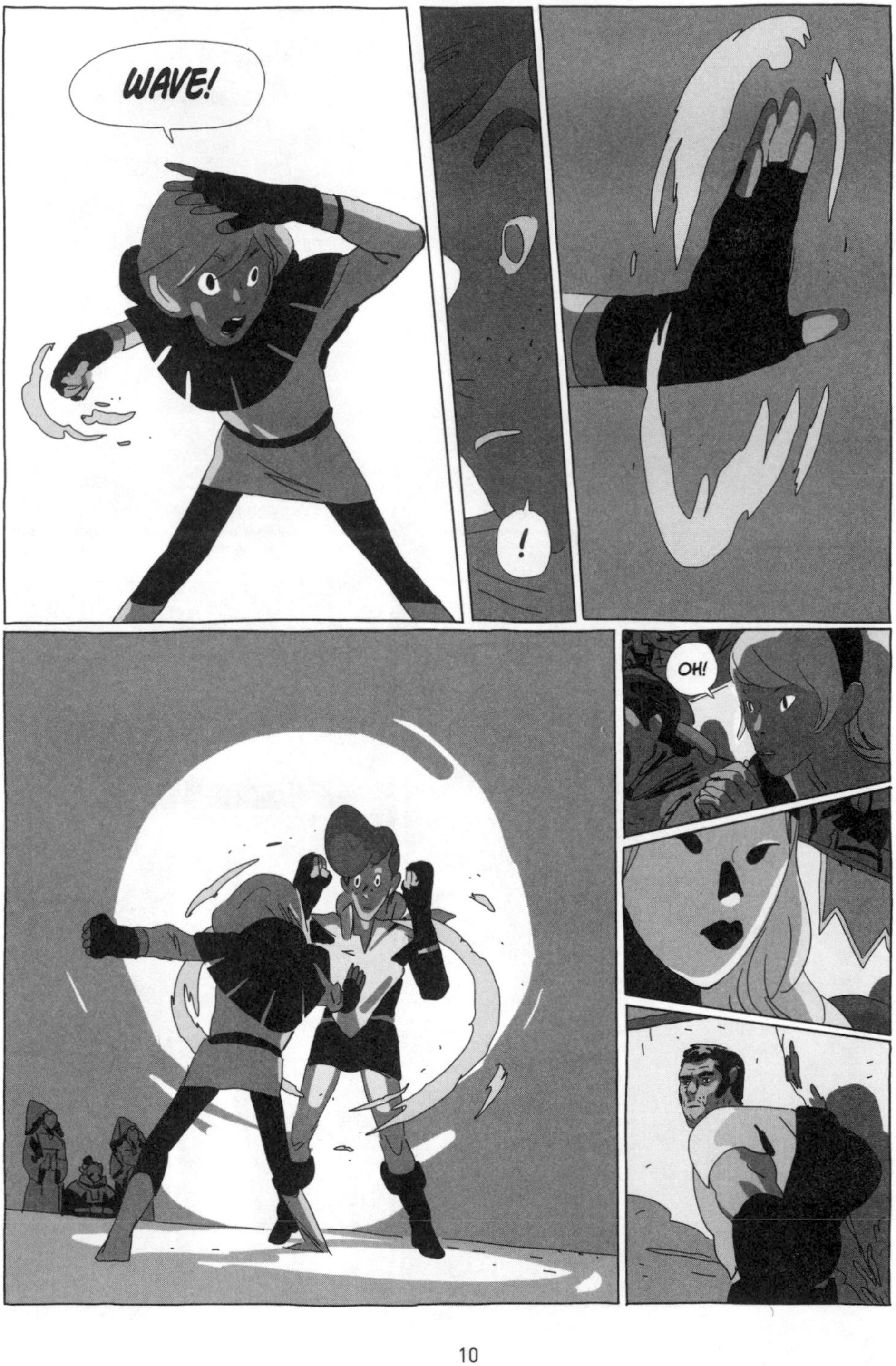
WAVE!
!
OH!

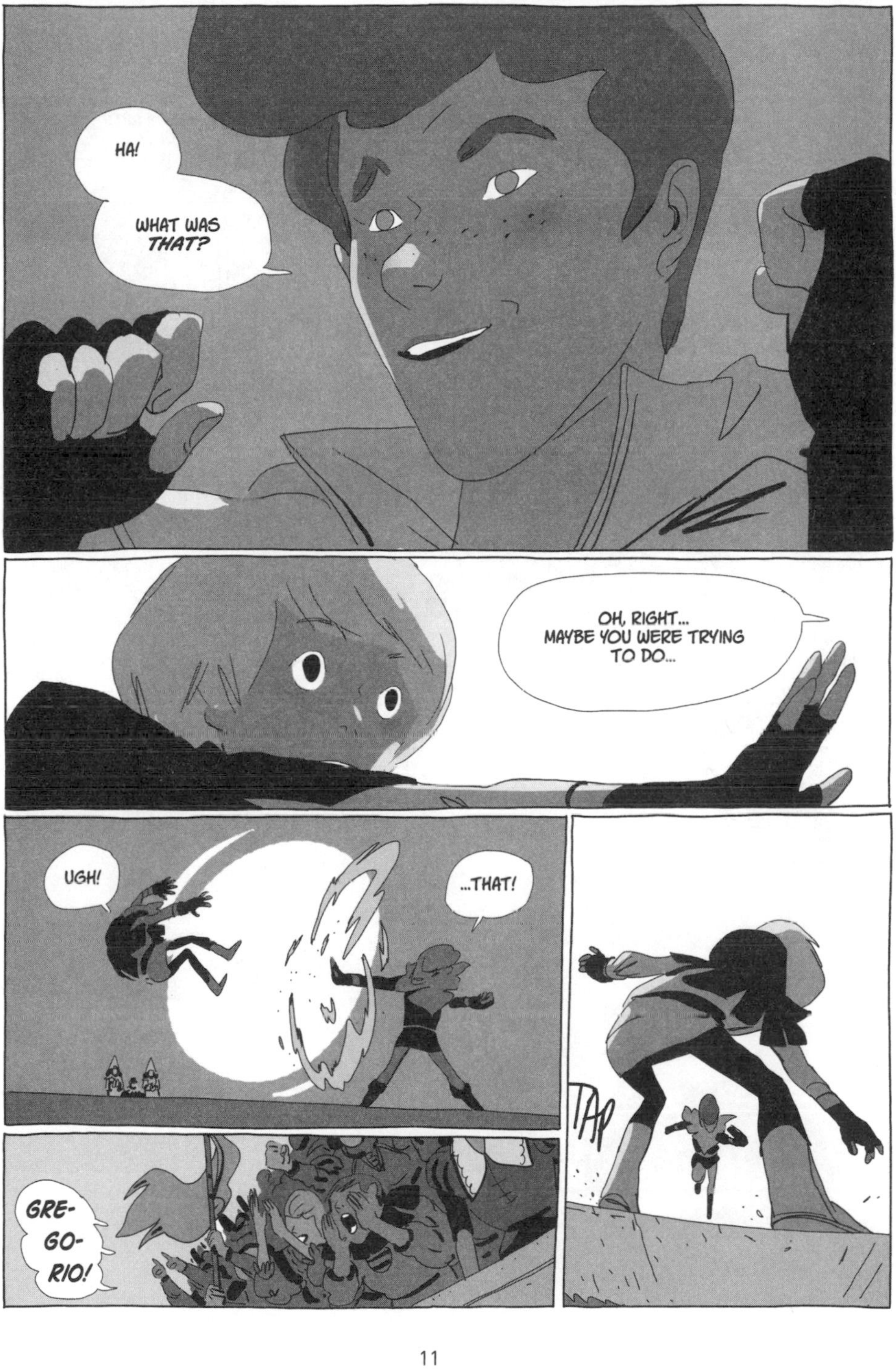
HA!
WHAT WAS THAT?
OH, RIGHT... MAYBE YOU WERE TRYING TO DO...
UGH!
...THAT!
TAP
GRE-GO-RIO!

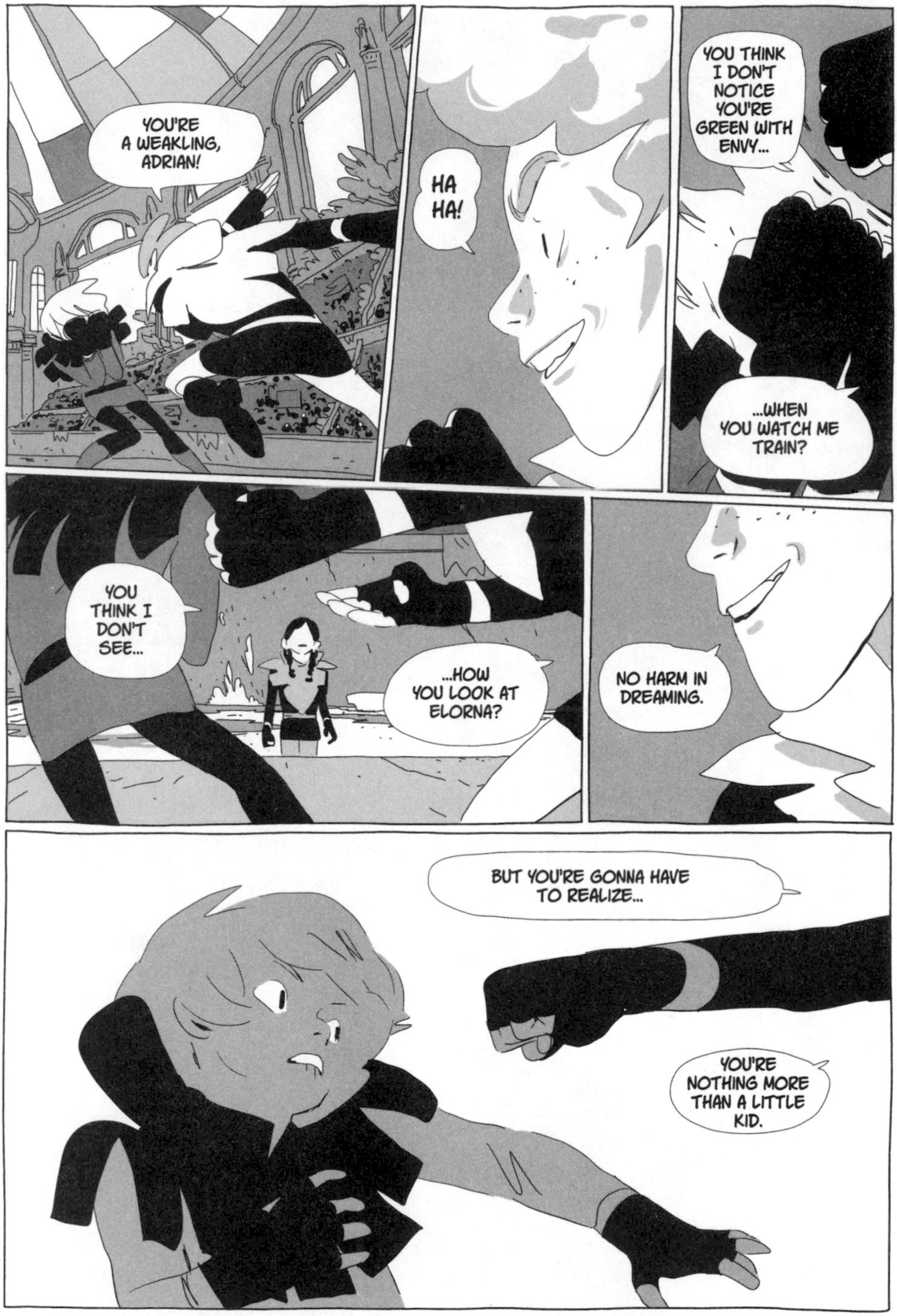
YOU'RE A WEAKLING, ADRIAN!
HA HA!
YOU THINK I DON'T NOTICE YOU'RE GREEN WITH ENVY...
...WHEN YOU WATCH ME TRAIN?
YOU THINK I DON'T SEE...
...HOW YOU LOOK AT ELORNA?
NO HARM IN DREAMING.
BUT YOU'RE GONNA HAVE TO REALIZE...
YOU'RE NOTHING MORE THAN A LITTLE KID.

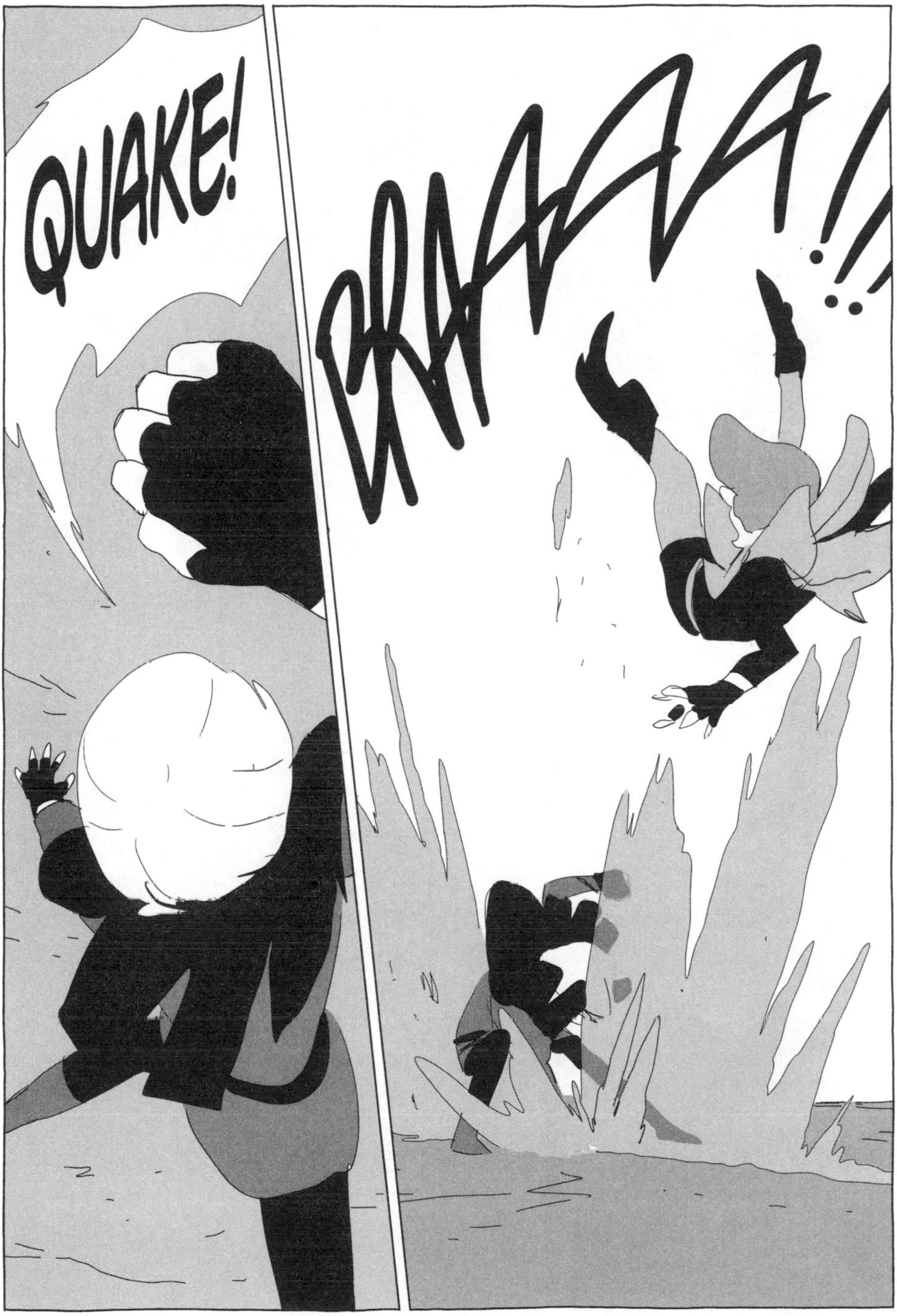
QUAKE!
BRAAAA!!!

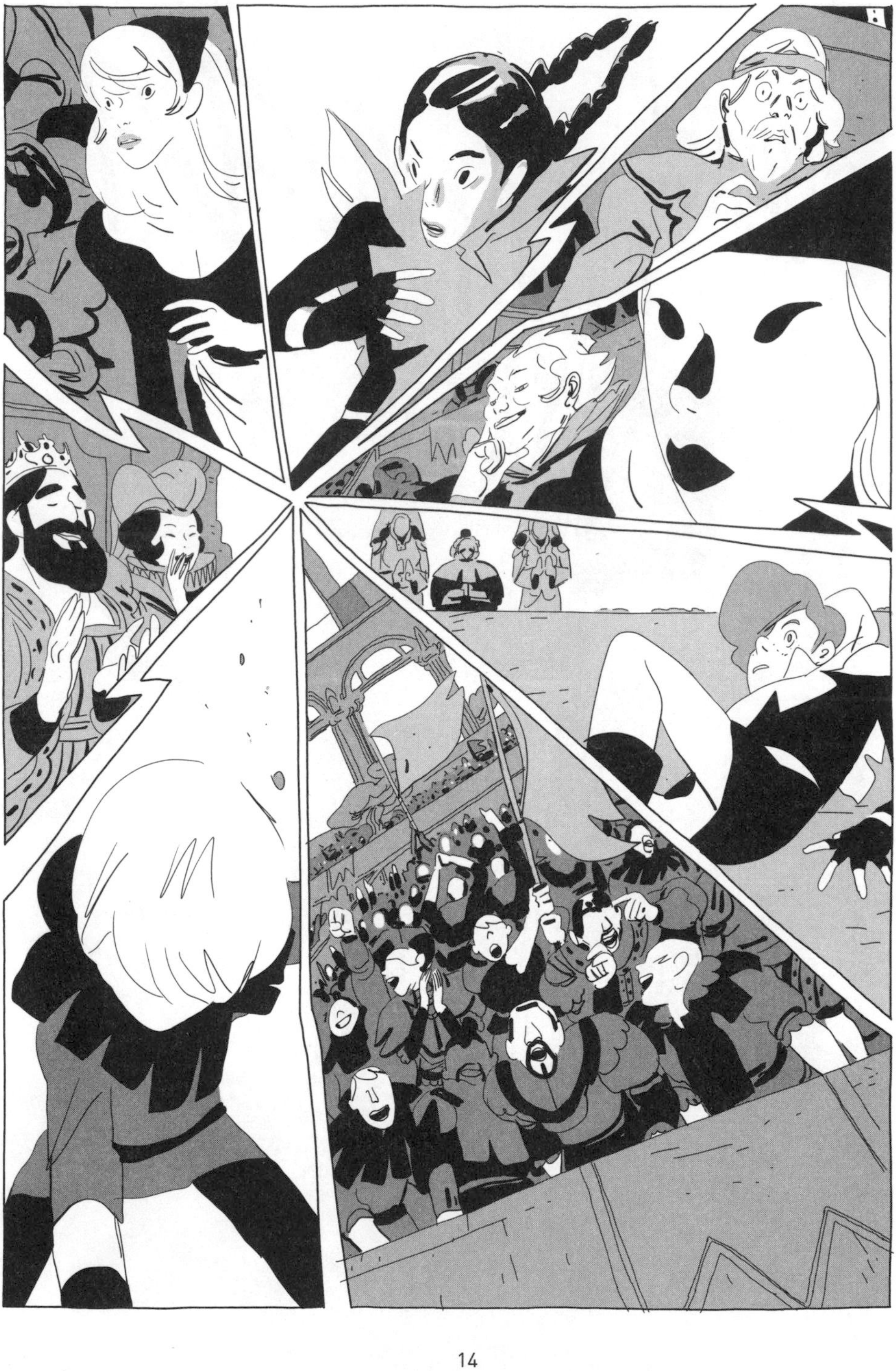

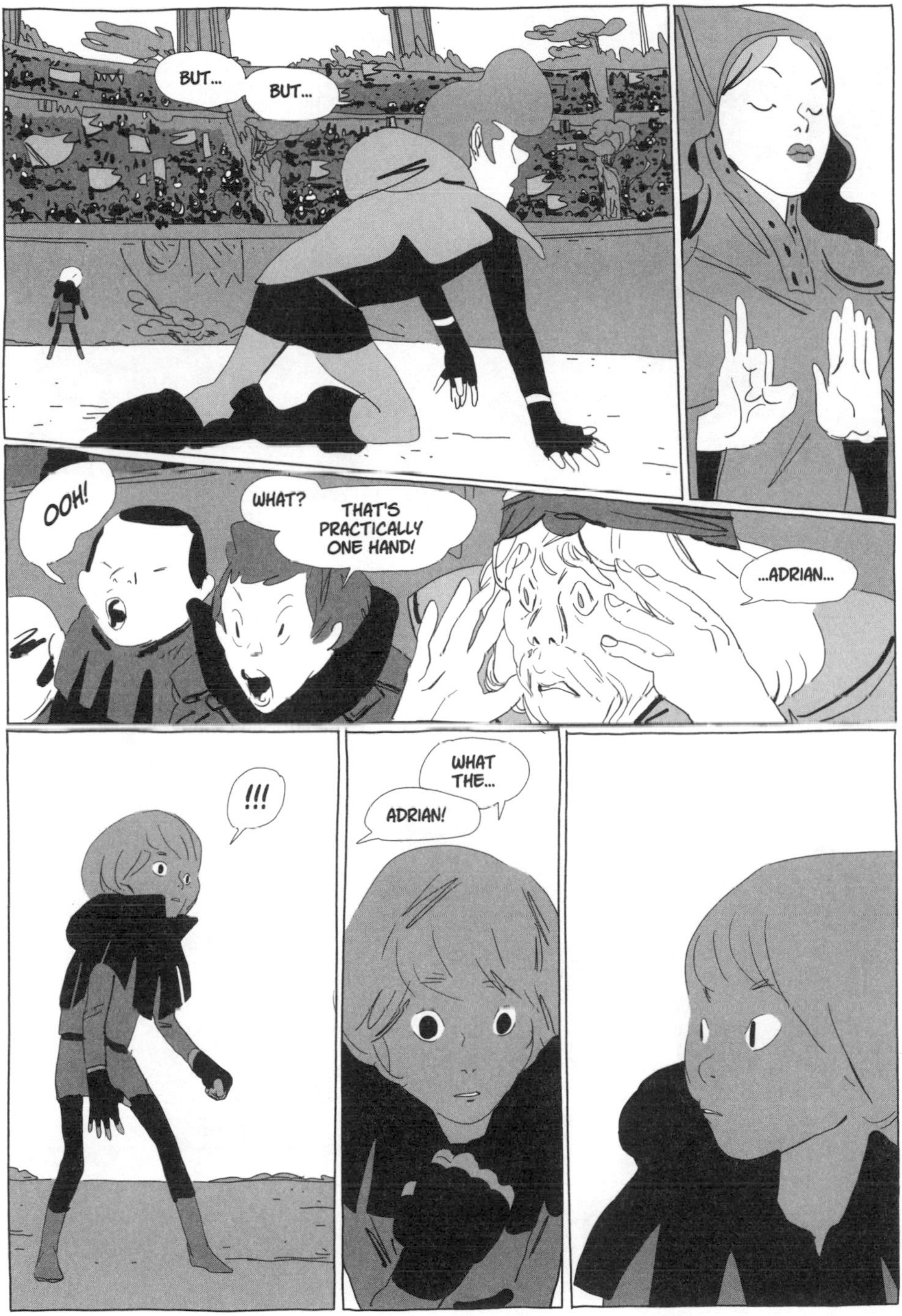
BUT...
BUT...
OOH!
WHAT?
THAT'S PRACTICALLY ONE HAND!
...ADRIAN...
!!!
WHAT THE...
ADRIAN!

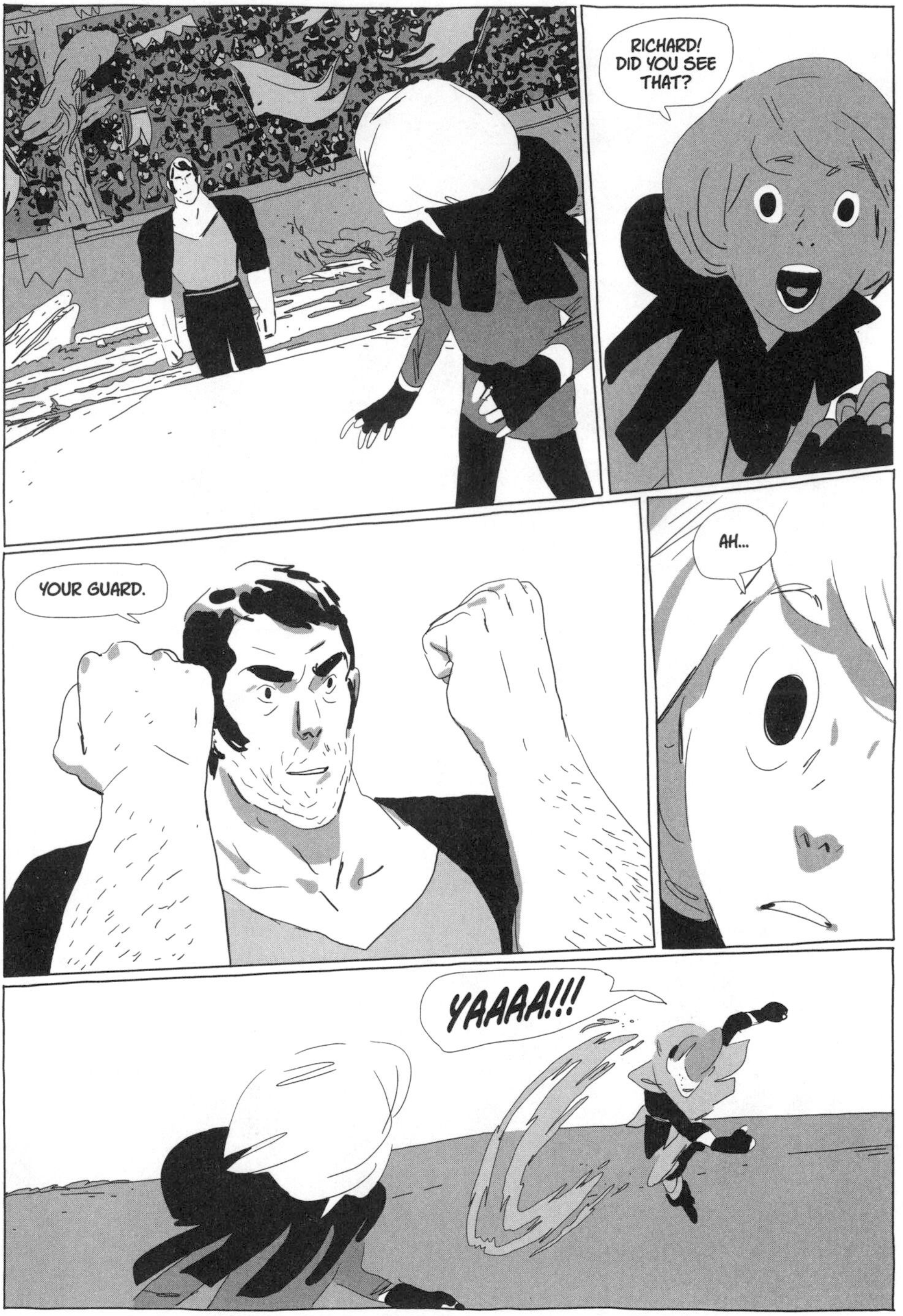
RICHARD! DID YOU SEE THAT?
YOUR GUARD.
AH...
YAAAA!!!

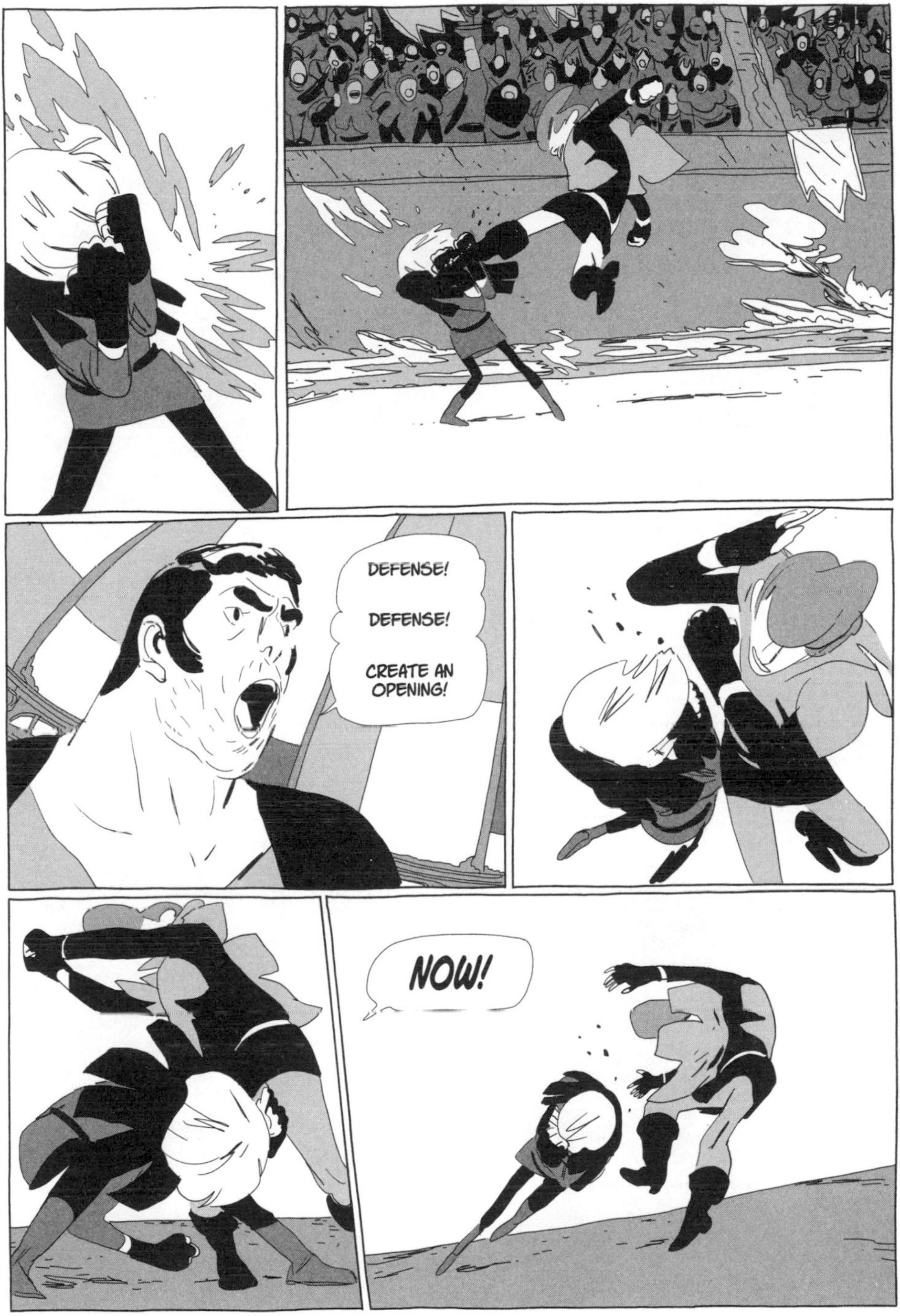
DEFENSE!
DEFENSE!
CREATE AN OPENING!
NOW!

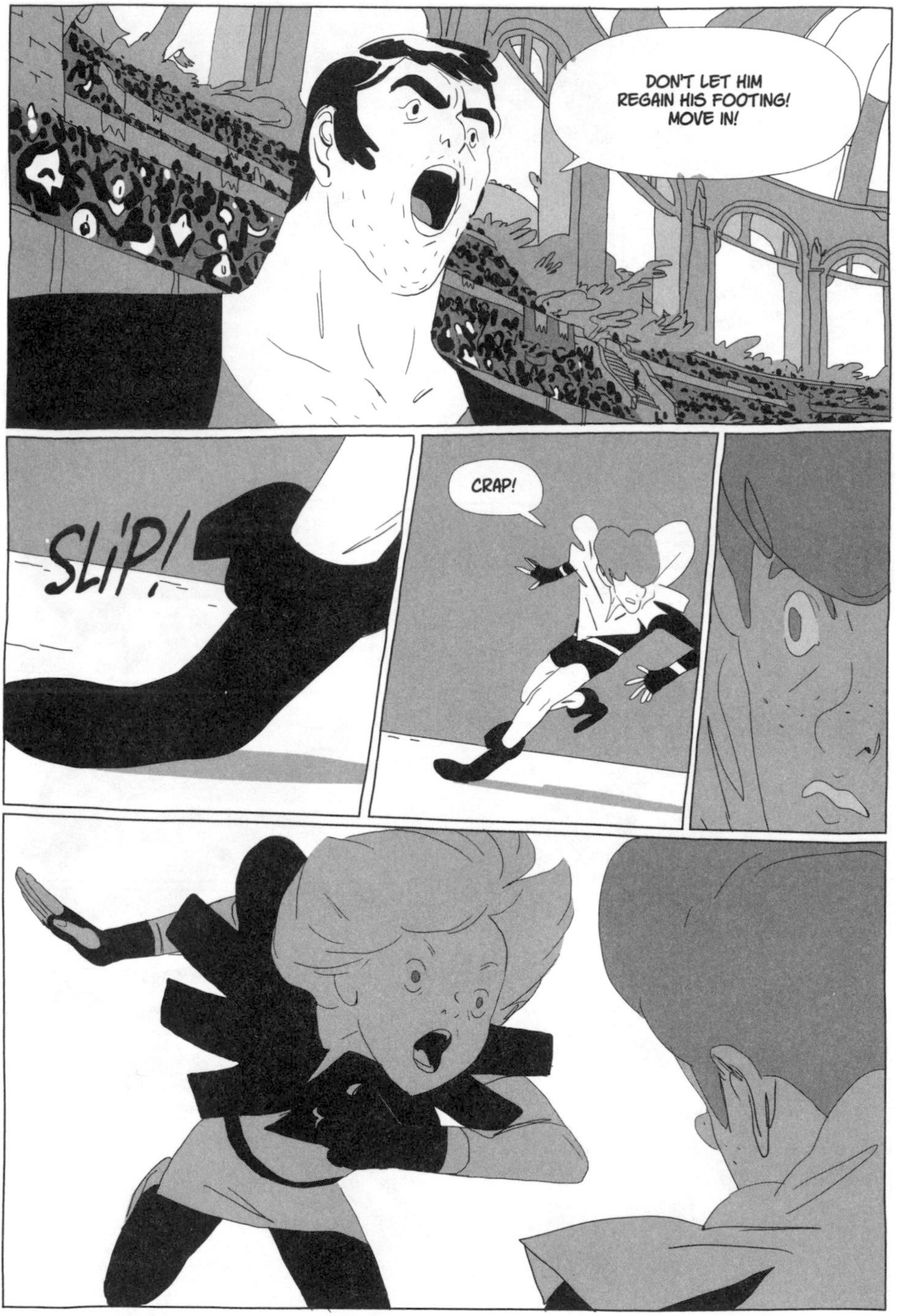
DON'T LET HIM REGAIN HIS FOOTING! MOVE IN!
SLIP!
CRAP!

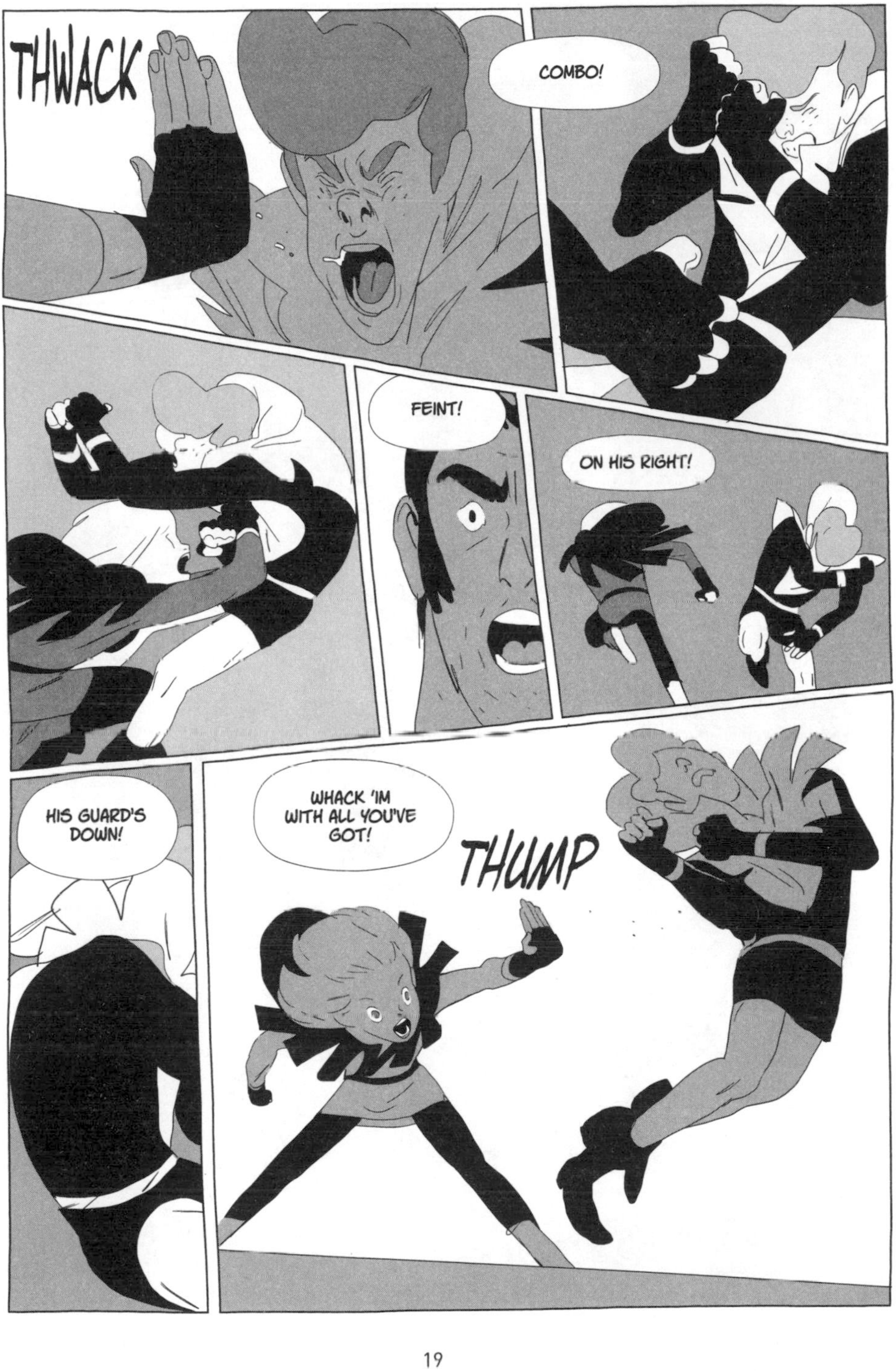
THWACK
COMBO!
FEINT!
ON HIS RIGHT!
HIS GUARD'S DOWN!
WHACK 'IM WITH ALL YOU'VE GOT!
THUMP

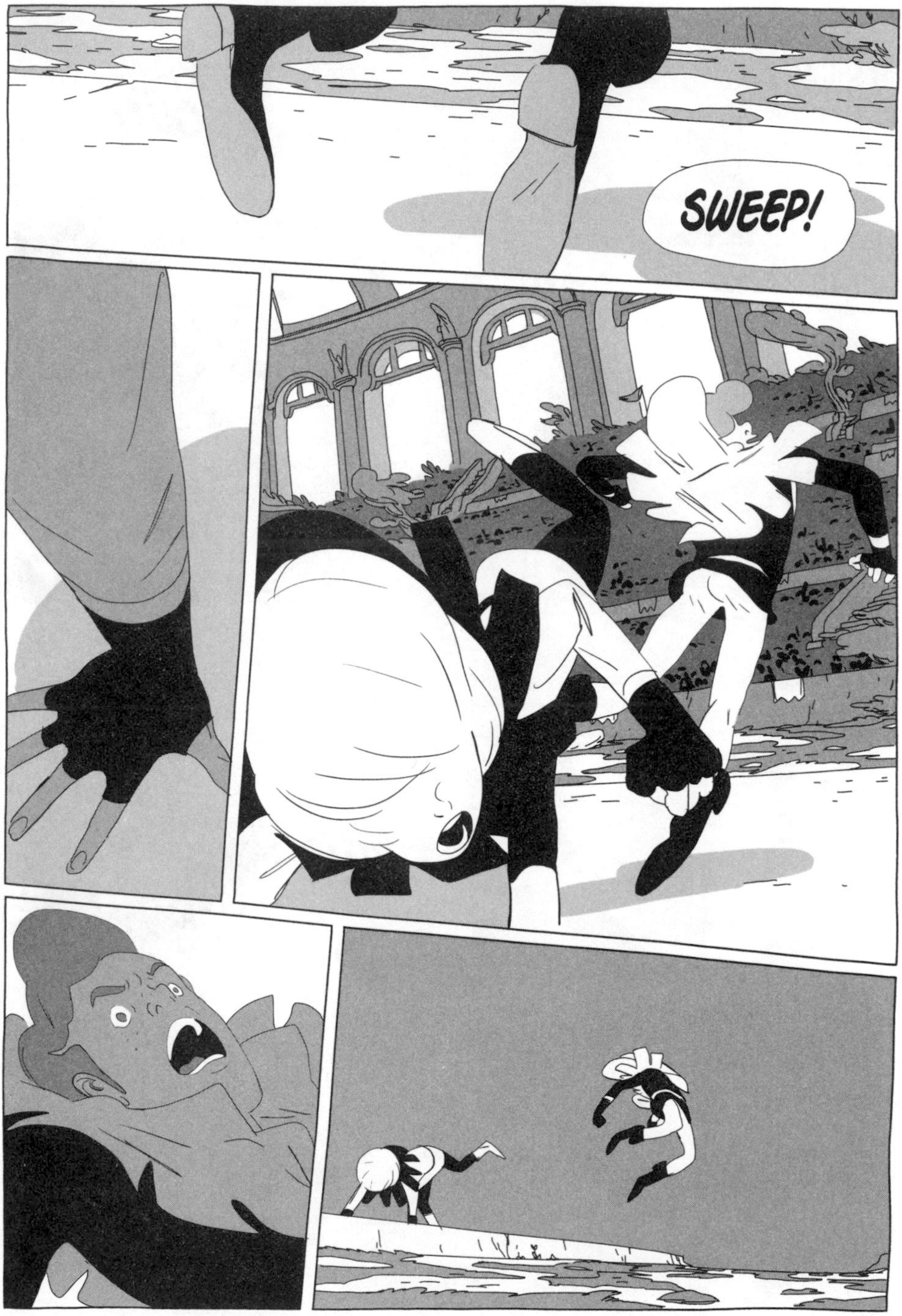
SWEEP!

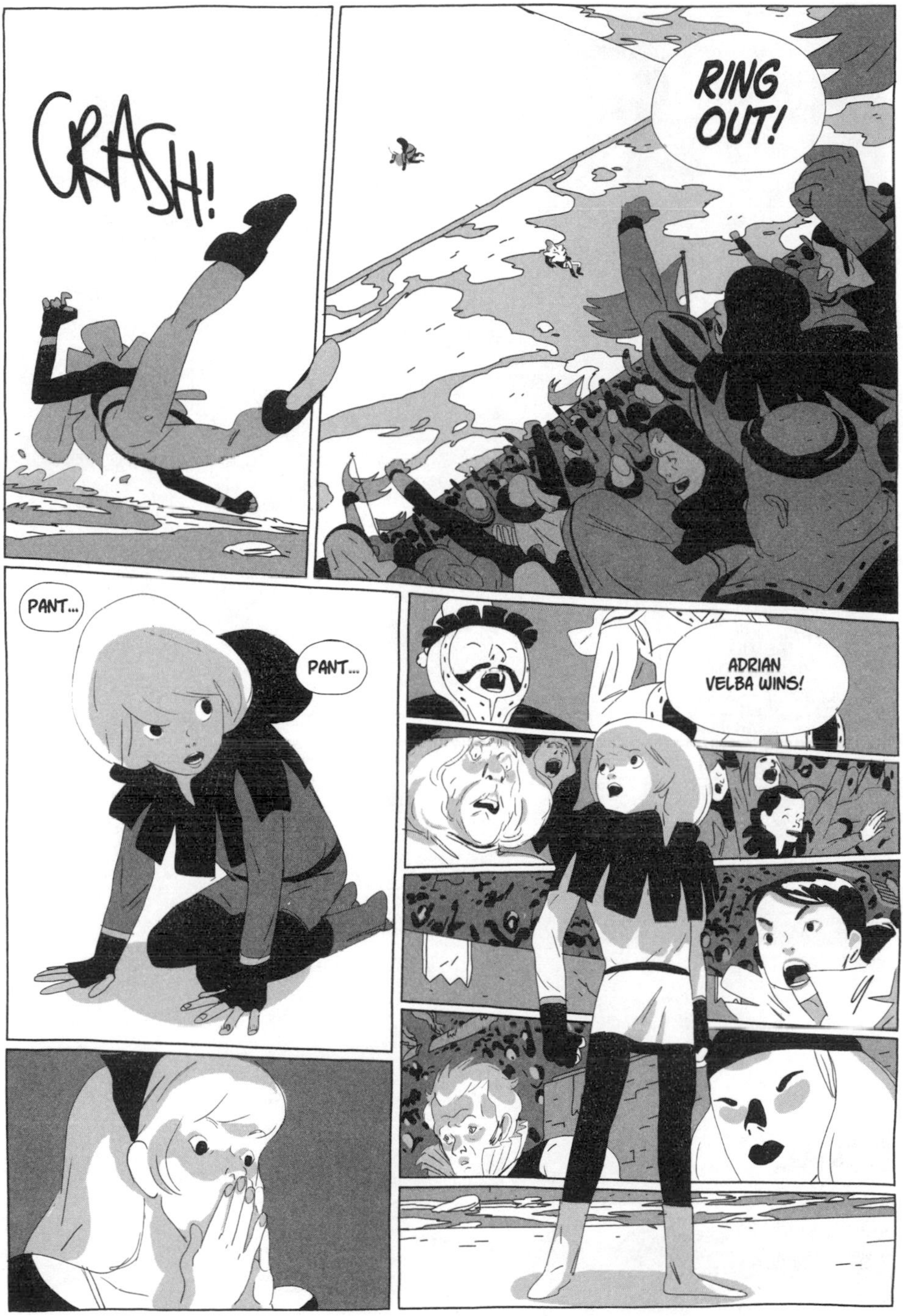
CRASH!
RING OUT!
PANT...
PANT...
ADRIAN VELBA WINS!

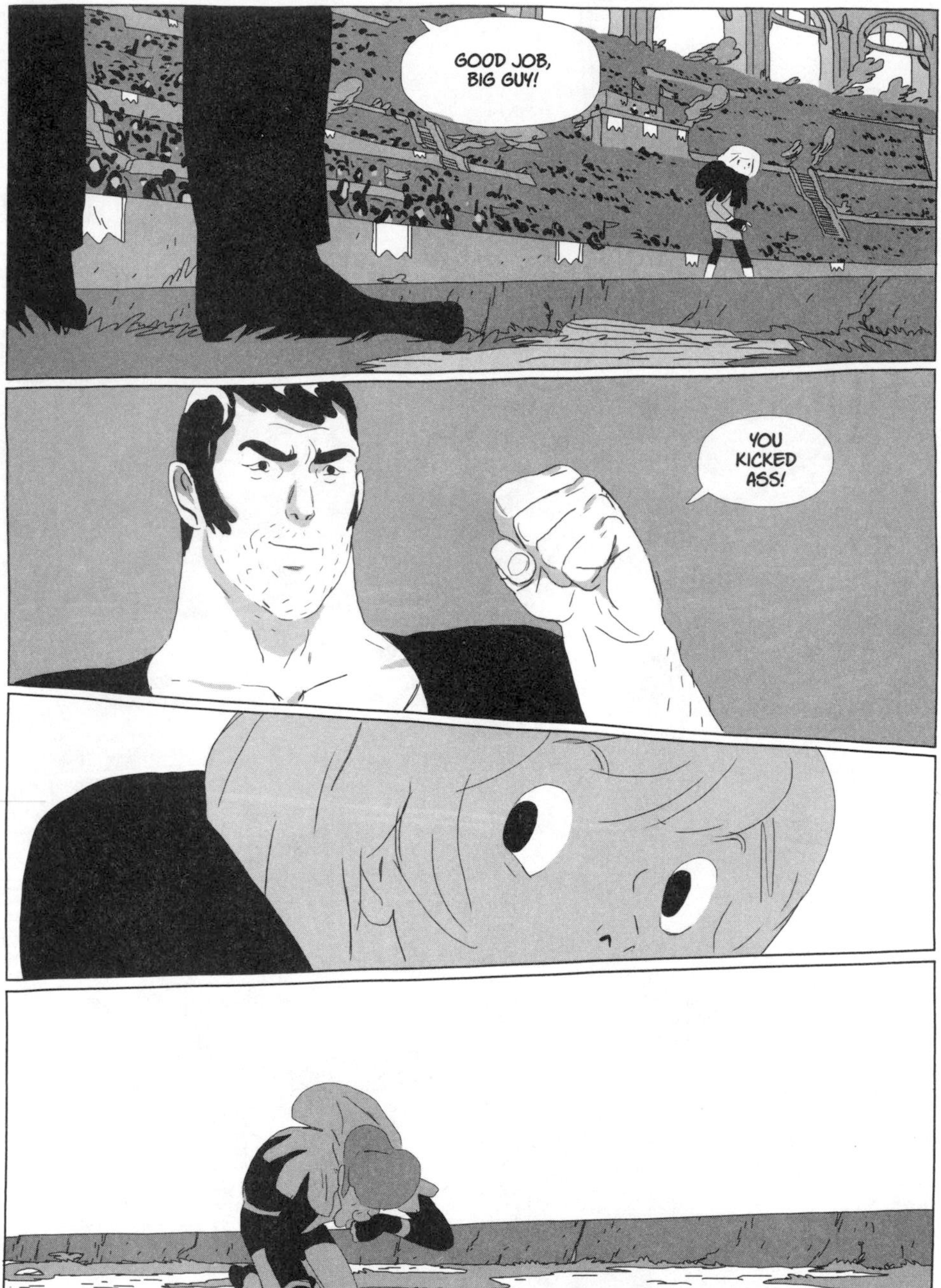
GOOD JOB, BIG GUY!
YOU KICKED ASS!

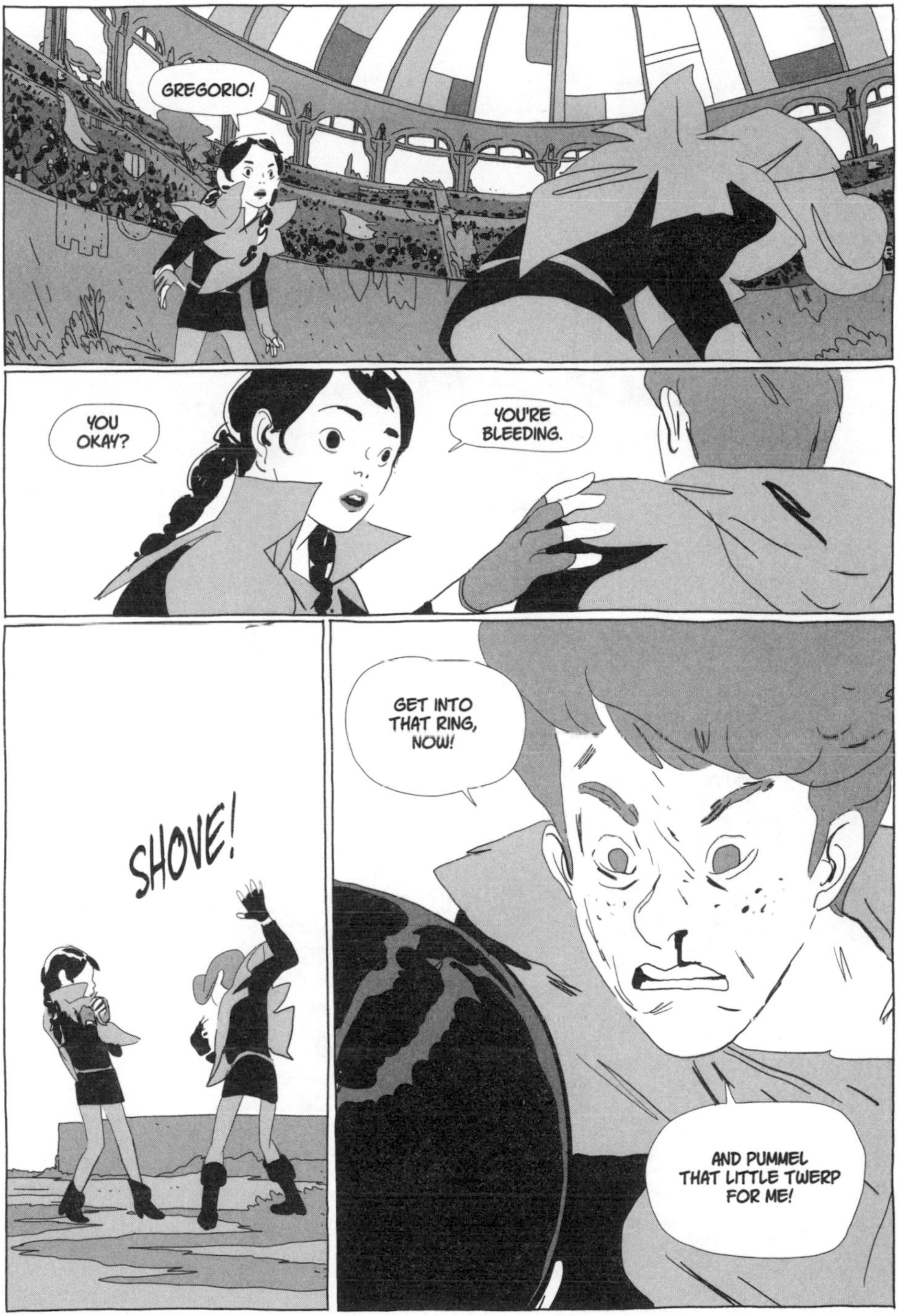
GREGORIO!
YOU OKAY?
YOU'RE BLEEDING.
SHOVE!
GET INTO THAT RING, NOW!
AND PUMMEL THAT LITTLE TWERP FOR ME!

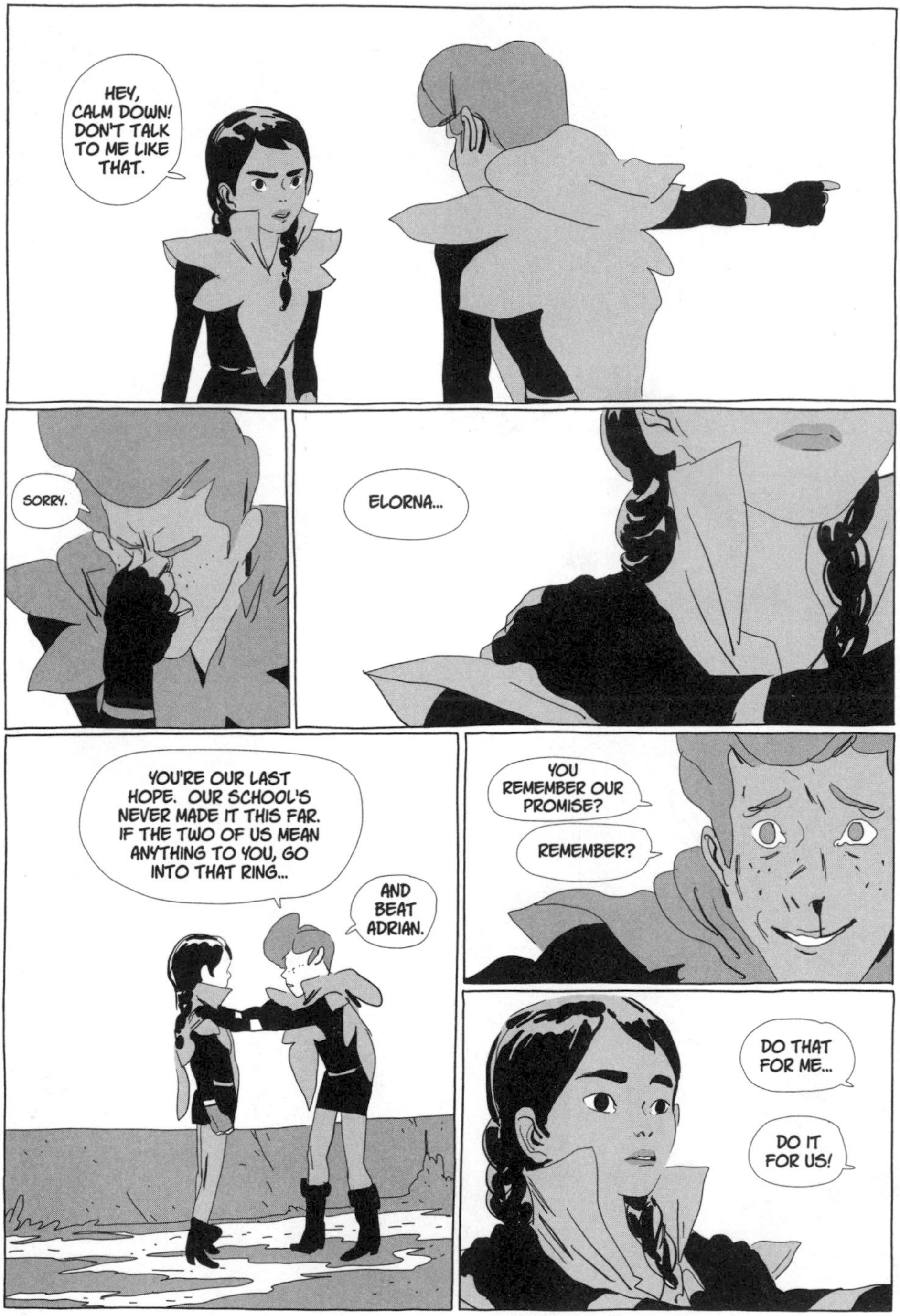
HEY, CALM DOWN! DON'T TALK TO ME LIKE THAT.
SORRY.
ELORNA...
YOU'RE OUR LAST HOPE. OUR SCHOOL'S NEVER MADE IT THIS FAR. IF THE TWO OF US MEAN ANYTHING TO YOU, GO INTO THAT RING...
AND BEAT ADRIAN.
YOU REMEMBER OUR PROMISE?
REMEMBER?
DO THAT FOR ME...
DO IT FOR US!

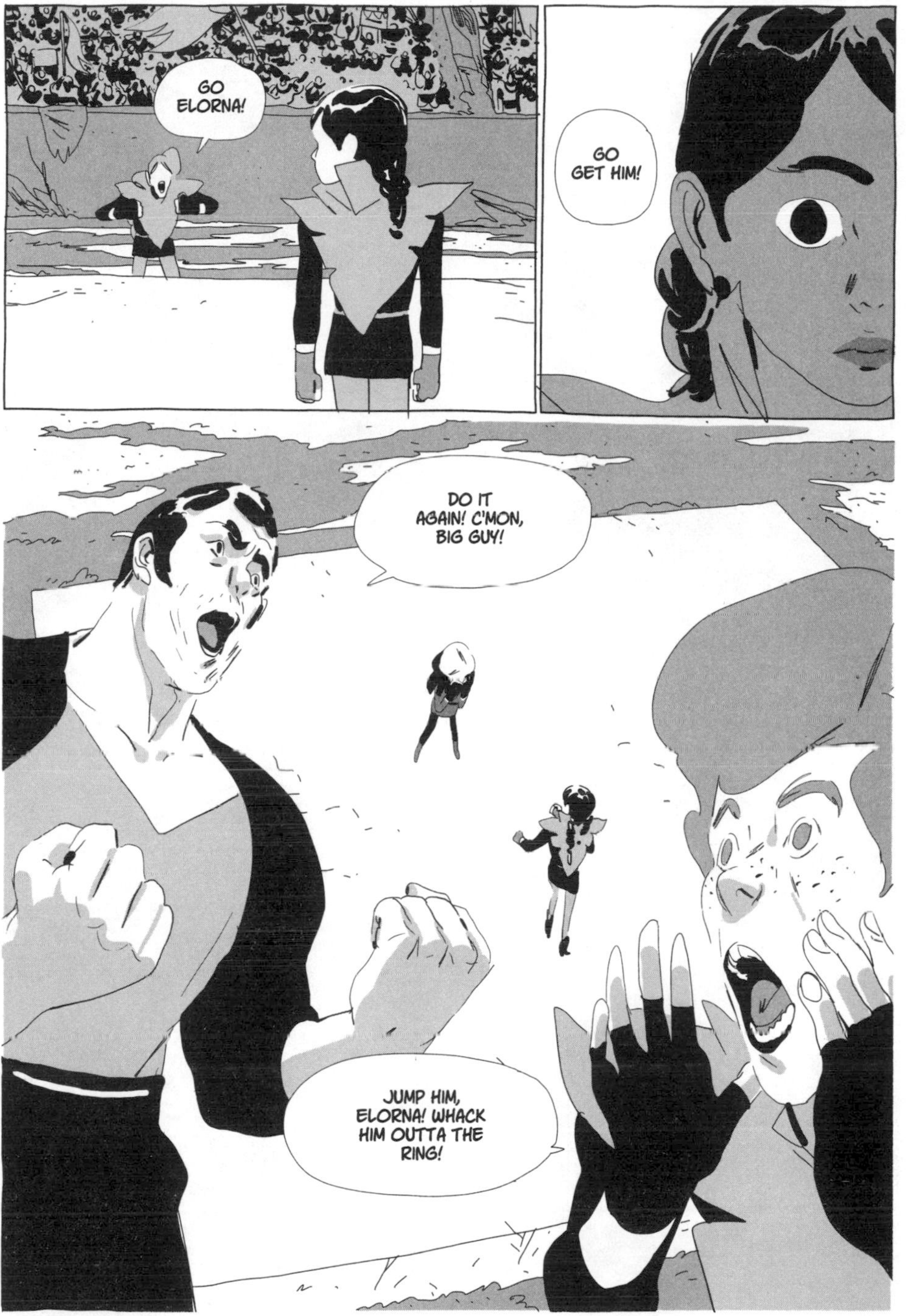
GO ELORNA!
GO GET HIM!
DO IT AGAIN! C'MON, BIG GUY!
JUMP HIM, ELORNA! WHACK HIM OUTTA THE RING!

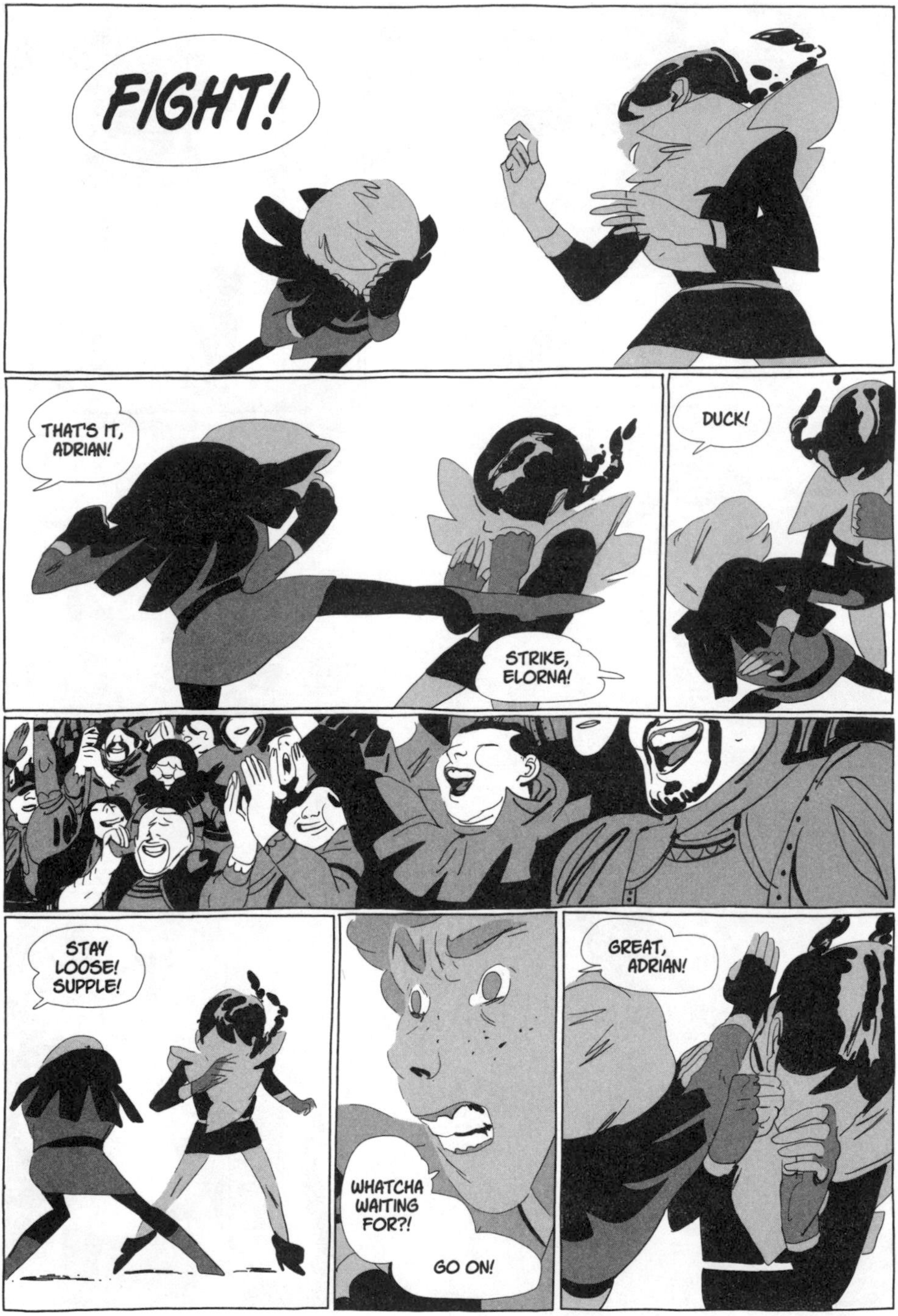
FIGHT!
THAT'S IT, ADRIAN!
STRIKE, ELORNA!
DUCK!
STAY LOOSE! SUPPLE!
WHATCHA WAITING FOR?!
GO ON!
GREAT, ADRIAN!

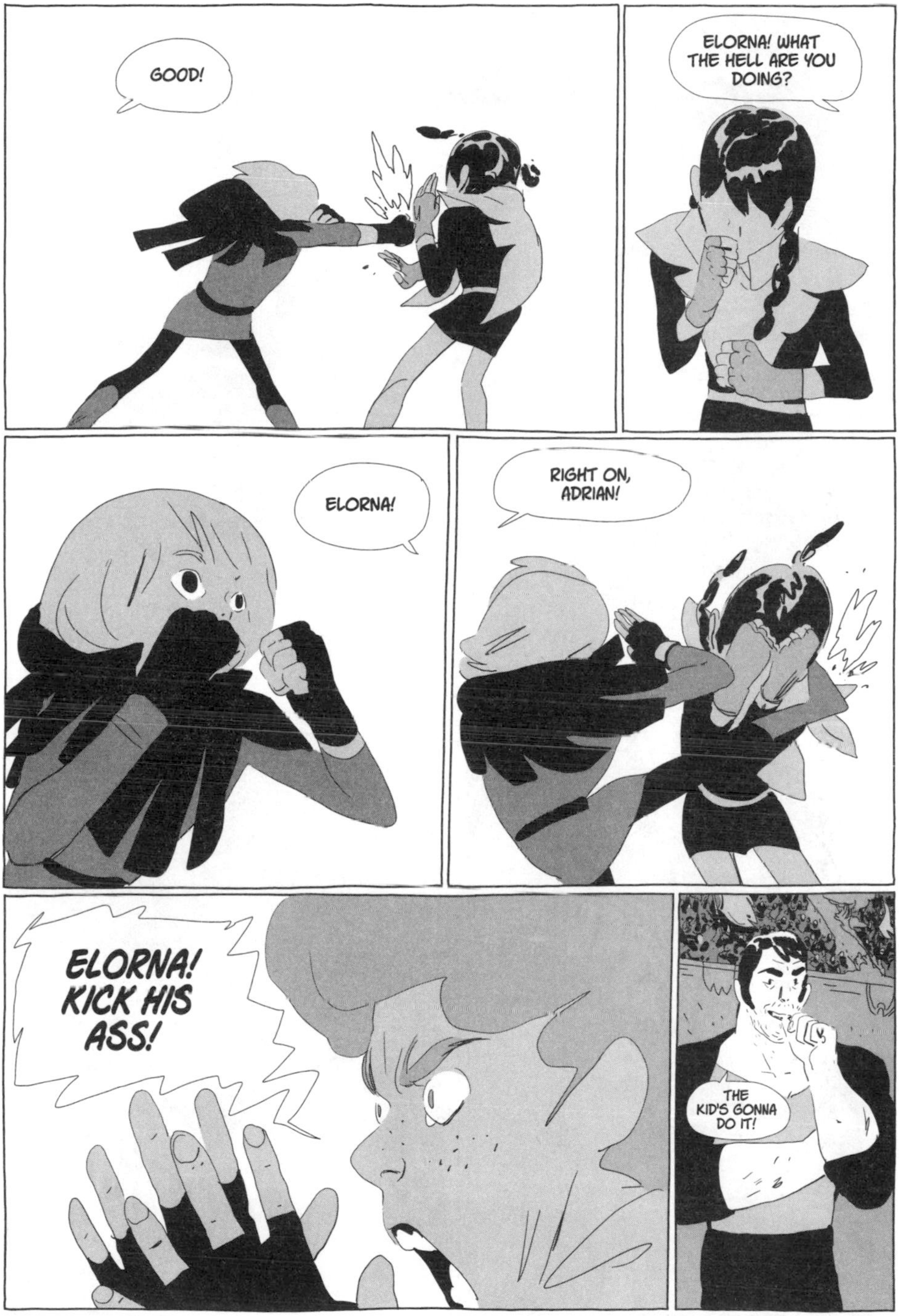
GOOD!
ELORNA! WHAT THE HELL ARE YOU DOING?
ELORNA!
RIGHT ON, ADRIAN!
ELORNA! KICK HIS ASS!
THE KID'S GONNA DO IT!

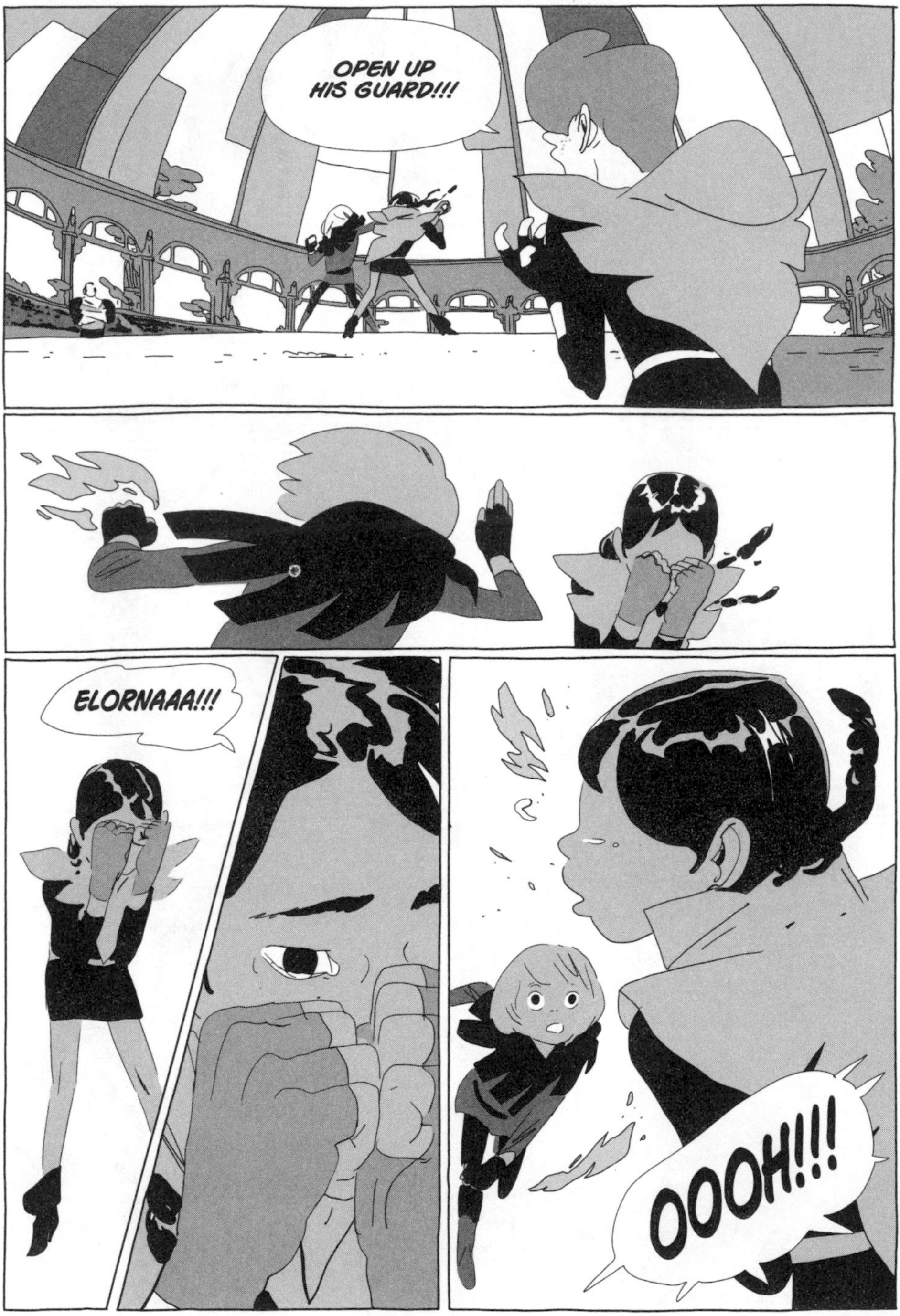
OPEN UP HIS GUARD!!!
ELORNAAA!!!
OOOH!!!

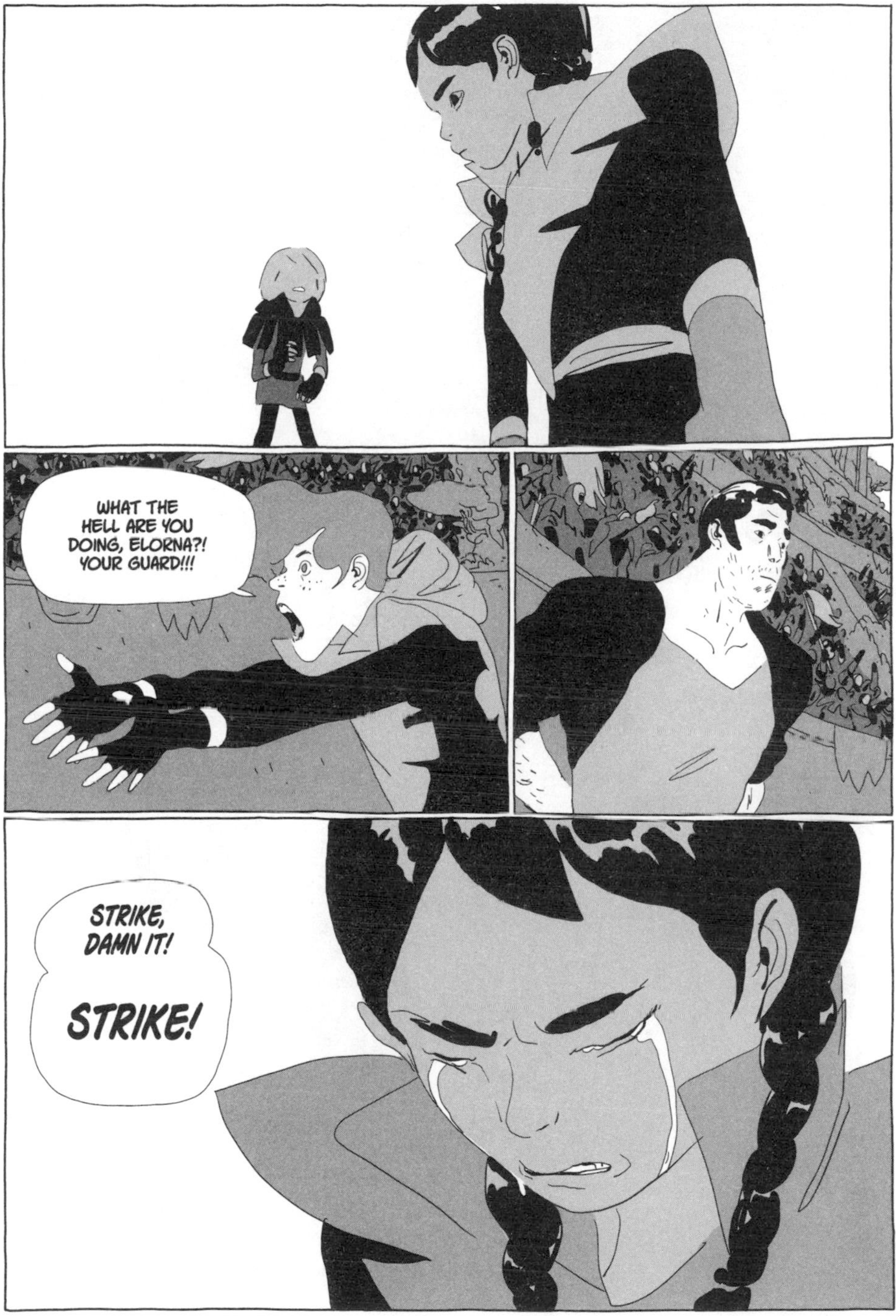
WHAT THE HELL ARE YOU DOING, ELORNA?! YOUR GUARD!!!
STRIKE, DAMN IT!
STRIKE!

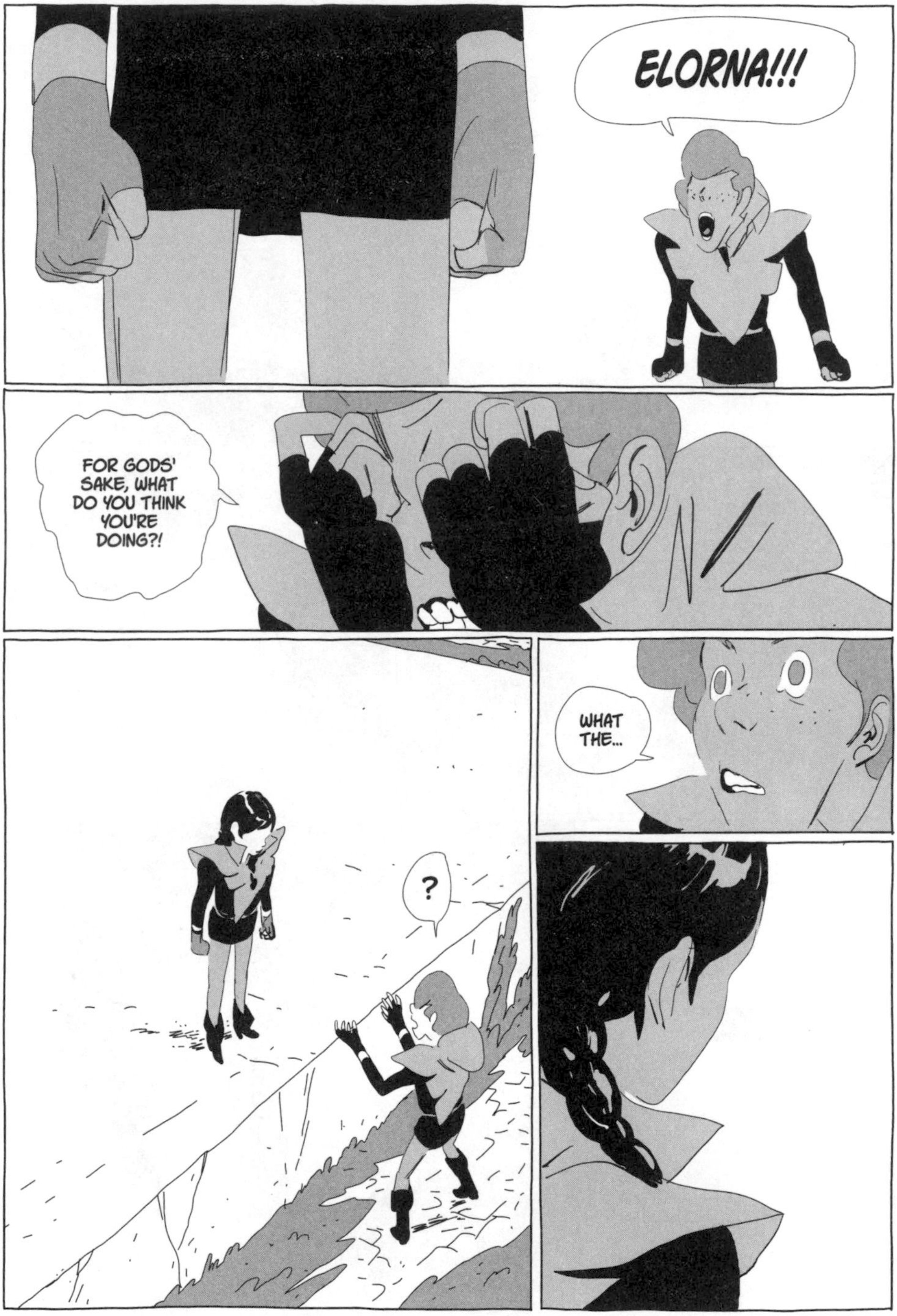
ELORNA!!!
FOR GODS' SAKE, WHAT DO YOU THINK YOU'RE DOING?!
WHAT THE...
?

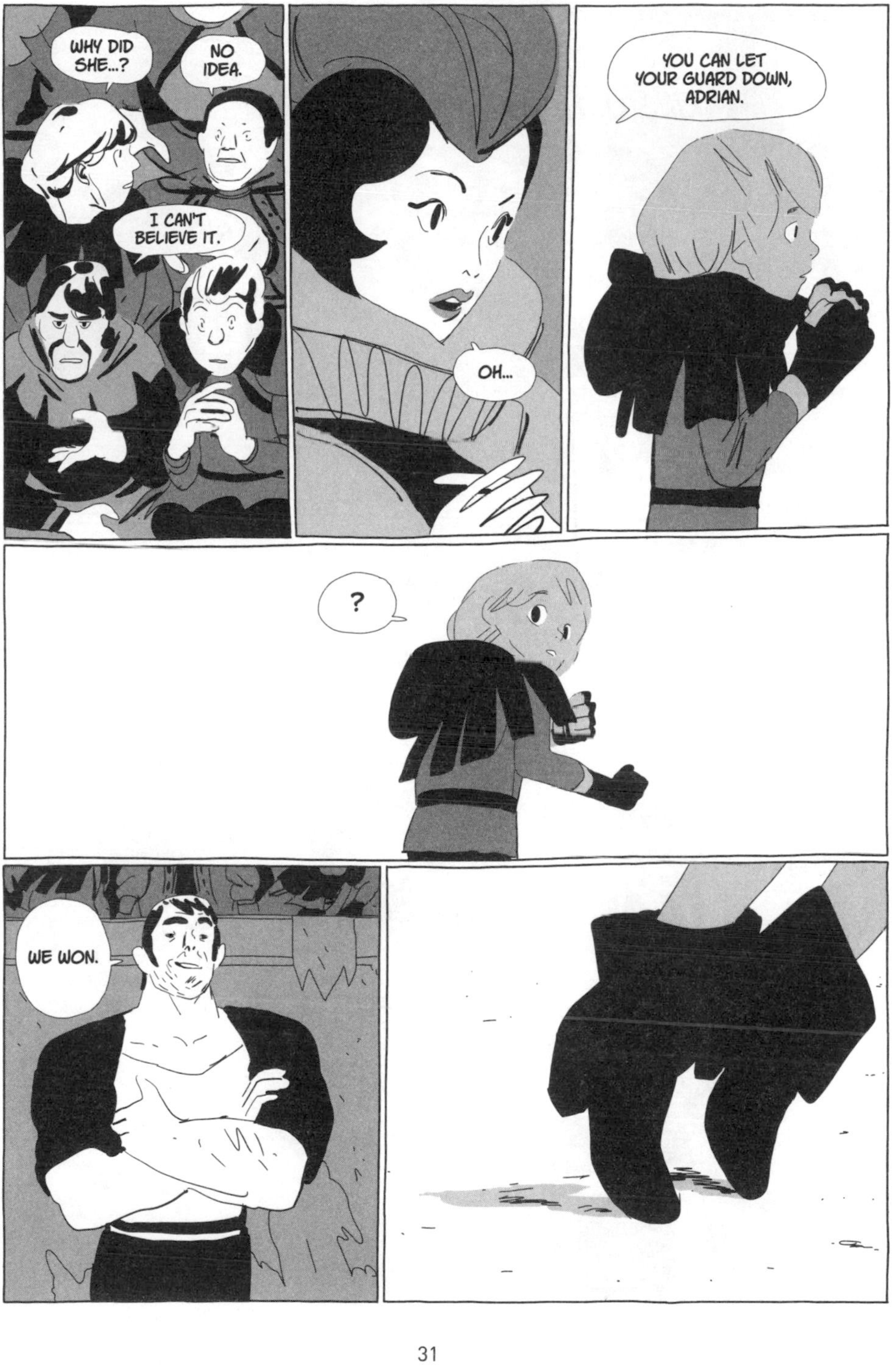
WHY DID SHE...?
NO IDEA.
I CAN'T BELIEVE IT.
OH...
YOU CAN LET YOUR GUARD DOWN, ADRIAN.
?
WE WON.

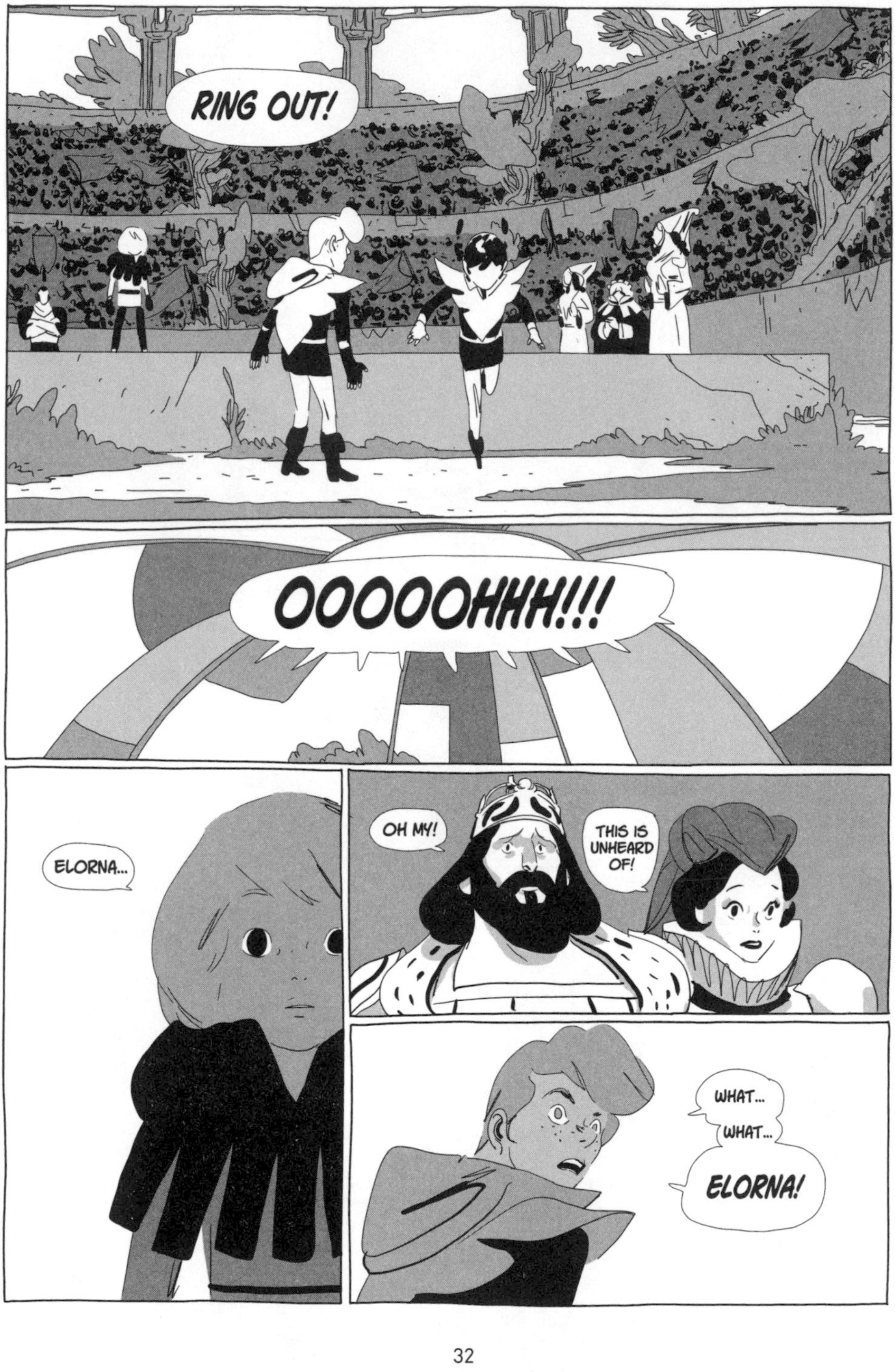
RING OUT!
OOOOOHHH!!!
ELORNA...
OH MY!
THIS IS UNHEARD OF!
WHAT...
WHAT...
ELORNA!

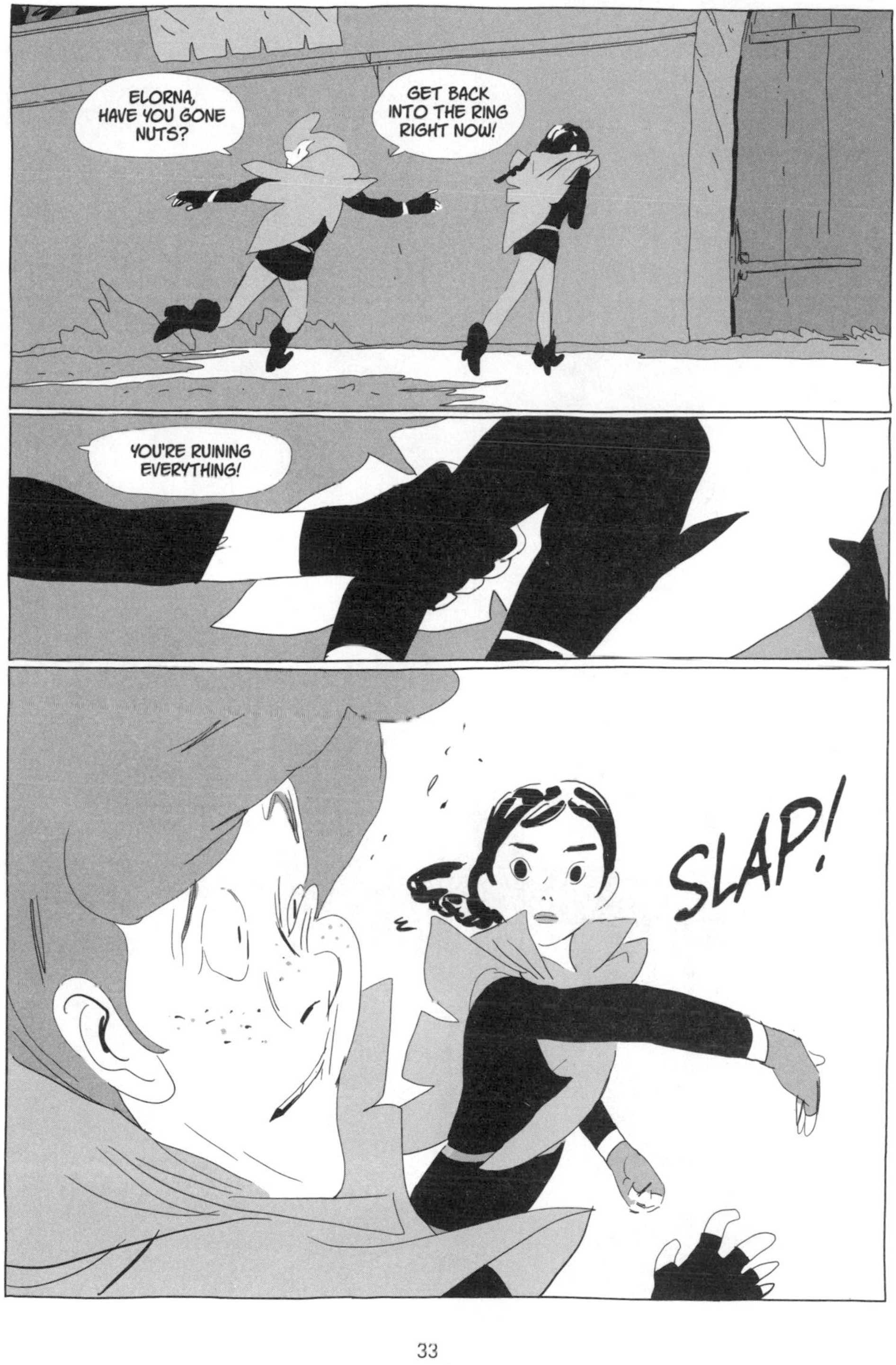
ELORNA, HAVE YOU GONE NUTS?
GET BACK INTO THE RING RIGHT NOW!
YOU'RE RUINING EVERYTHING!
SLAP!

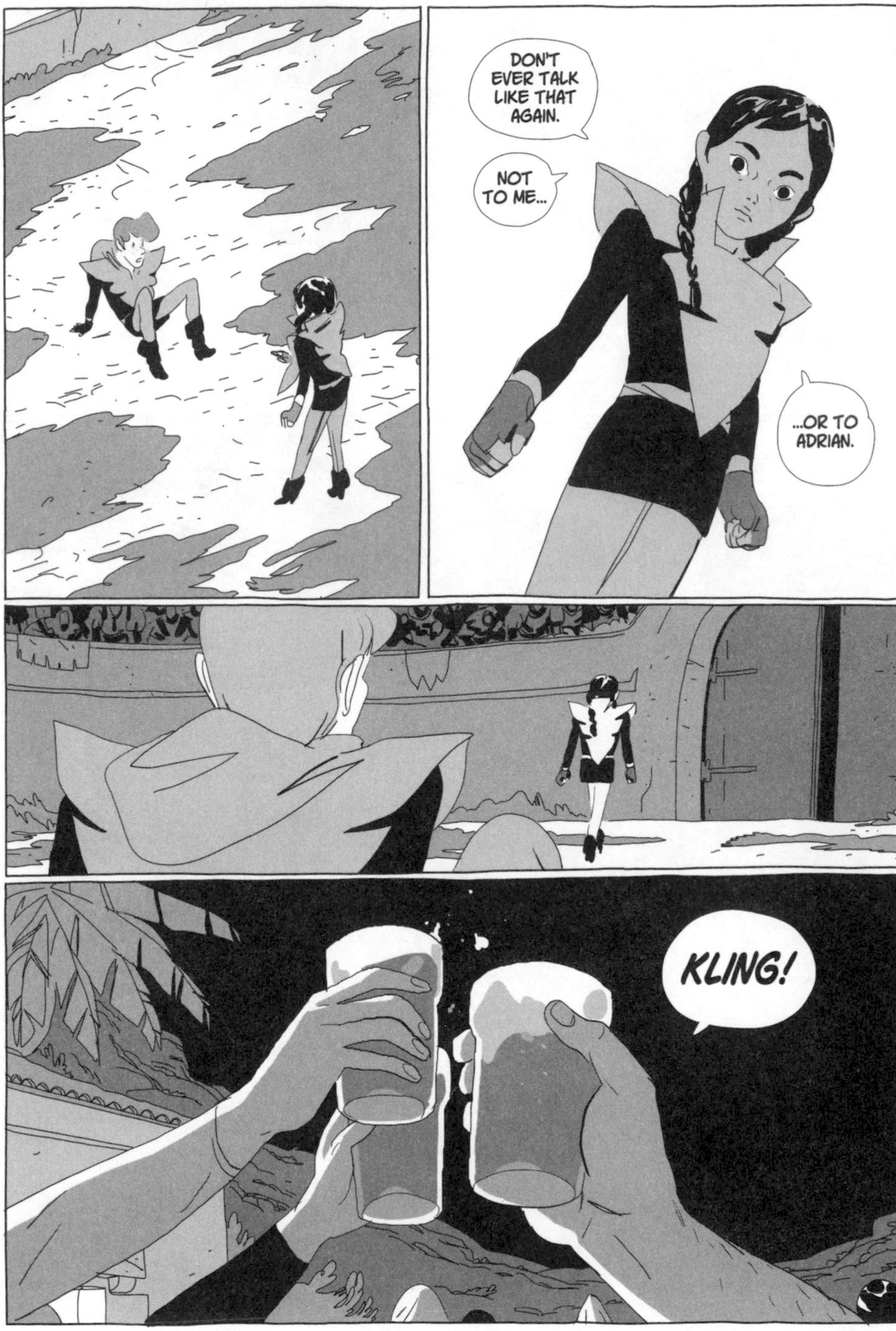
DON'T EVER TALK LIKE THAT AGAIN.
NOT TO ME...
...OR TO ADRIAN.
KLING!

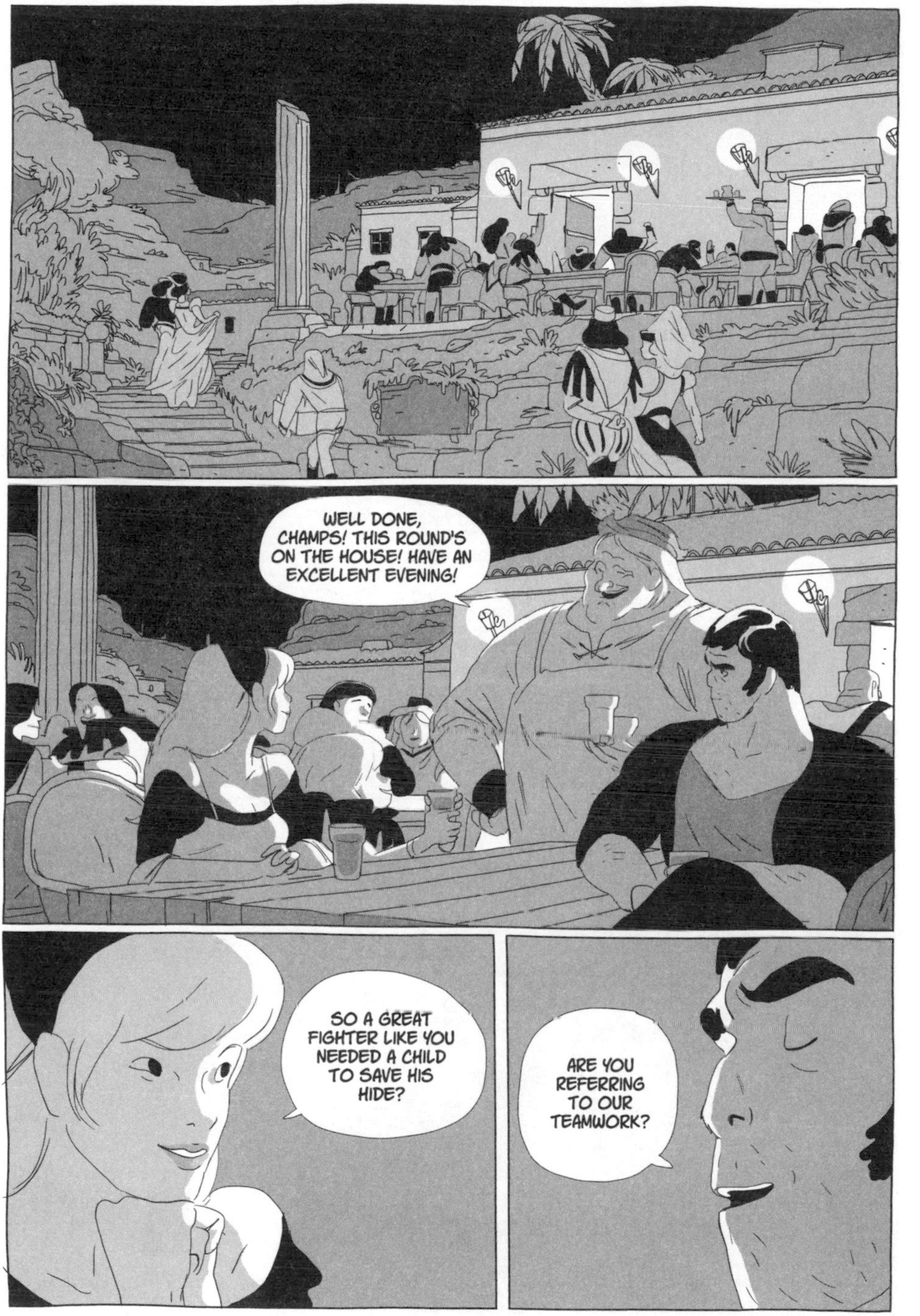
WELL DONE, CHAMPS! THIS ROUND'S ON THE HOUSE! HAVE AN EXCELLENT EVENING!
SO A GREAT FIGHTER LIKE YOU NEEDED A CHILD TO SAVE HIS HIDE?
ARE YOU REFERRING TO OUR TEAMWORK?

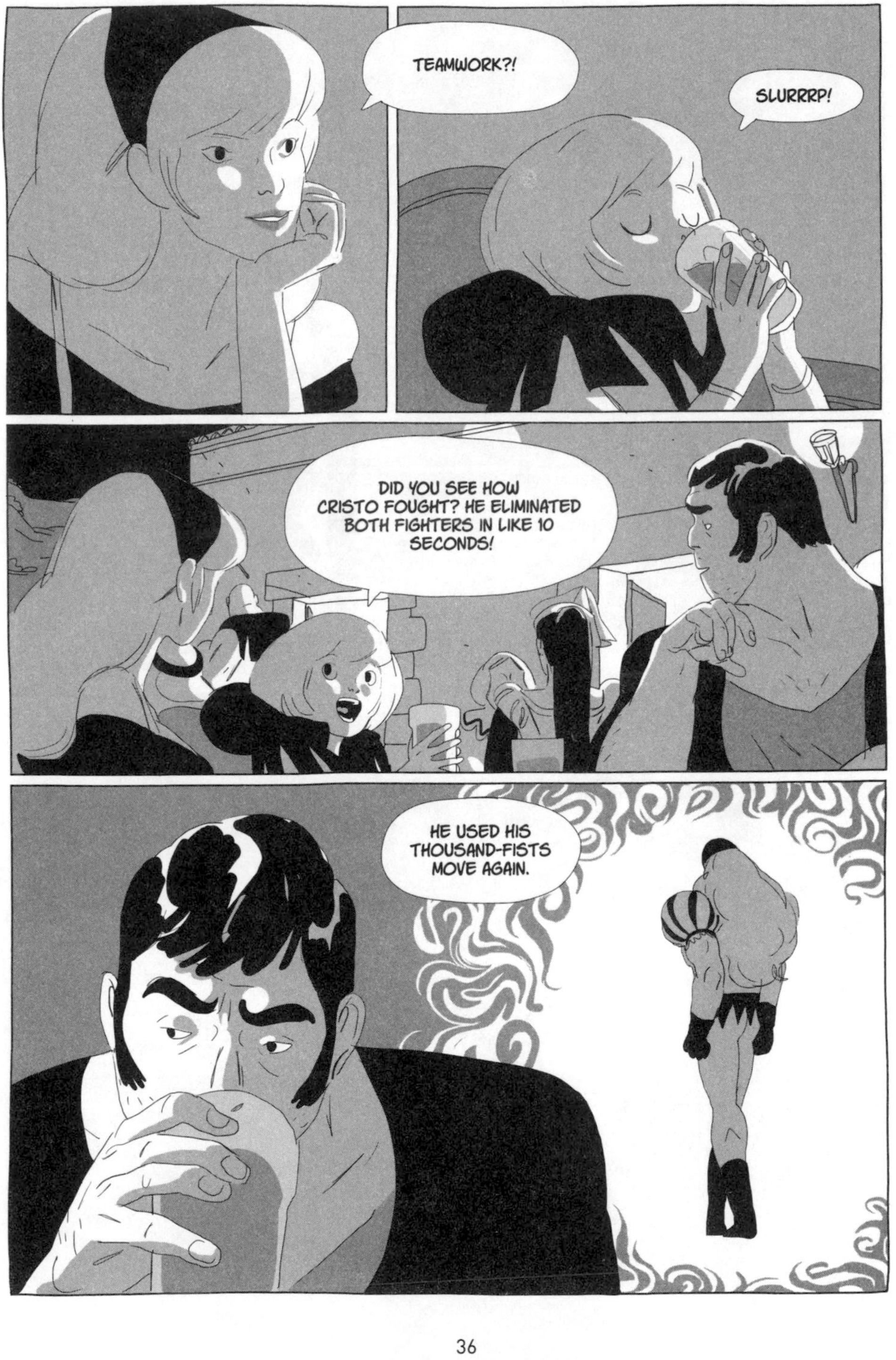
TEAMWORK?!
SLURRRP!
DID YOU SEE HOW CRISTO FOUGHT? HE ELIMINATED BOTH FIGHTERS IN LIKE 10 SECONDS!
HE USED HIS THOUSAND-FISTS MOVE AGAIN.

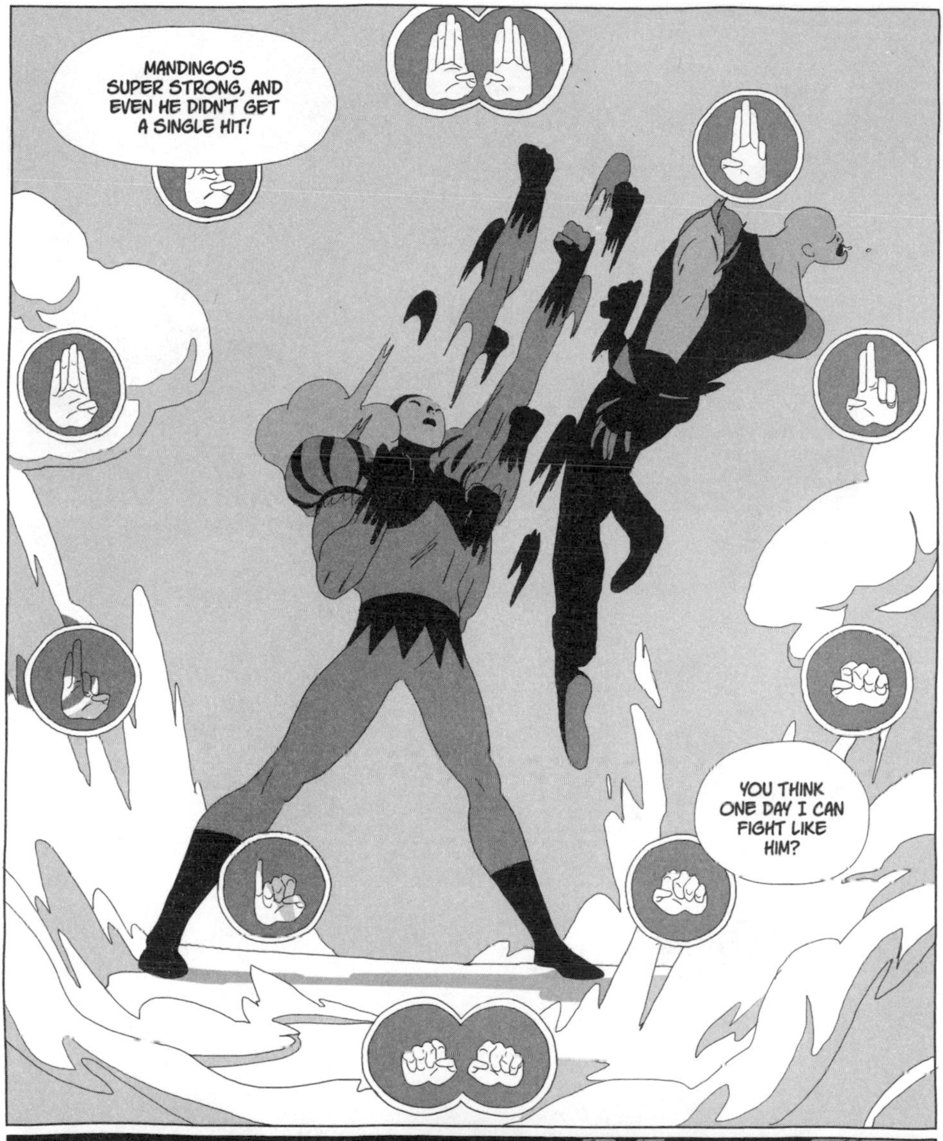
MANDINGO'S SUPER STRONG, AND EVEN HE DIDN'T GET A SINGLE HIT!
YOU THINK ONE DAY I CAN FIGHT LIKE HIM?

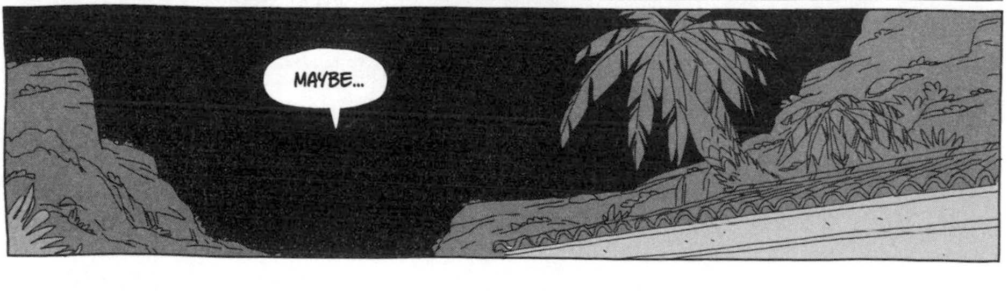
MAYBE...

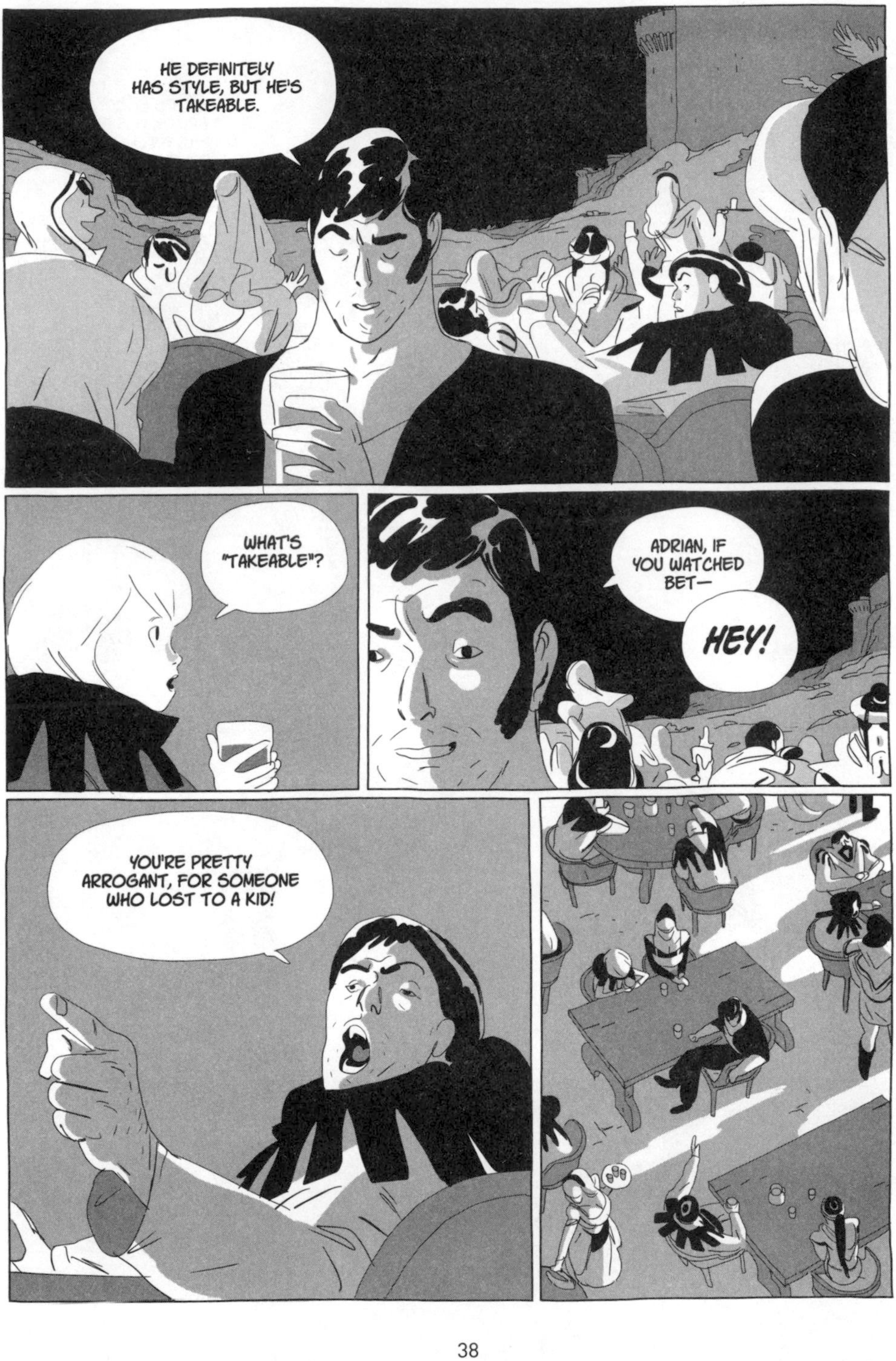
HE DEFINITELY HAS STYLE, BUT HE'S TAKEABLE.
WHAT'S "TAKEABLE"?
ADRIAN, IF YOU WATCHED BET—
HEY!
YOU'RE PRETTY ARROGANT, FOR SOMEONE WHO LOST TO A KID!

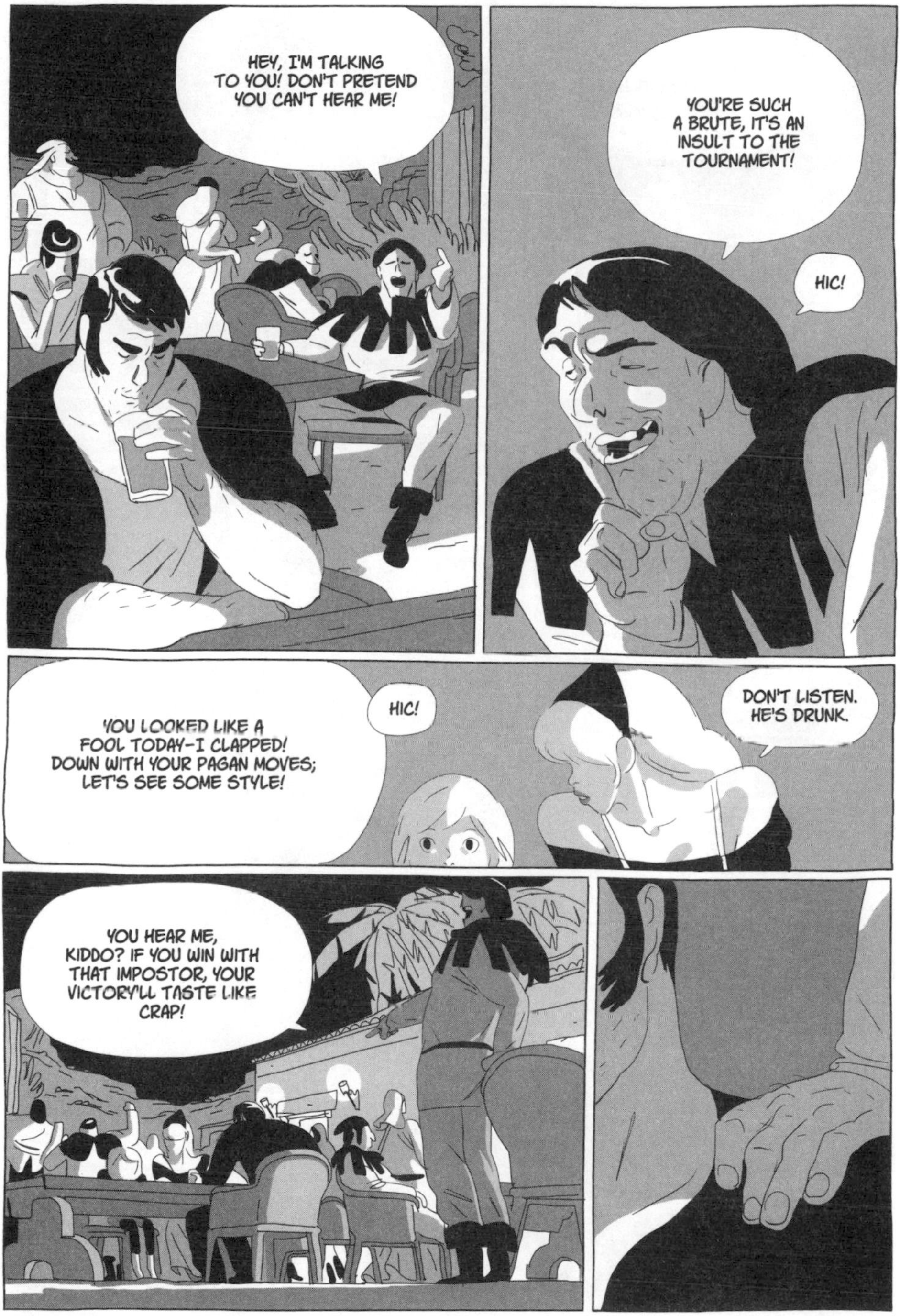
HEY, I'M TALKING TO YOU! DON'T PRETEND YOU CAN'T HEAR ME!
YOU'RE SUCH A BRUTE, IT'S AN INSULT TO THE TOURNAMENT!
HIC!
YOU LOOKED LIKE A FOOL TODAY–I CLAPPED! DOWN WITH YOUR PAGAN MOVES; LET'S SEE SOME STYLE!
HIC!
DON'T LISTEN. HE'S DRUNK.
YOU HEAR ME, KIDDO? IF YOU WIN WITH THAT IMPOSTOR, YOUR VICTORY'LL TASTE LIKE CRAP!

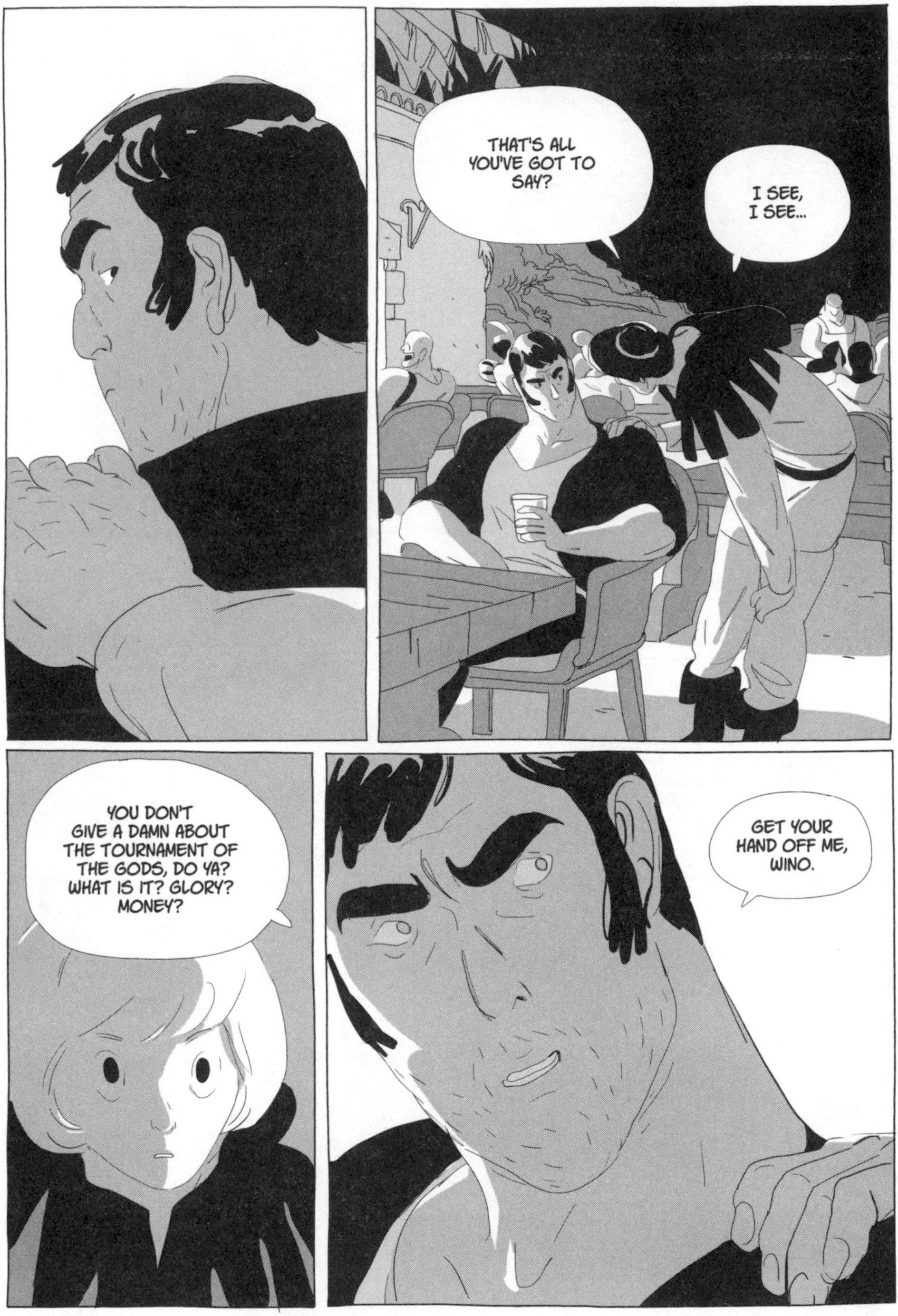
THAT'S ALL YOU'VE GOT TO SAY?
I SEE, I SEE...
YOU DON'T GIVE A DAMN ABOUT THE TOURNAMENT OF THE GODS, DO YA? WHAT IS IT? GLORY? MONEY?
GET YOUR HAND OFF ME, WINO.

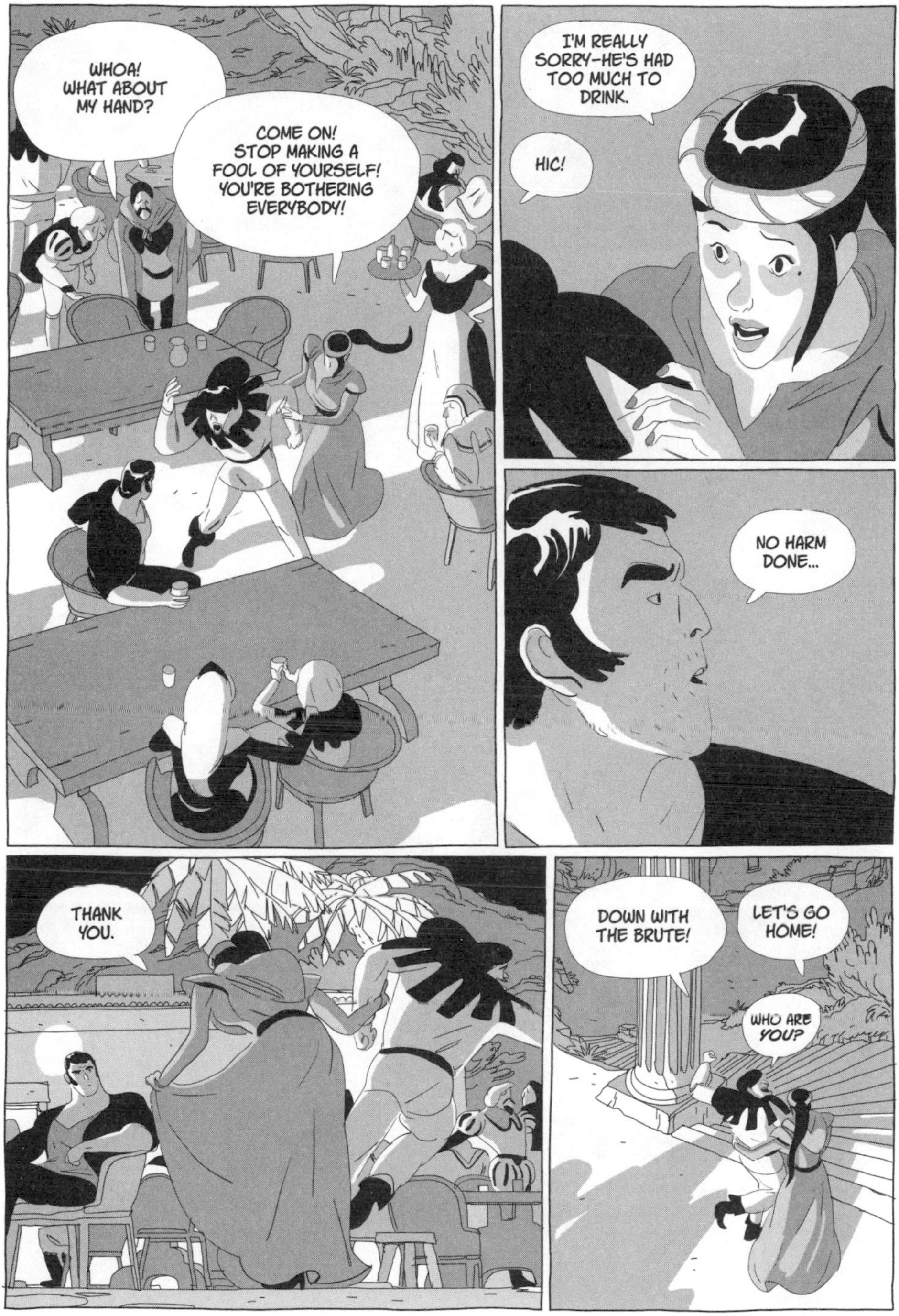
WHOA! WHAT ABOUT MY HAND?
COME ON! STOP MAKING A FOOL OF YOURSELF! YOU'RE BOTHERING EVERYBODY!
I'M REALLY SORRY—HE'S HAD TOO MUCH TO DRINK.
HIC!
NO HARM DONE...
THANK YOU.
DOWN WITH THE BRUTE!
LET'S GO HOME!
WHO ARE YOU?

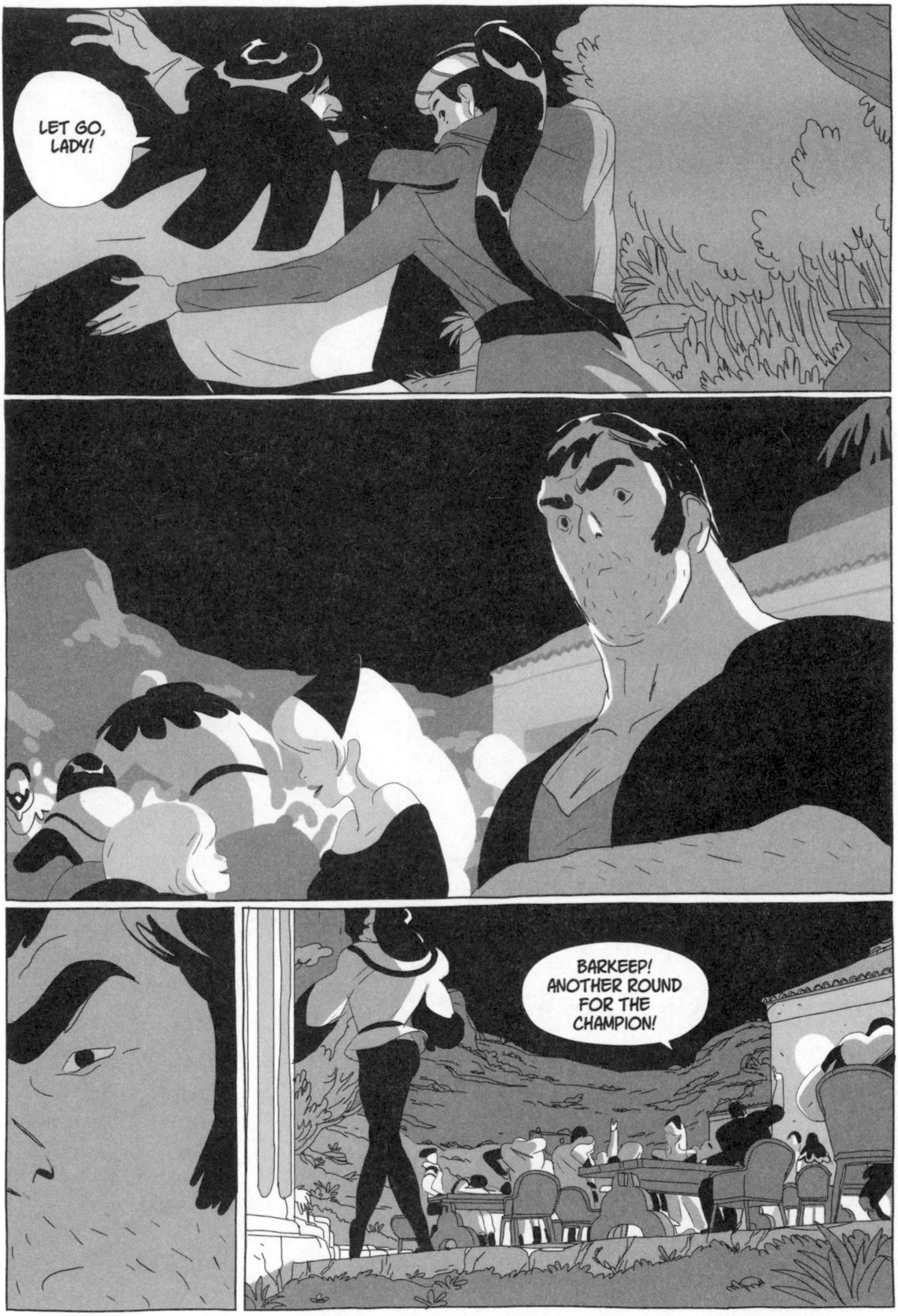
LET GO, LADY!
BARKEEP! ANOTHER ROUND FOR THE CHAMPION!

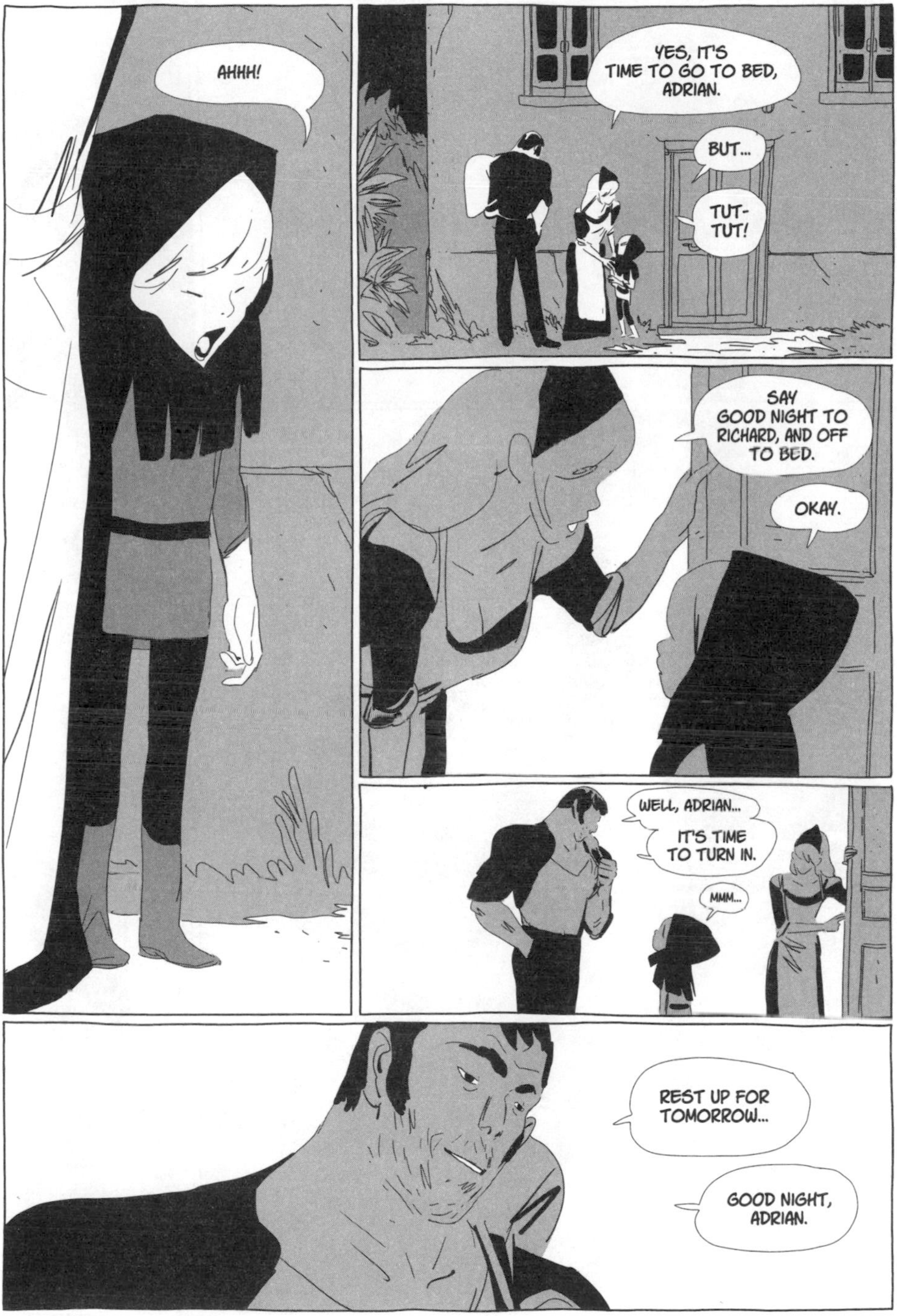
AHHH!
YES, IT'S TIME TO GO TO BED, ADRIAN.
BUT...
TUT-TUT!
SAY GOOD NIGHT TO RICHARD, AND OFF TO BED.
OKAY.
WELL, ADRIAN...
IT'S TIME TO TURN IN.
MMM...
REST UP FOR TOMORROW...
GOOD NIGHT, ADRIAN.

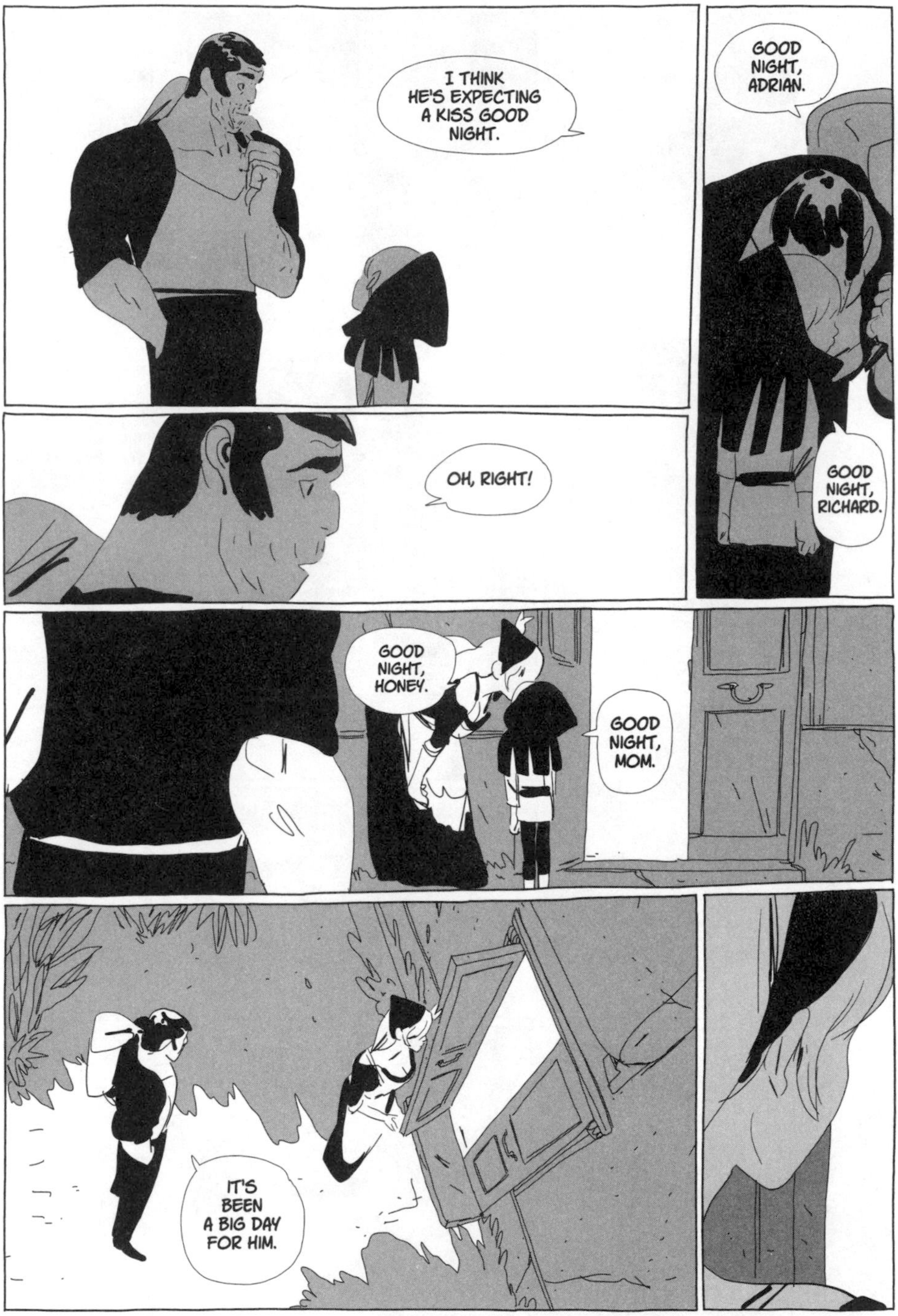
I THINK HE'S EXPECTING A KISS GOOD NIGHT.
OH, RIGHT!
GOOD NIGHT, ADRIAN.
GOOD NIGHT, RICHARD.
GOOD NIGHT, HONEY.
GOOD NIGHT, MOM.
IT'S BEEN A BIG DAY FOR HIM.

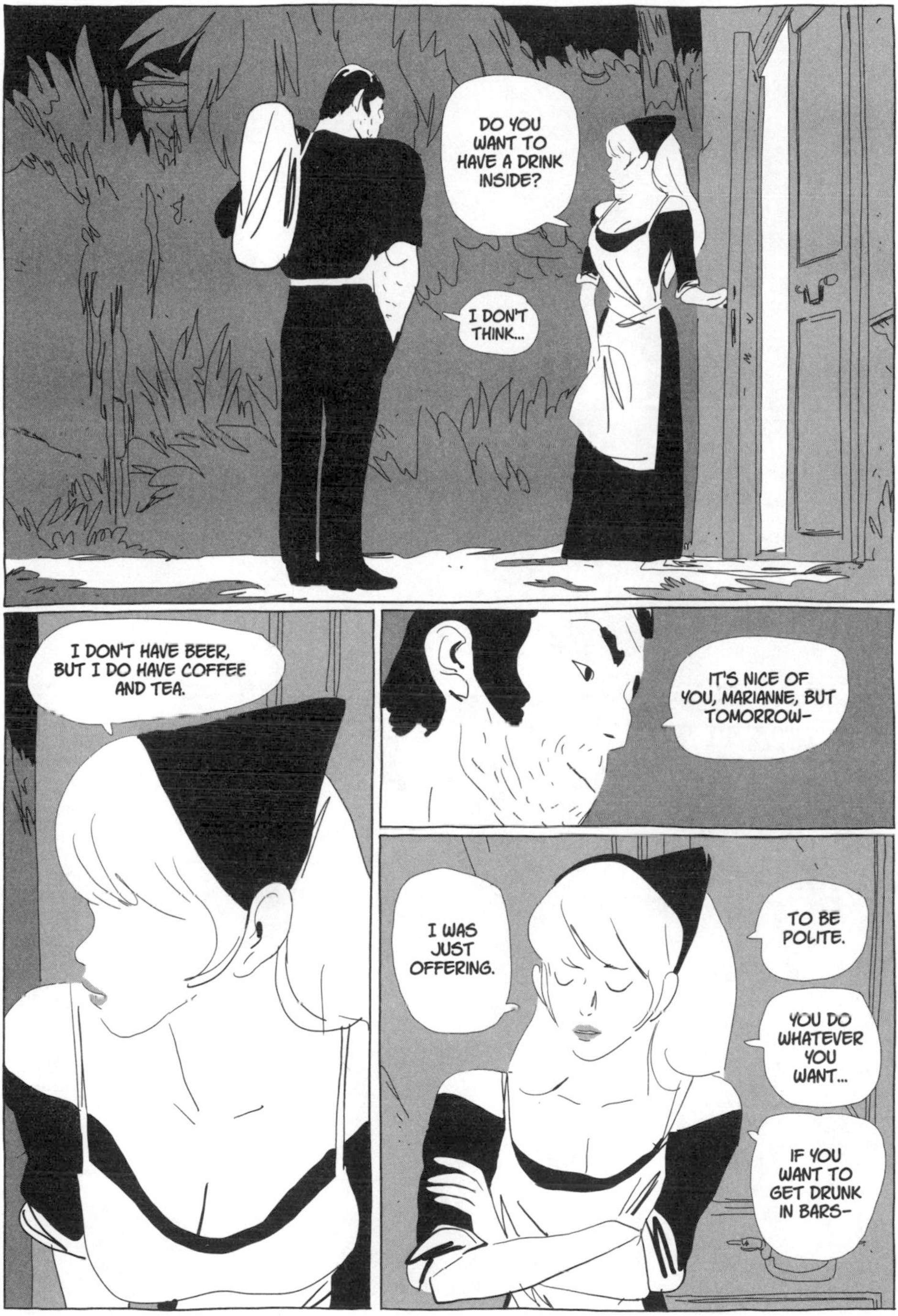
DO YOU WANT TO HAVE A DRINK INSIDE?
I DON'T THINK...
I DON'T HAVE BEER, BUT I DO HAVE COFFEE AND TEA.
IT'S NICE OF YOU, MARIANNE, BUT TOMORROW-
I WAS JUST OFFERING.
TO BE POLITE.
YOU DO WHATEVER YOU WANT...
IF YOU WANT TO GET DRUNK IN BARS-

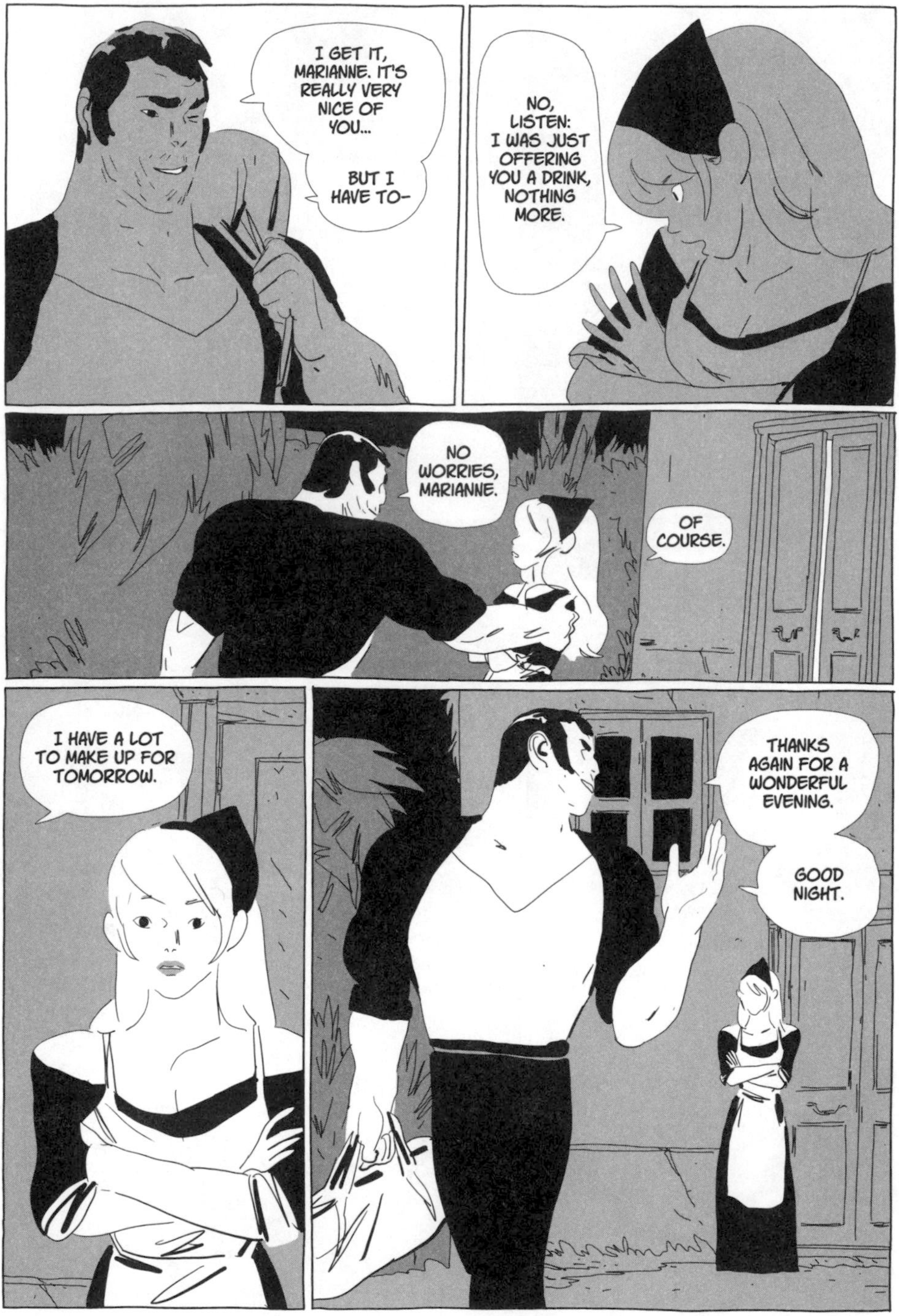
I GET IT, MARIANNE. IT'S REALLY VERY NICE OF YOU...
BUT I HAVE TO-
NO, LISTEN: I WAS JUST OFFERING YOU A DRINK, NOTHING MORE.
NO WORRIES, MARIANNE.
OF COURSE.
I HAVE A LOT TO MAKE UP FOR TOMORROW.
THANKS AGAIN FOR A WONDERFUL EVENING.
GOOD NIGHT.

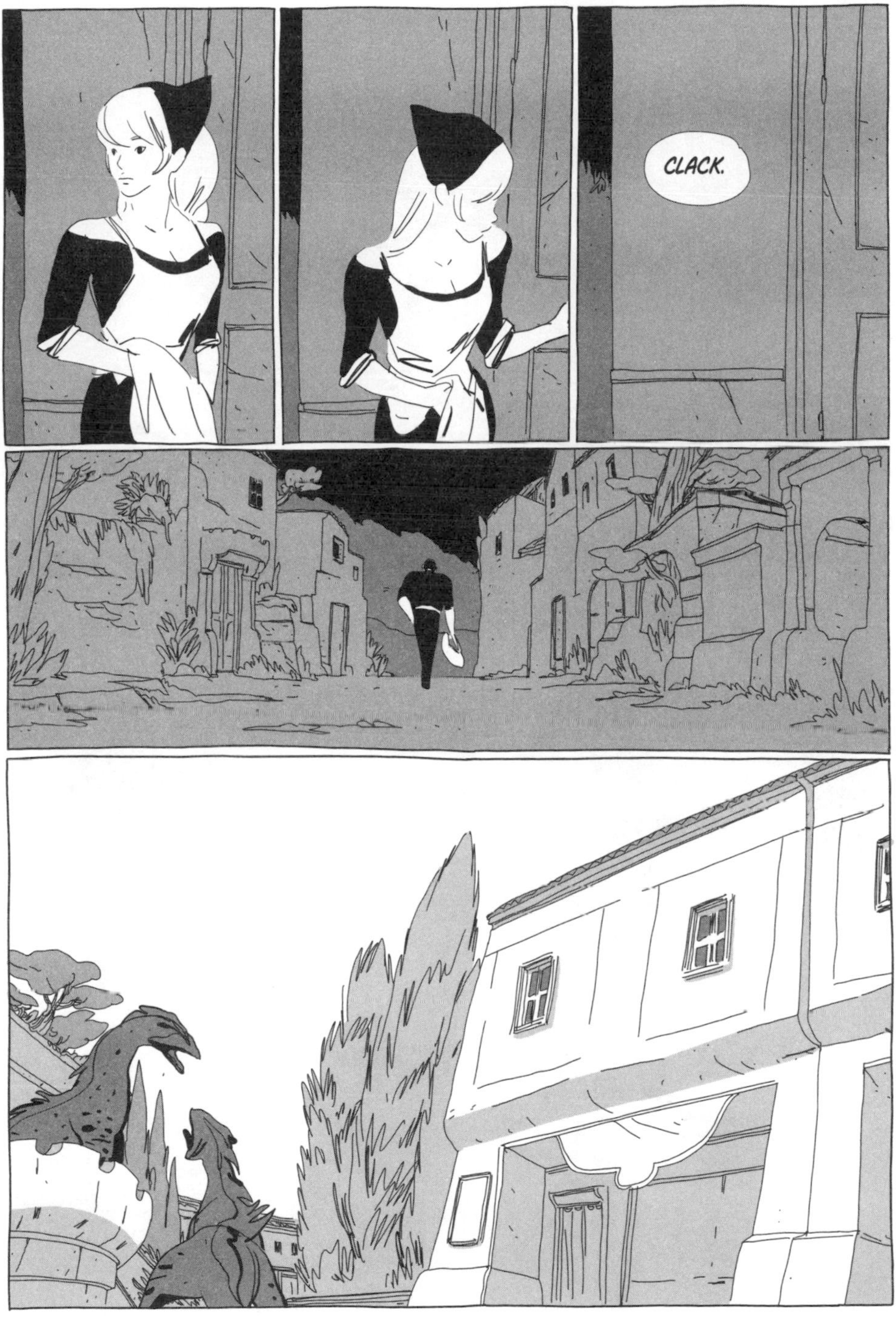
CLACK.

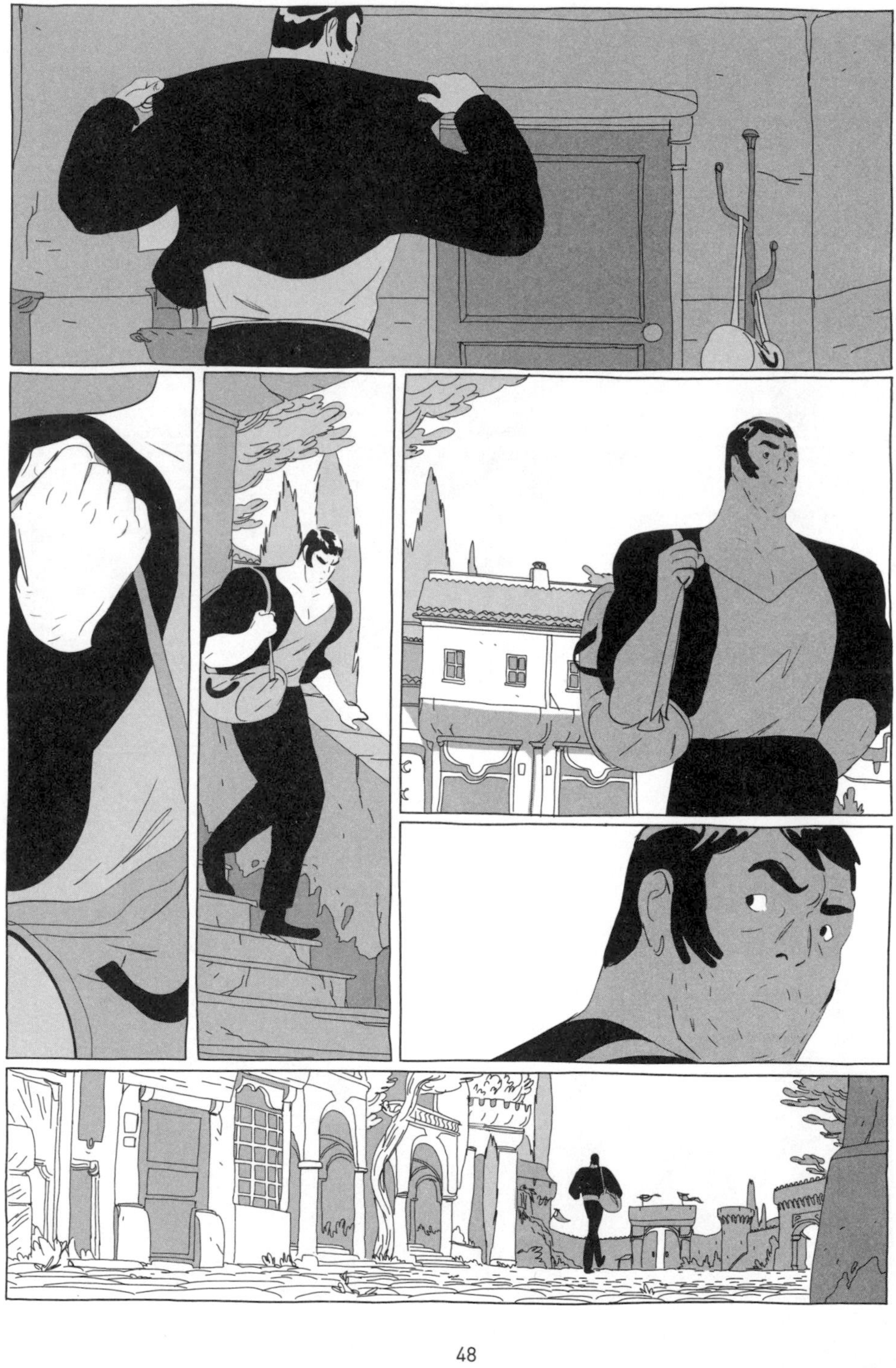

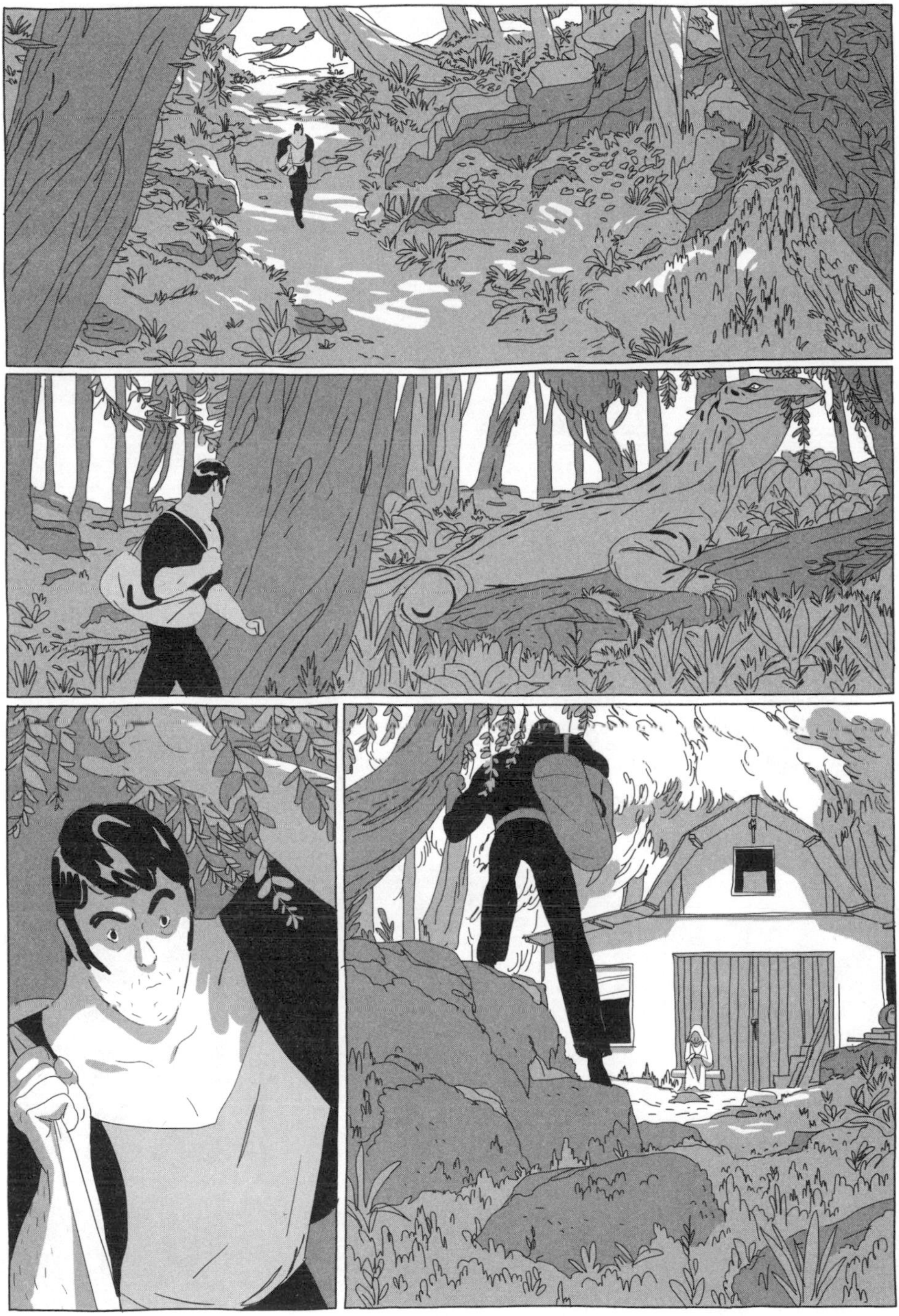

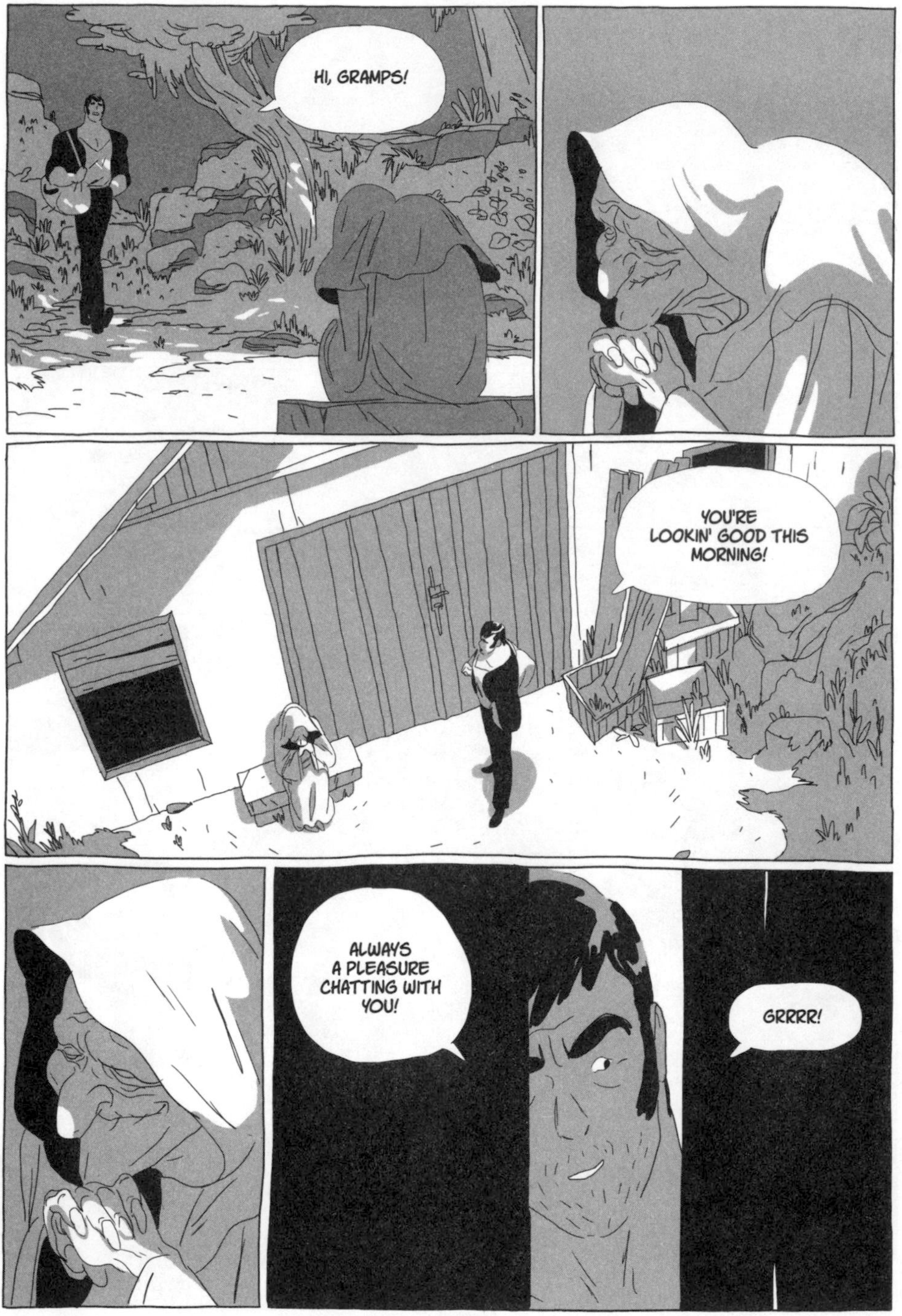
HI, GRAMPS!
YOU'RE LOOKIN' GOOD THIS MORNING!
ALWAYS A PLEASURE CHATTING WITH YOU!
GRRRR!

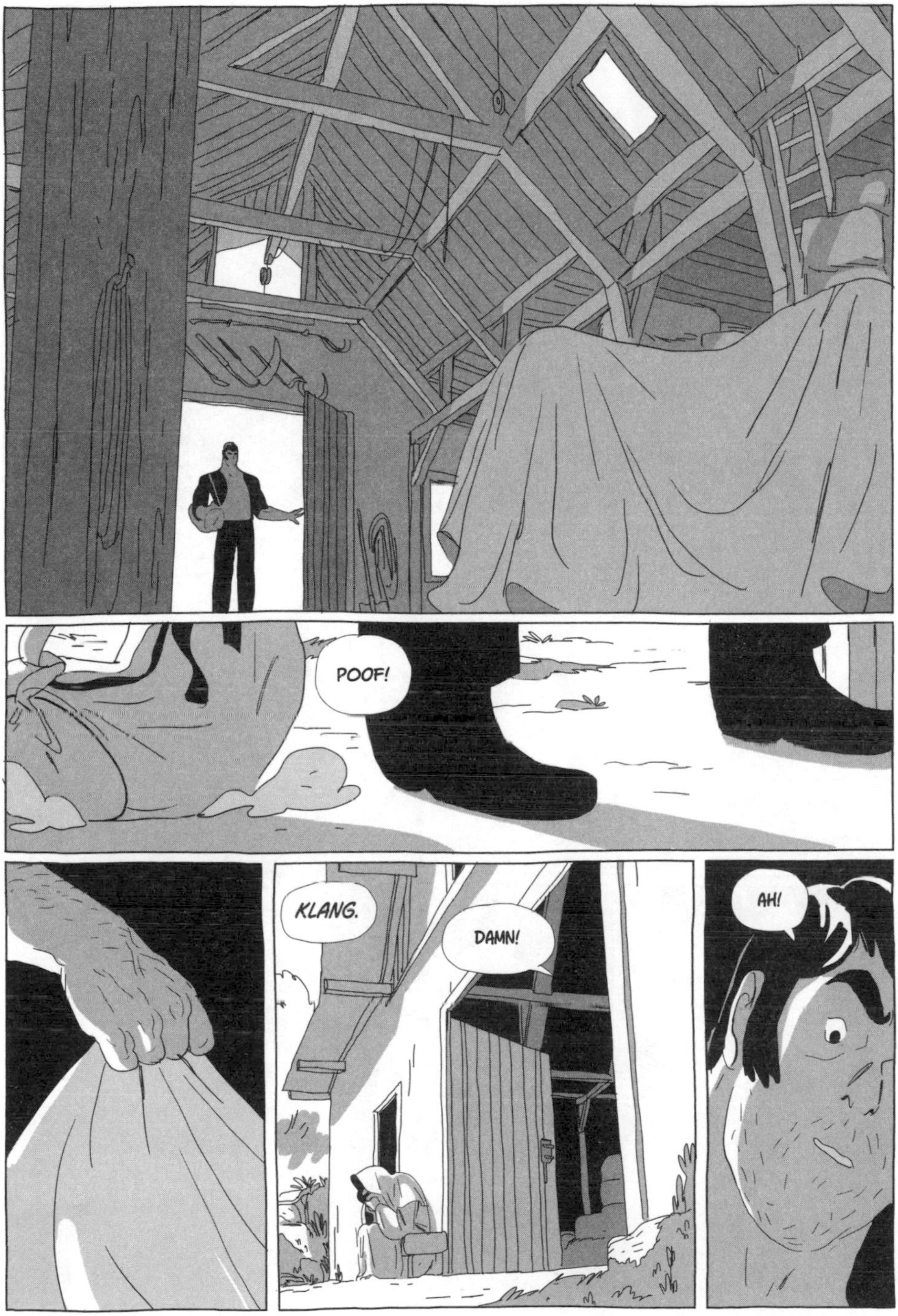
POOF!
KLANG.
DAMN!
AH!

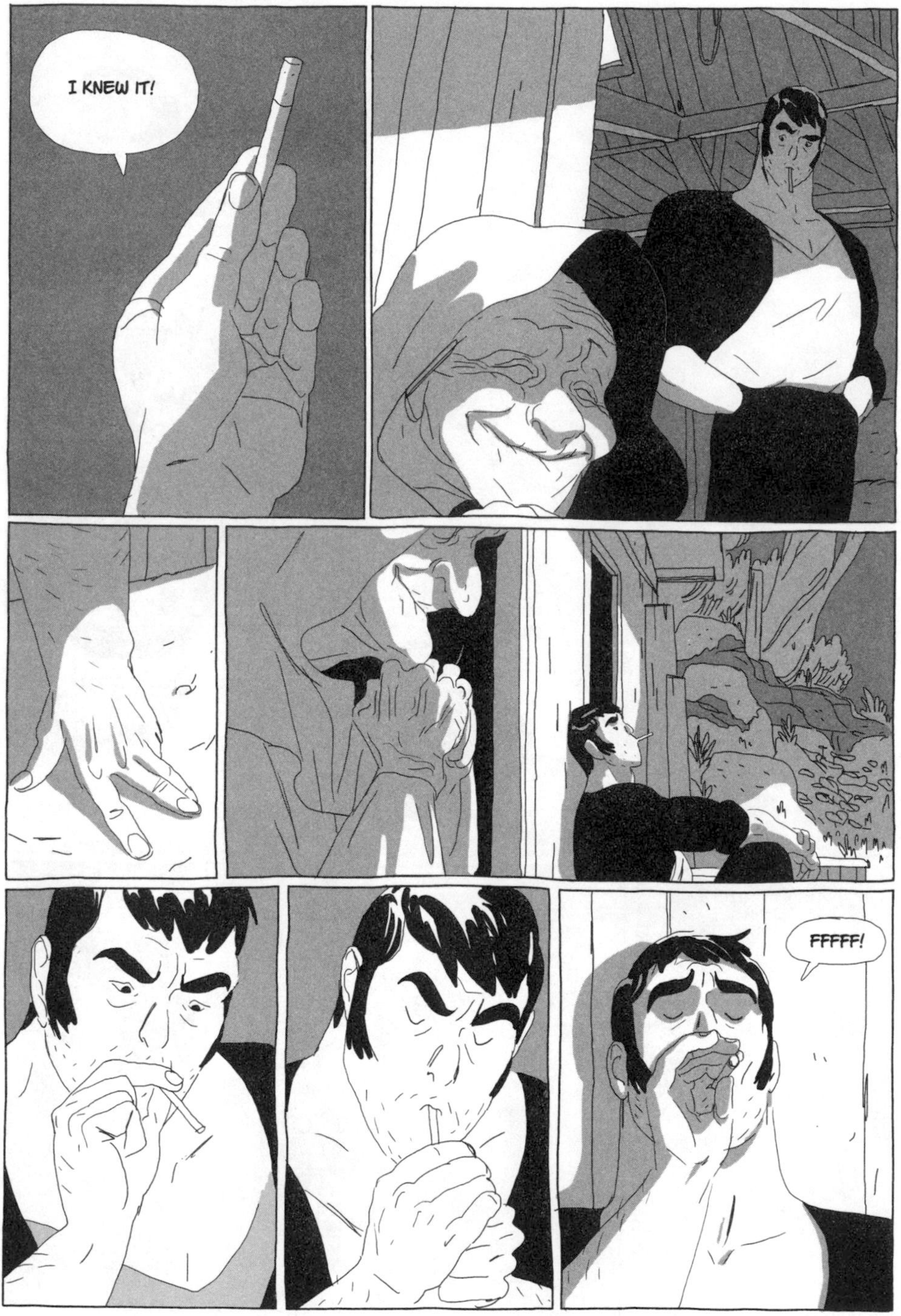
I KNEW IT!
FFFFF!

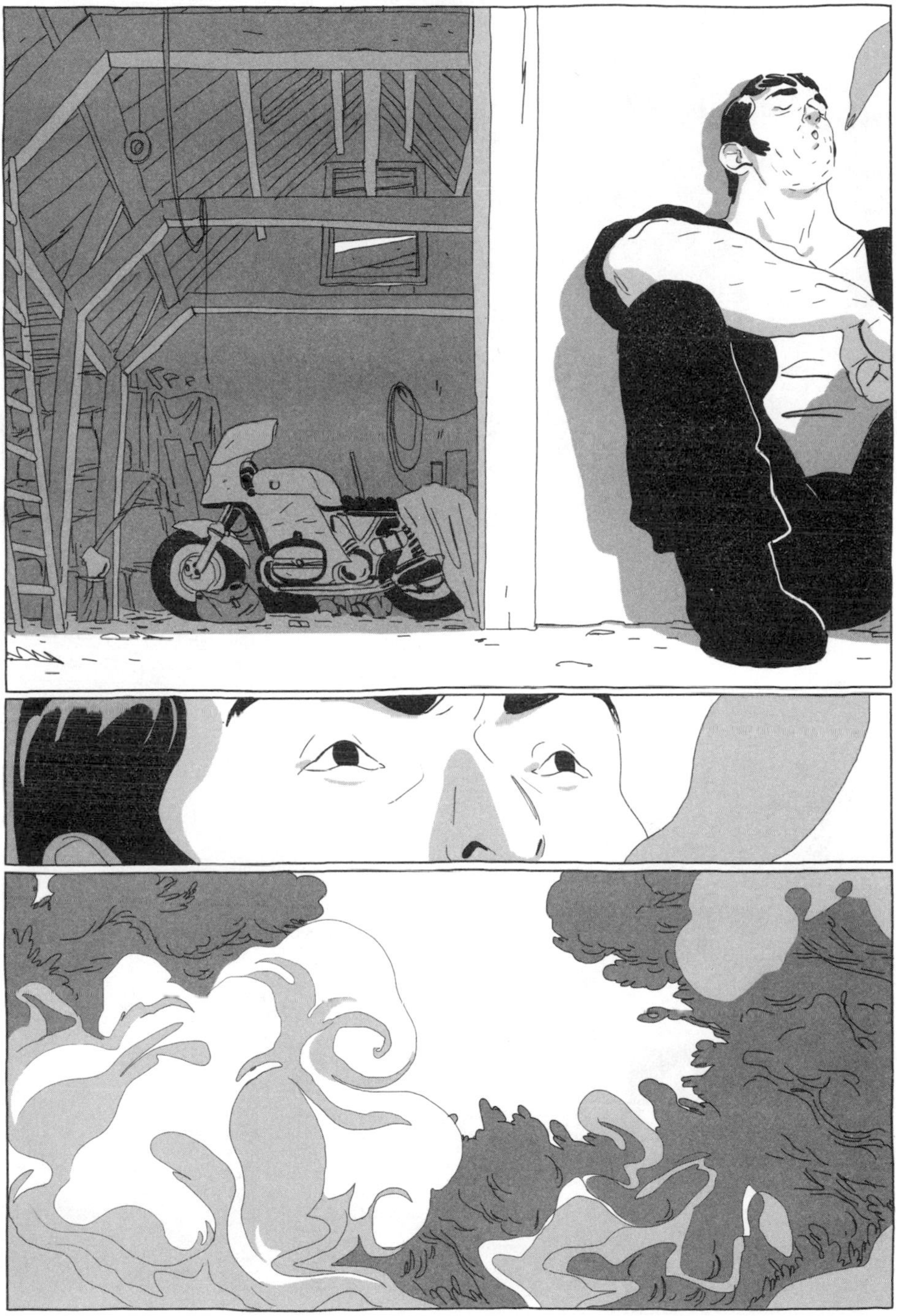

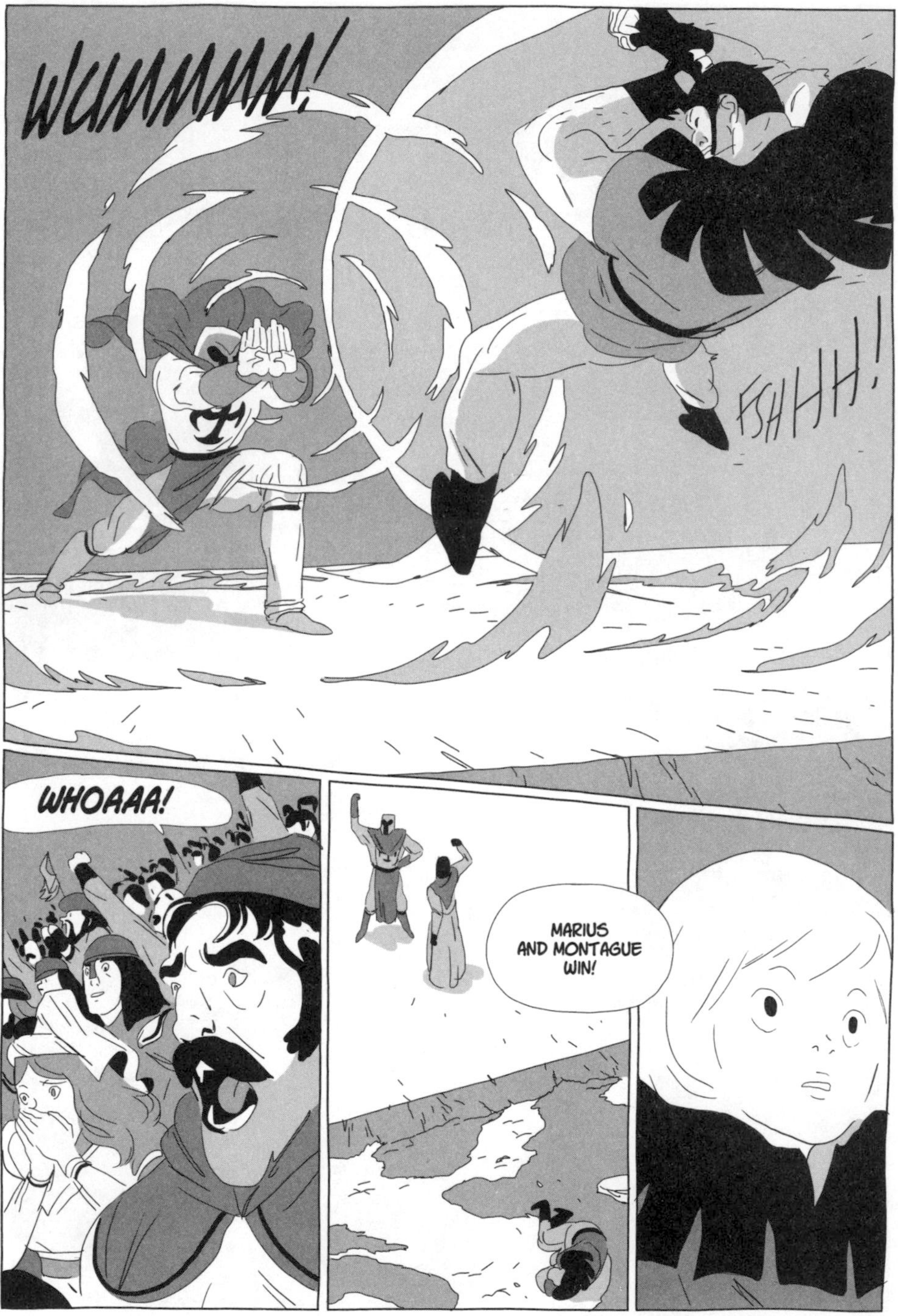
WUMMMM!
FSHHH!
WHOAAA!
MARIUS AND MONTAGUE WIN!

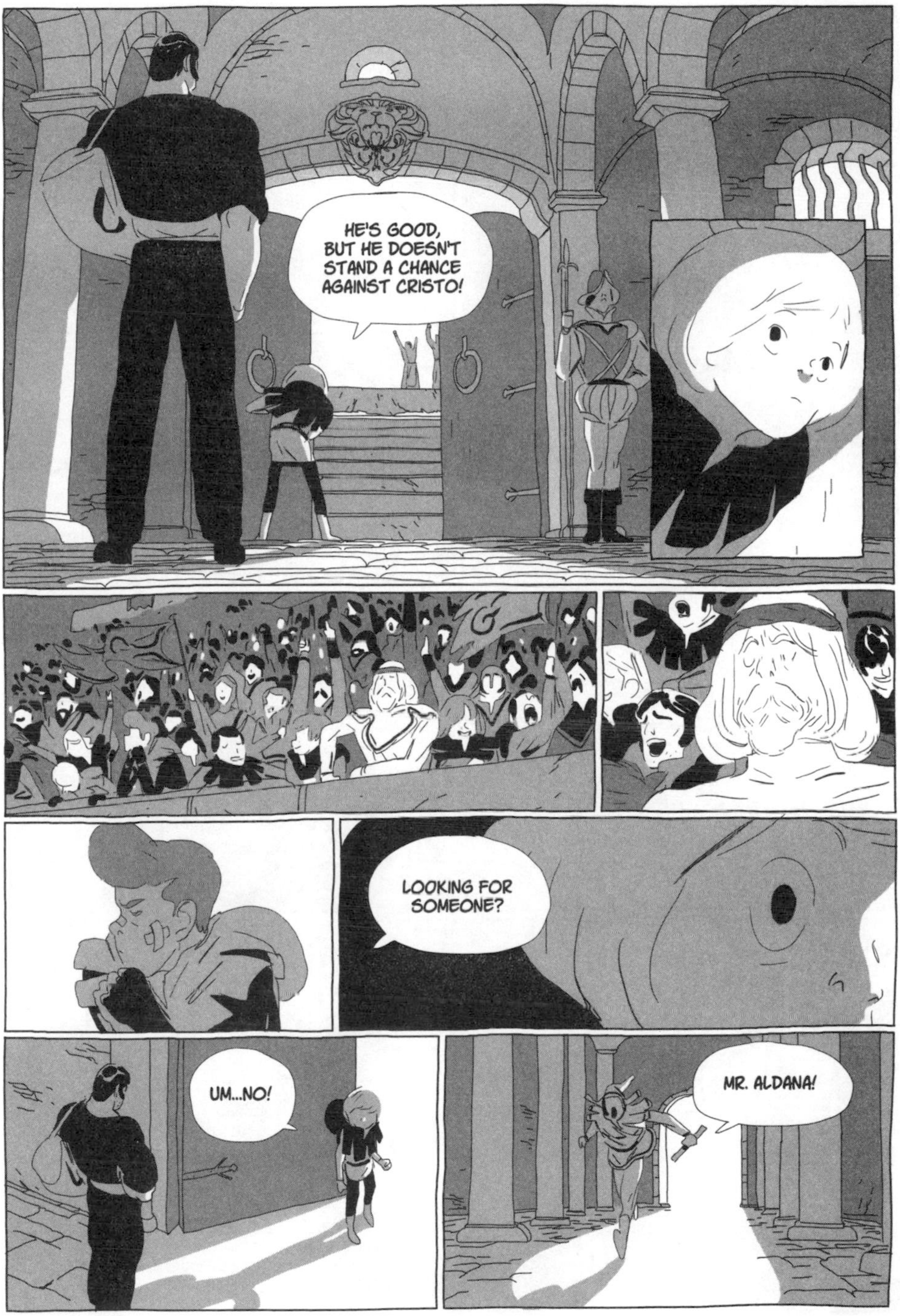
HE'S GOOD, BUT HE DOESN'T STAND A CHANCE AGAINST CRISTO!
LOOKING FOR SOMEONE?
UM...NO!
MR. ALDANA!

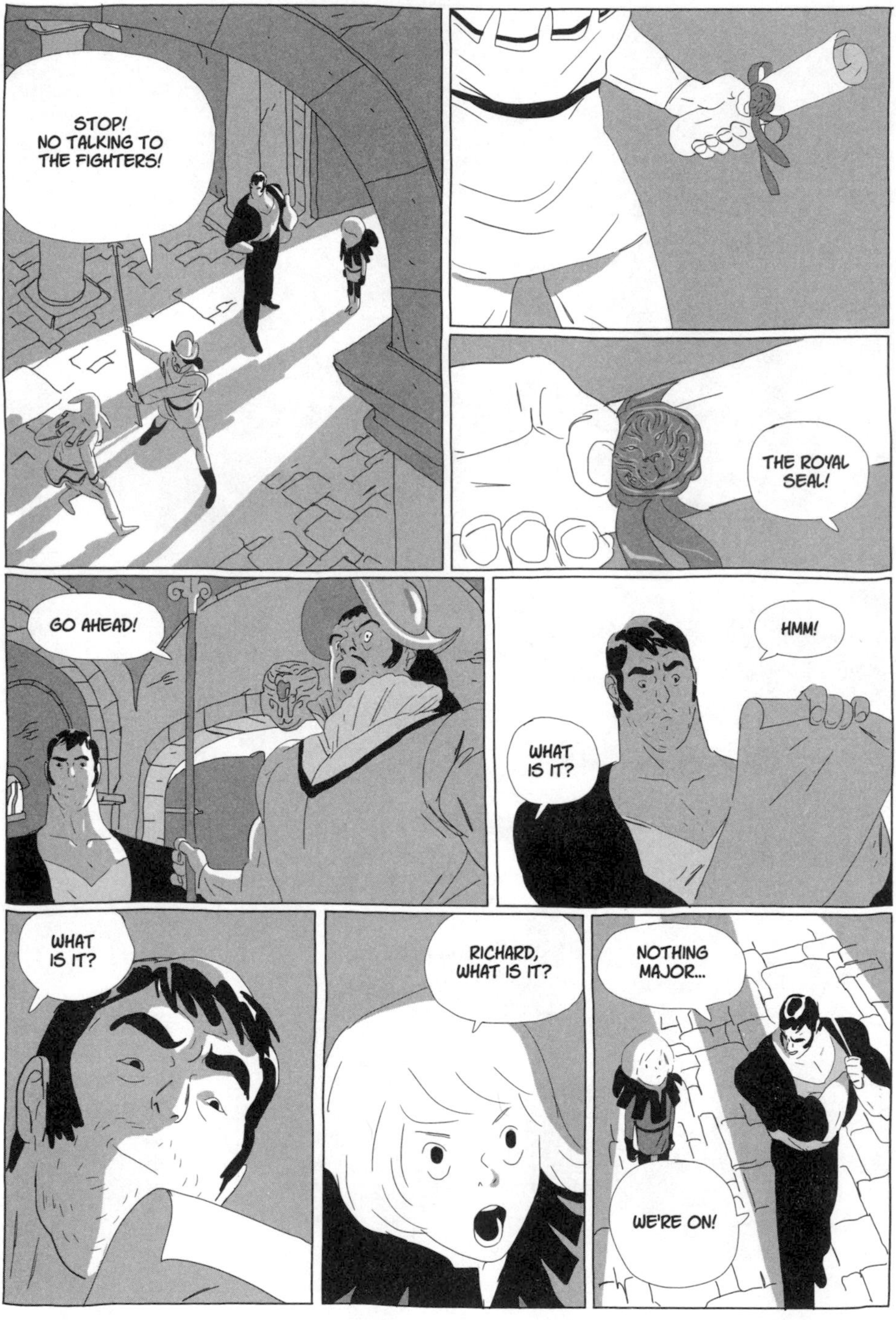
STOP!
NO TALKING TO THE FIGHTERS!
THE ROYAL SEAL!
GO AHEAD!
HMM!
WHAT IS IT?
WHAT IS IT?
RICHARD, WHAT IS IT?
NOTHING MAJOR...
WE'RE ON!

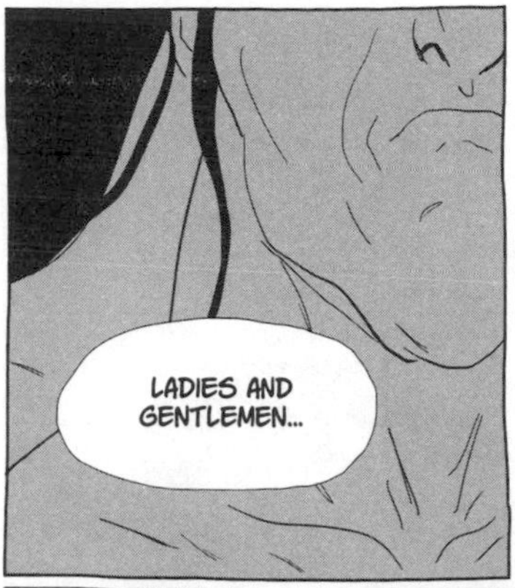
LADIES AND GENTLEMEN...

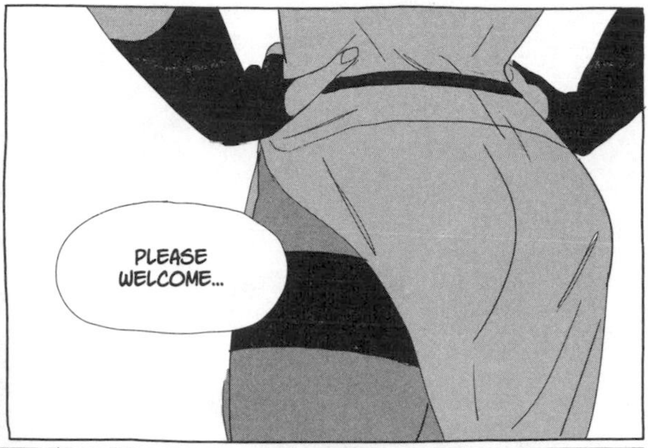
PLEASE WELCOME...

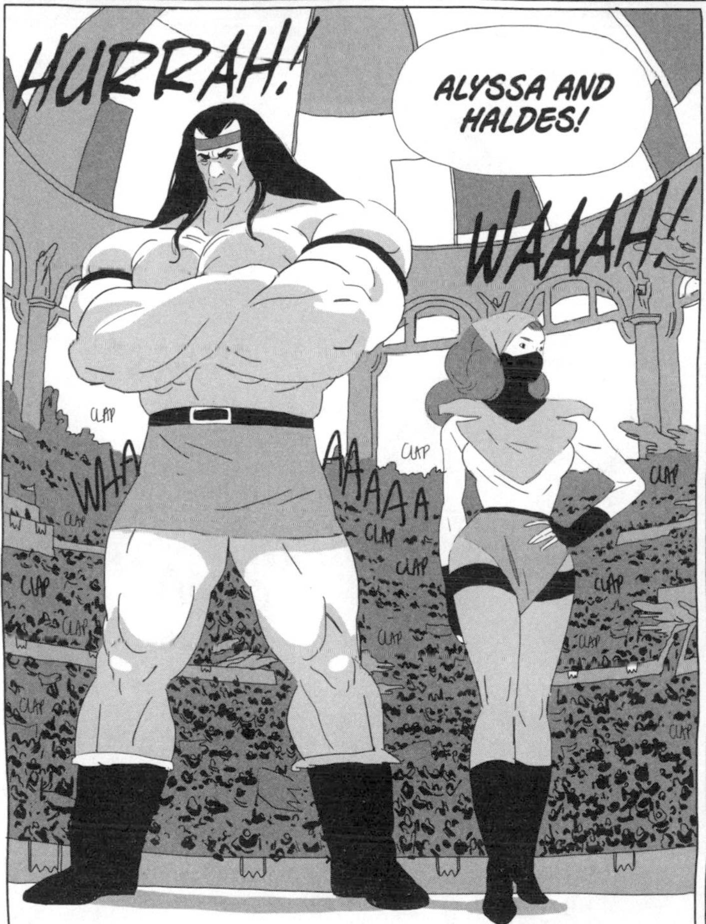
HURRAH!
ALYSSA AND HALDES!
WAAAH!
WHA
AAAAA
CLAP
CLAP
CLAP

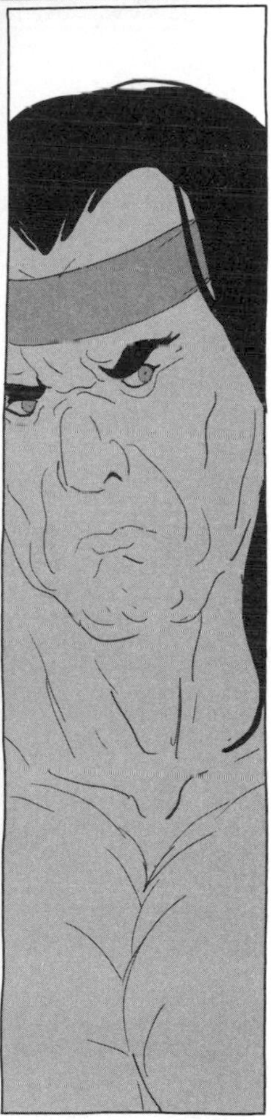

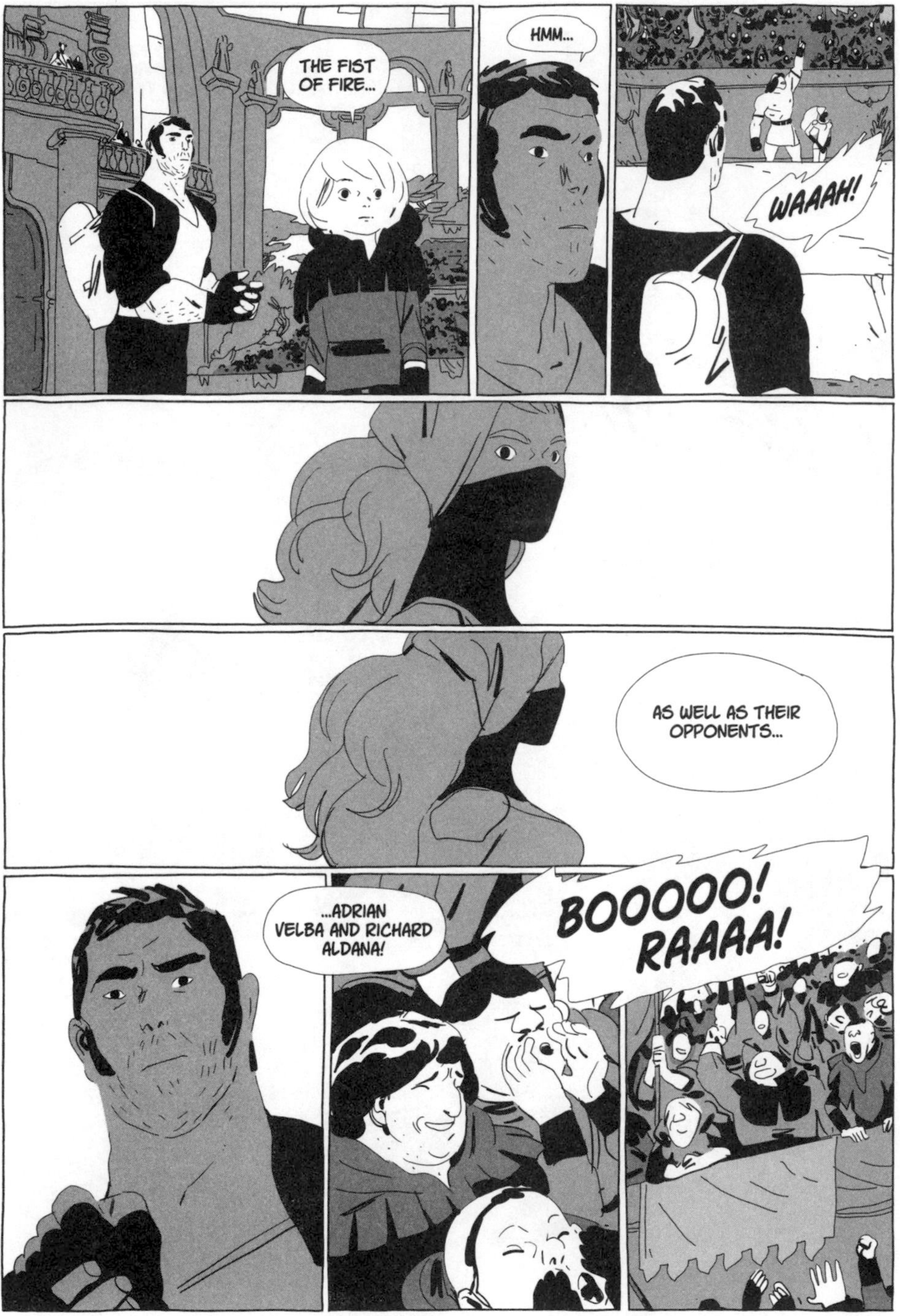
THE FIST OF FIRE...
HMM...
WAAAH!
AS WELL AS THEIR OPPONENTS...
...ADRIAN VELBA AND RICHARD ALDANA!
BOOOOO! RAAAA!

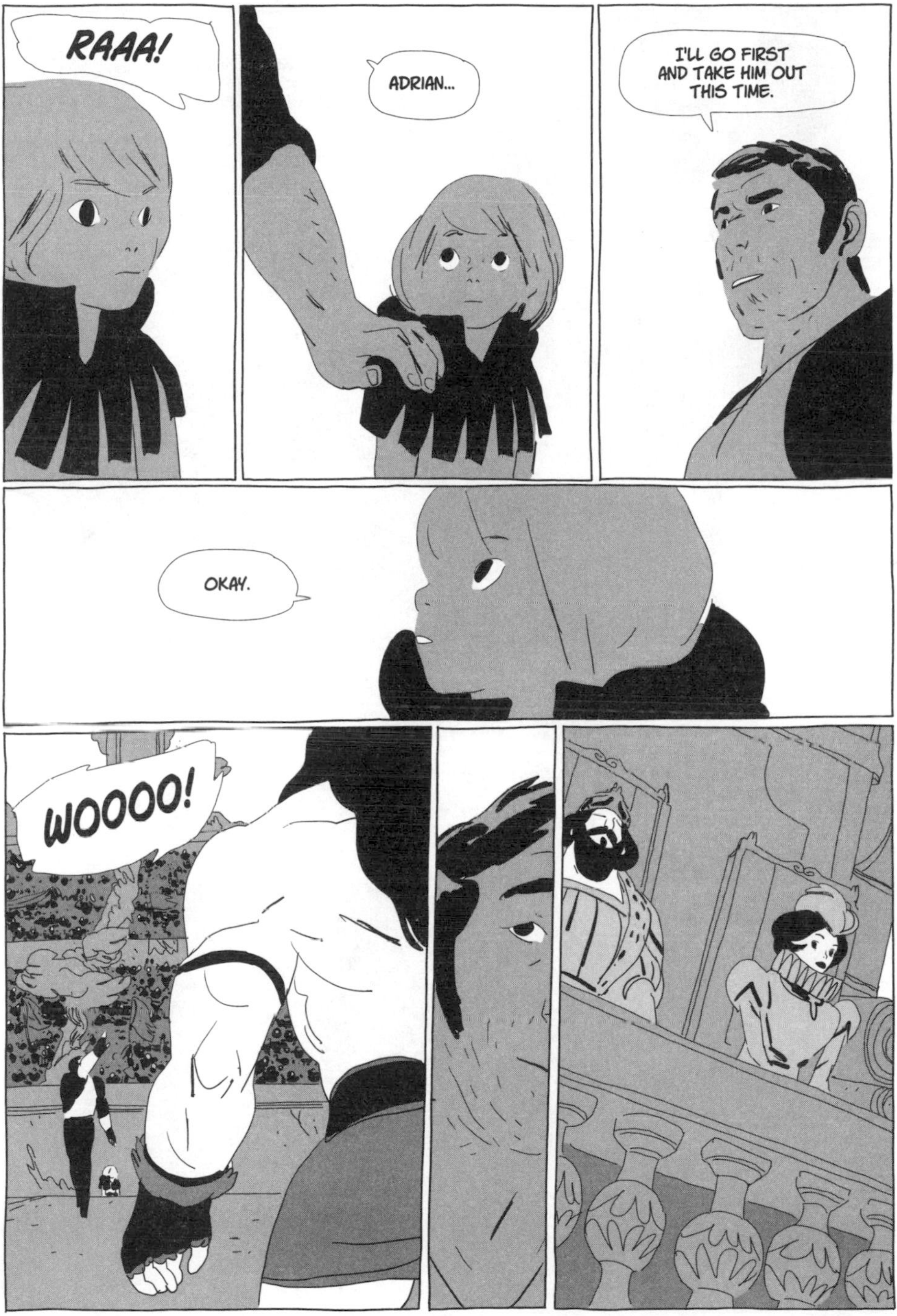
RAAA!
ADRIAN...
I'LL GO FIRST AND TAKE HIM OUT THIS TIME.
OKAY.
WOOOO!

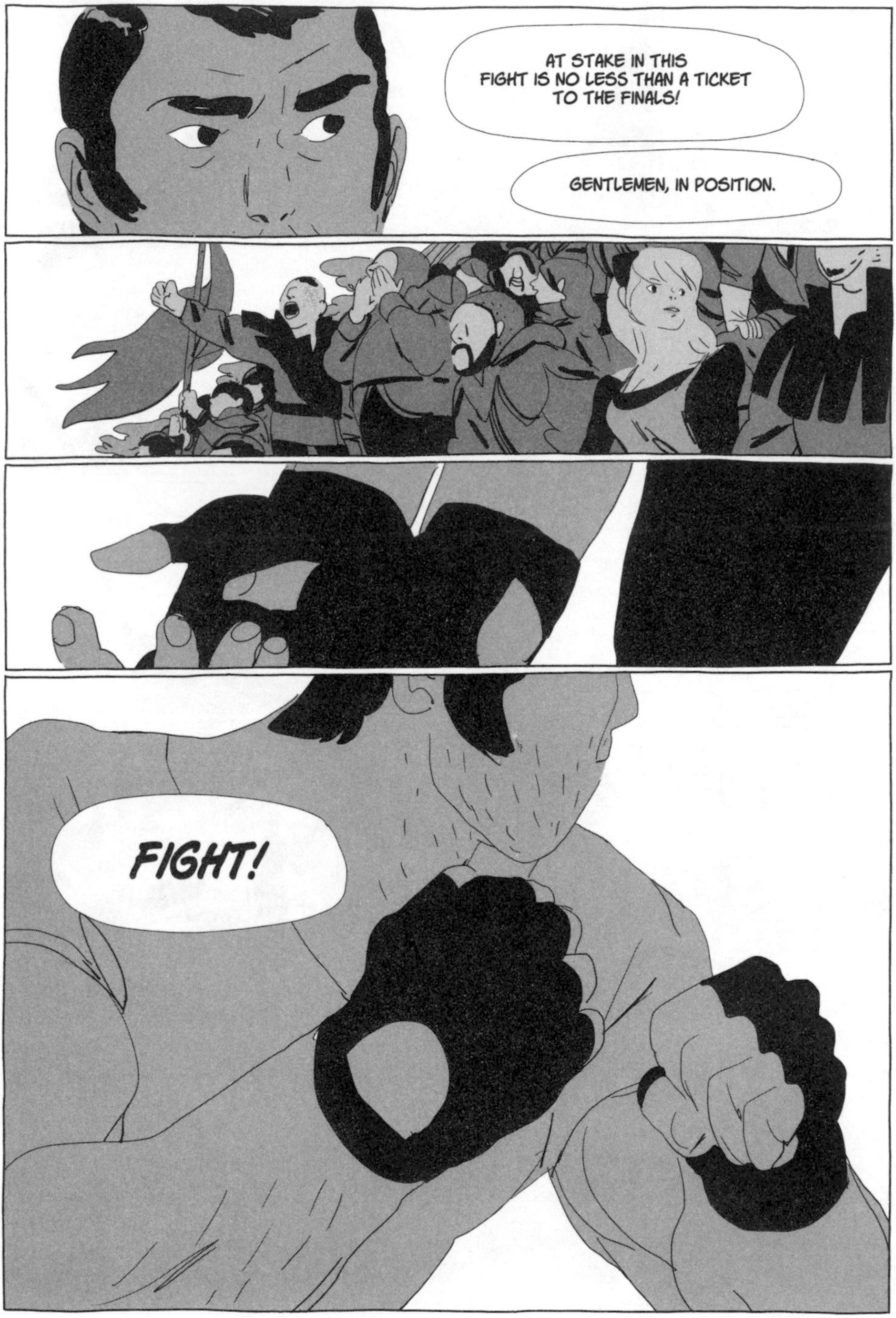
AT STAKE IN THIS FIGHT IS NO LESS THAN A TICKET TO THE FINALS!
GENTLEMEN, IN POSITION.
FIGHT!

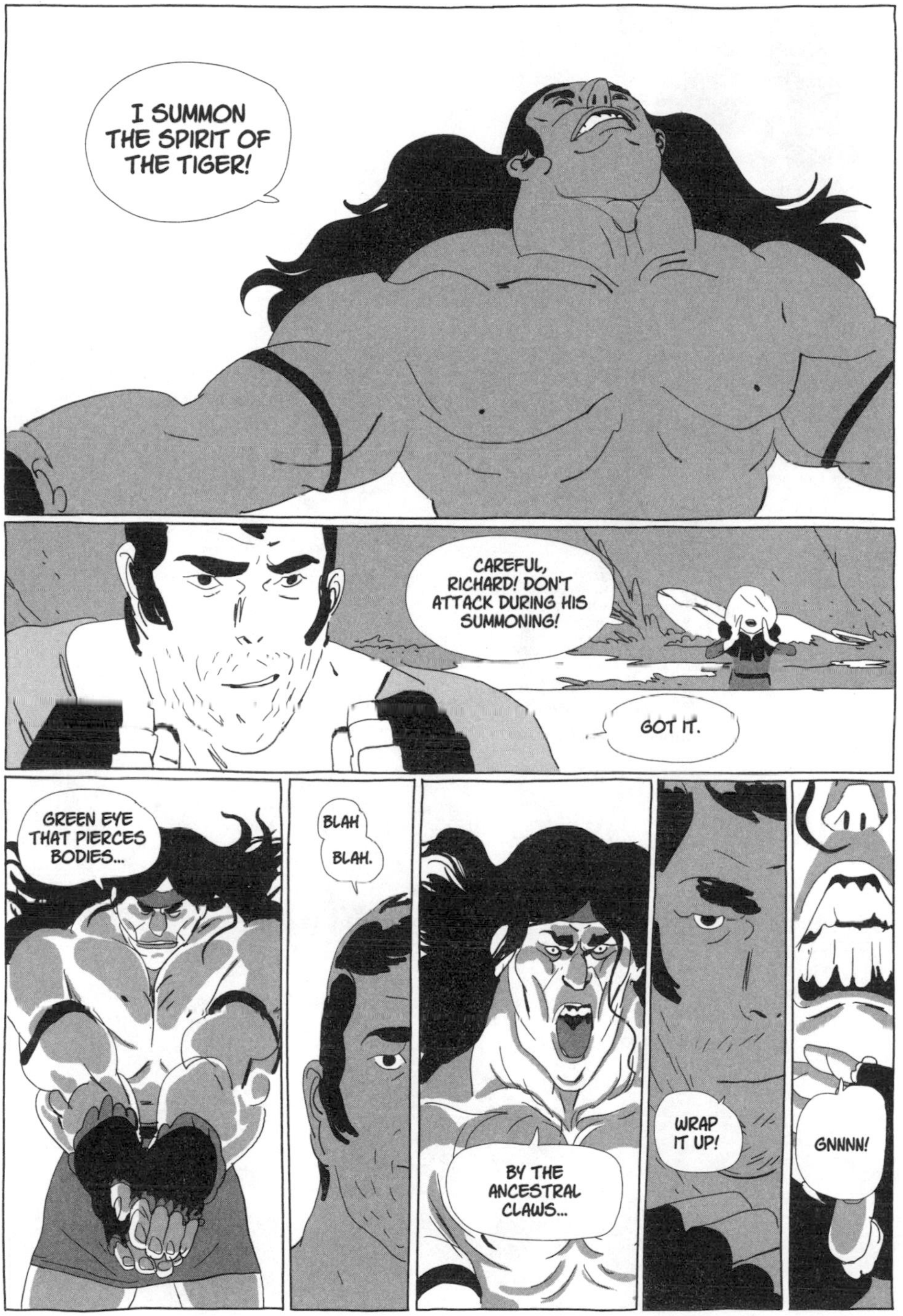
I SUMMON THE SPIRIT OF THE TIGER!
CAREFUL, RICHARD! DON'T ATTACK DURING HIS SUMMONING!
GOT IT.
GREEN EYE THAT PIERCES BODIES...
BLAH
BLAH.
BY THE ANCESTRAL CLAWS...
WRAP IT UP!
GNNNN!

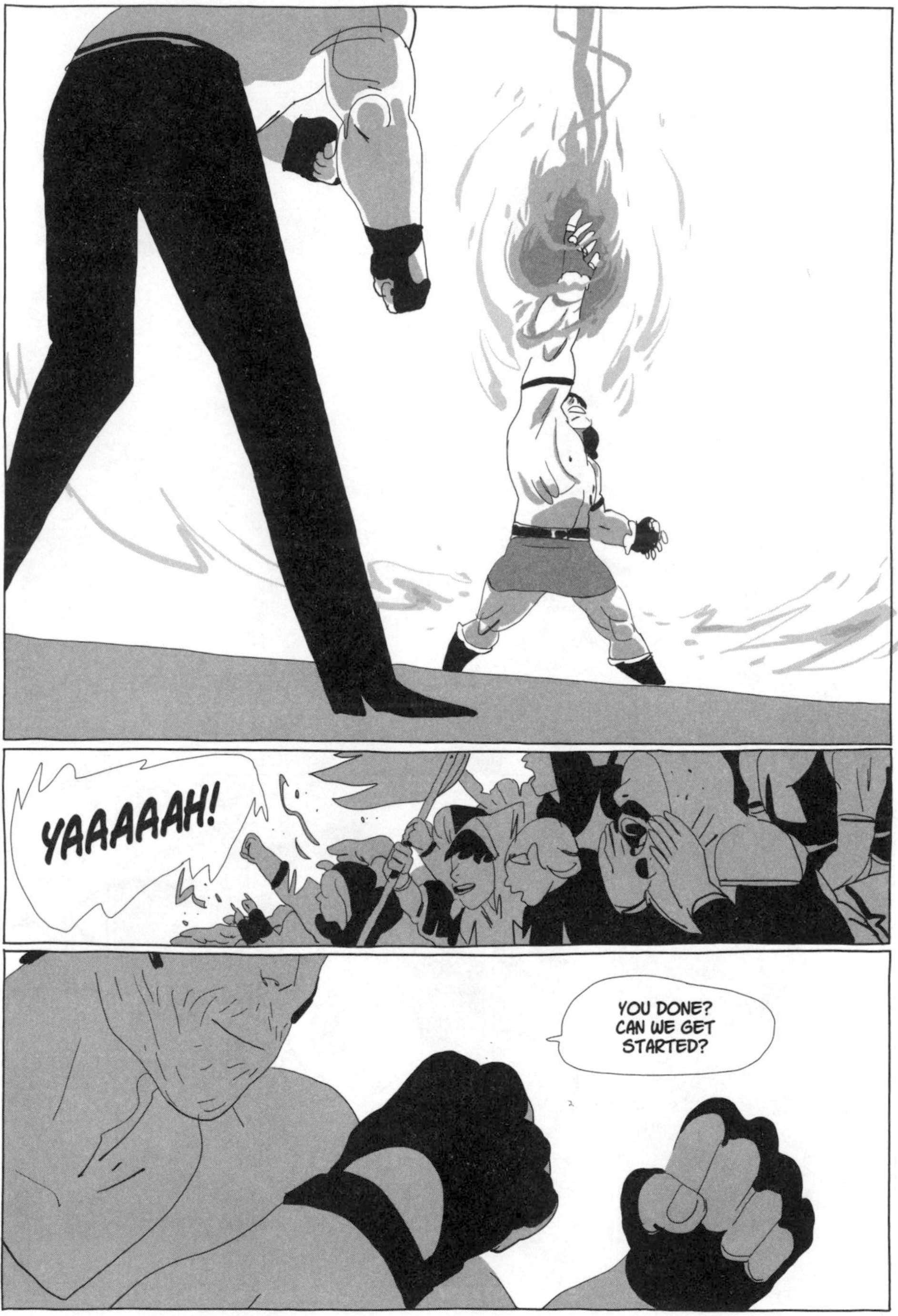
YAAAAAH!
YOU DONE? CAN WE GET STARTED?

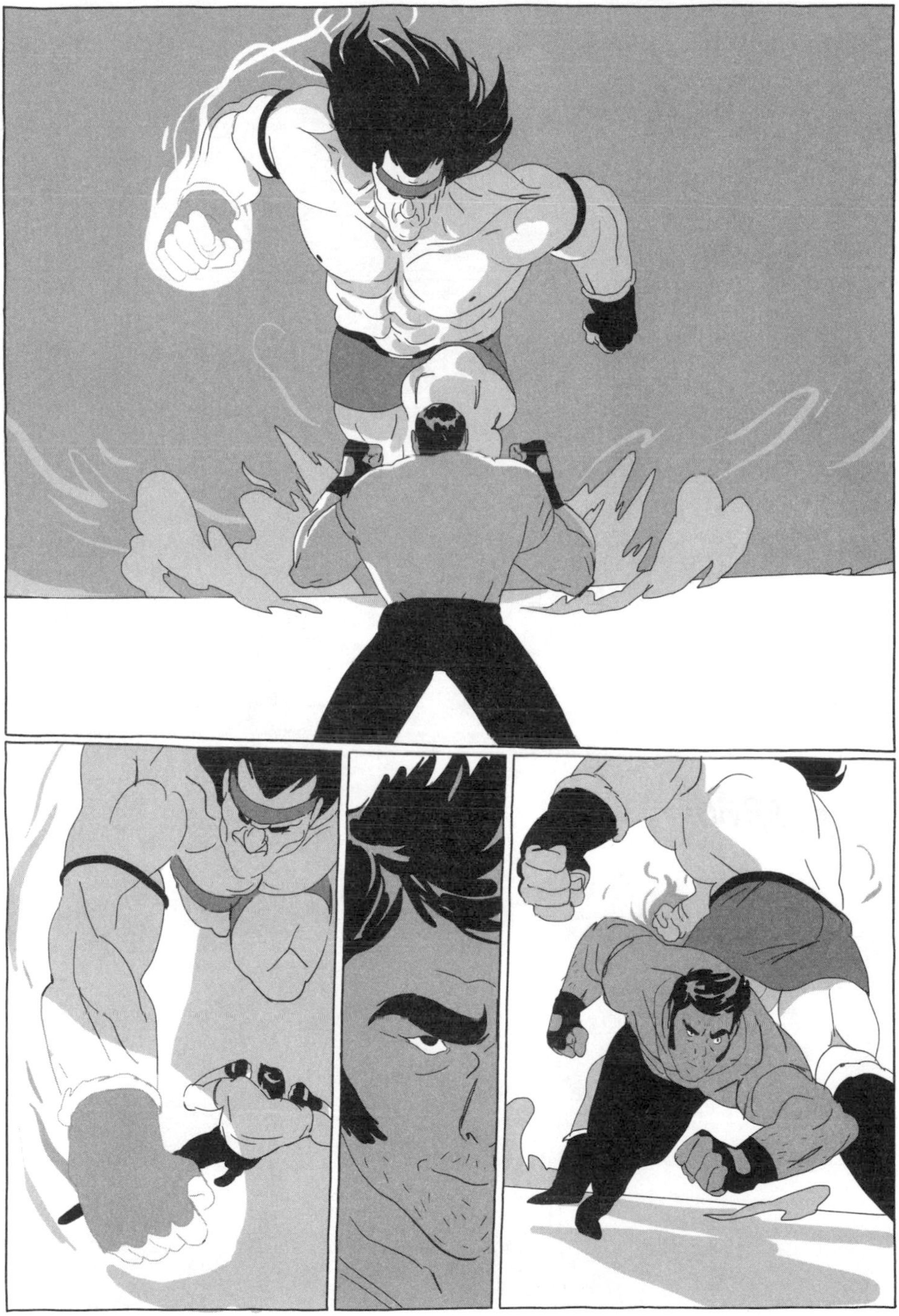

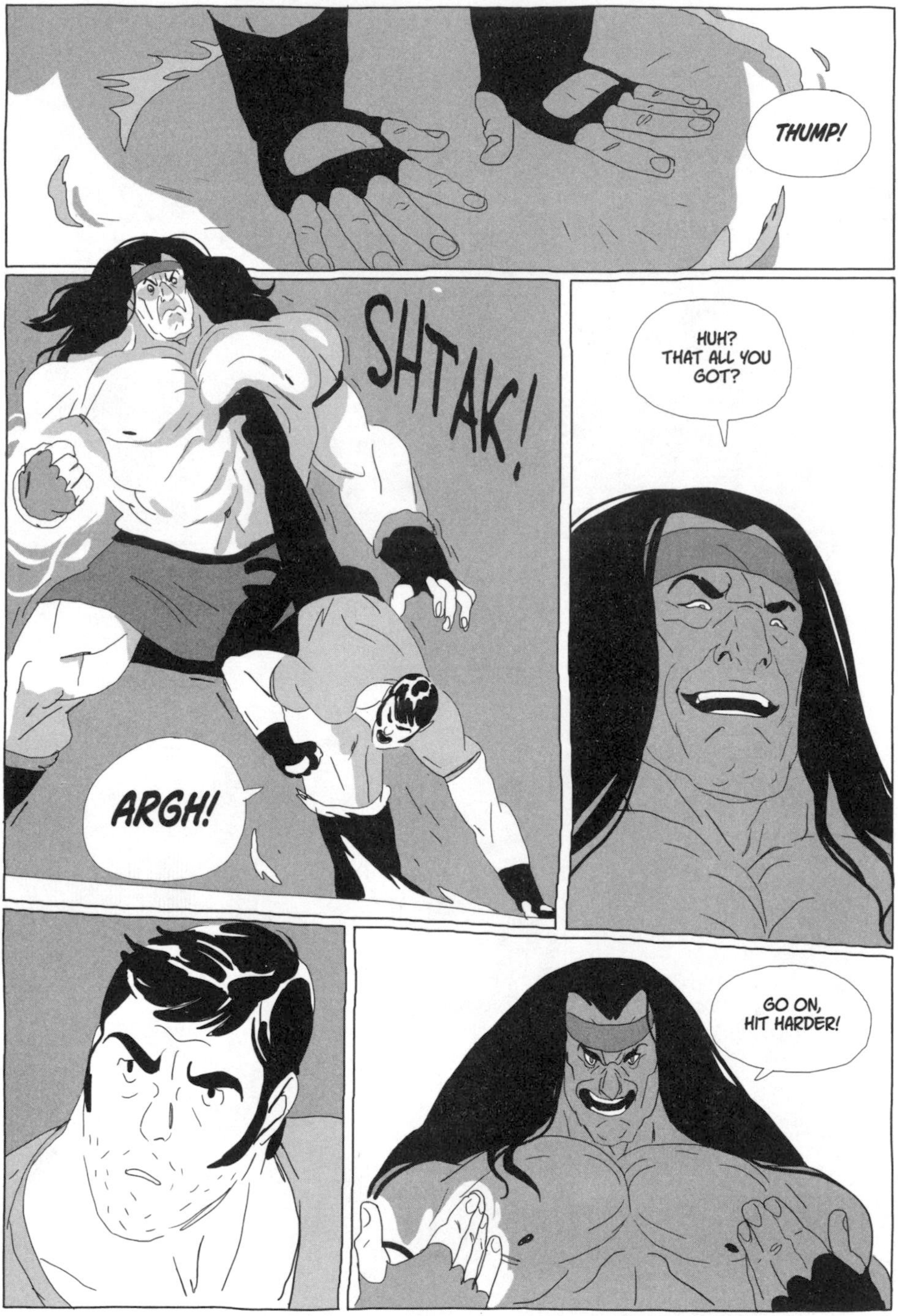
THUMP!
SHTAK!
ARGH!
HUH? THAT ALL YOU GOT?
GO ON, HIT HARDER!

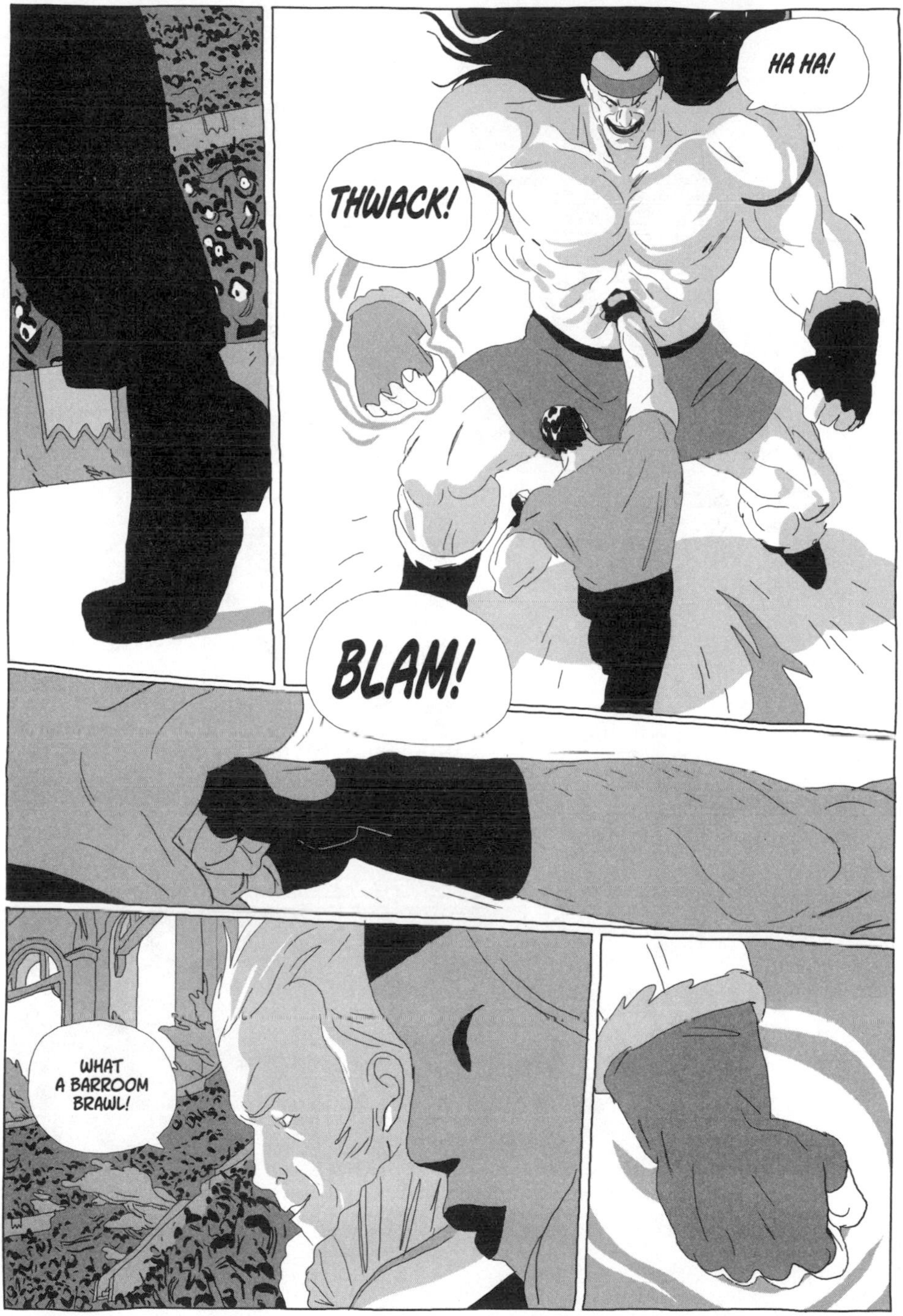
HA HA!
THWACK!
BLAM!
WHAT A BARROOM BRAWL!

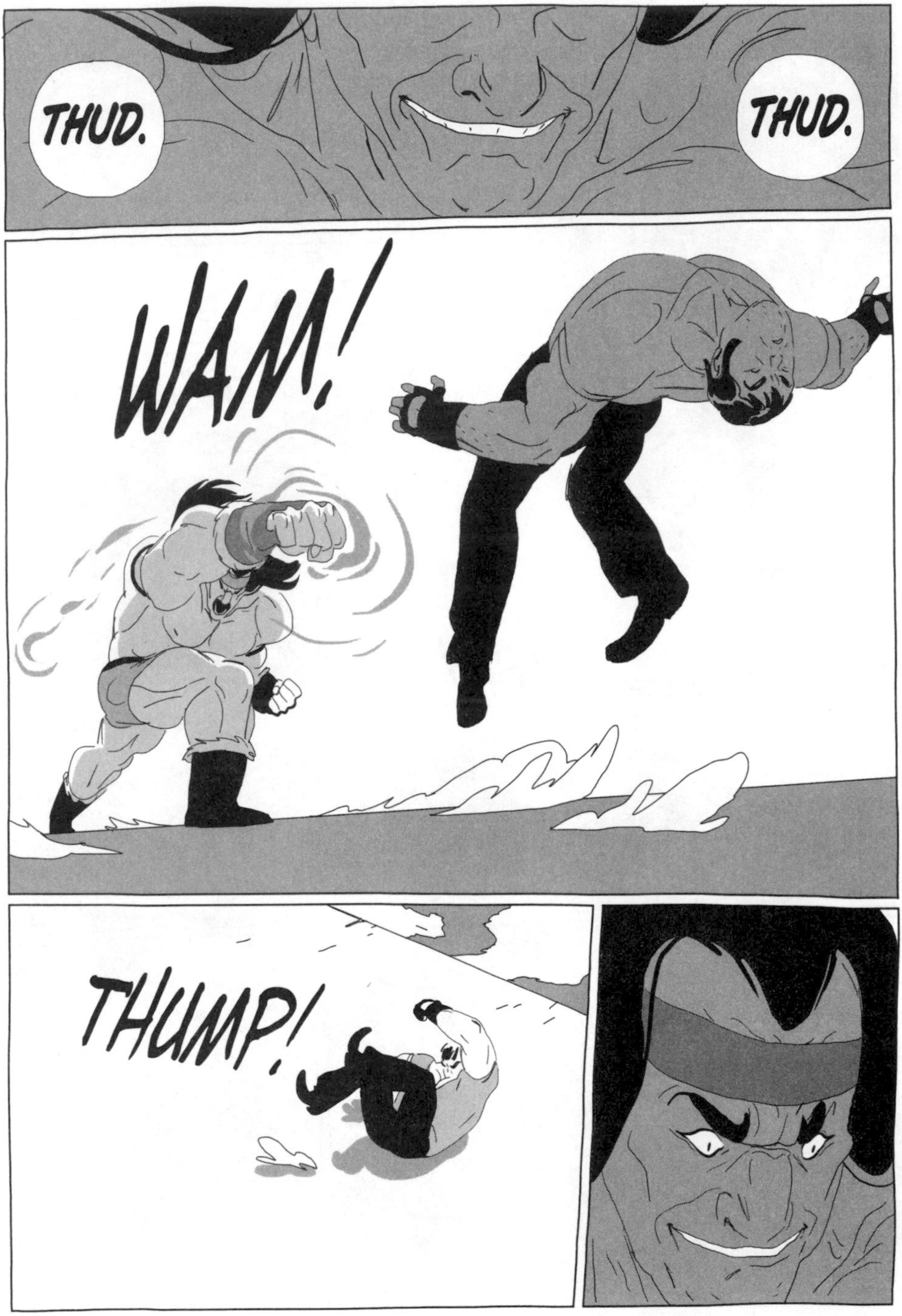
THUD.
THUD.
WAM!
THUMP!

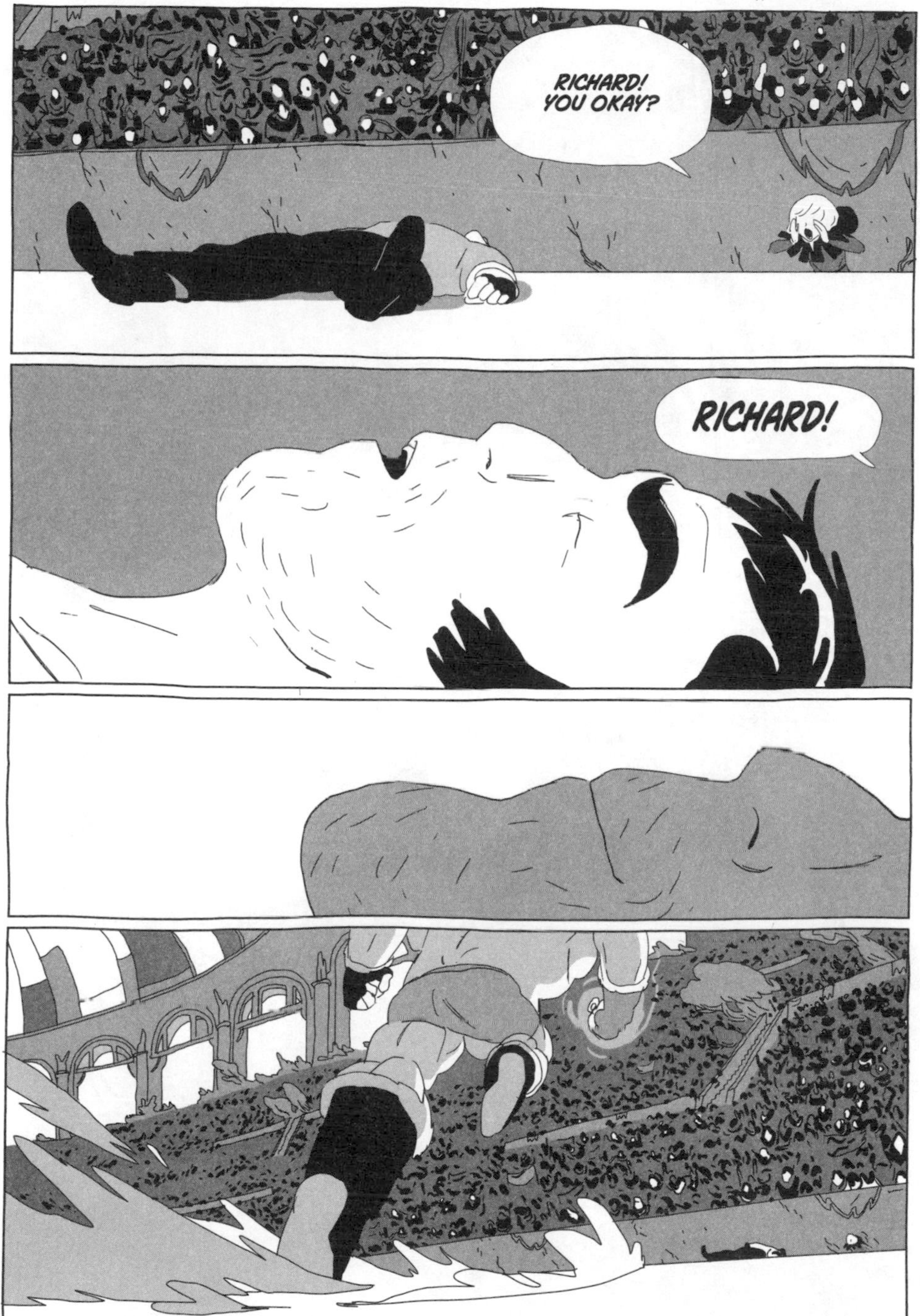
RICHARD!
YOU OKAY?
RICHARD!

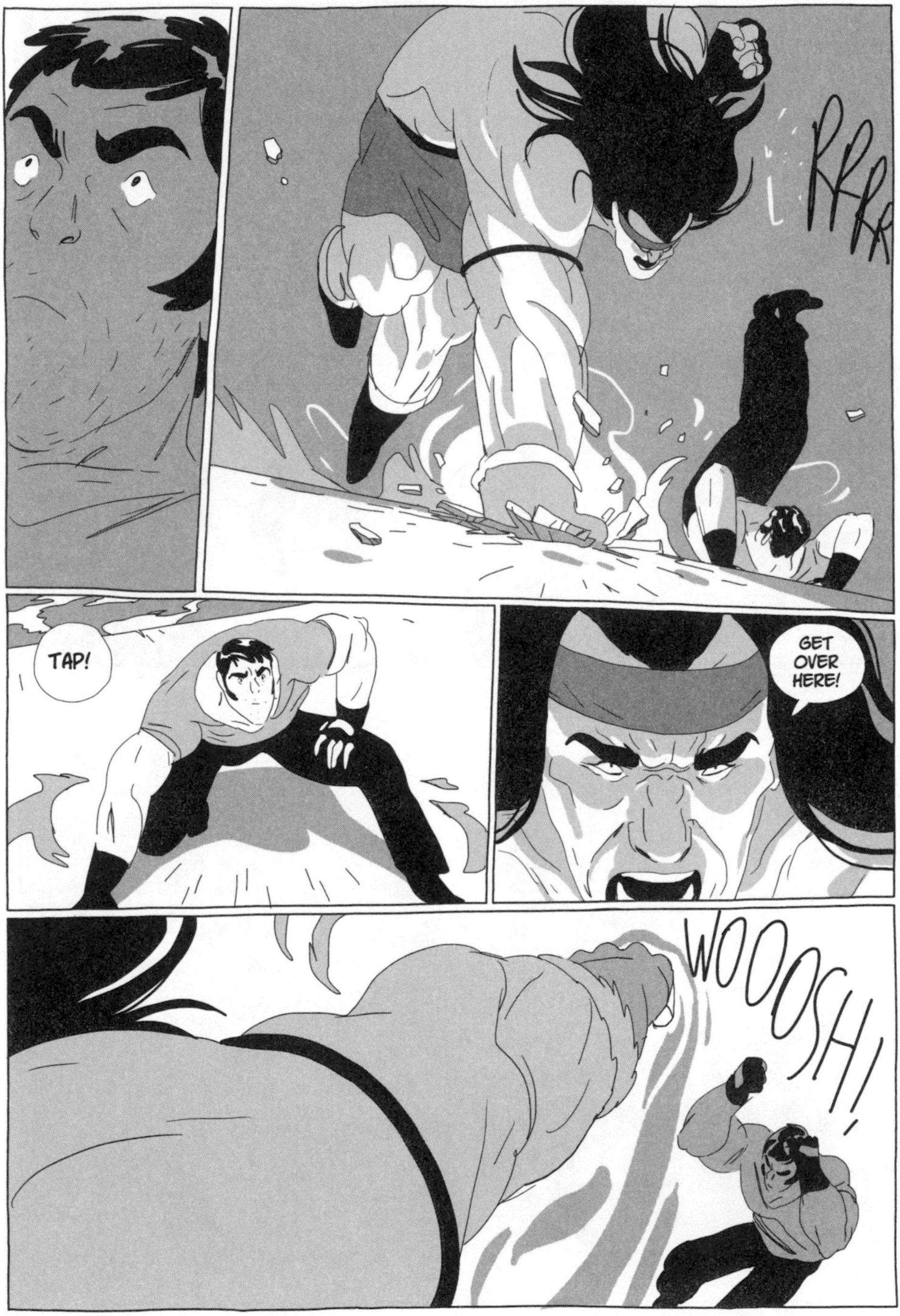
RRRR
TAP!
GET OVER HERE!
WOOOSH!

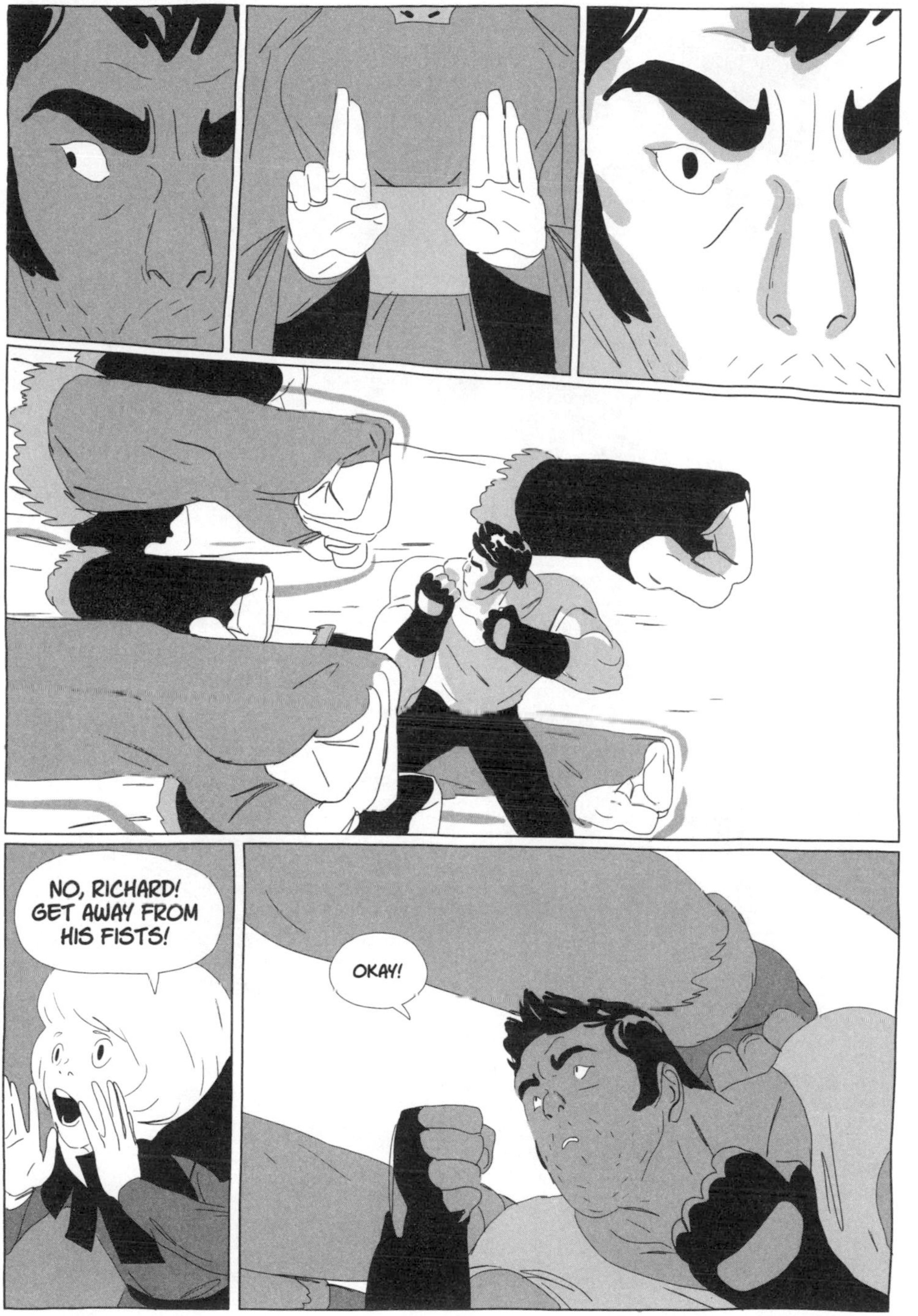
NO, RICHARD! GET AWAY FROM HIS FISTS!
OKAY!

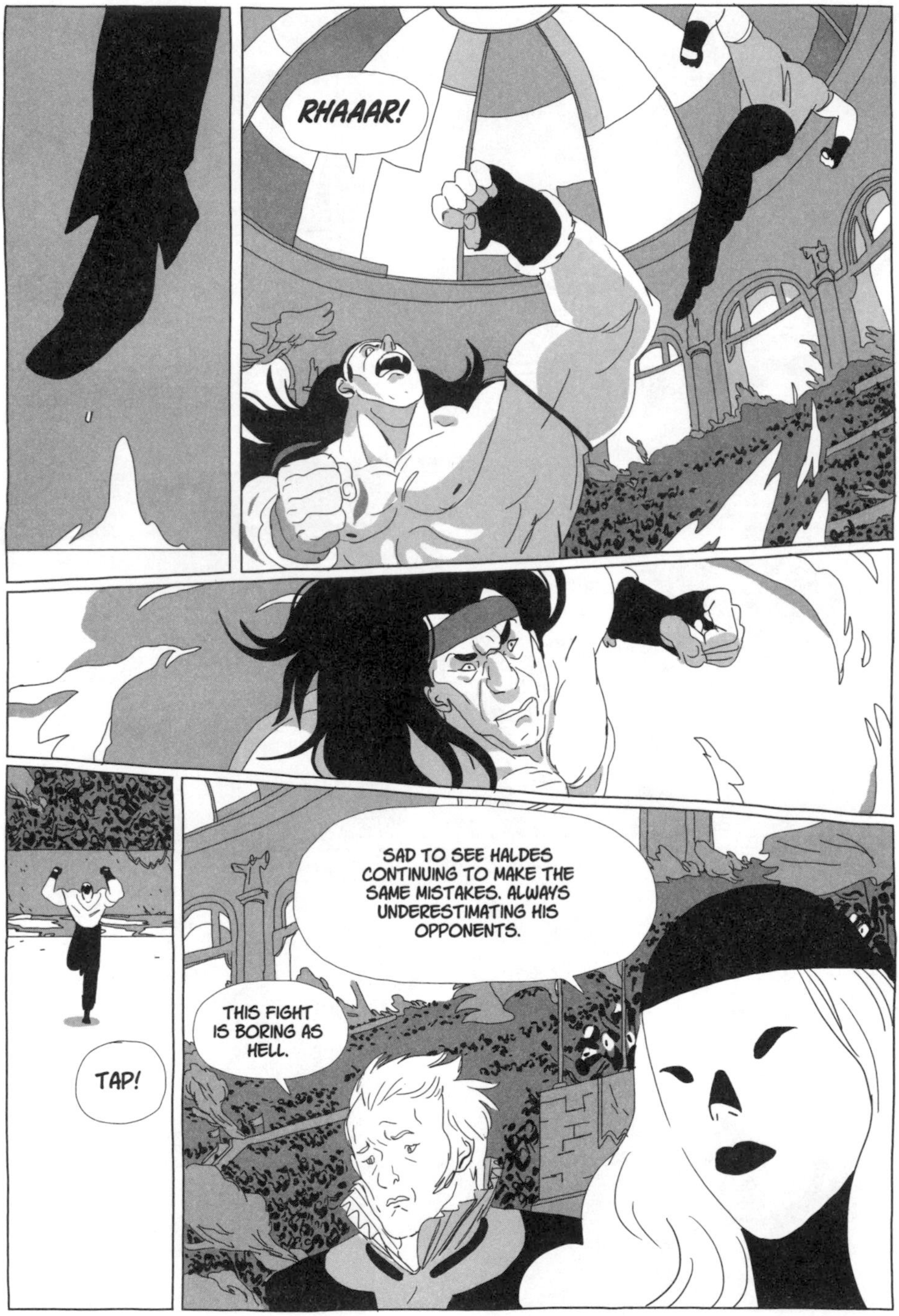
RHAAAR!
TAP!
SAD TO SEE HALDES CONTINUING TO MAKE THE SAME MISTAKES. ALWAYS UNDERESTIMATING HIS OPPONENTS.
THIS FIGHT IS BORING AS HELL.

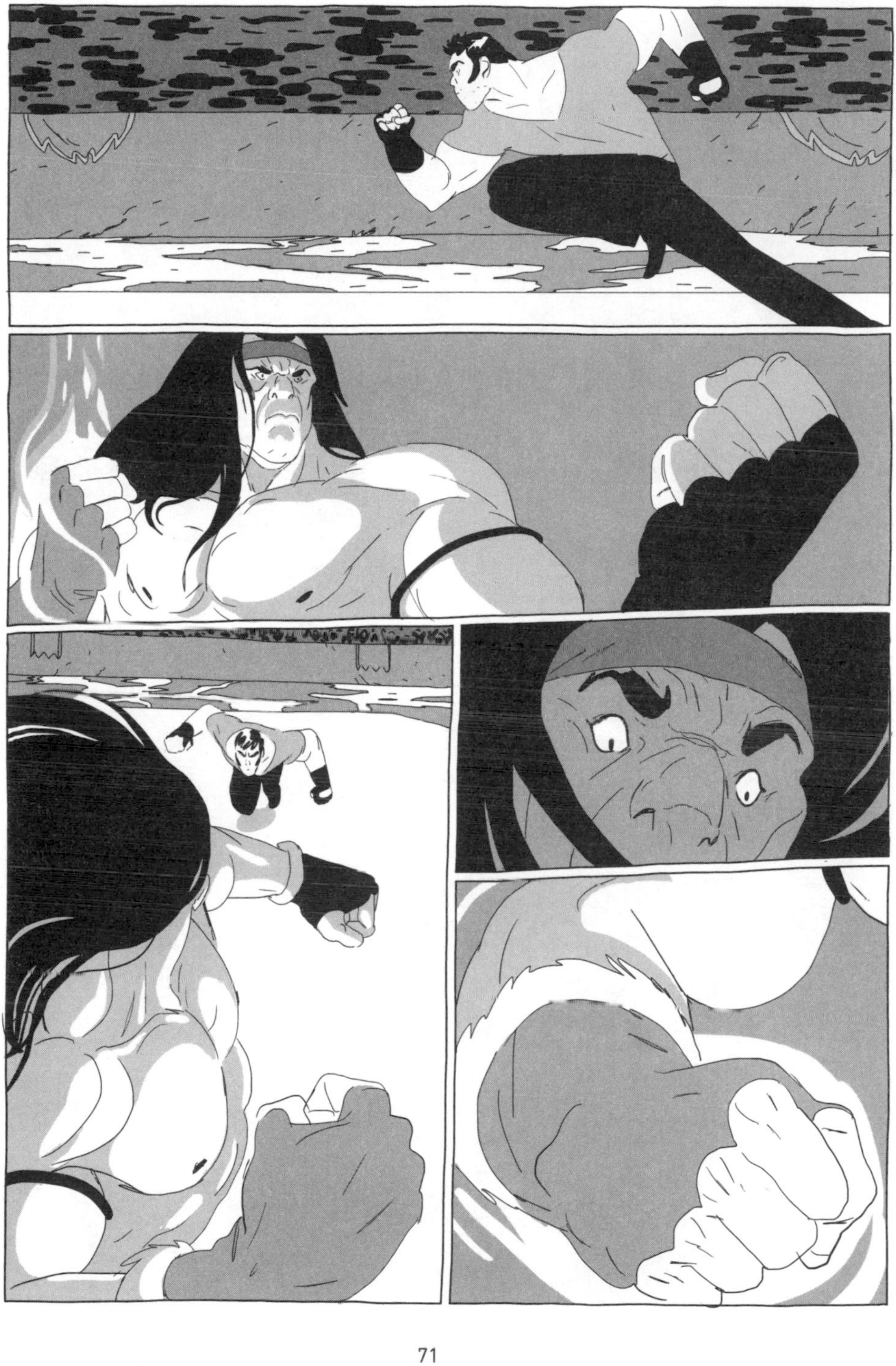

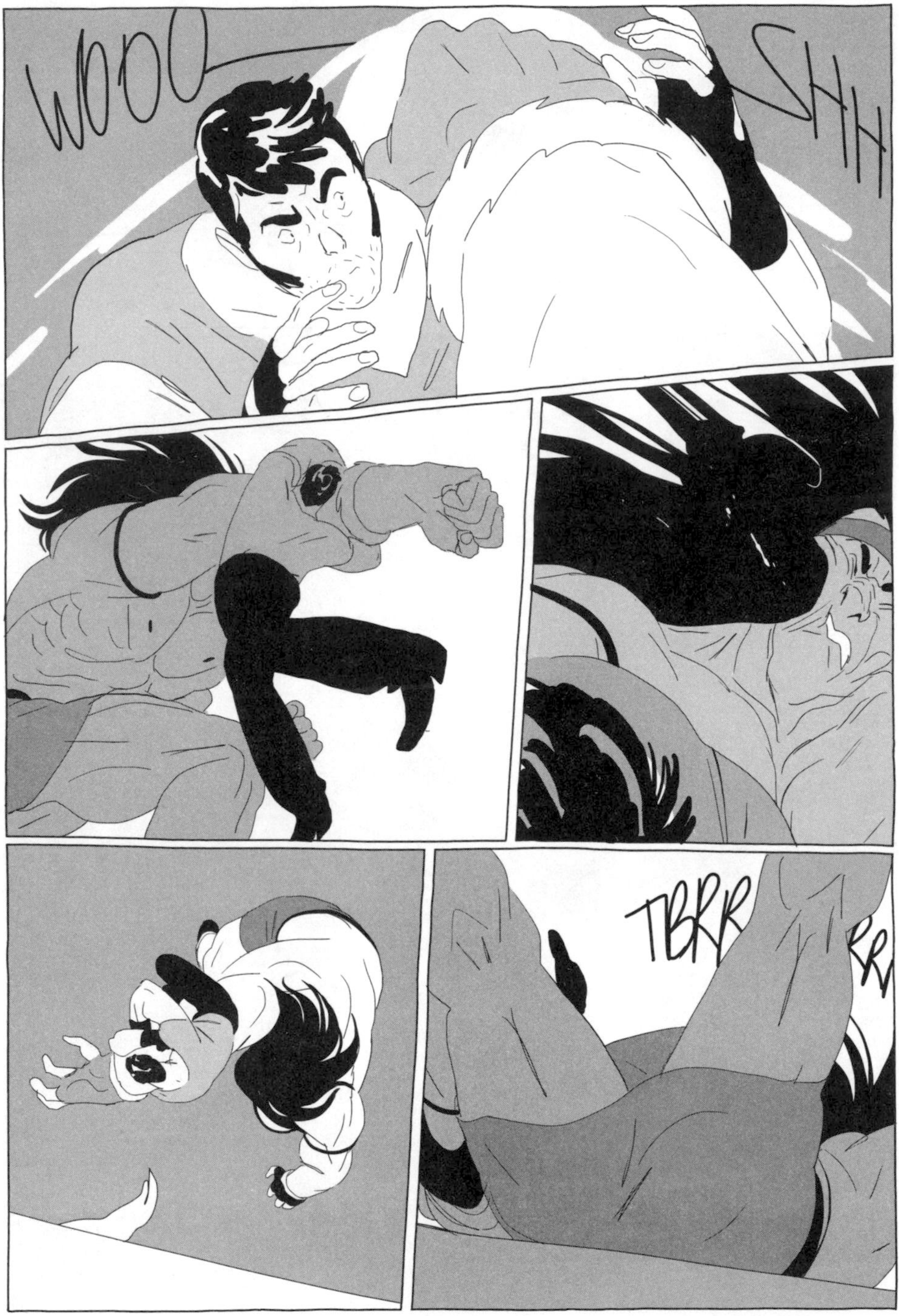
WOOO
SHH
TBRR
RRR

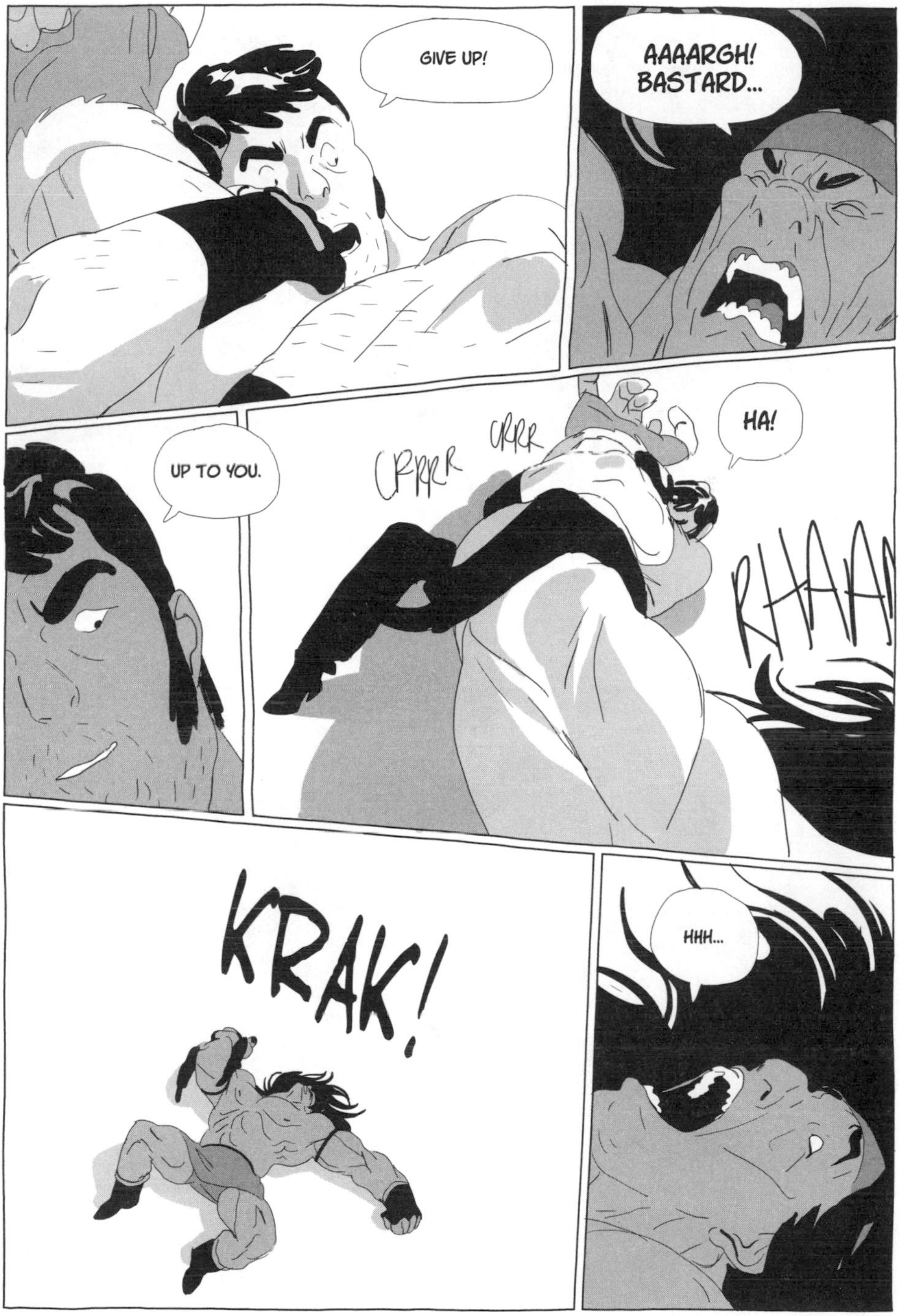
GIVE UP!
AAAARGH! BASTARD...
UP TO YOU.
CRRRR
CRRR
HA!
KRAK!
HHH...

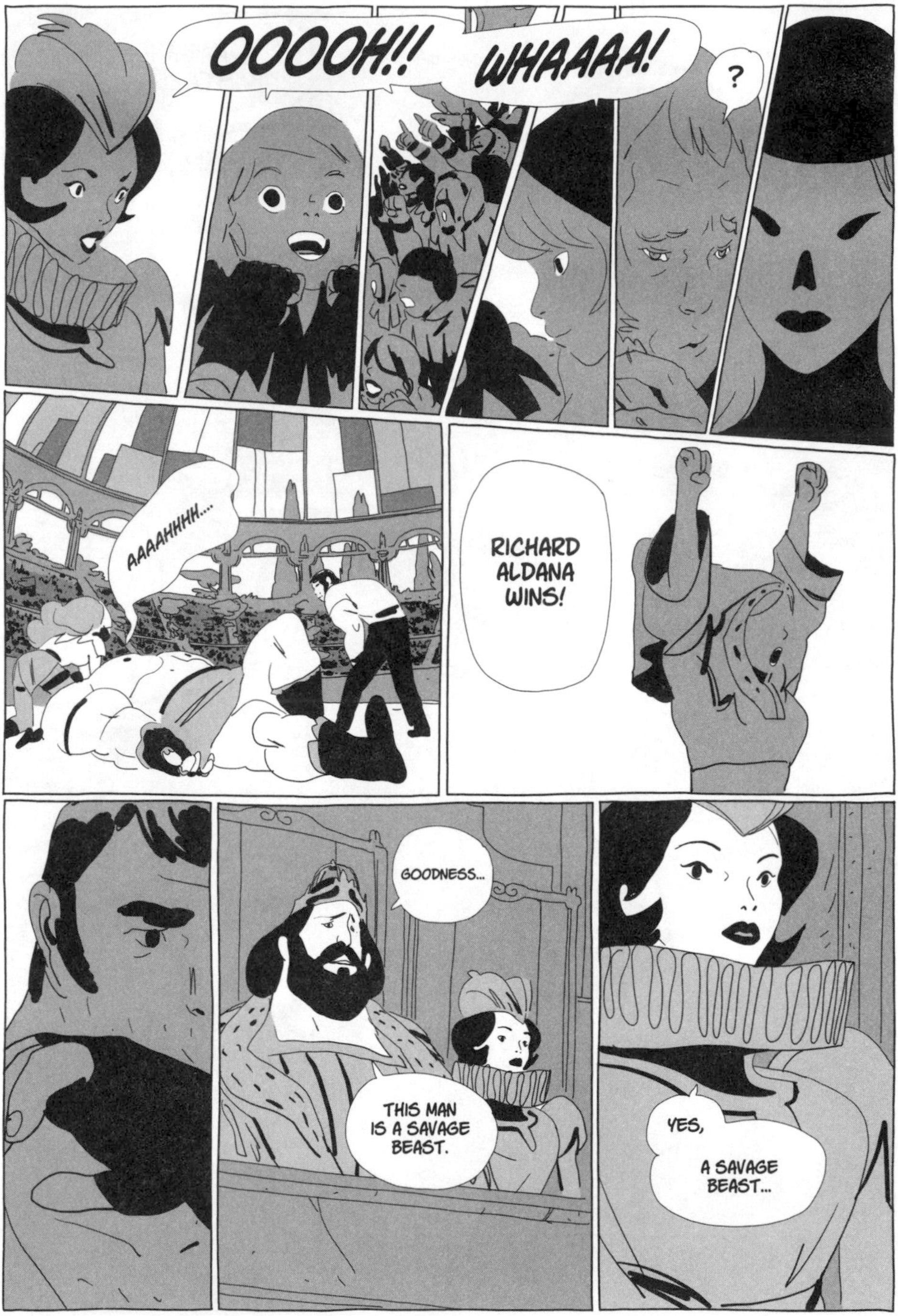
OOOOH!!
WHAAAA!
?
AAAAHHHH....
RICHARD ALDANA WINS!
GOODNESS...
THIS MAN IS A SAVAGE BEAST.
YES,
A SAVAGE BEAST...

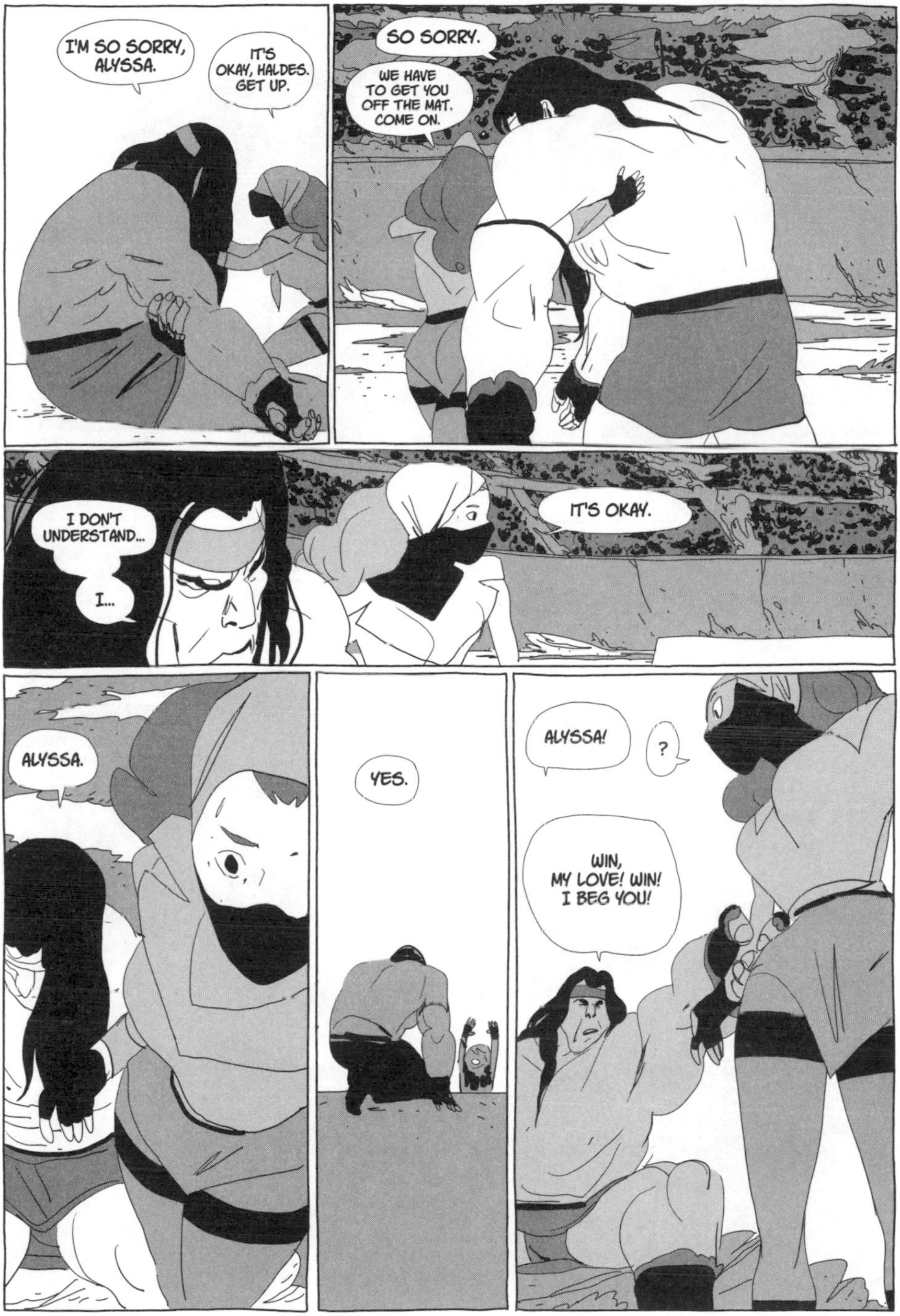
I'M SO SORRY, ALYSSA.
IT'S OKAY, HALDES. GET UP.
SO SORRY.
WE HAVE TO GET YOU OFF THE MAT. COME ON.
I DON'T UNDERSTAND...
I...
IT'S OKAY.
ALYSSA.
YES.
ALYSSA!
?
WIN, MY LOVE! WIN! I BEG YOU!

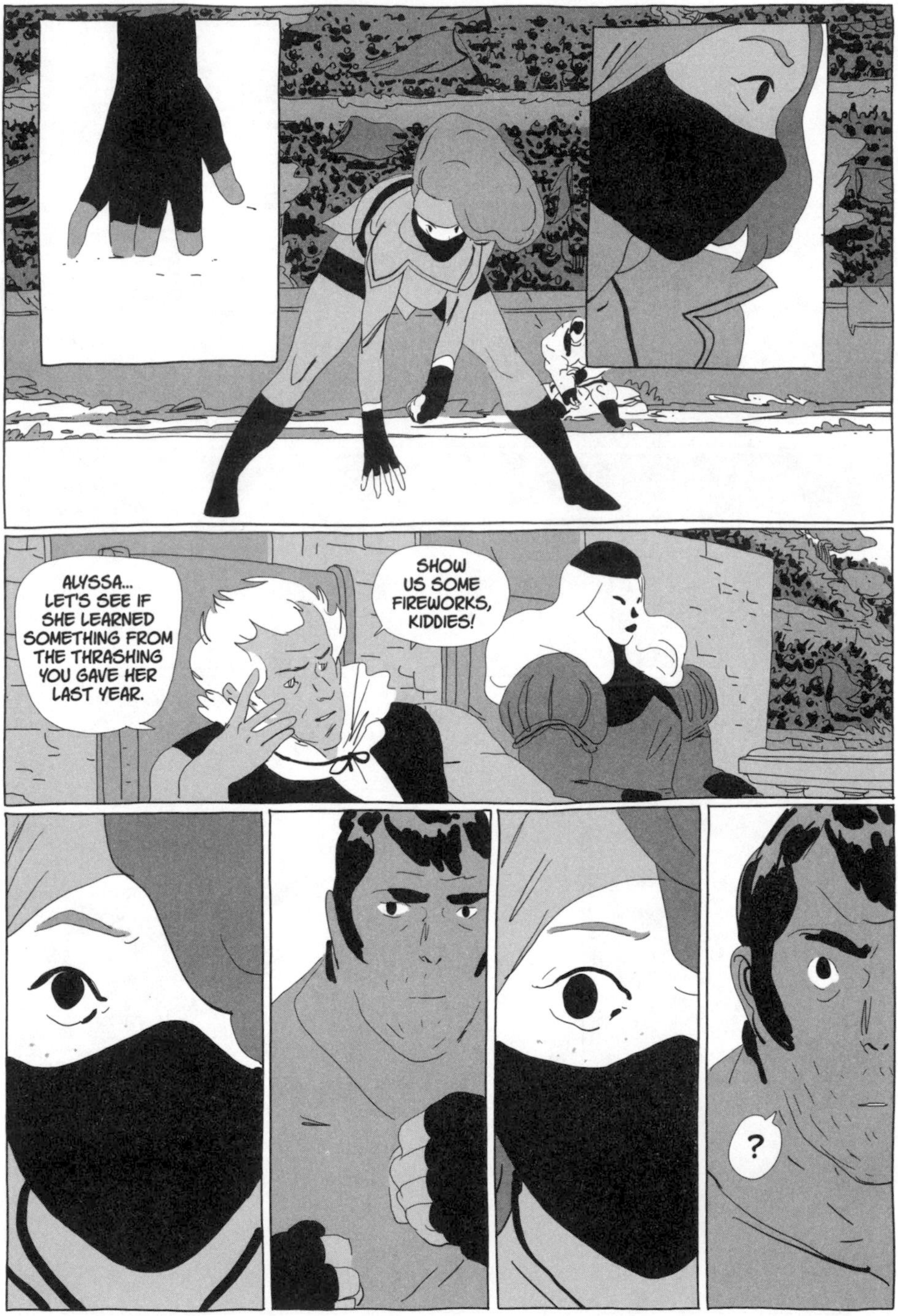
ALYSSA... LET'S SEE IF SHE LEARNED SOMETHING FROM THE THRASHING YOU GAVE HER LAST YEAR.
SHOW US SOME FIREWORKS, KIDDIES!
?

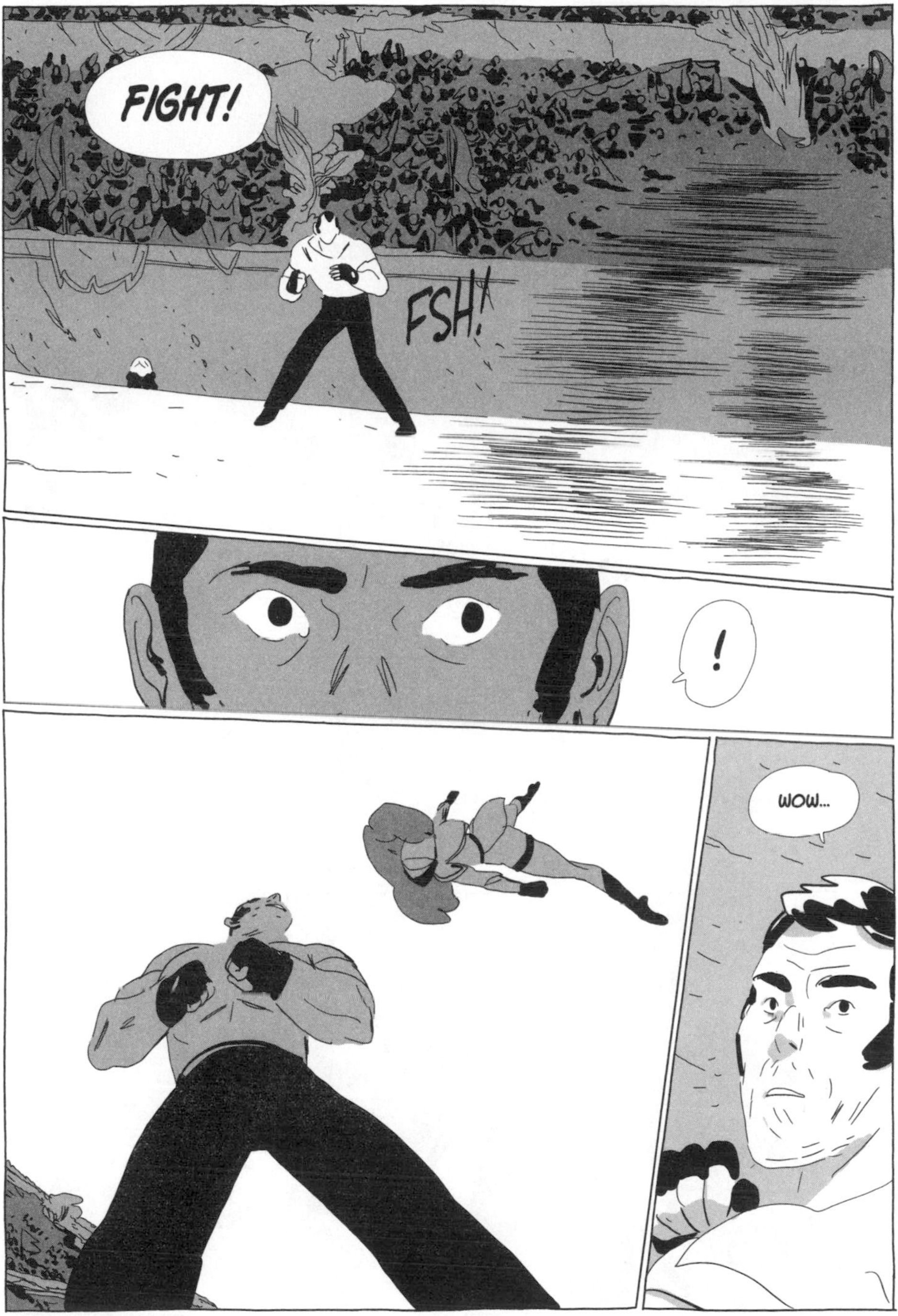
FIGHT!
FSH!
!
WOW...

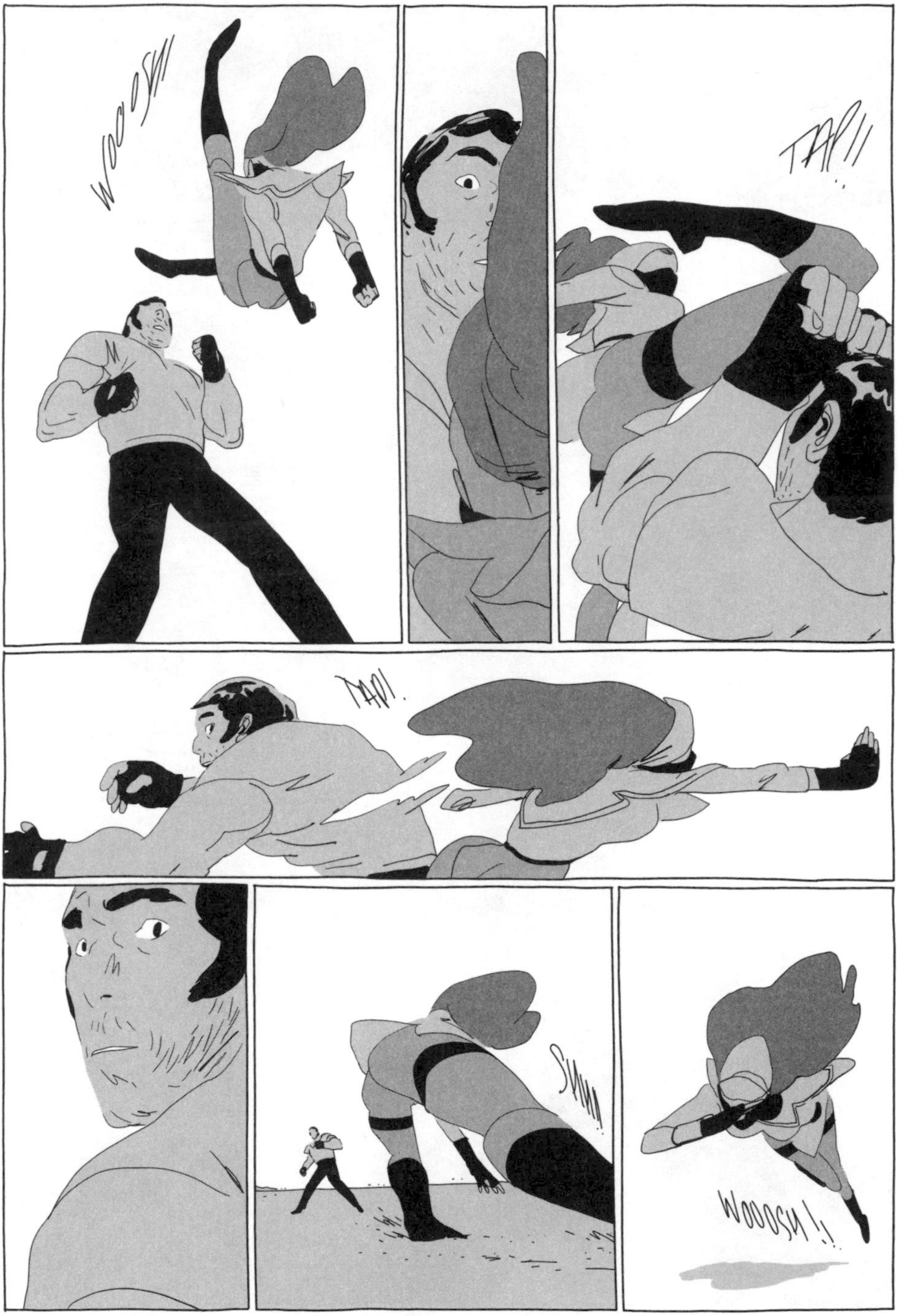
WOOOSH
TAP!!
TAP!
SHHH!!
WOOOSH!!

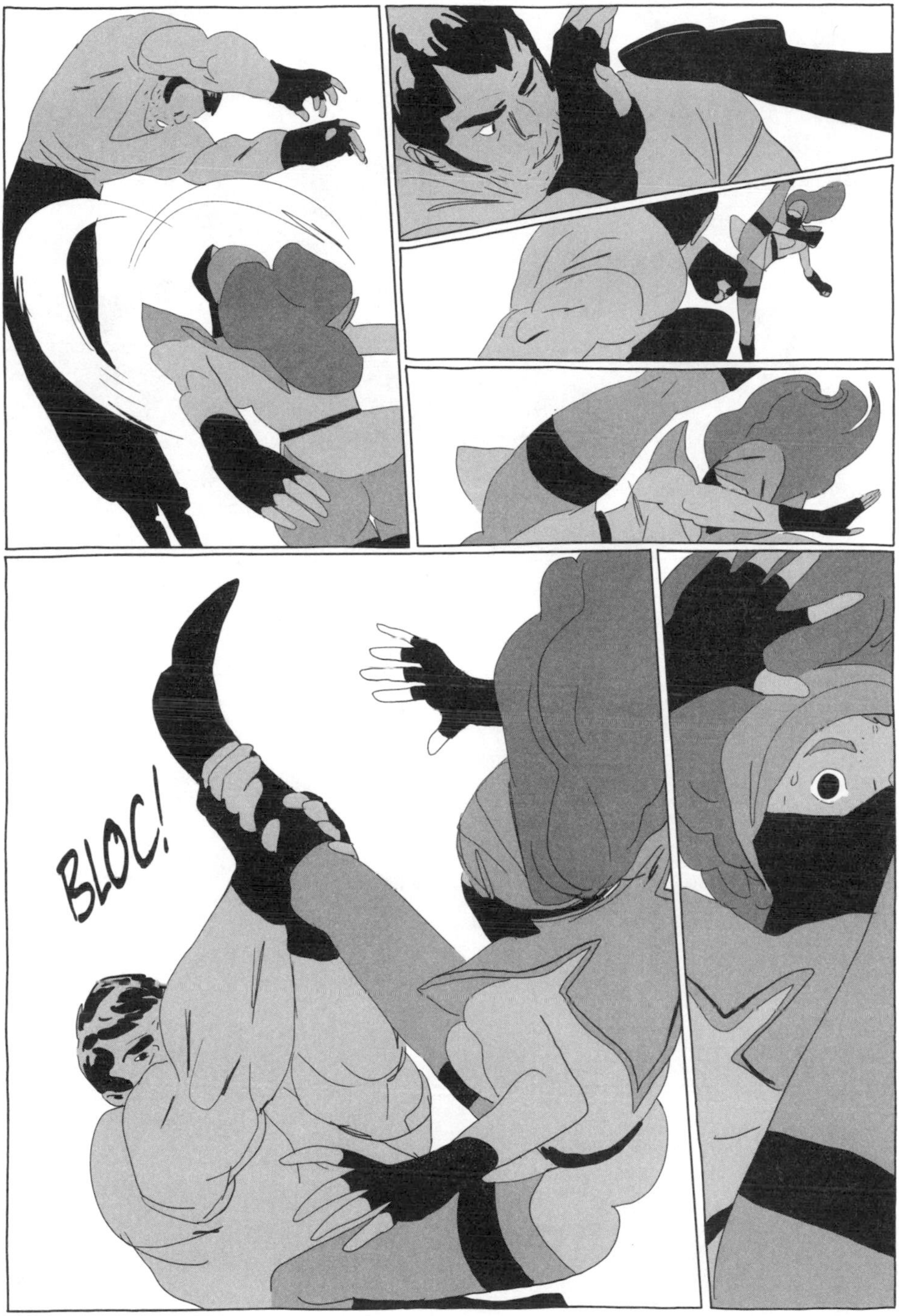
BLOC!

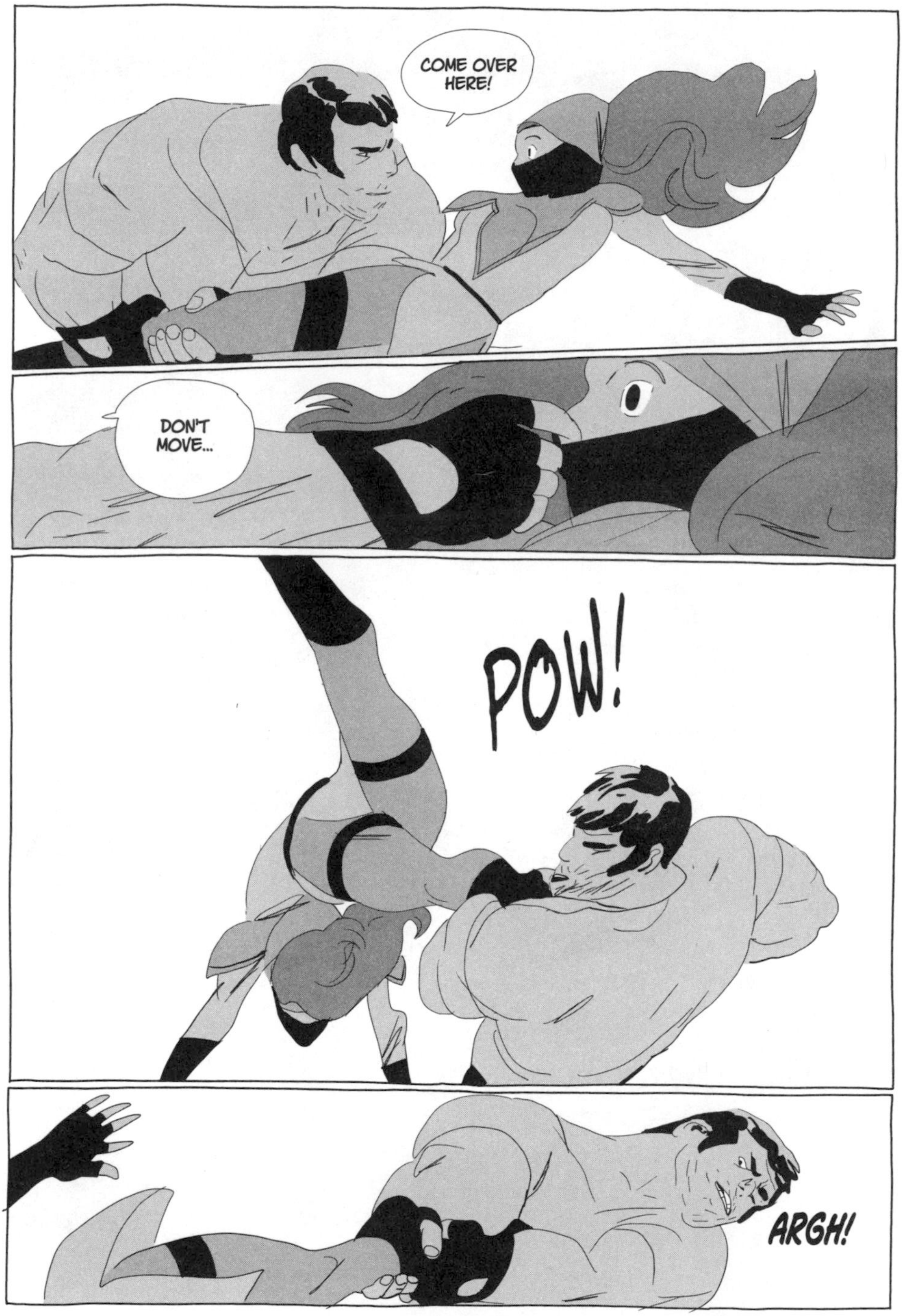
COME OVER HERE!
DON'T MOVE...
POW!
ARGH!

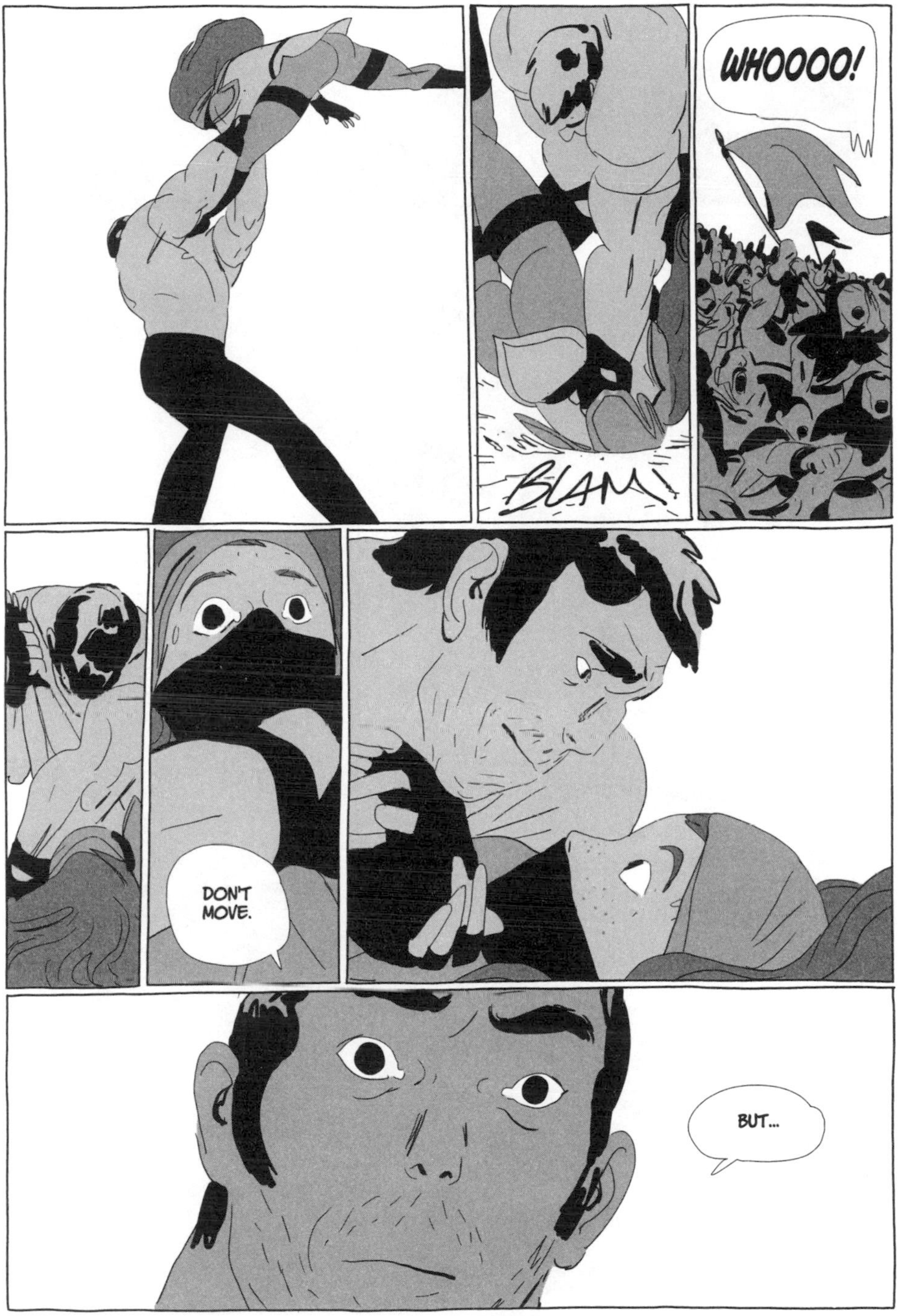
WHOOOO!
BLAM!
DON'T MOVE.
BUT...

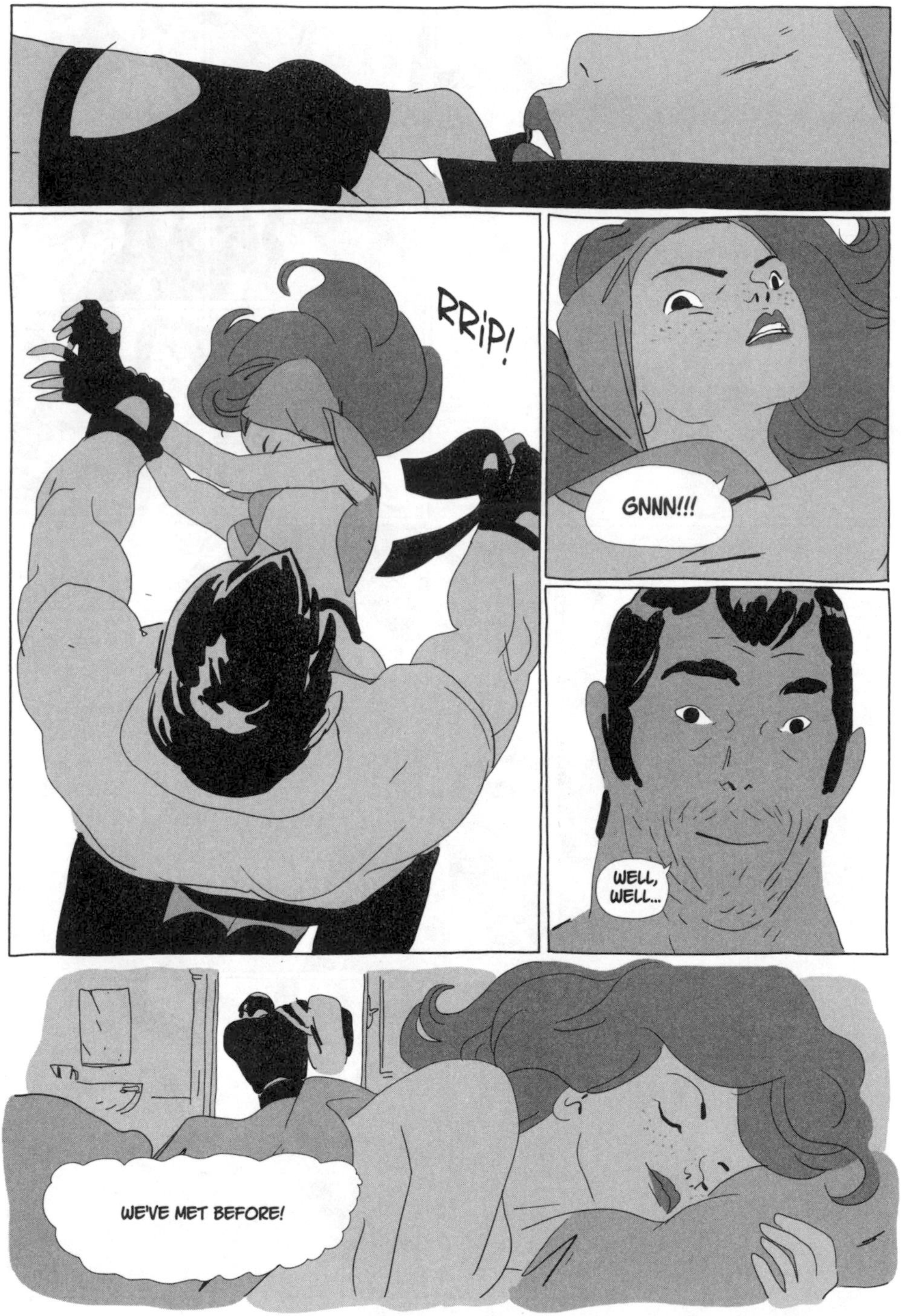
RRIP!
GNNN!!!
WELL, WELL...
WE'VE MET BEFORE!

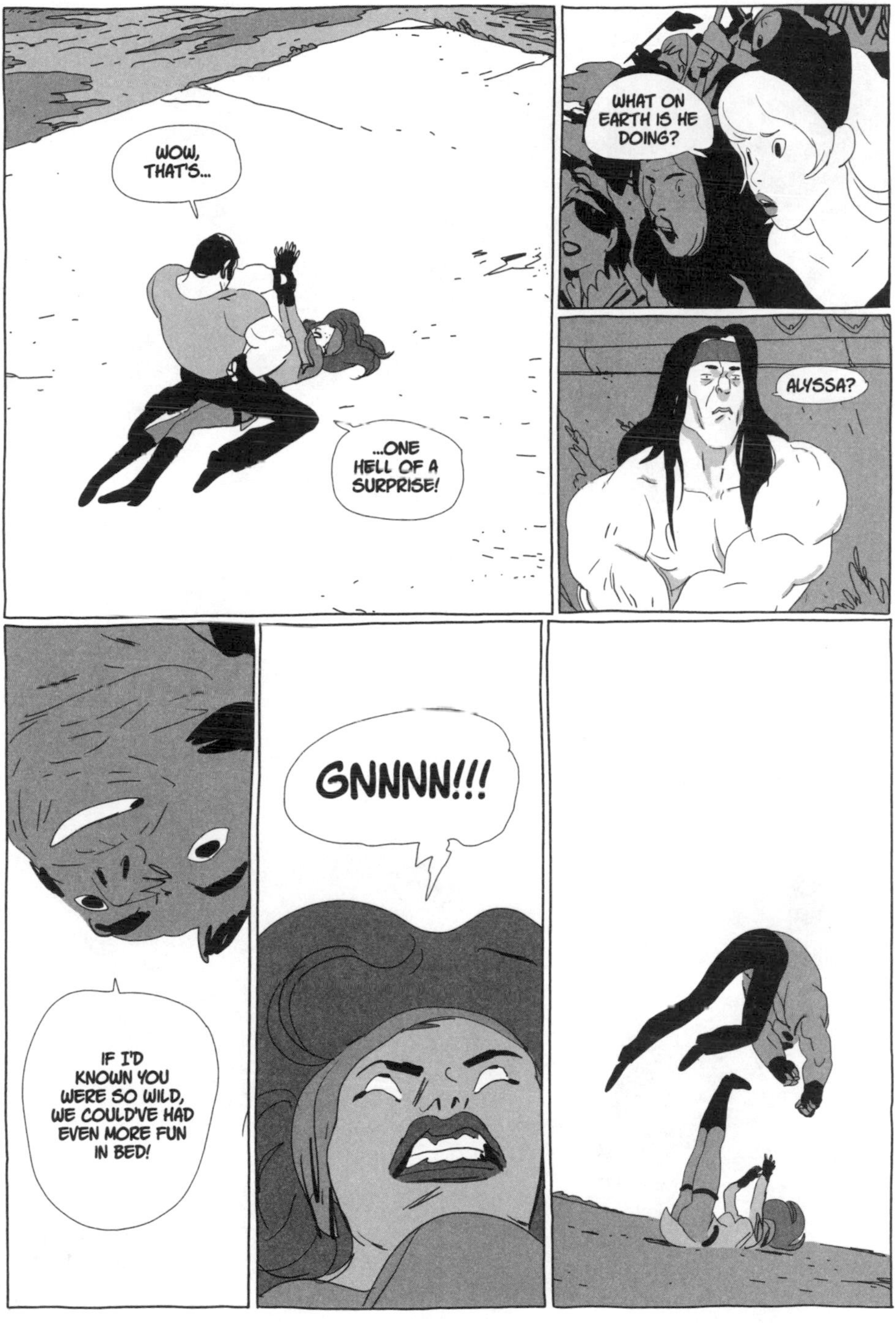

WOW, THAT'S...
...ONE HELL OF A SURPRISE!
WHAT ON EARTH IS HE DOING?
ALYSSA?
IF I'D KNOWN YOU WERE SO WILD, WE COULD'VE HAD EVEN MORE FUN IN BED!
GNNNN!!!

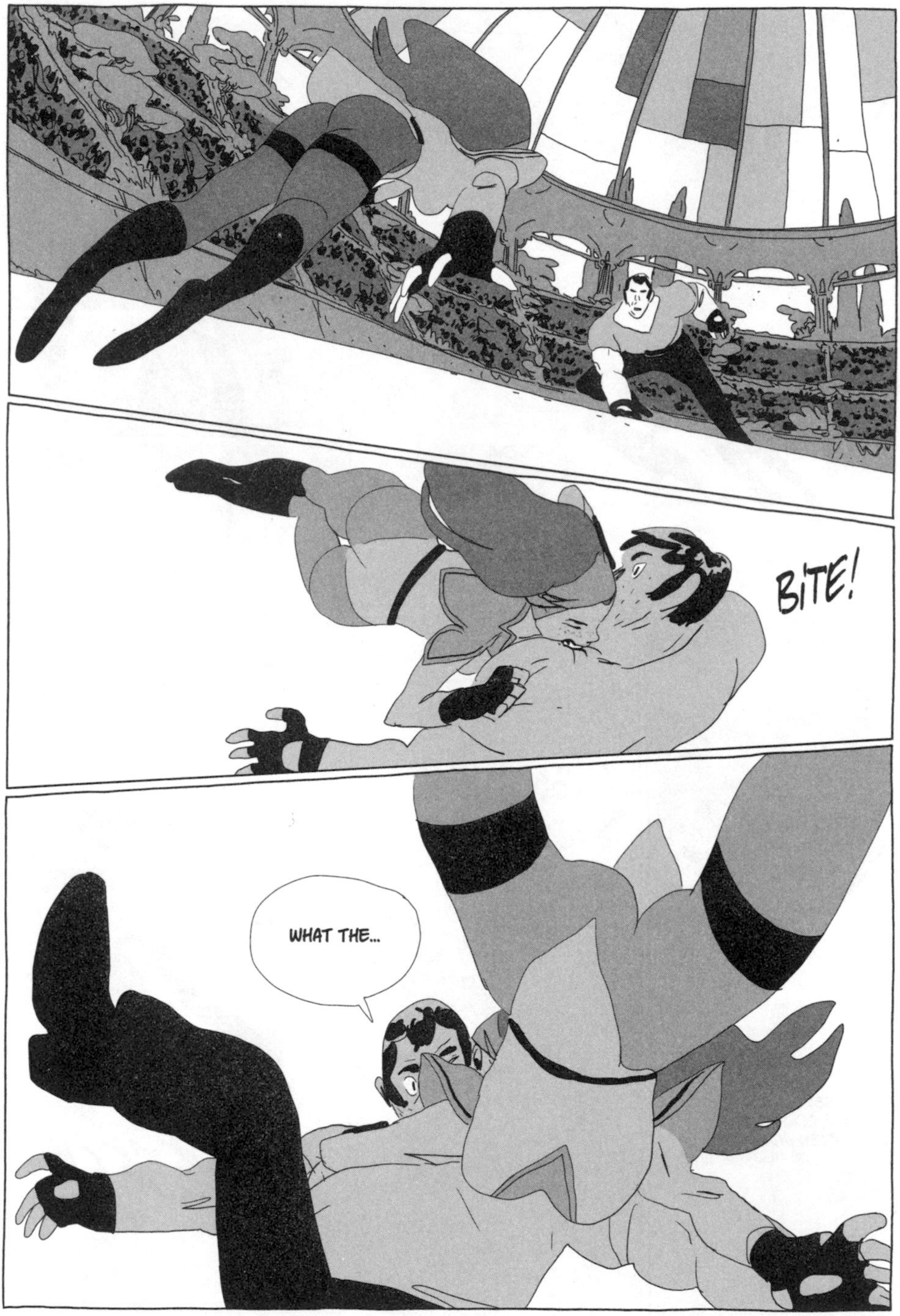
BITE!
WHAT THE...

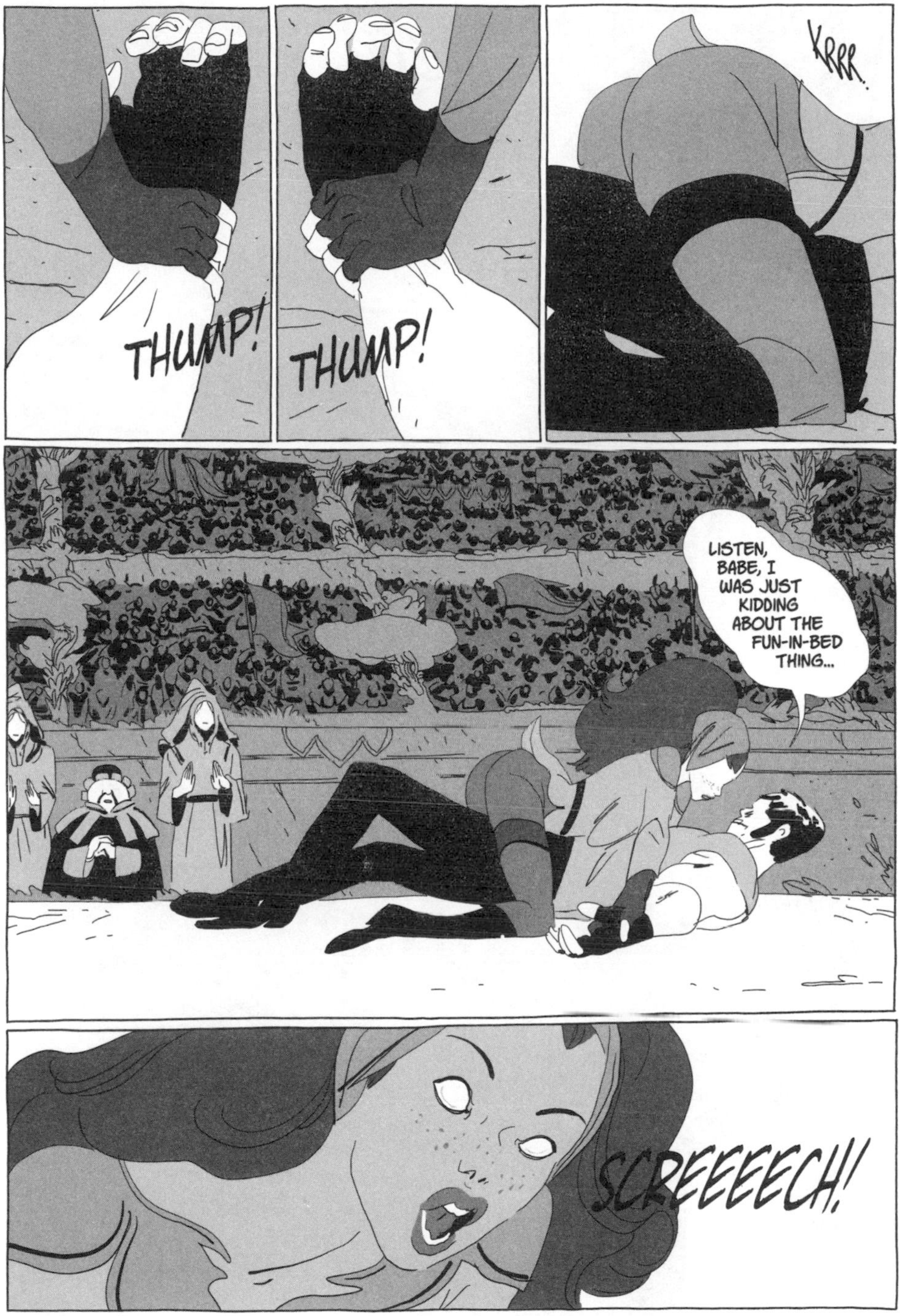
THUMP!
THUMP!
KRRR..
LISTEN, BABE, I WAS JUST KIDDING ABOUT THE FUN-IN-BED THING...
SCREEEEECH!

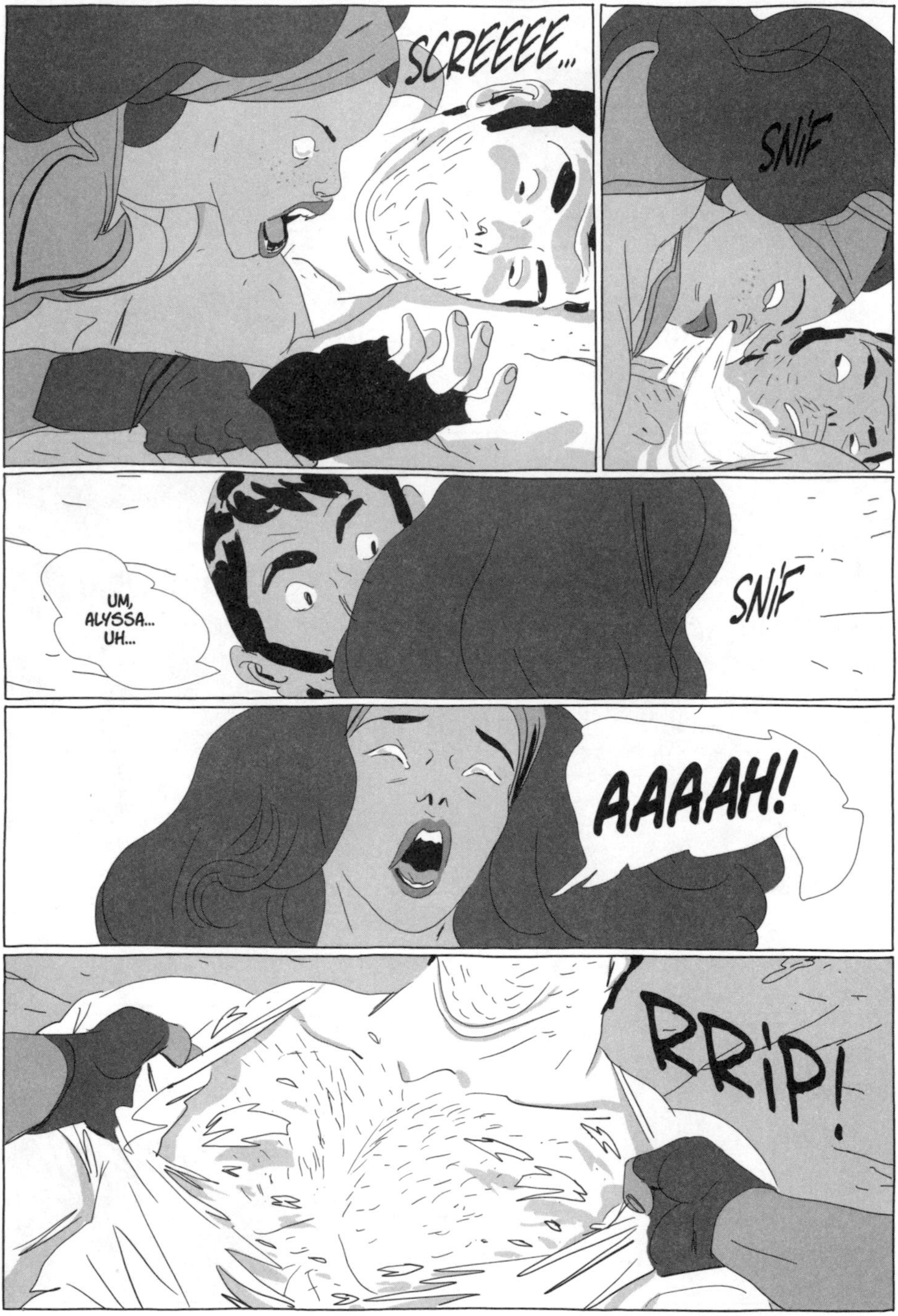
SCREEEE...
SNIF
UM, ALYSSA... UH...
SNIF
AAAAH!
RRIP!

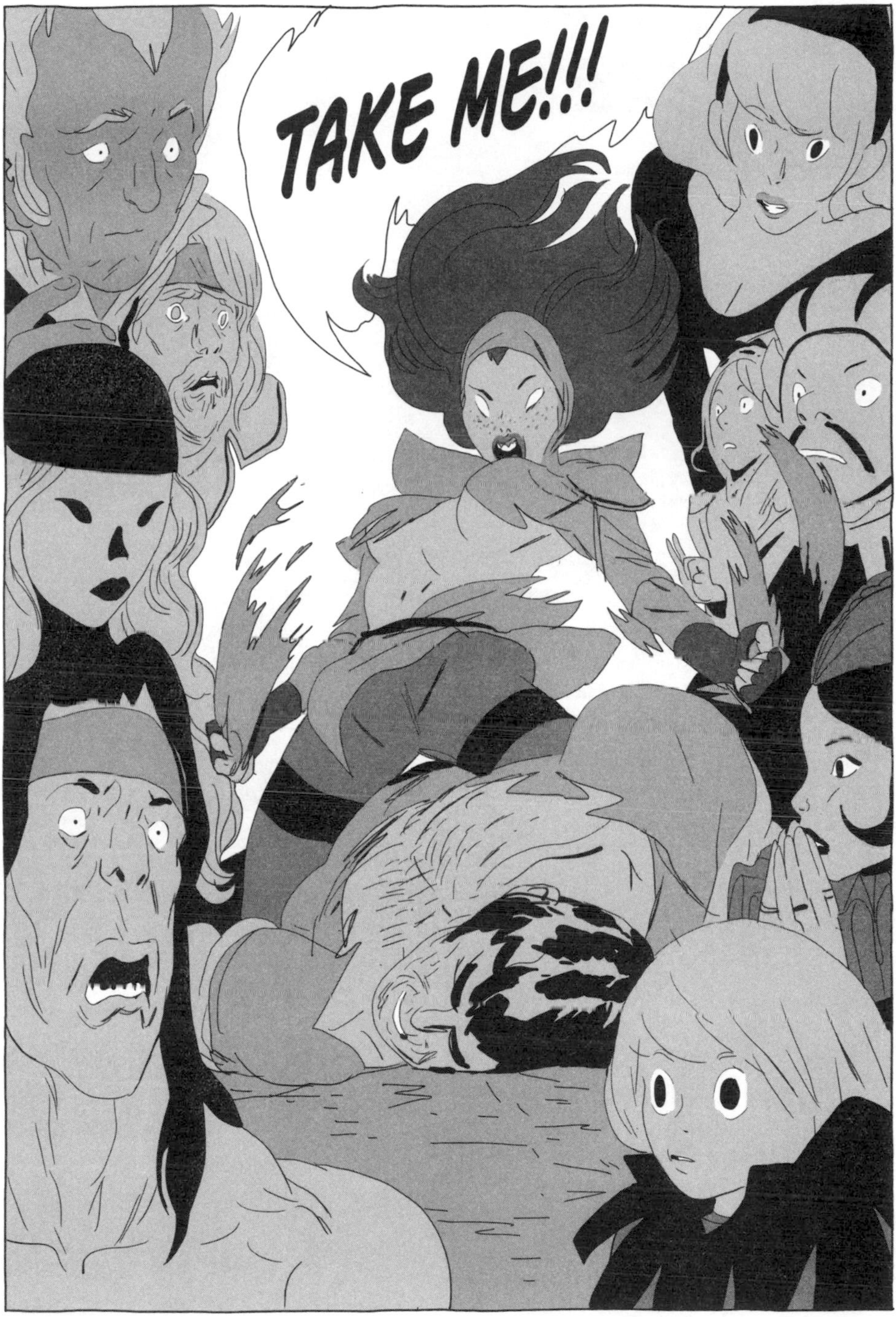
TAKE ME!!!

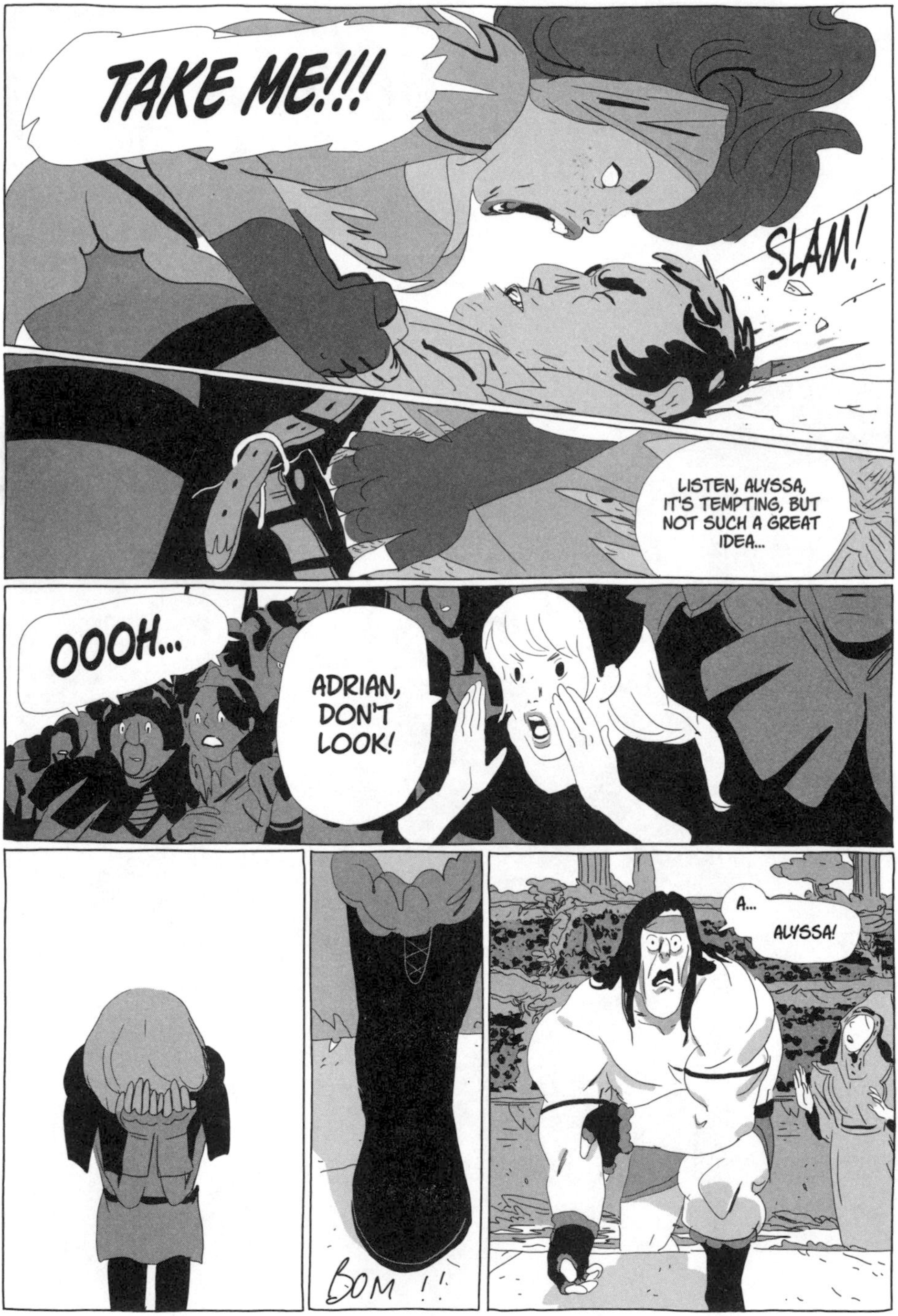
TAKE ME!!!
SLAM!
LISTEN, ALYSSA, IT'S TEMPTING, BUT NOT SUCH A GREAT IDEA...
OOOH...
ADRIAN, DON'T LOOK!
BOM !!
A...
ALYSSA!

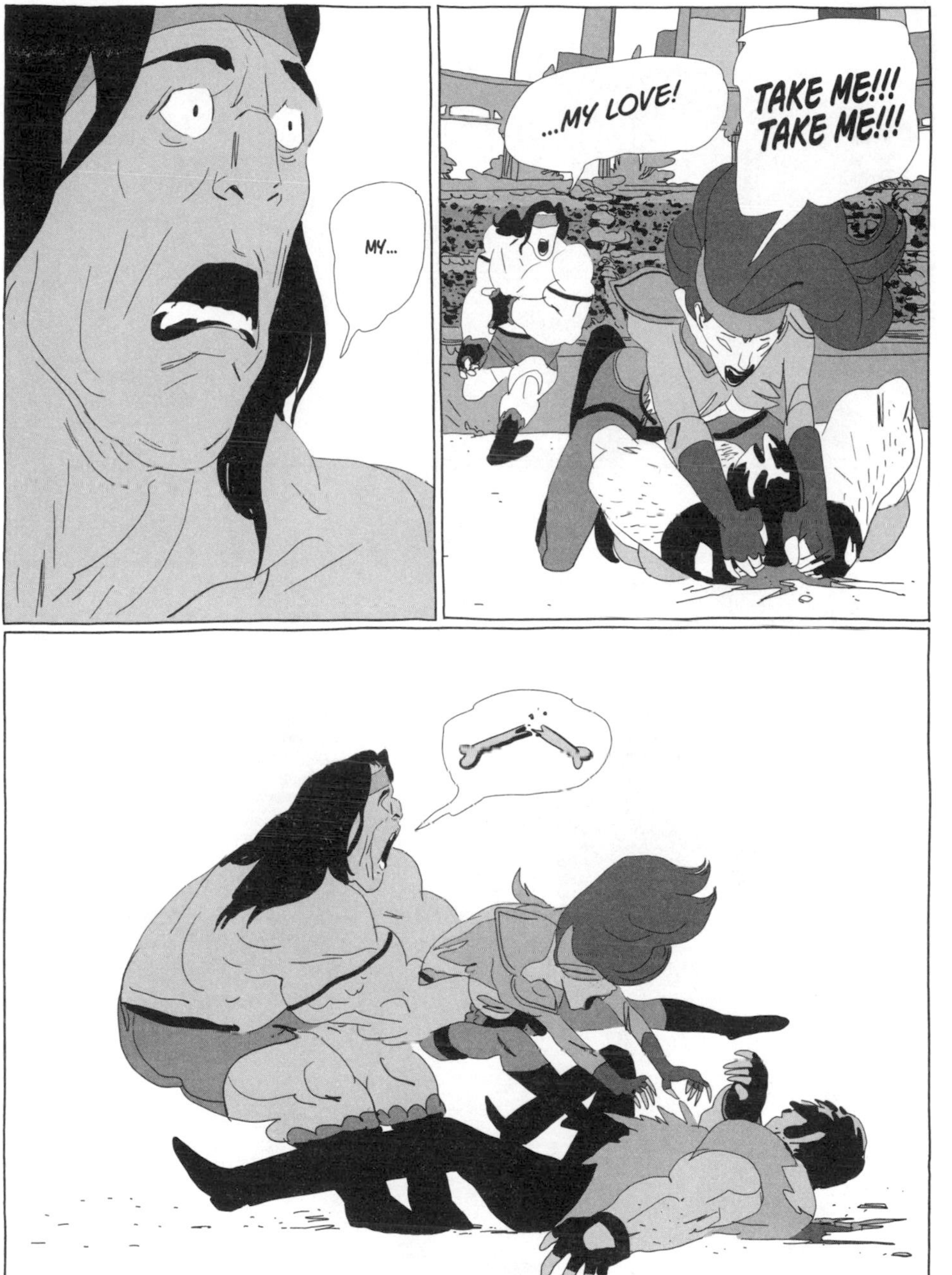
MY...
...MY LOVE!
TAKE ME!!! TAKE ME!!!

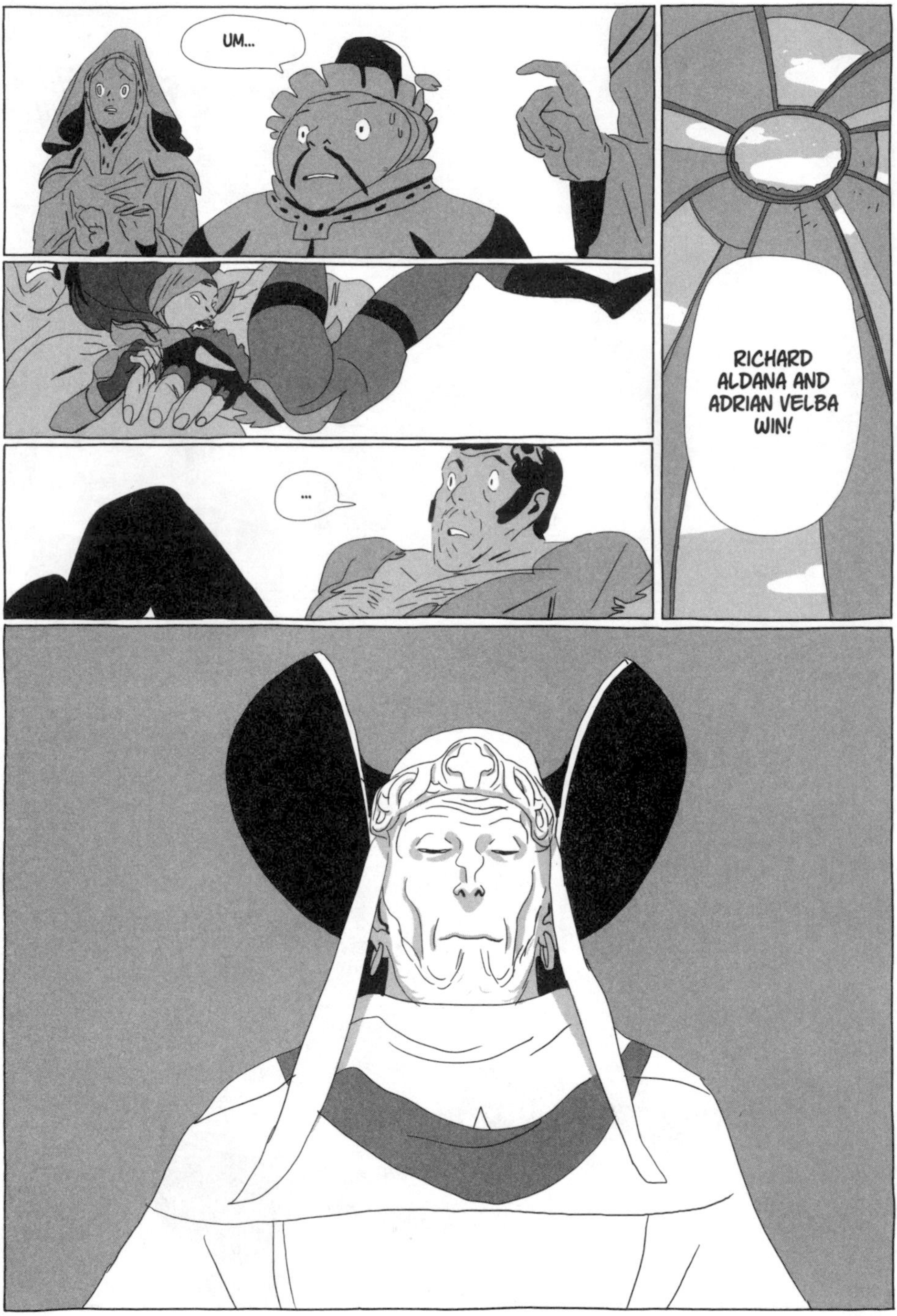
UM...
...
RICHARD ALDANA AND ADRIAN VELBA WIN!

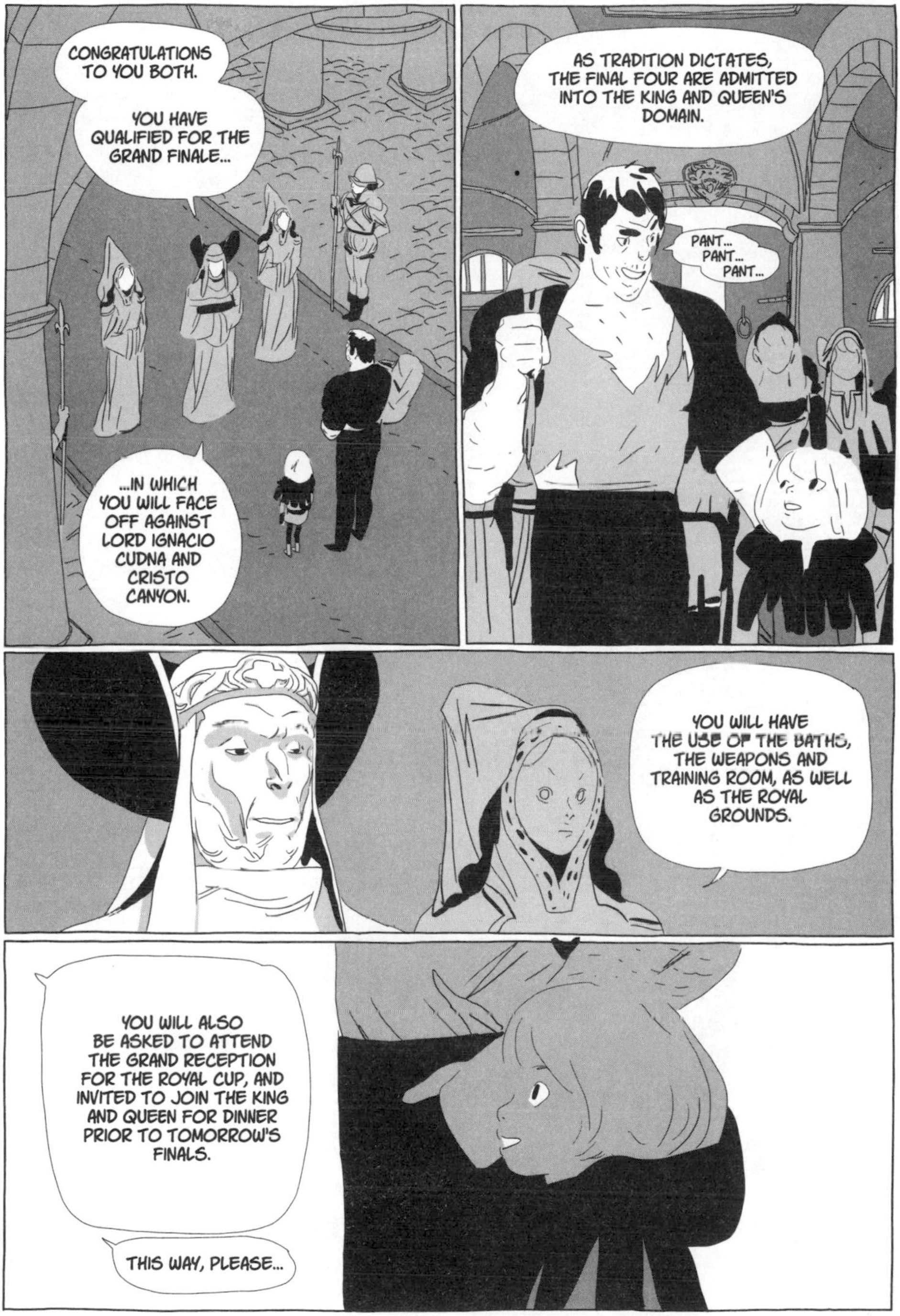
CONGRATULATIONS TO YOU BOTH.
YOU HAVE QUALIFIED FOR THE GRAND FINALE...
...IN WHICH YOU WILL FACE OFF AGAINST LORD IGNACIO CUDNA AND CRISTO CANYON.
AS TRADITION DICTATES, THE FINAL FOUR ARE ADMITTED INTO THE KING AND QUEEN'S DOMAIN.
PANT... PANT... PANT...
YOU WILL HAVE THE USE OF THE BATHS, THE WEAPONS AND TRAINING ROOM, AS WELL AS THE ROYAL GROUNDS.
YOU WILL ALSO BE ASKED TO ATTEND THE GRAND RECEPTION FOR THE ROYAL CUP, AND INVITED TO JOIN THE KING AND QUEEN FOR DINNER PRIOR TO TOMORROW'S FINALS.
THIS WAY, PLEASE...

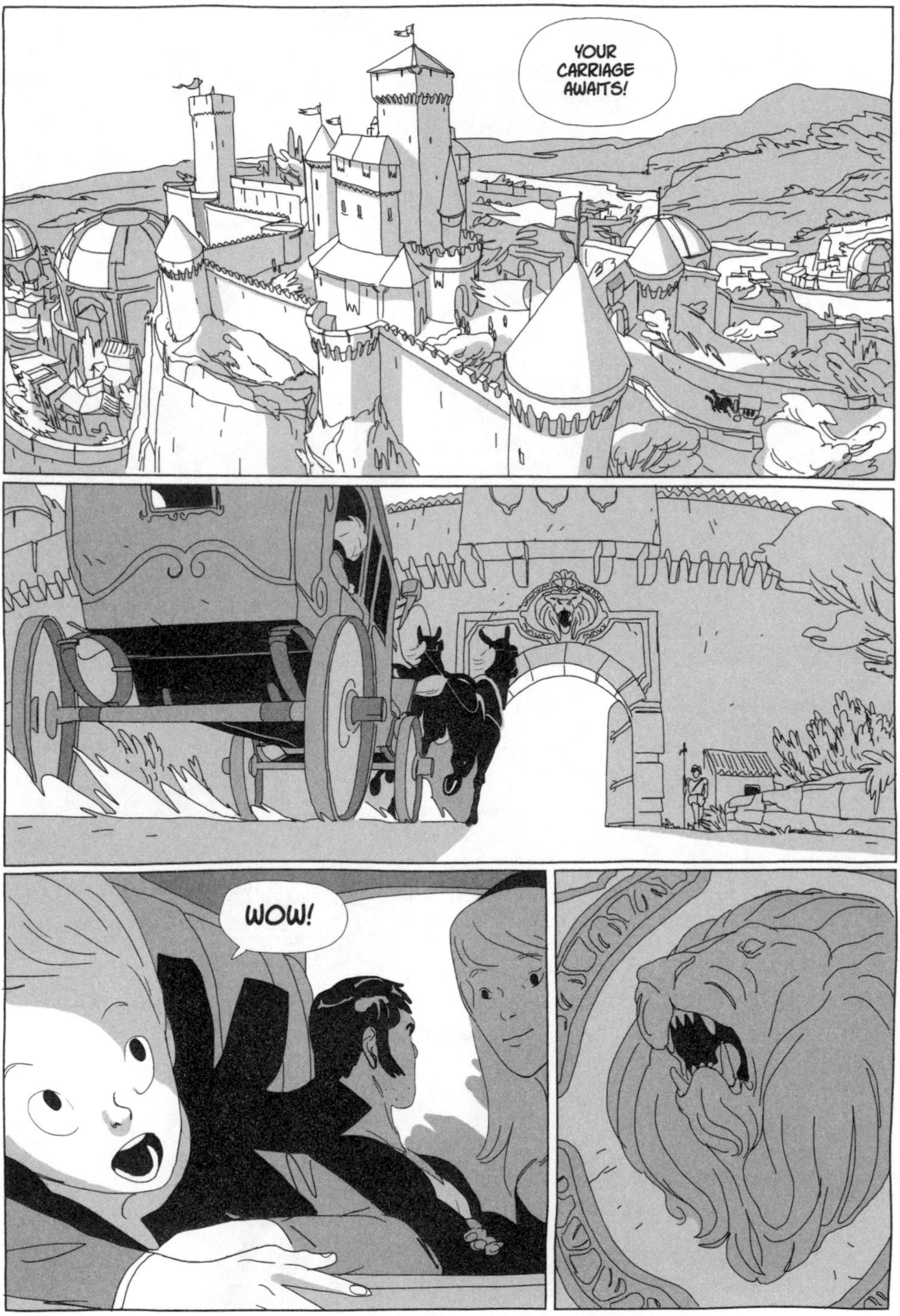
YOUR CARRIAGE AWAITS!
WOW!

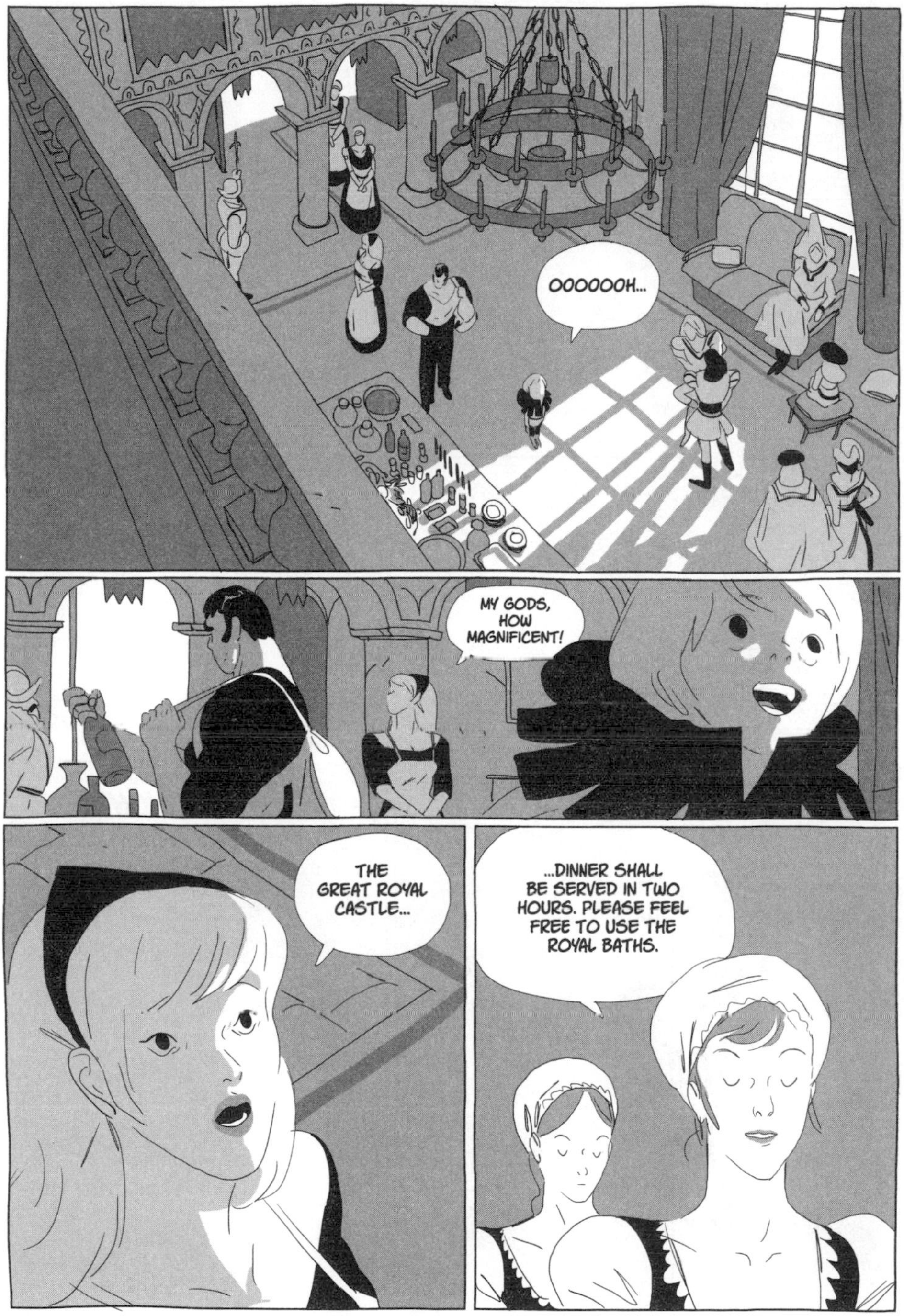
OOOOOOH...
MY GODS, HOW MAGNIFICENT!
THE GREAT ROYAL CASTLE...
...DINNER SHALL BE SERVED IN TWO HOURS. PLEASE FEEL FREE TO USE THE ROYAL BATHS.

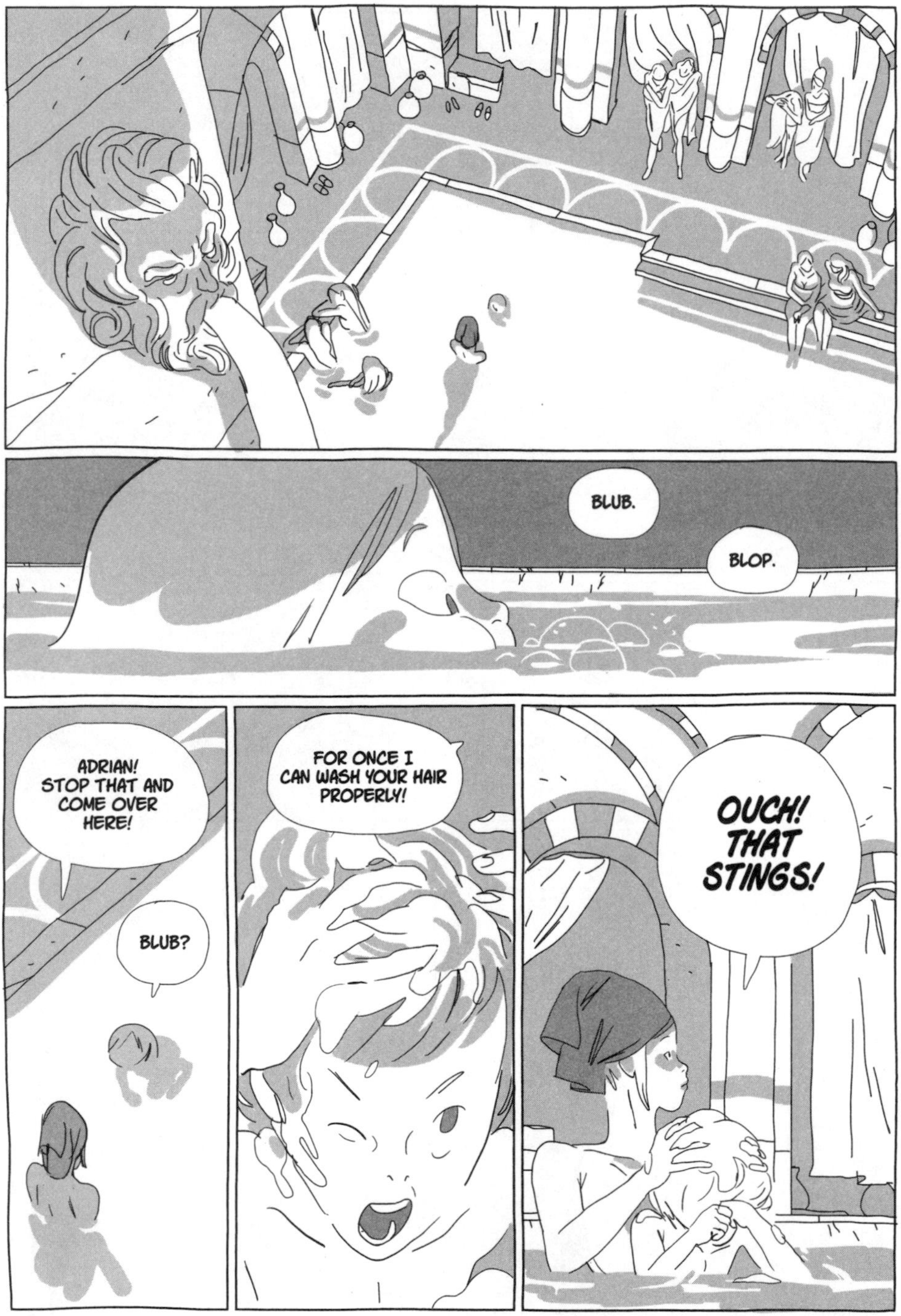
BLUB.
BLOP.
ADRIAN! STOP THAT AND COME OVER HERE!
BLUB?
FOR ONCE I CAN WASH YOUR HAIR PROPERLY!
OUCH! THAT STINGS!

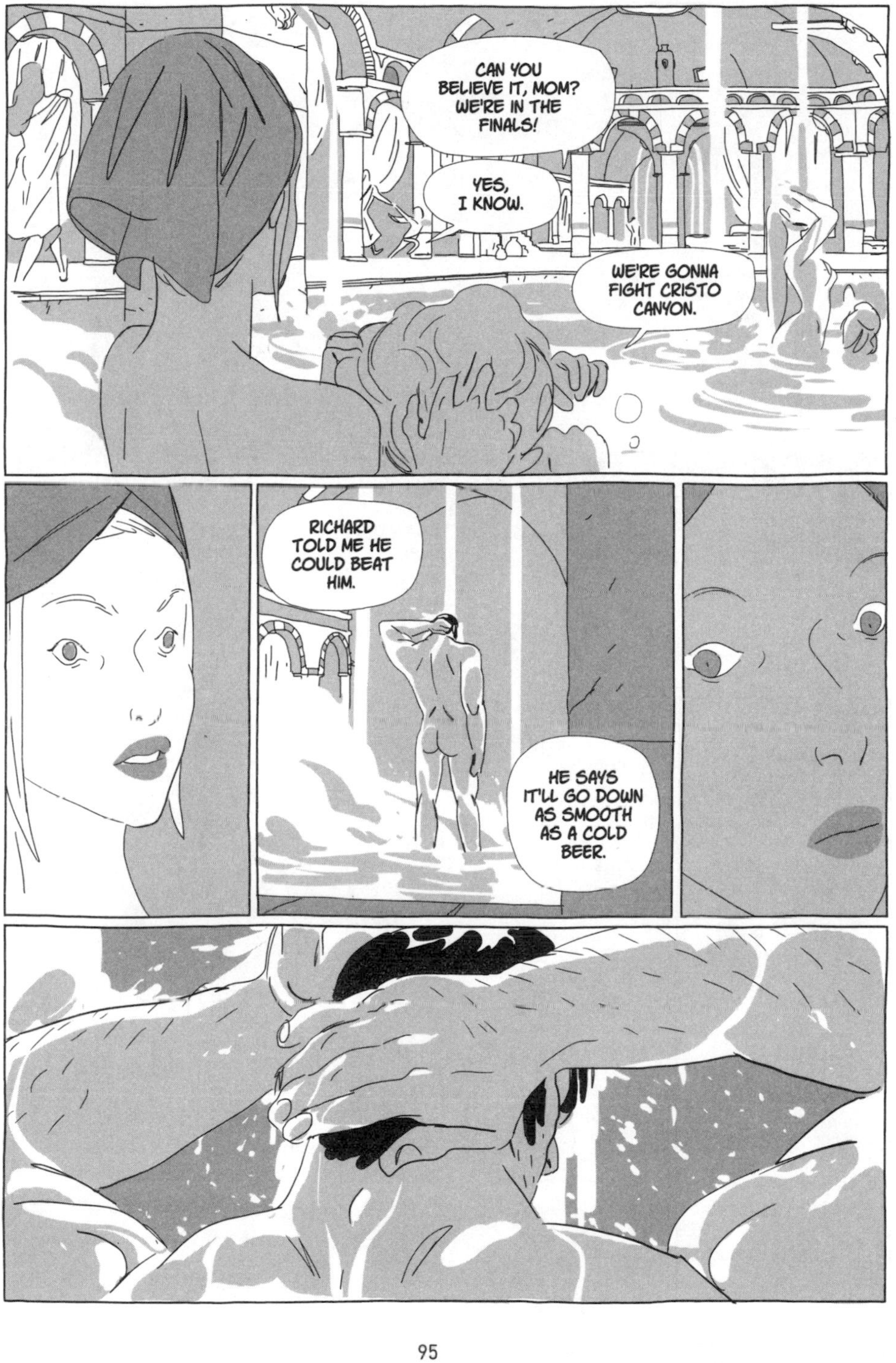
CAN YOU BELIEVE IT, MOM? WE'RE IN THE FINALS!
YES, I KNOW.
WE'RE GONNA FIGHT CRISTO CANYON.
RICHARD TOLD ME HE COULD BEAT HIM.
HE SAYS IT'LL GO DOWN AS SMOOTH AS A COLD BEER.

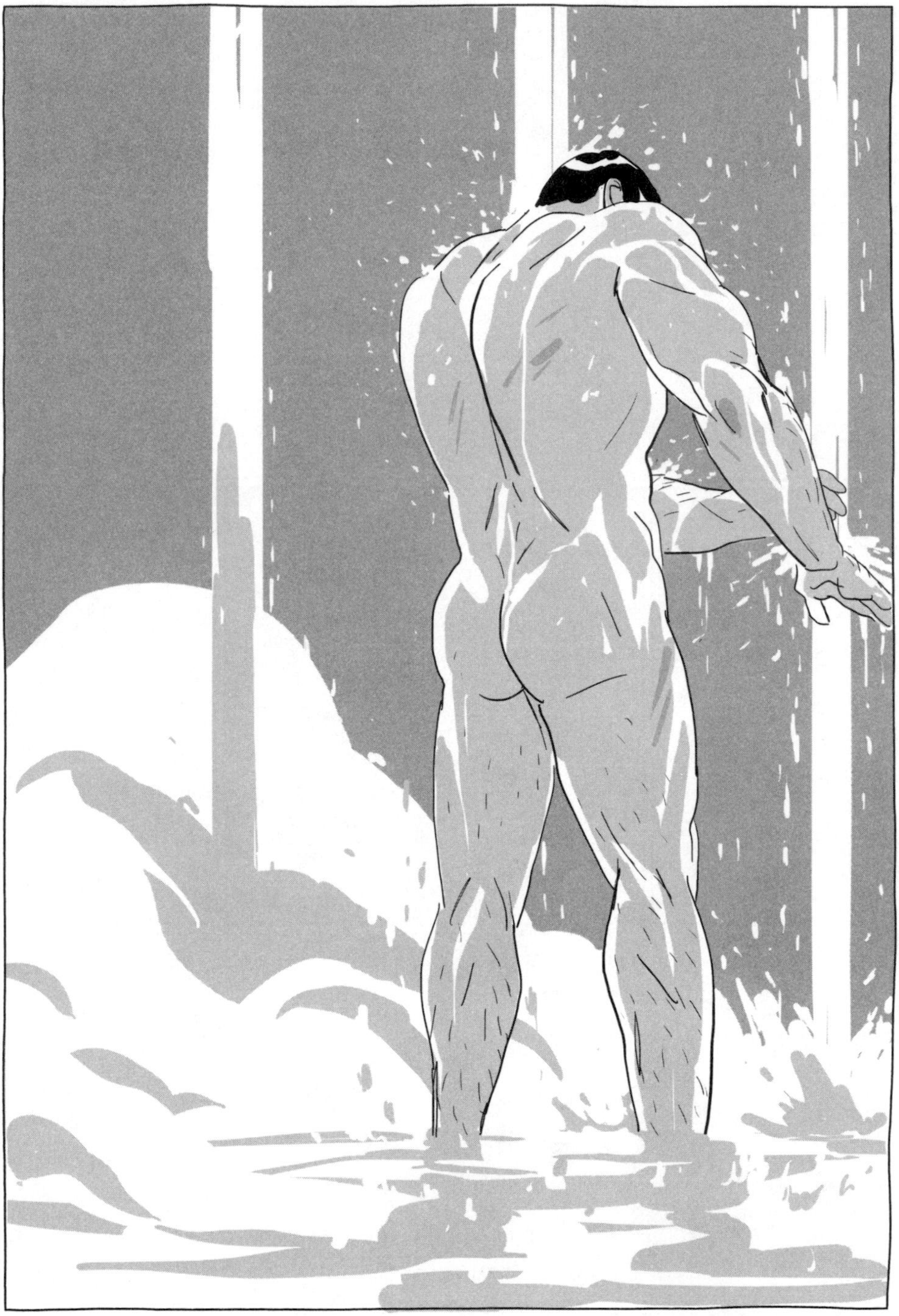

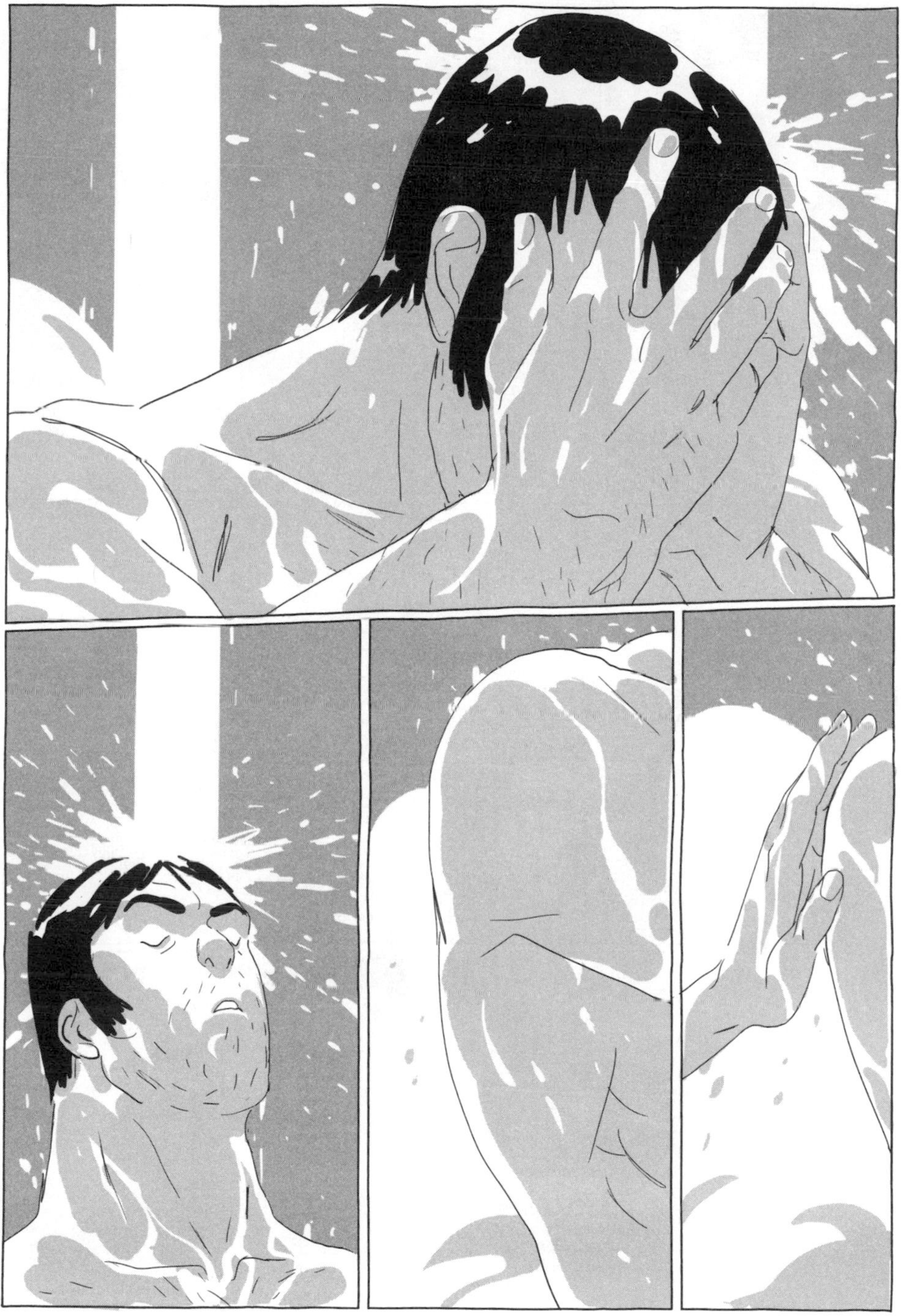

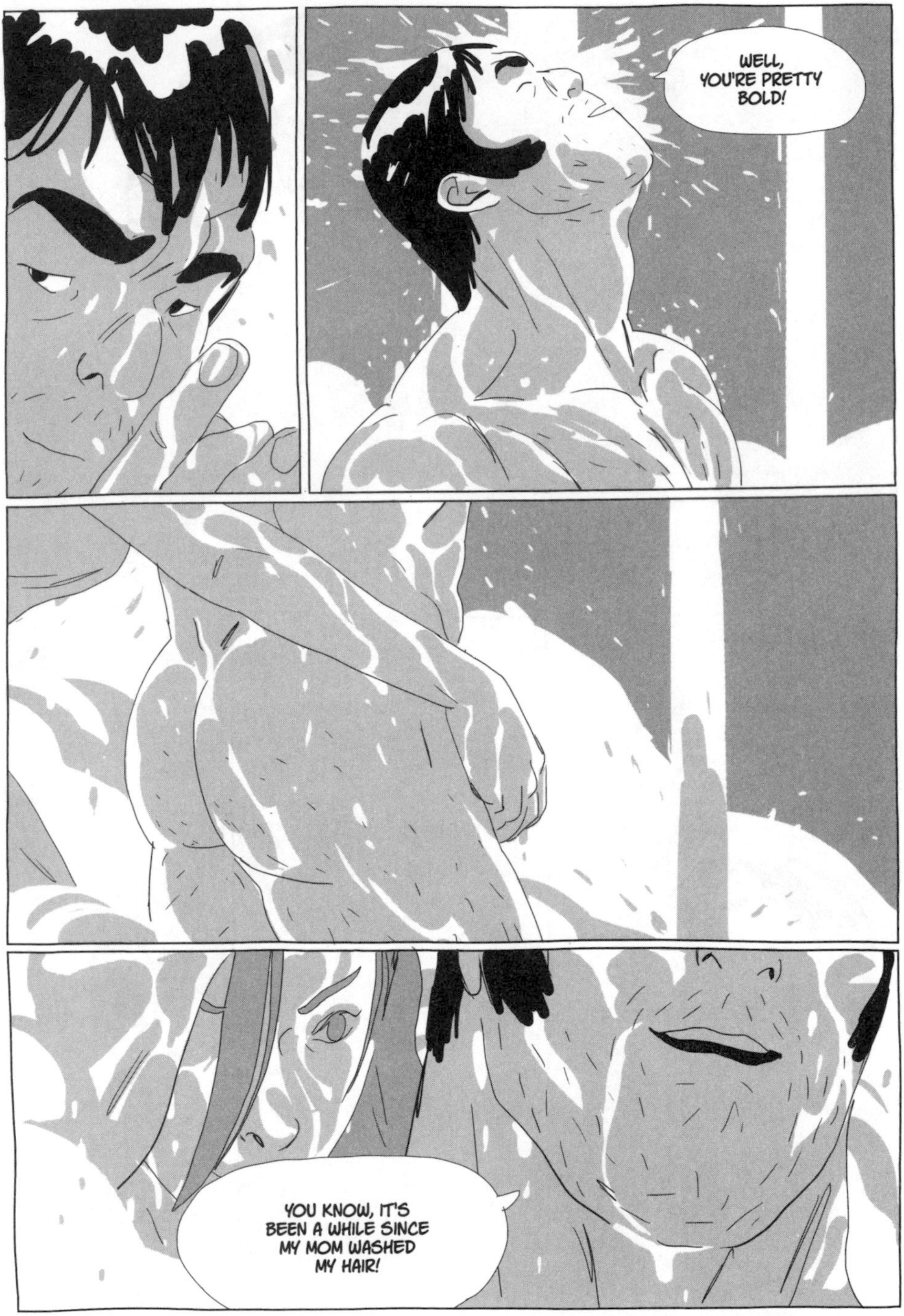
WELL, YOU'RE PRETTY BOLD!
YOU KNOW, IT'S BEEN A WHILE SINCE MY MOM WASHED MY HAIR!

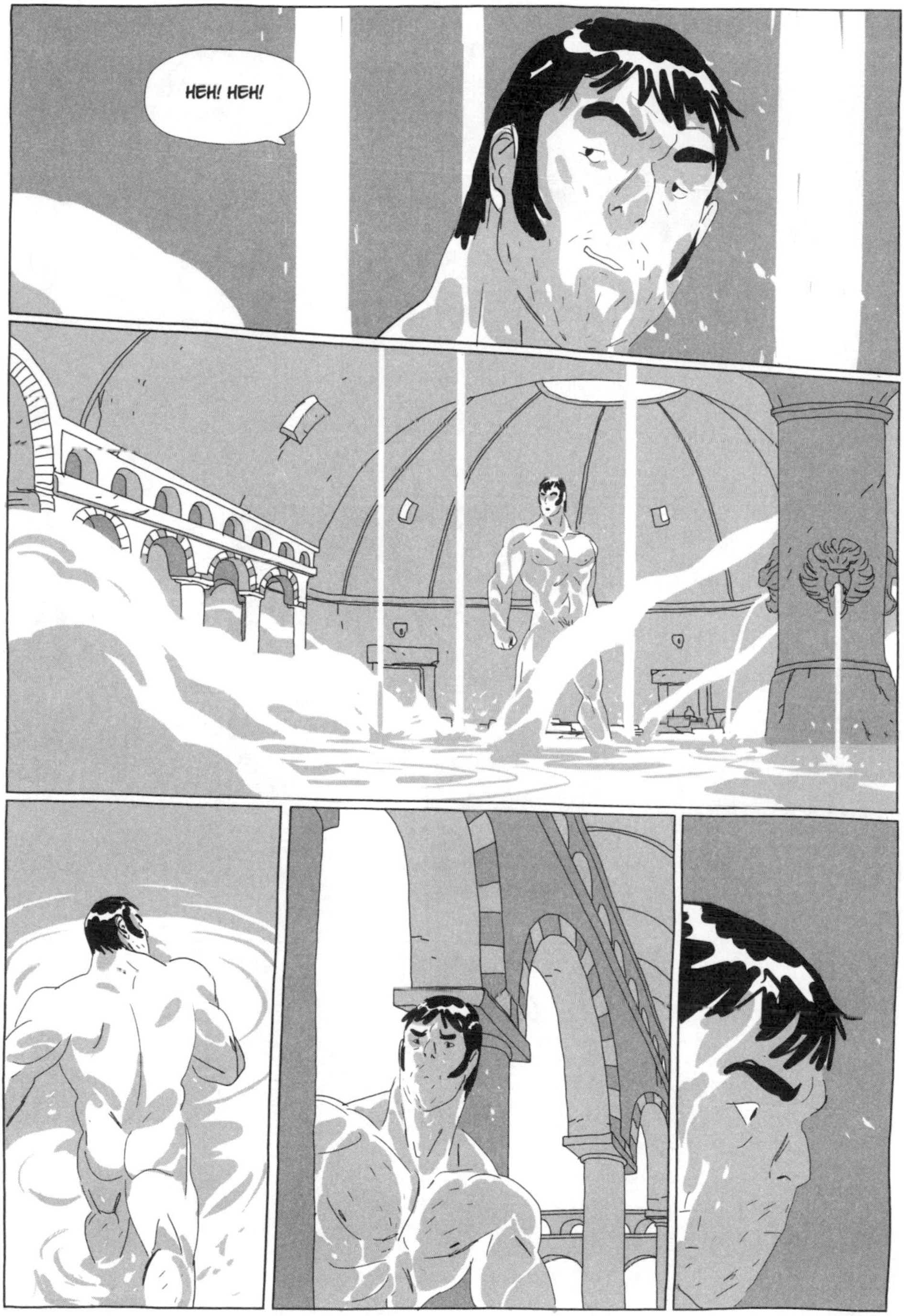
HEH! HEH!

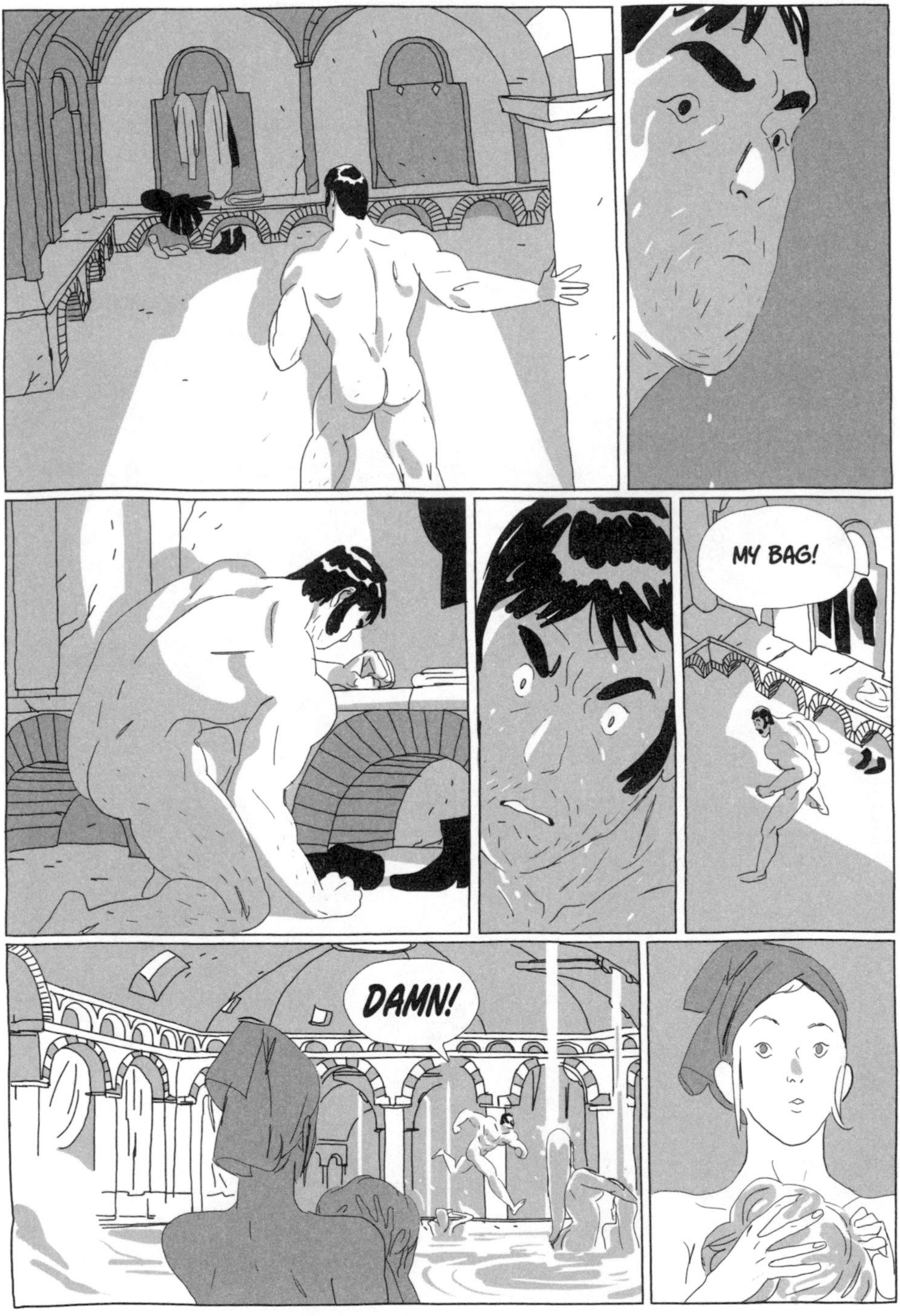
MY BAG!
DAMN!

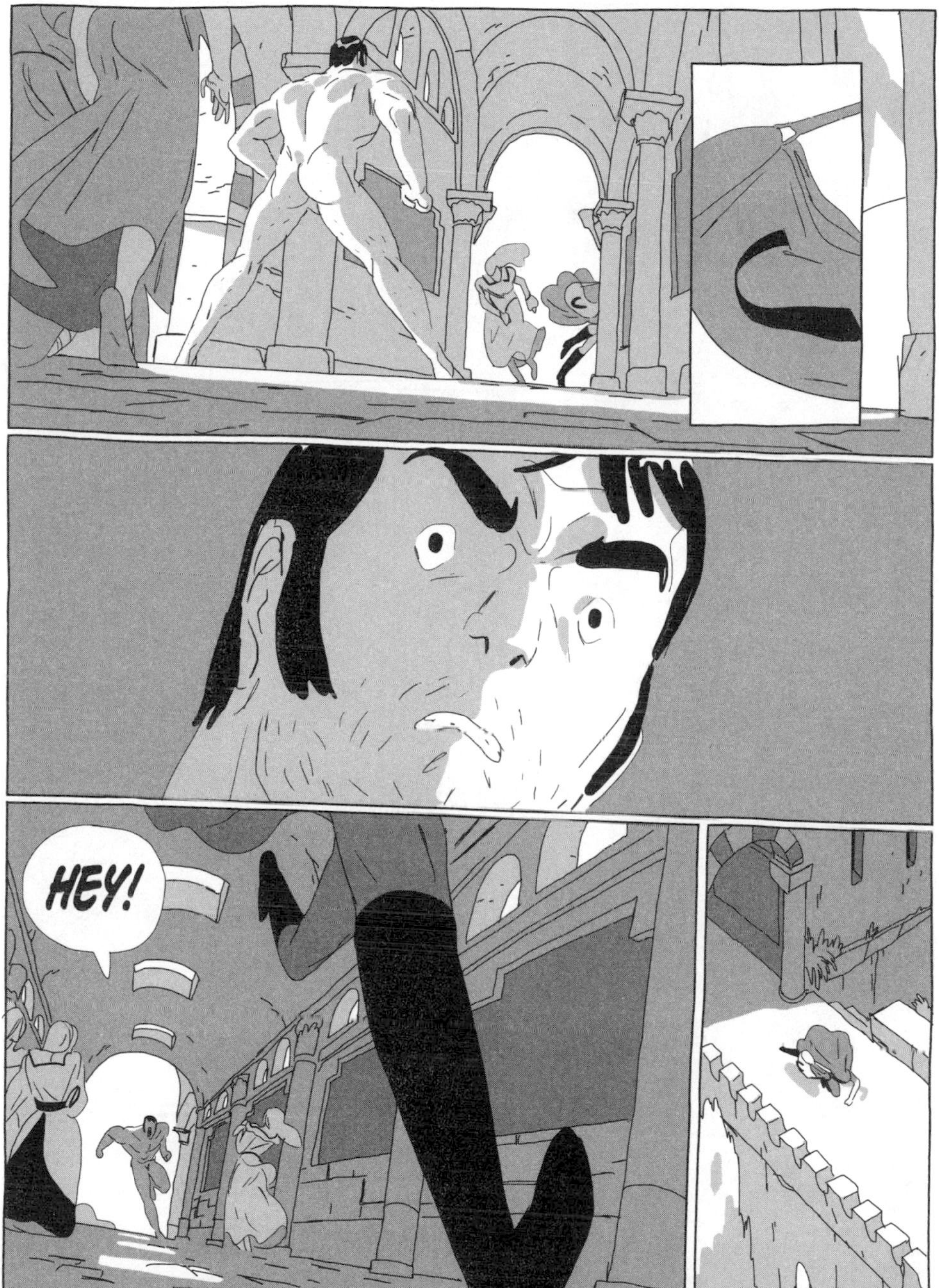
HEY!

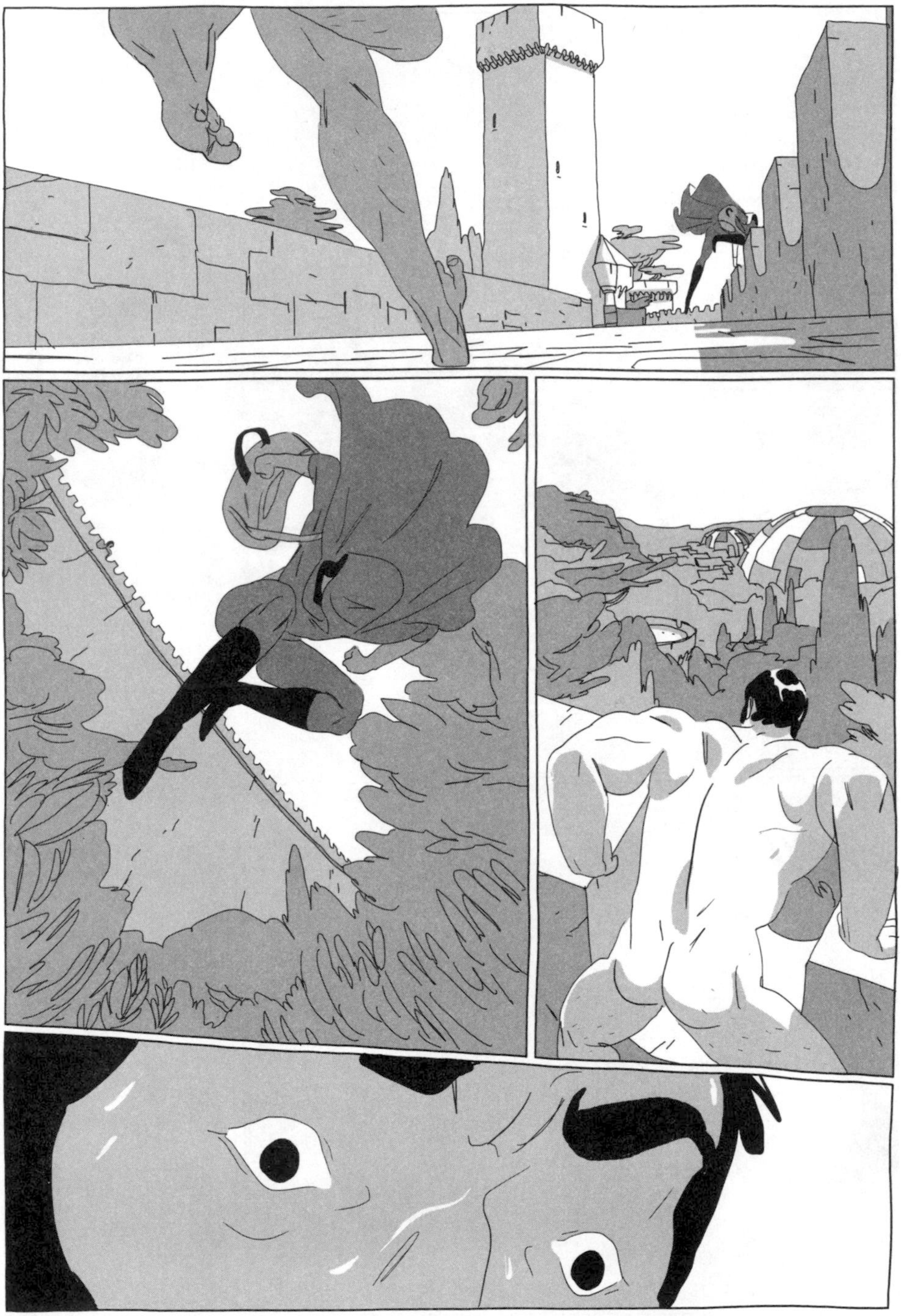

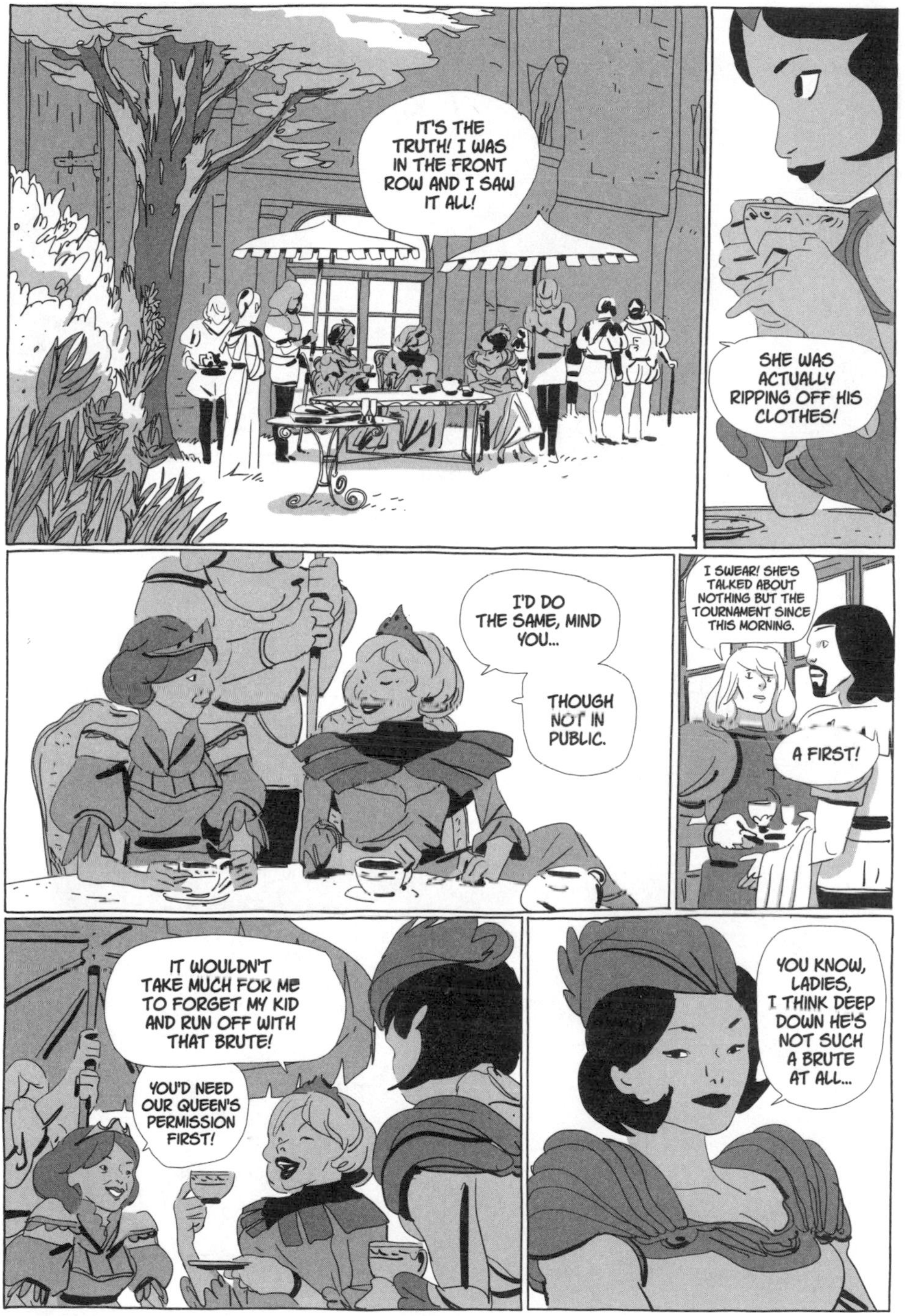
IT'S THE TRUTH! I WAS IN THE FRONT ROW AND I SAW IT ALL!
SHE WAS ACTUALLY RIPPING OFF HIS CLOTHES!
I'D DO THE SAME, MIND YOU...
THOUGH NOT IN PUBLIC.
I SWEAR! SHE'S TALKED ABOUT NOTHING BUT THE TOURNAMENT SINCE THIS MORNING.
A FIRST!
IT WOULDN'T TAKE MUCH FOR ME TO FORGET MY KID AND RUN OFF WITH THAT BRUTE!
YOU'D NEED OUR QUEEN'S PERMISSION FIRST!
YOU KNOW, LADIES, I THINK DEEP DOWN HE'S NOT SUCH A BRUTE AT ALL...

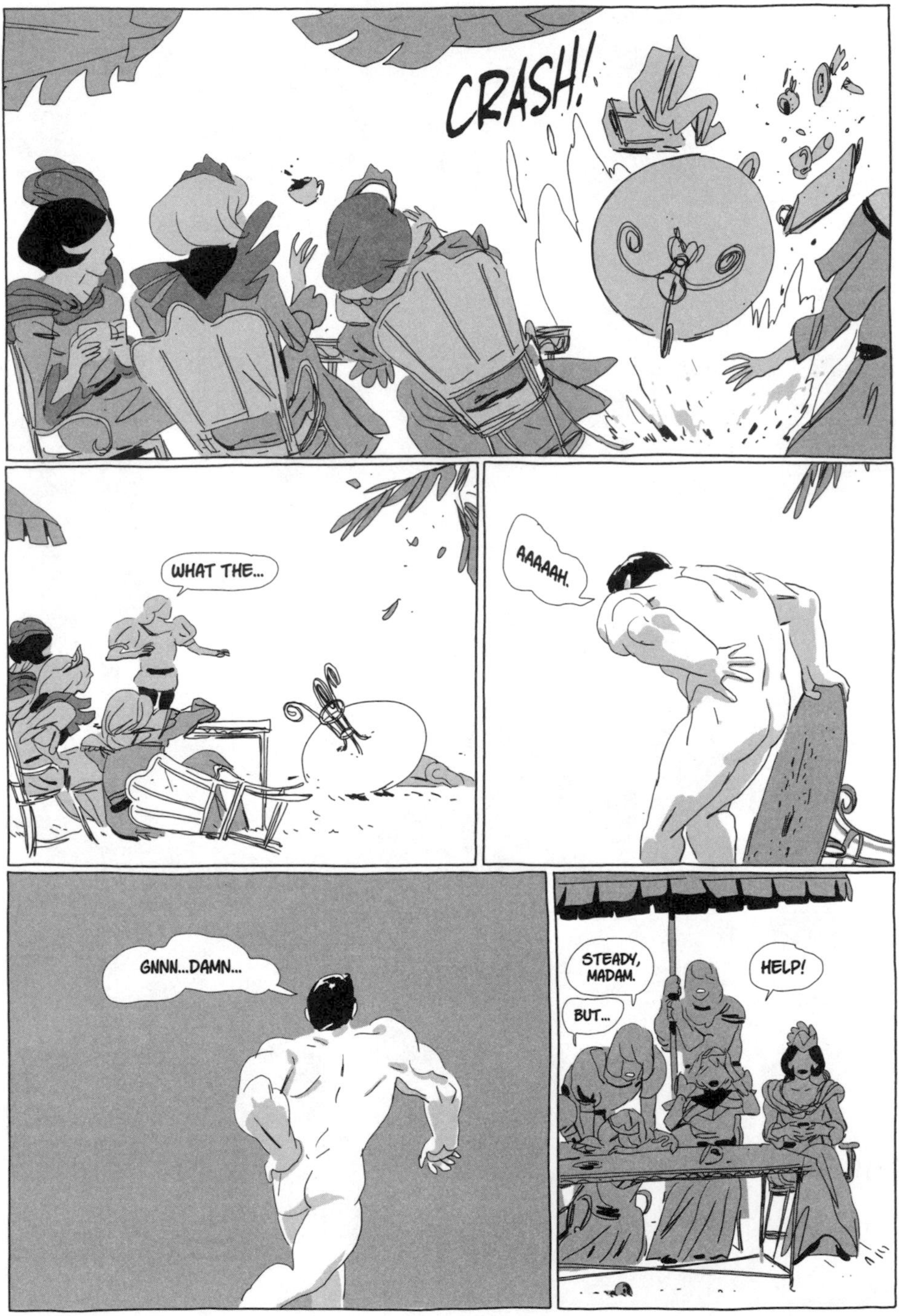
CRASH!
WHAT THE...
AAAAAH.
GNNN...DAMN...
STEADY, MADAM.
BUT...
HELP!

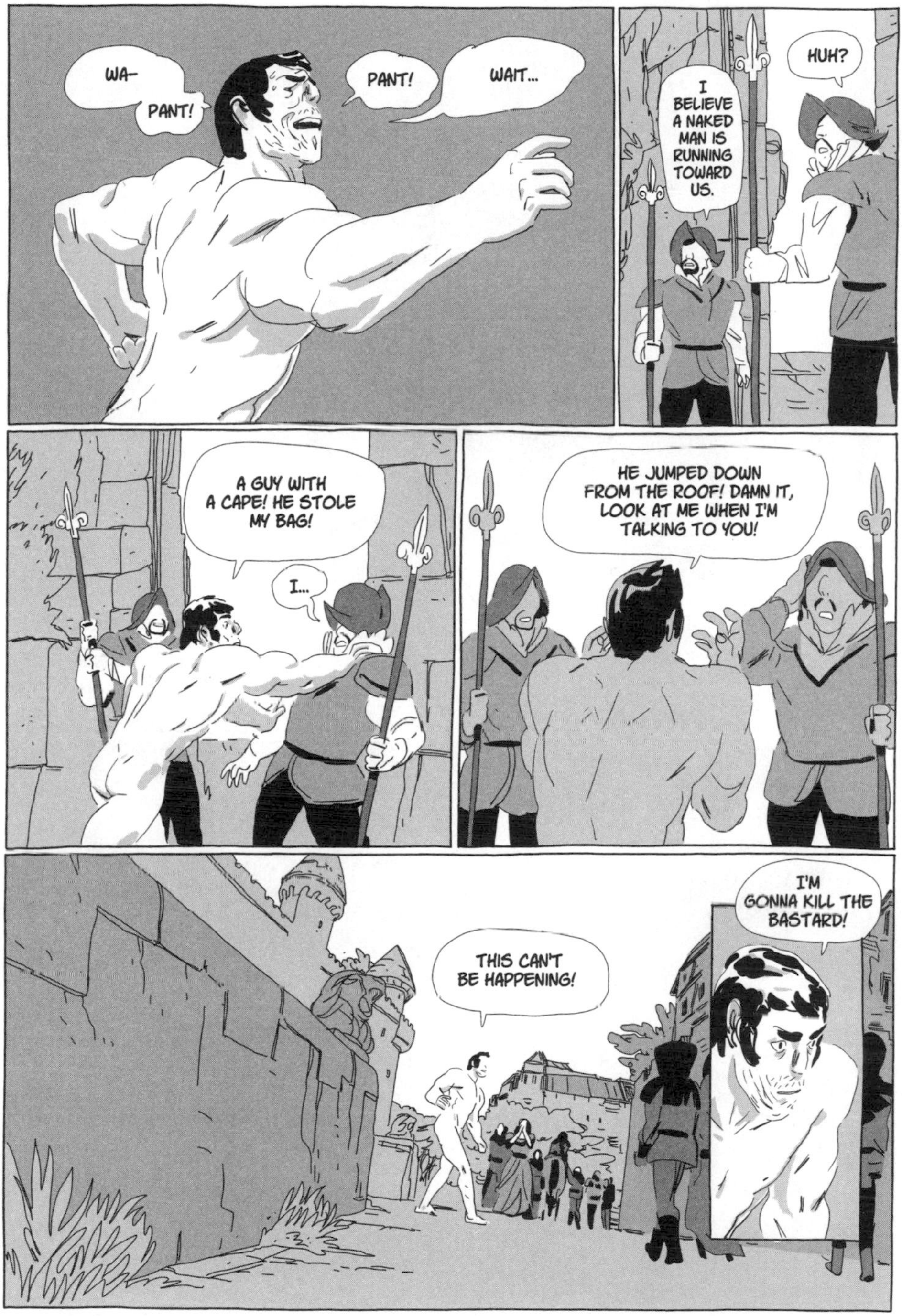
WA-
PANT!
PANT!
WAIT...
I BELIEVE A NAKED MAN IS RUNNING TOWARD US.
HUH?
A GUY WITH A CAPE! HE STOLE MY BAG!
I...
HE JUMPED DOWN FROM THE ROOF! DAMN IT, LOOK AT ME WHEN I'M TALKING TO YOU!
THIS CAN'T BE HAPPENING!
I'M GONNA KILL THE BASTARD!

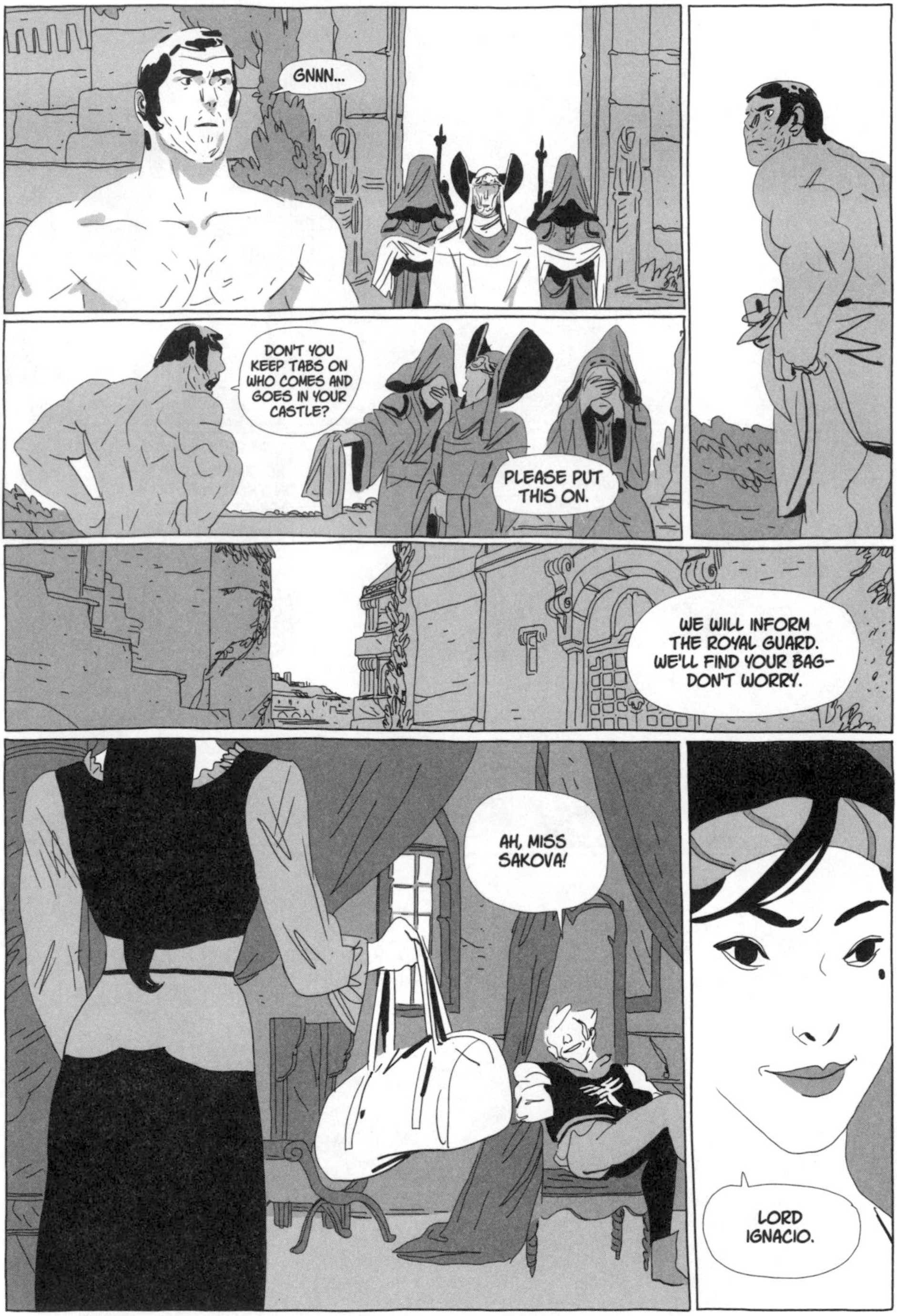
GNNN...
DON'T YOU KEEP TABS ON WHO COMES AND GOES IN YOUR CASTLE?
PLEASE PUT THIS ON.
WE WILL INFORM THE ROYAL GUARD. WE'LL FIND YOUR BAG-DON'T WORRY.
AH, MISS SAKOVA!
LORD IGNACIO.

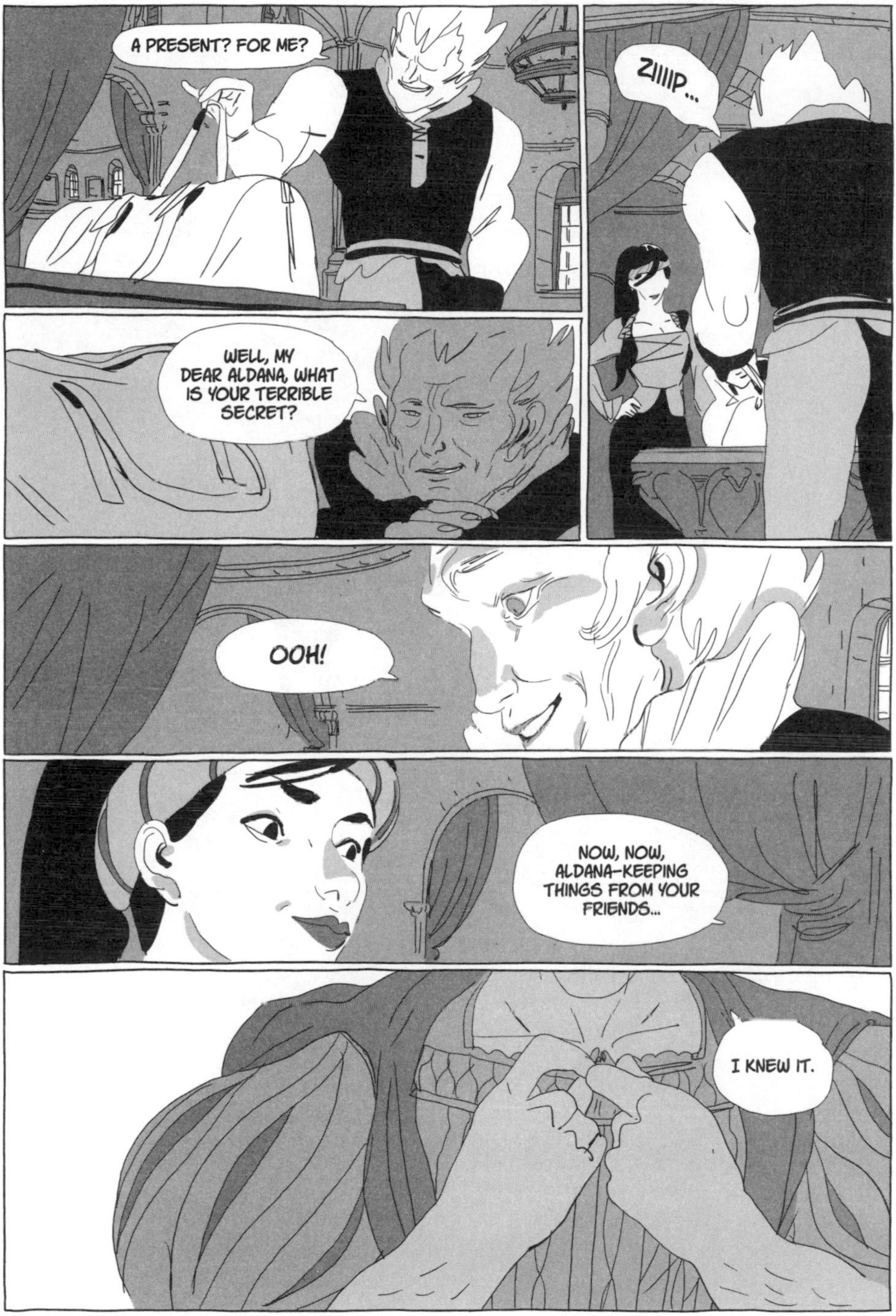
A PRESENT? FOR ME?
ZIIIIP...
WELL, MY DEAR ALDANA, WHAT IS YOUR TERRIBLE SECRET?
OOH!
NOW, NOW, ALDANA—KEEPING THINGS FROM YOUR FRIENDS...
I KNEW IT.

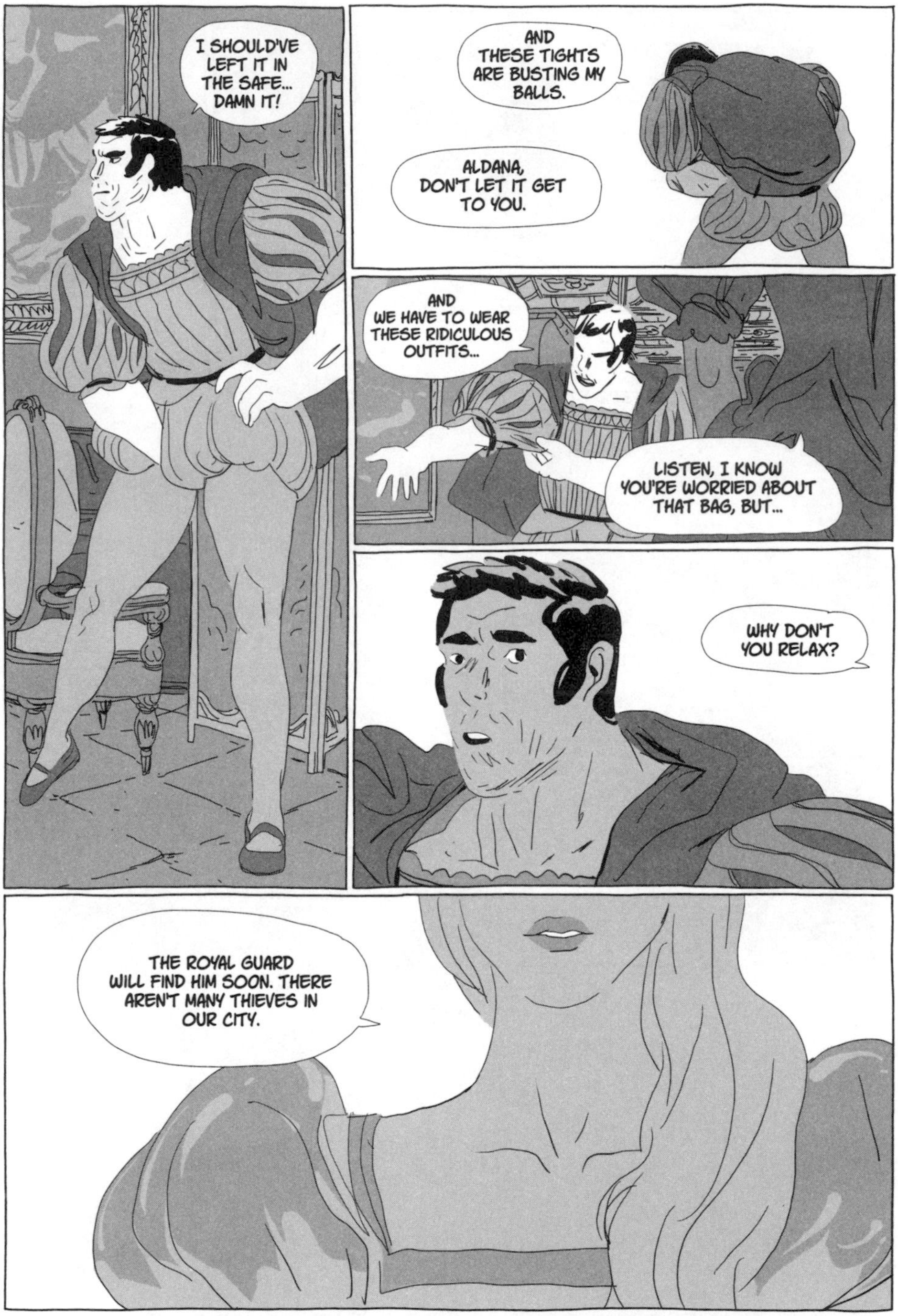
I SHOULD'VE LEFT IT IN THE SAFE... DAMN IT!
AND THESE TIGHTS ARE BUSTING MY BALLS.
ALDANA, DON'T LET IT GET TO YOU.
AND WE HAVE TO WEAR THESE RIDICULOUS OUTFITS...
LISTEN, I KNOW YOU'RE WORRIED ABOUT THAT BAG, BUT...
WHY DON'T YOU RELAX?
THE ROYAL GUARD WILL FIND HIM SOON. THERE AREN'T MANY THIEVES IN OUR CITY.

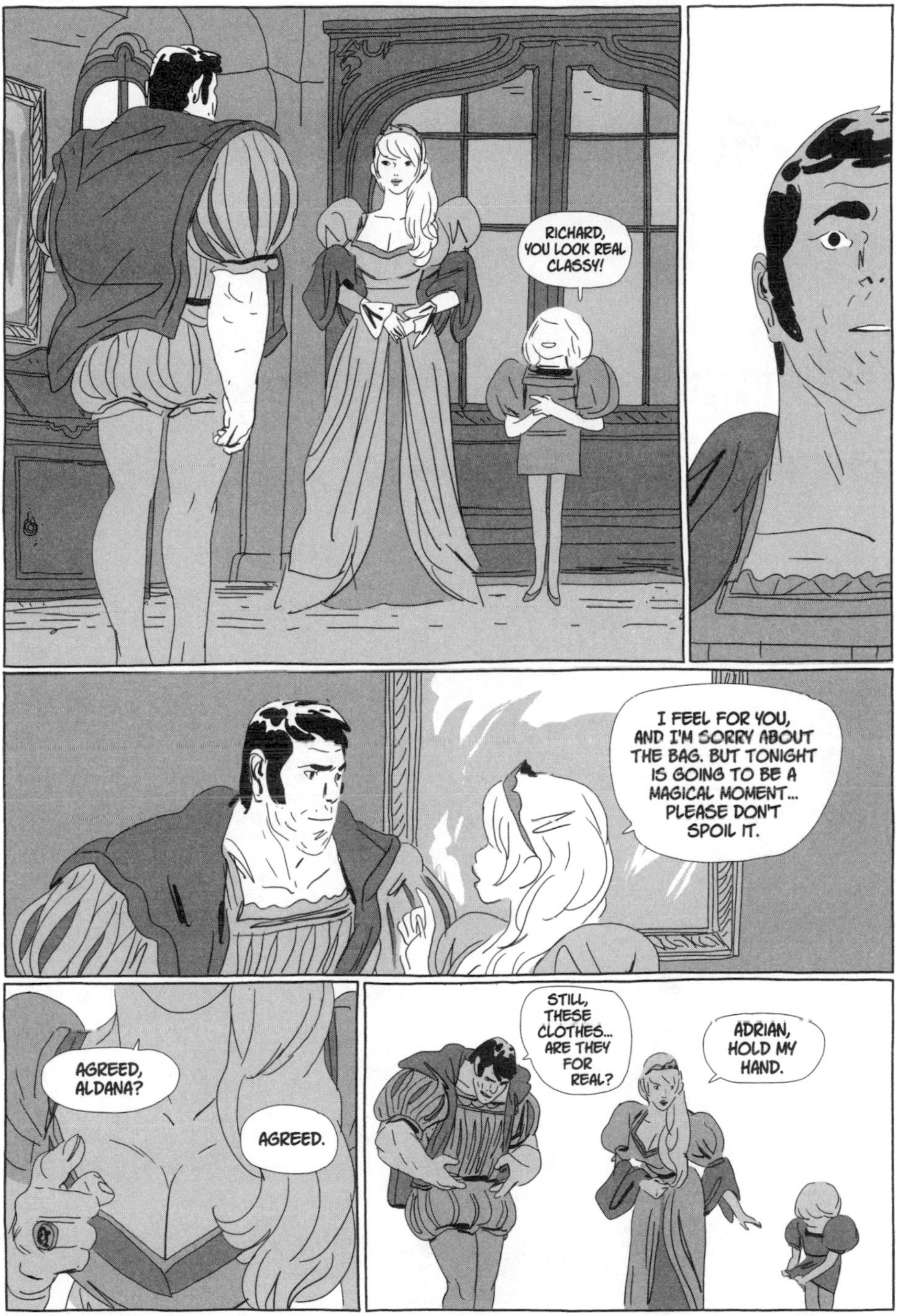
RICHARD, YOU LOOK REAL CLASSY!
I FEEL FOR YOU, AND I'M SORRY ABOUT THE BAG. BUT TONIGHT IS GOING TO BE A MAGICAL MOMENT... PLEASE DON'T SPOIL IT.
AGREED, ALDANA?
AGREED.
STILL, THESE CLOTHES... ARE THEY FOR REAL?
ADRIAN, HOLD MY HAND.

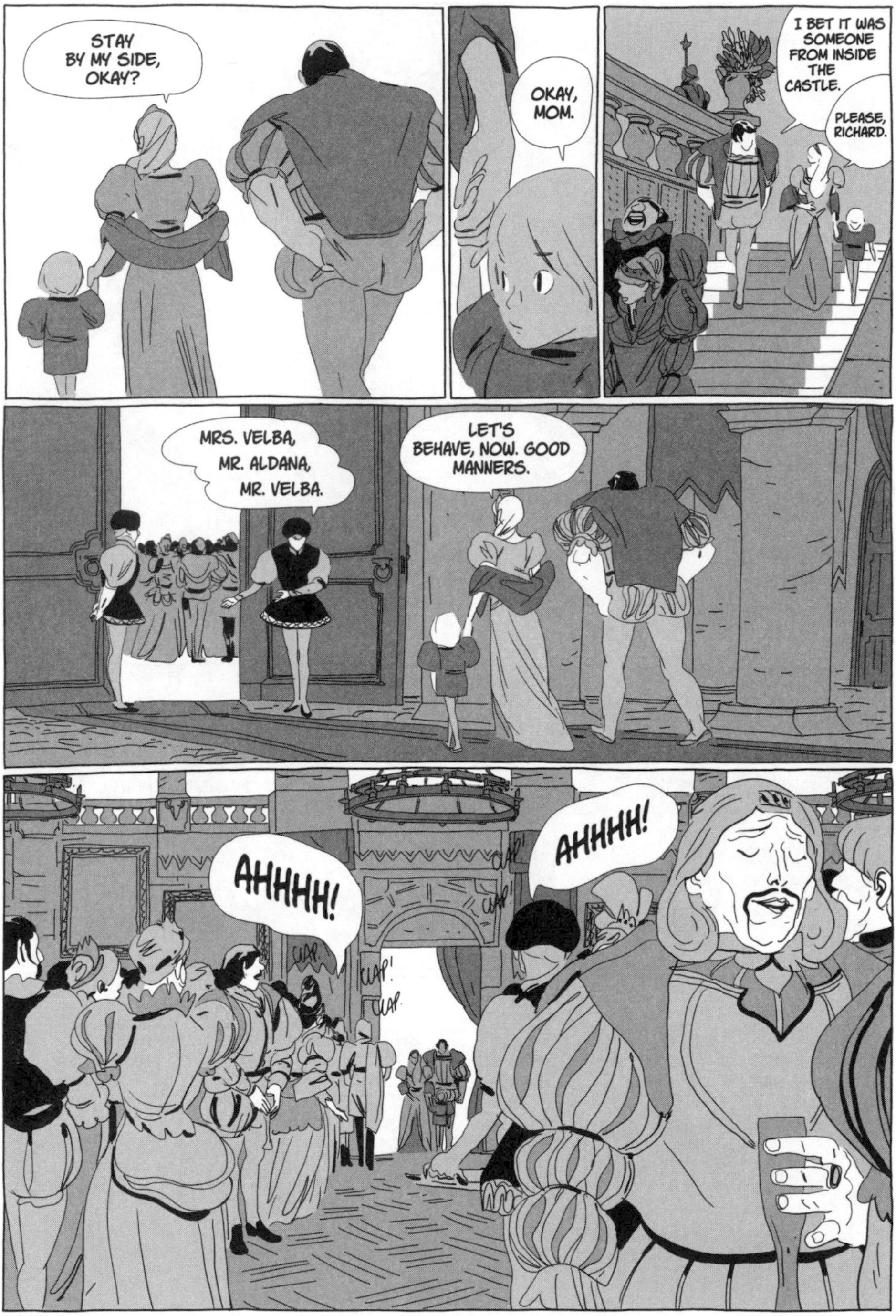
STAY BY MY SIDE, OKAY?
OKAY, MOM.
I BET IT WAS SOMEONE FROM INSIDE THE CASTLE.
PLEASE, RICHARD.
MRS. VELBA, MR. ALDANA, MR. VELBA.
LET'S BEHAVE, NOW. GOOD MANNERS.
AHHHH!
CLAP!
CLAP!
CLAP!
CLAP!
CLAP!
AHHHH!

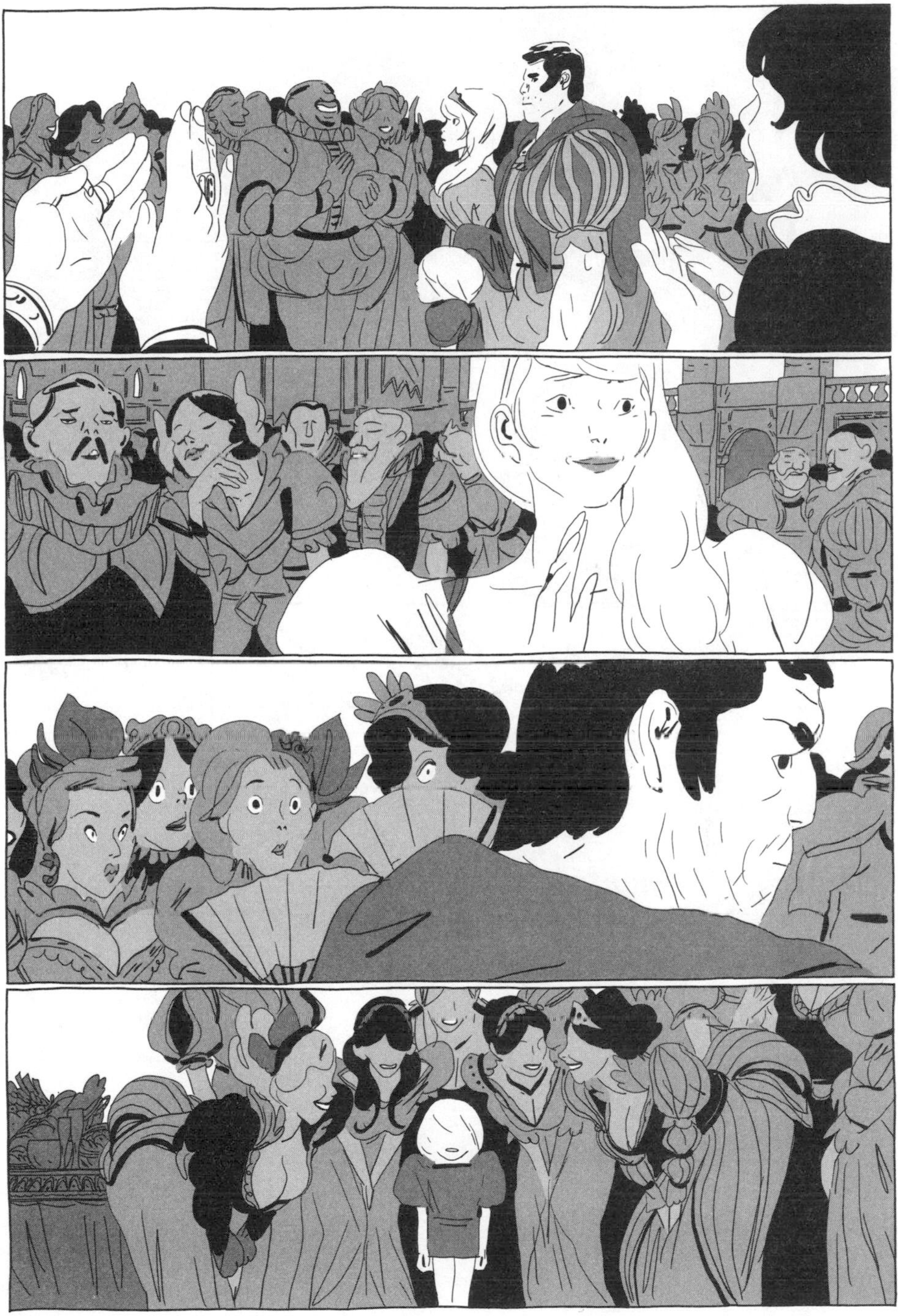

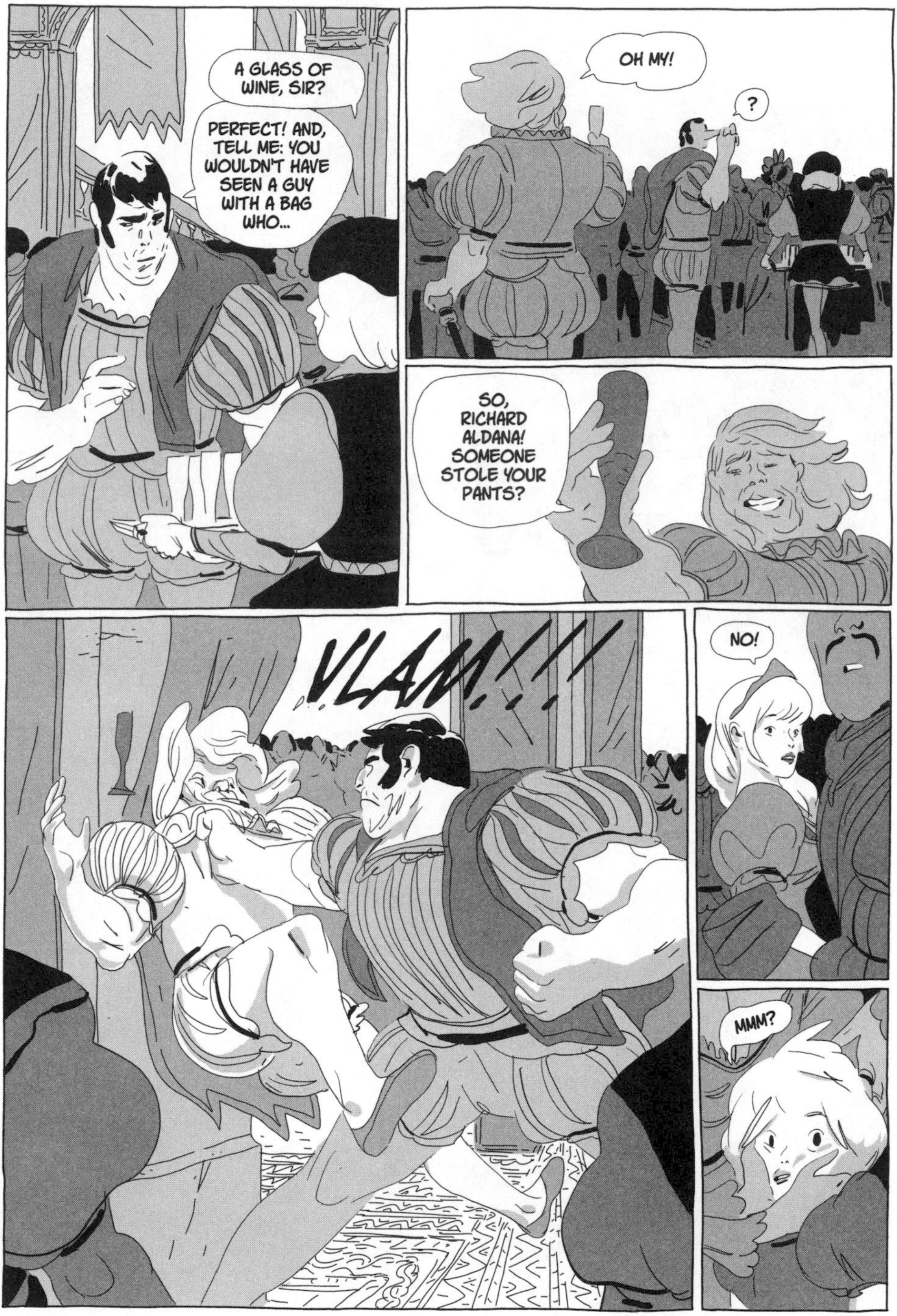
A GLASS OF WINE, SIR?
PERFECT! AND, TELL ME: YOU WOULDN'T HAVE SEEN A GUY WITH A BAG WHO...
OH MY!
?
SO, RICHARD ALDANA! SOMEONE STOLE YOUR PANTS?
VLAM!!!!
NO!
MMM?

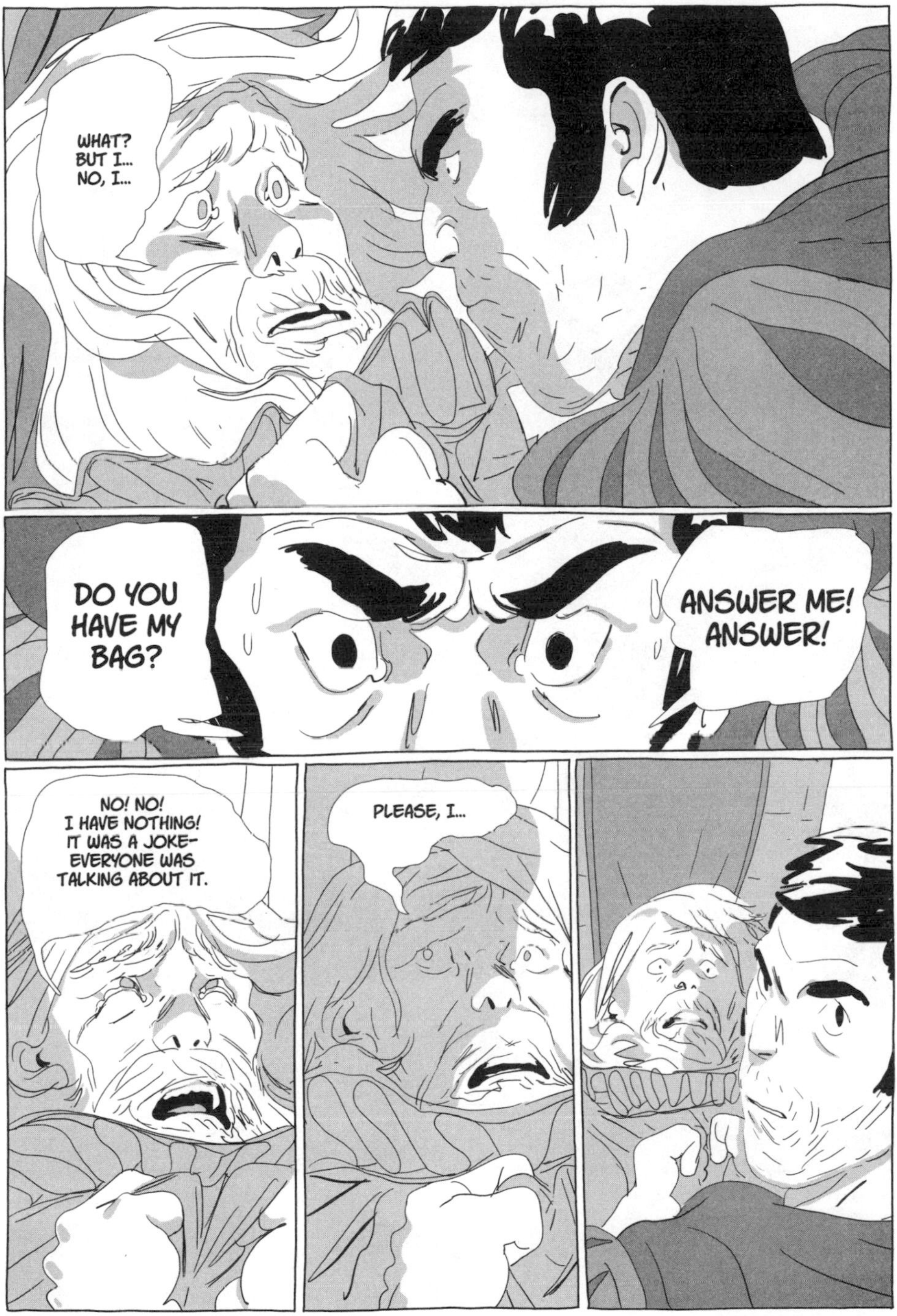
WHAT? BUT I... NO, I...
DO YOU HAVE MY BAG?
ANSWER ME! ANSWER!
NO! NO! I HAVE NOTHING! IT WAS A JOKE- EVERYONE WAS TALKING ABOUT IT.
PLEASE, I...

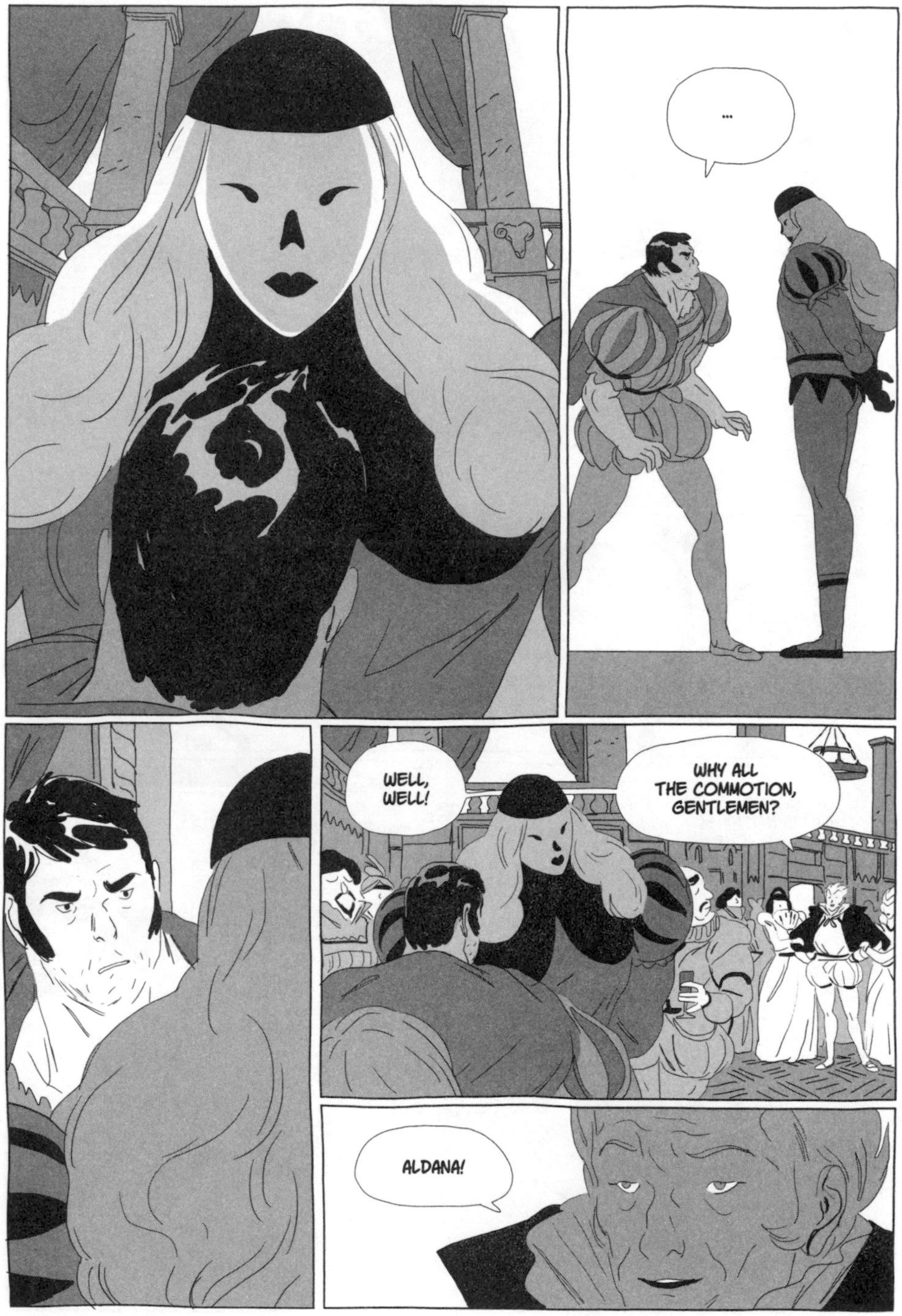
...
WELL, WELL!
WHY ALL THE COMMOTION, GENTLEMEN?
ALDANA!

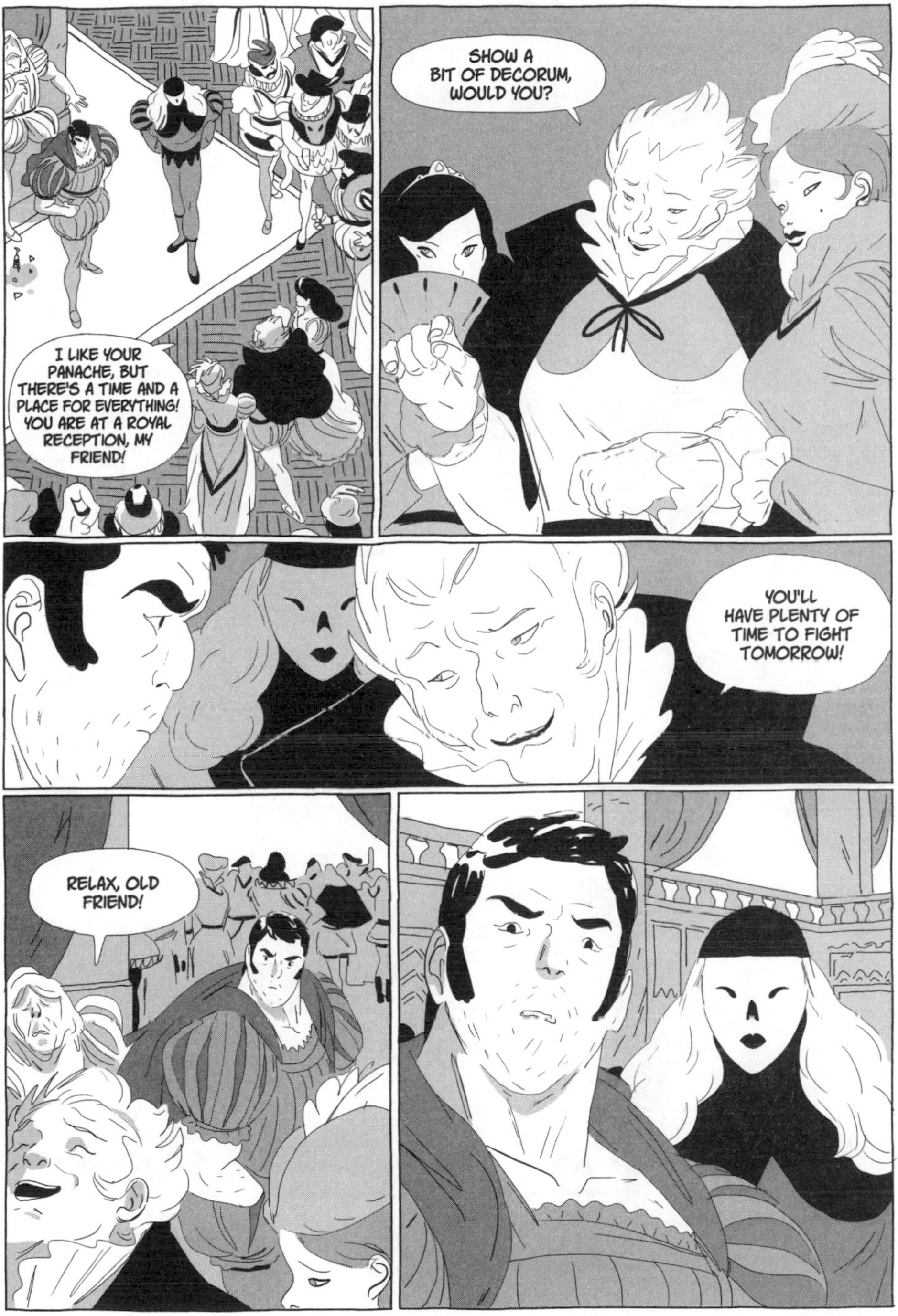
I LIKE YOUR PANACHE, BUT THERE'S A TIME AND A PLACE FOR EVERYTHING! YOU ARE AT A ROYAL RECEPTION, MY FRIEND!
SHOW A BIT OF DECORUM, WOULD YOU?
YOU'LL HAVE PLENTY OF TIME TO FIGHT TOMORROW!
RELAX, OLD FRIEND!

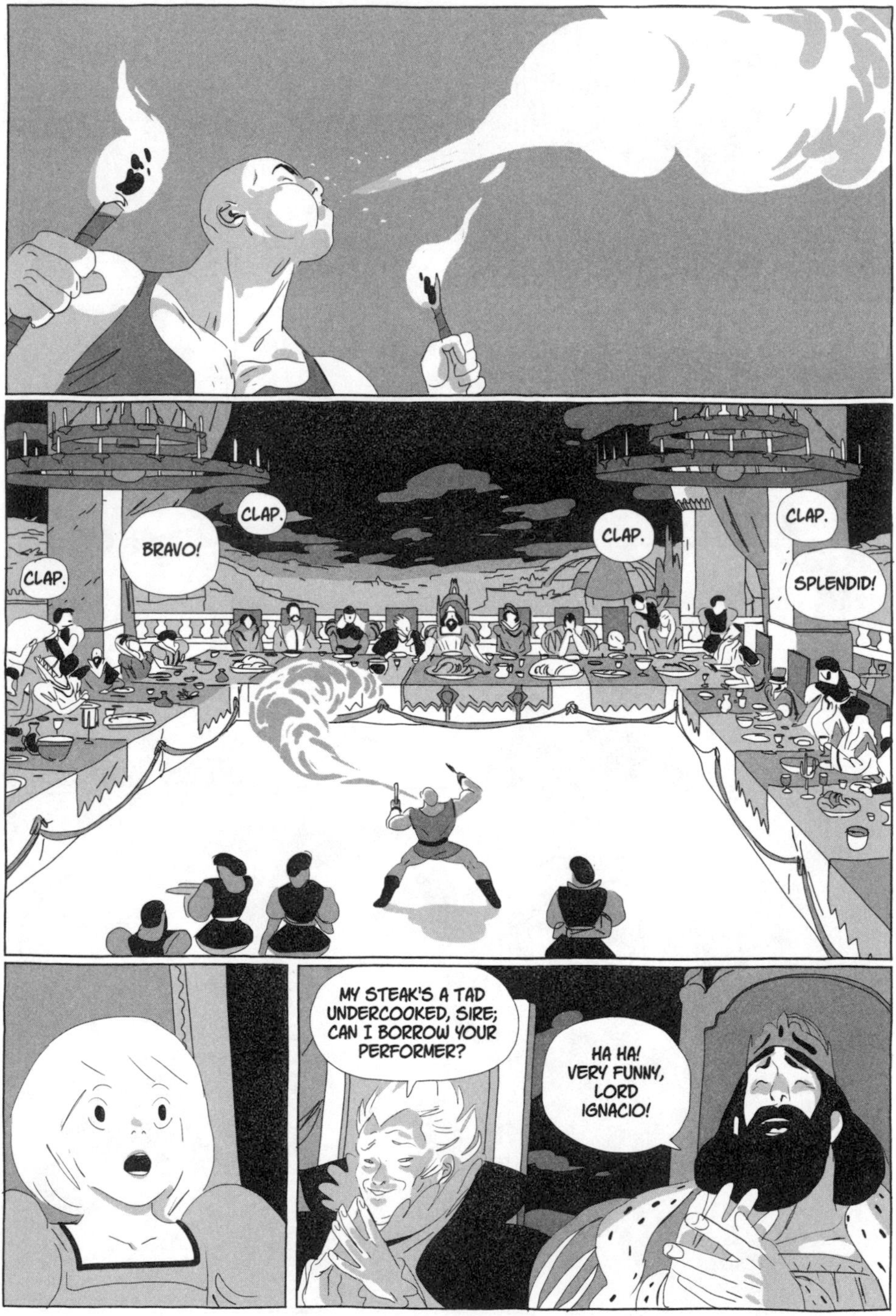
CLAP.
BRAVO!
CLAP.
CLAP.
CLAP.
SPLENDID!
MY STEAK'S A TAD UNDERCOOKED, SIRE; CAN I BORROW YOUR PERFORMER?
HA HA! VERY FUNNY, LORD IGNACIO!

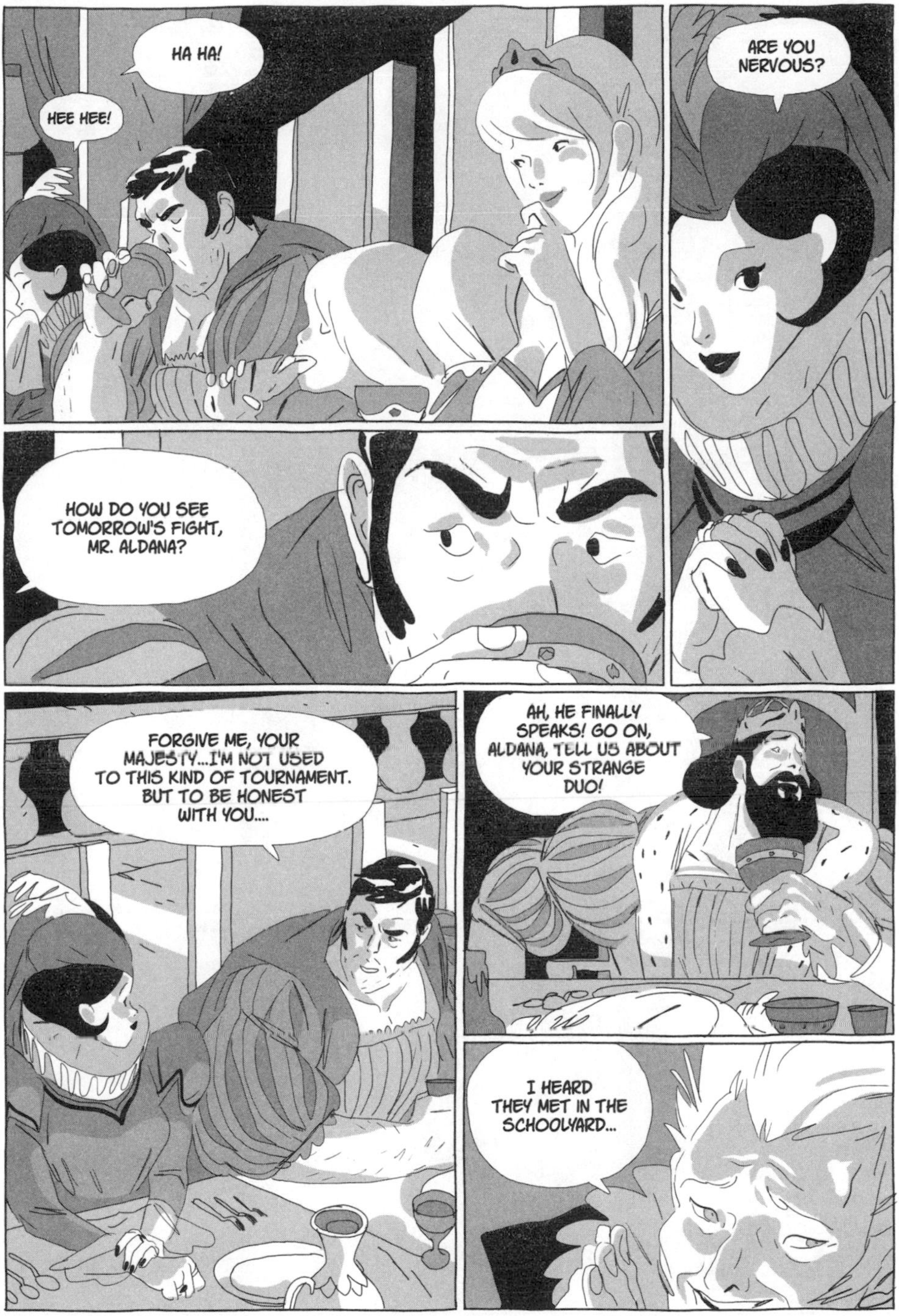
HA HA!
HEE HEE!
ARE YOU NERVOUS?
HOW DO YOU SEE TOMORROW'S FIGHT, MR. ALDANA?
FORGIVE ME, YOUR MAJESTY...I'M NOT USED TO THIS KIND OF TOURNAMENT. BUT TO BE HONEST WITH YOU....
AH, HE FINALLY SPEAKS! GO ON, ALDANA, TELL US ABOUT YOUR STRANGE DUO!
I HEARD THEY MET IN THE SCHOOLYARD...

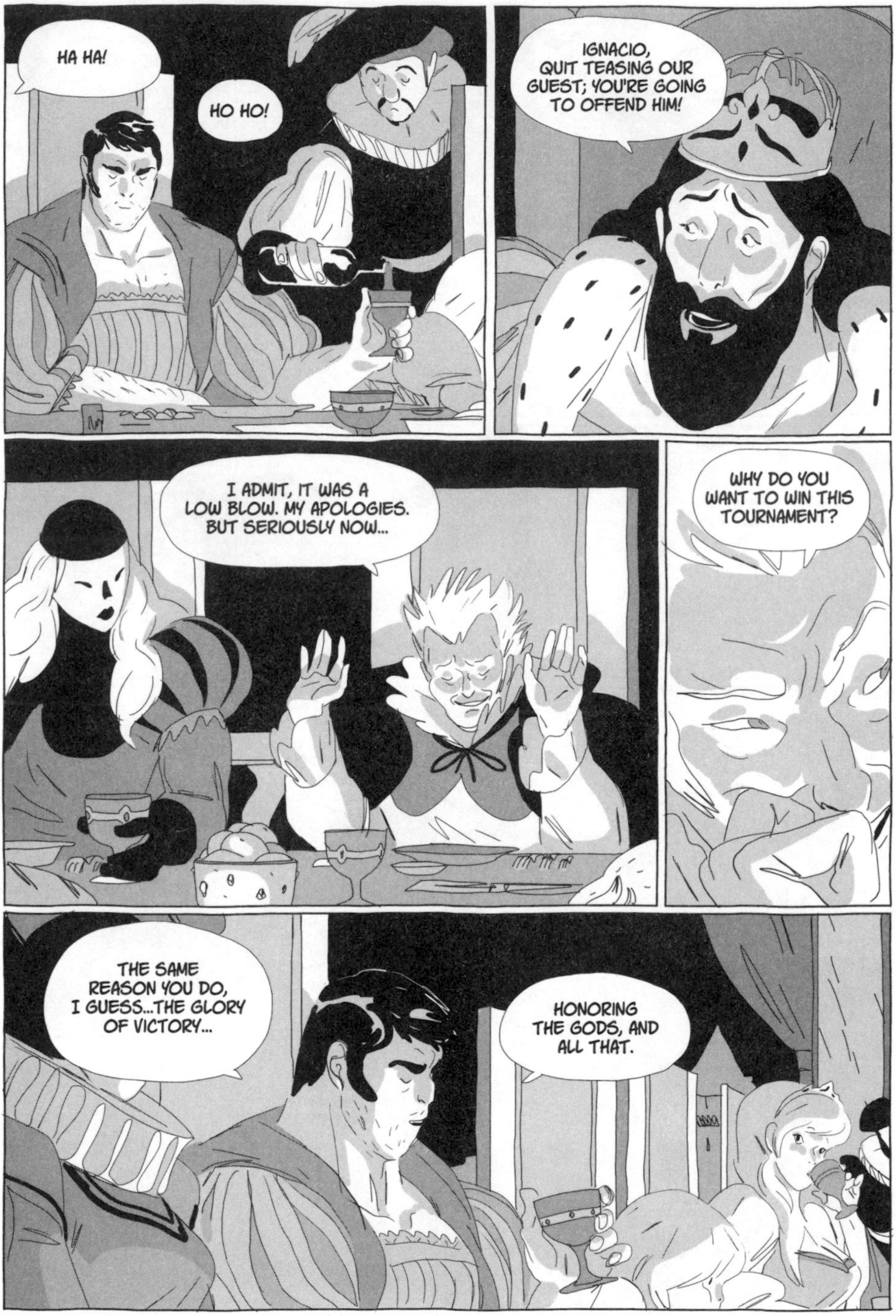
HA HA!
HO HO!
IGNACIO, QUIT TEASING OUR GUEST; YOU'RE GOING TO OFFEND HIM!
I ADMIT, IT WAS A LOW BLOW. MY APOLOGIES. BUT SERIOUSLY NOW...
WHY DO YOU WANT TO WIN THIS TOURNAMENT?
THE SAME REASON YOU DO, I GUESS...THE GLORY OF VICTORY...
HONORING THE GODS, AND ALL THAT.

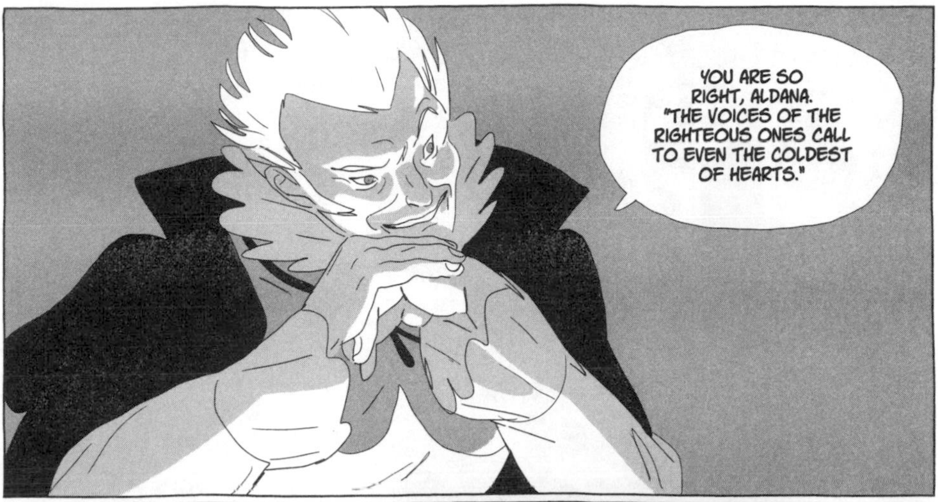
YOU ARE SO RIGHT, ALDANA. "THE VOICES OF THE RIGHTEOUS ONES CALL TO EVEN THE COLDEST OF HEARTS."

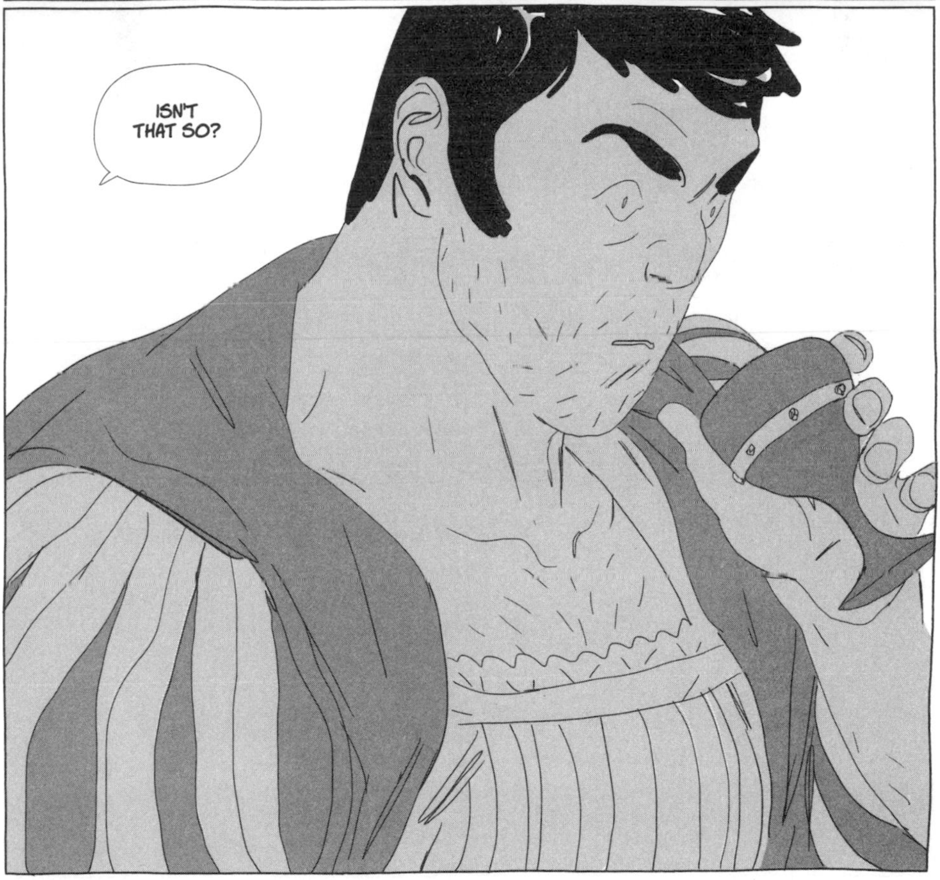
ISN'T THAT SO?

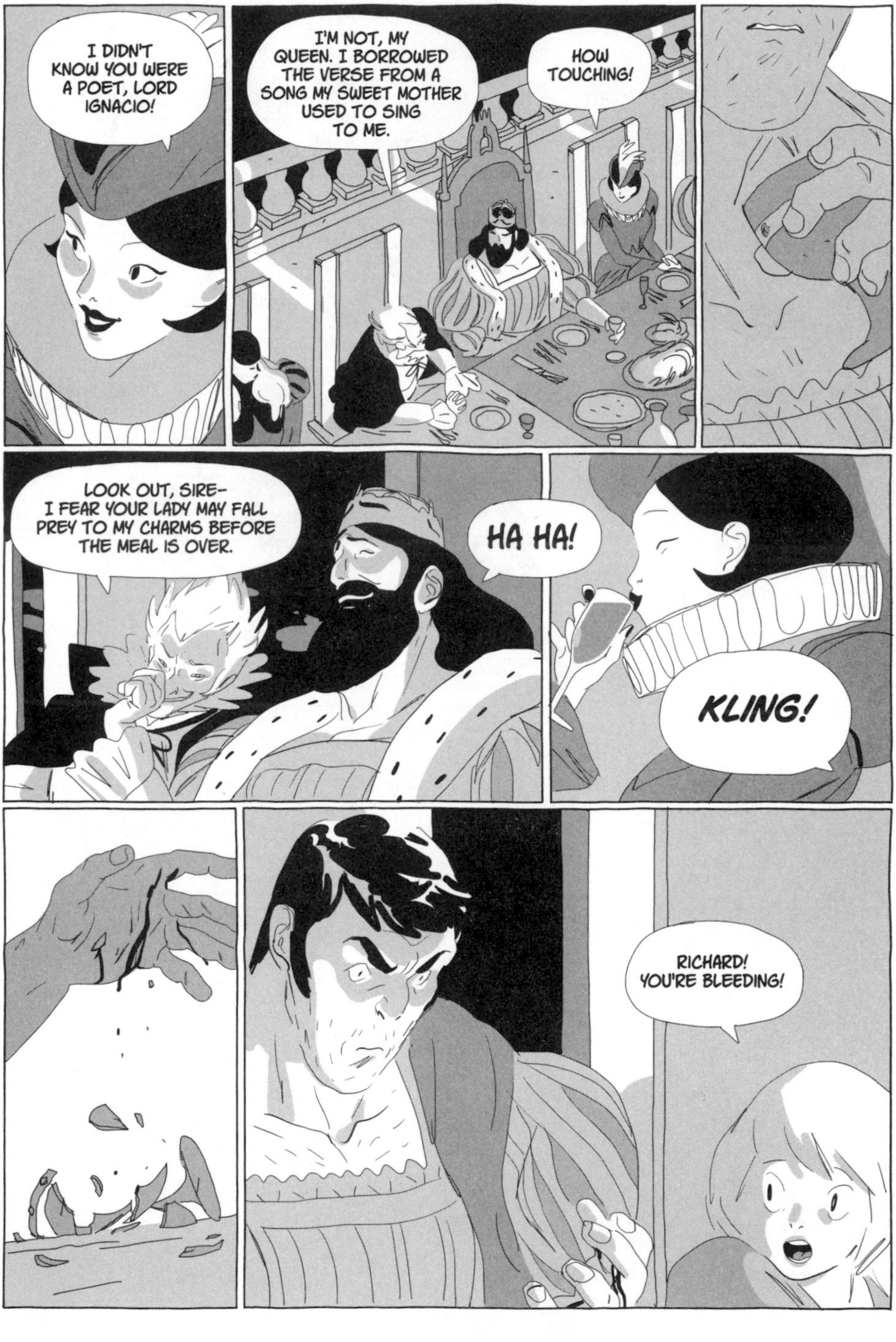
I DIDN'T KNOW YOU WERE A POET, LORD IGNACIO!
I'M NOT, MY QUEEN. I BORROWED THE VERSE FROM A SONG MY SWEET MOTHER USED TO SING TO ME.
HOW TOUCHING!
LOOK OUT, SIRE- I FEAR YOUR LADY MAY FALL PREY TO MY CHARMS BEFORE THE MEAL IS OVER.
HA HA!
KLING!
RICHARD! YOU'RE BLEEDING!

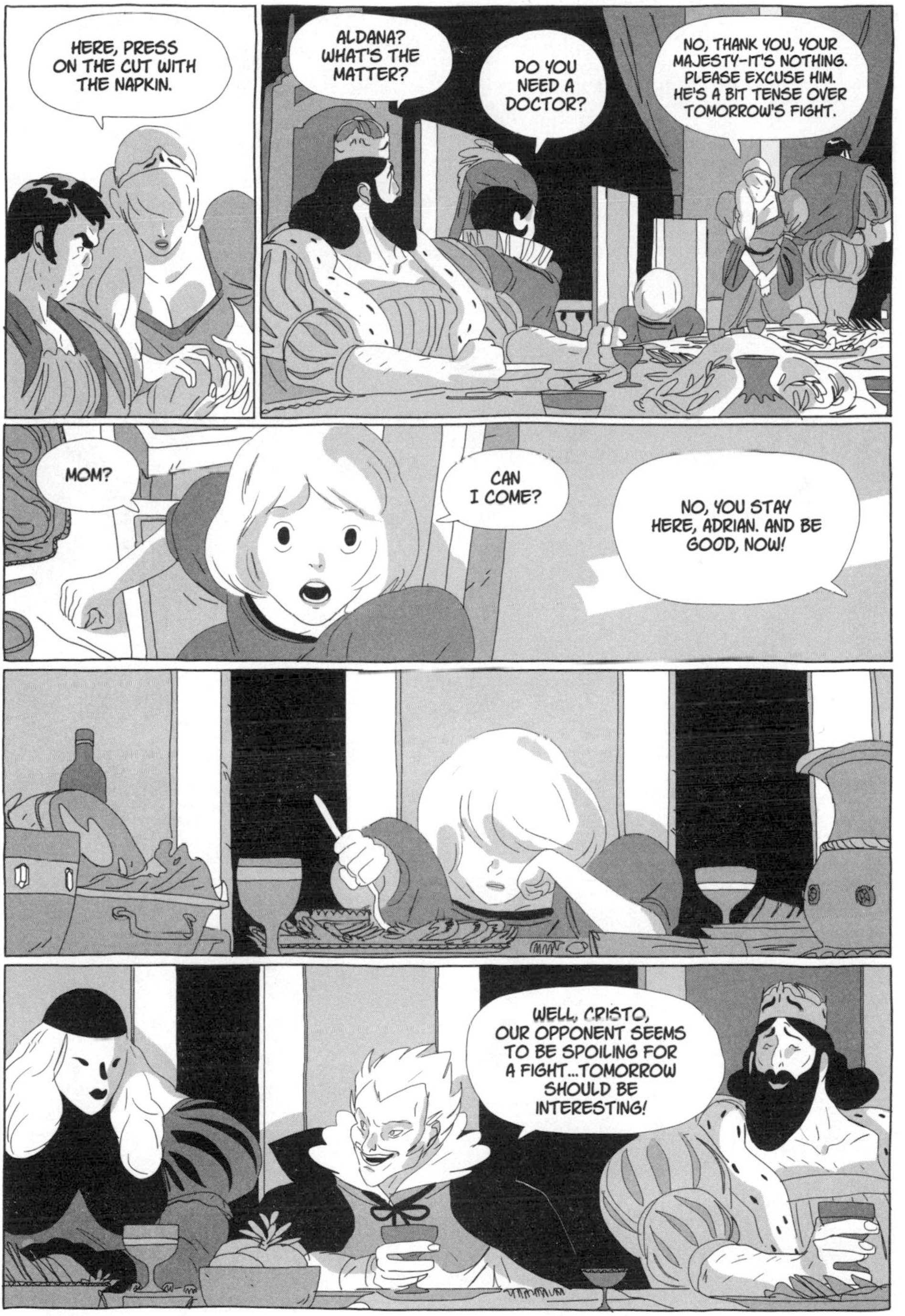
HERE, PRESS ON THE CUT WITH THE NAPKIN.
ALDANA? WHAT'S THE MATTER?
DO YOU NEED A DOCTOR?
NO, THANK YOU, YOUR MAJESTY–IT'S NOTHING. PLEASE EXCUSE HIM. HE'S A BIT TENSE OVER TOMORROW'S FIGHT.
MOM?
CAN I COME?
NO, YOU STAY HERE, ADRIAN. AND BE GOOD, NOW!
WELL, CRISTO, OUR OPPONENT SEEMS TO BE SPOILING FOR A FIGHT...TOMORROW SHOULD BE INTERESTING!

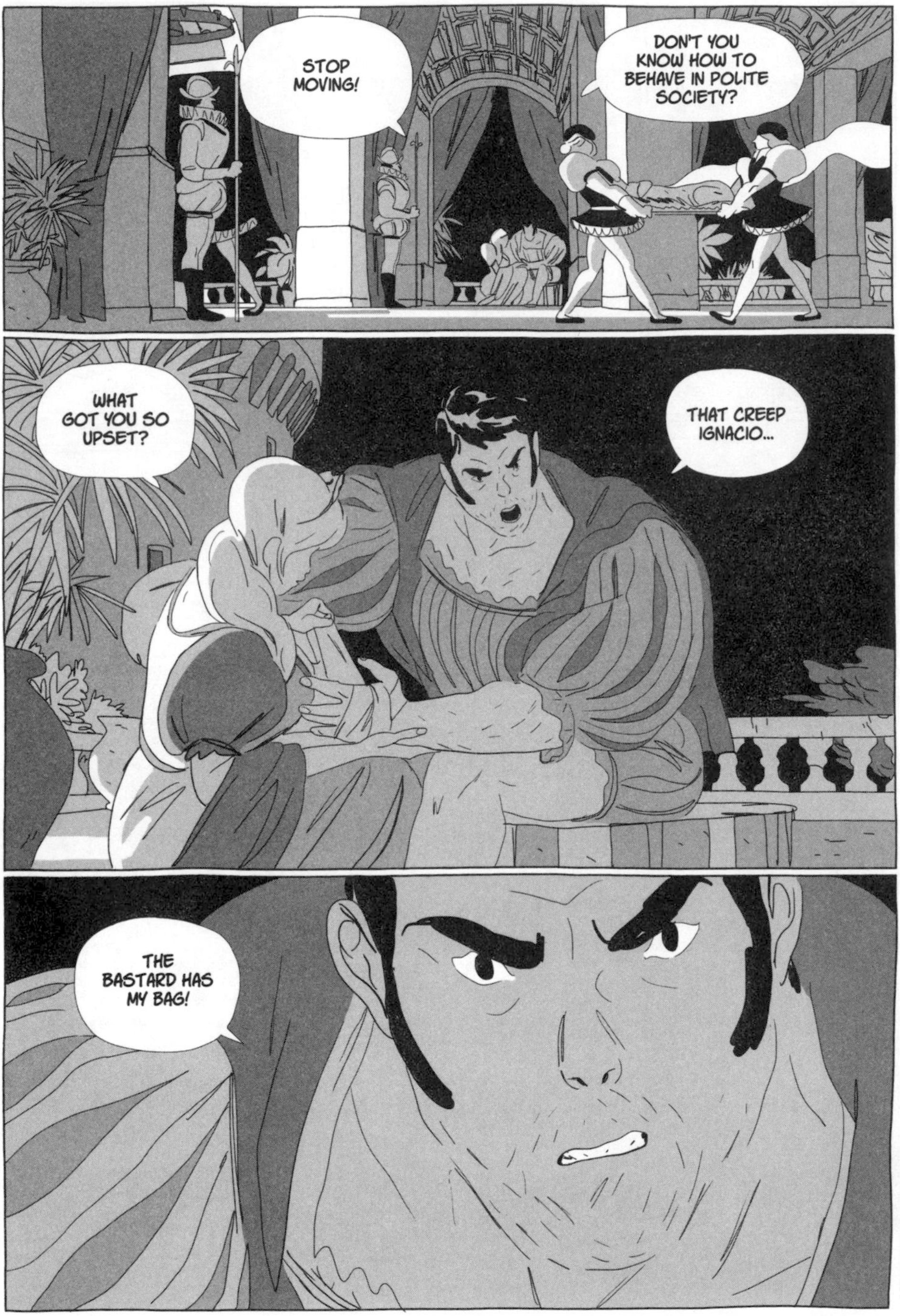
STOP MOVING!
DON'T YOU KNOW HOW TO BEHAVE IN POLITE SOCIETY?
WHAT GOT YOU SO UPSET?
THAT CREEP IGNACIO...
THE BASTARD HAS MY BAG!

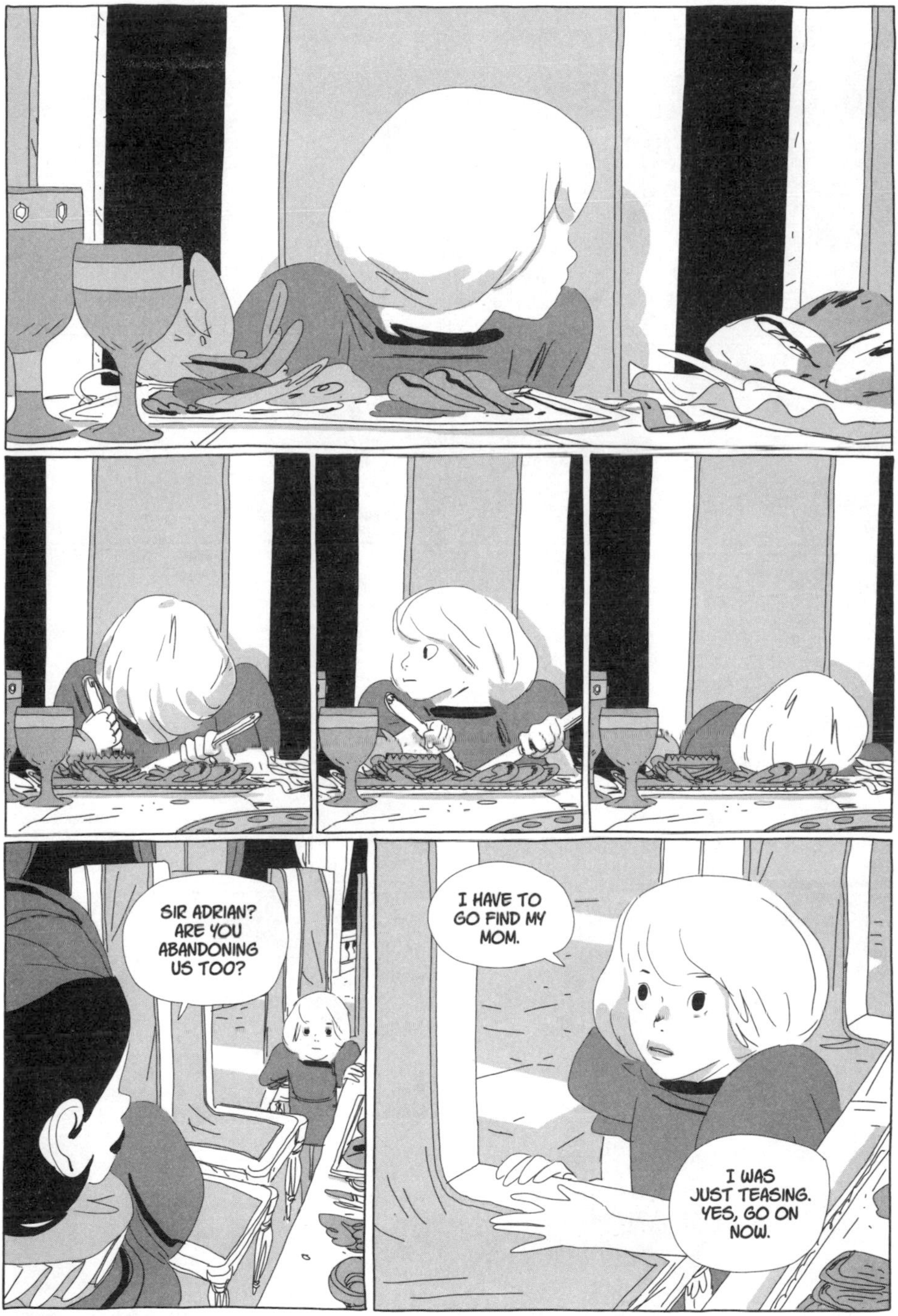
SIR ADRIAN? ARE YOU ABANDONING US TOO?
I HAVE TO GO FIND MY MOM.
I WAS JUST TEASING. YES, GO ON NOW.

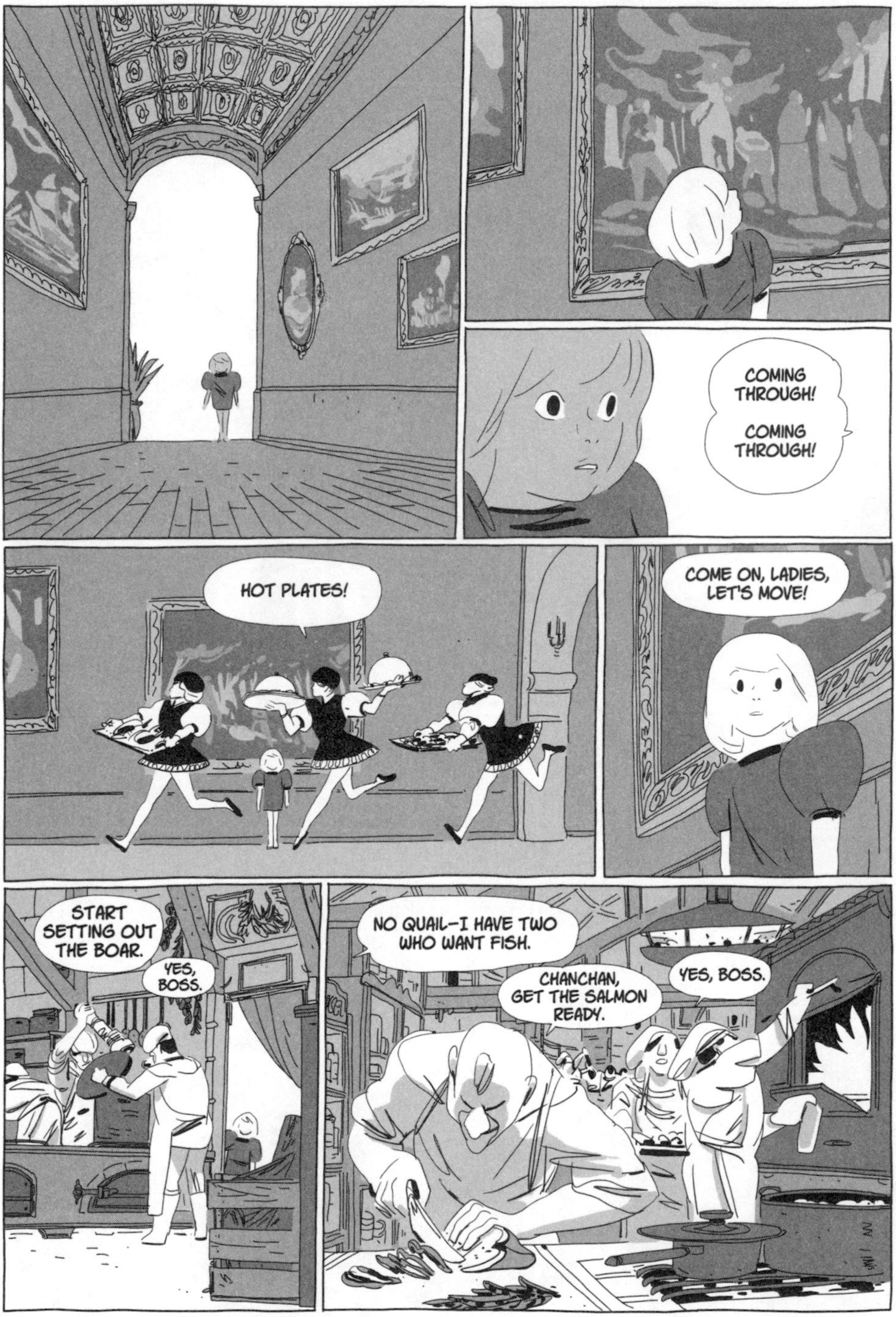
COMING THROUGH!
COMING THROUGH!
HOT PLATES!
COME ON, LADIES, LET'S MOVE!
START SETTING OUT THE BOAR.
YES, BOSS.
NO QUAIL—I HAVE TWO WHO WANT FISH.
CHANCHAN, GET THE SALMON READY.
YES, BOSS.

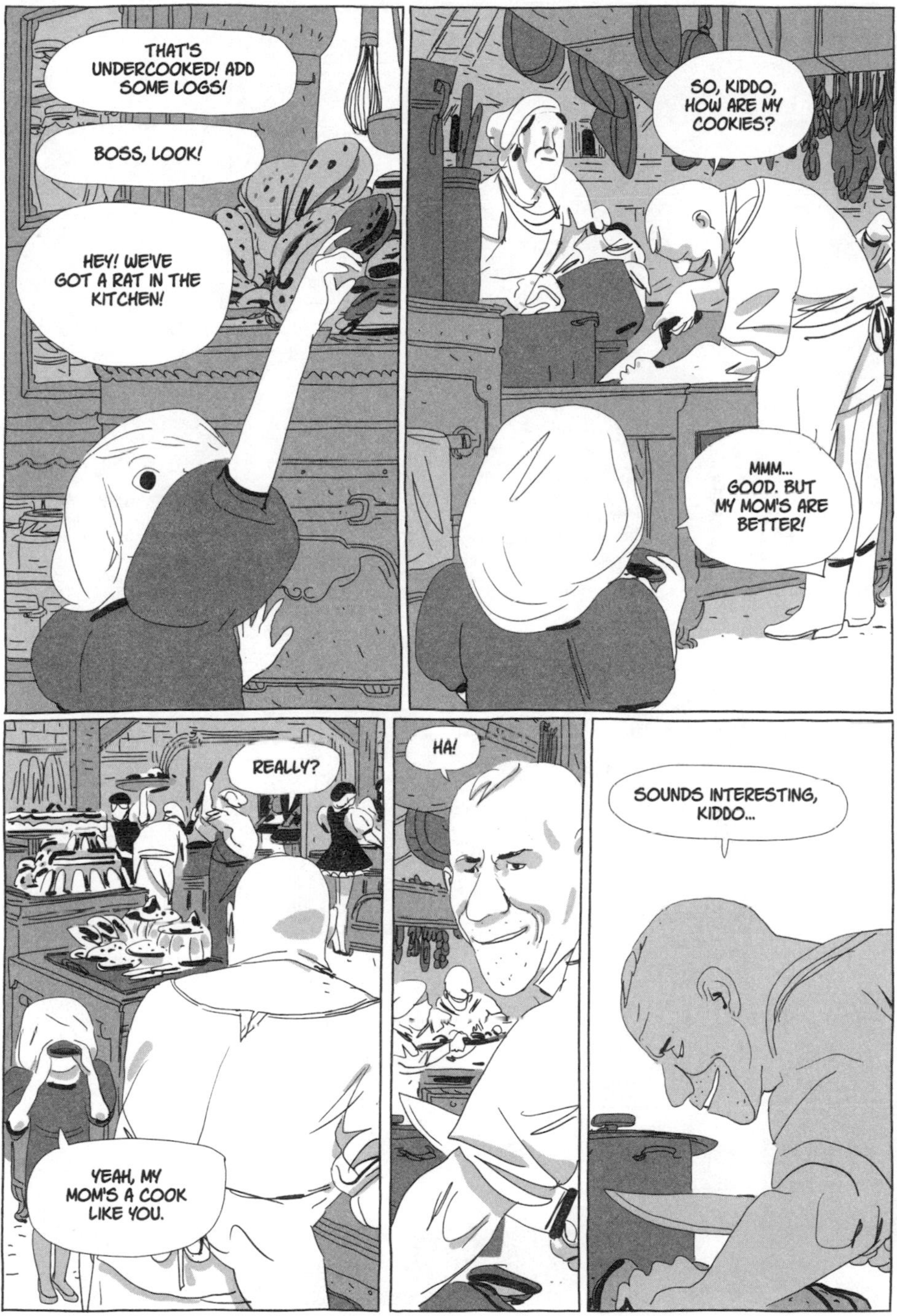
THAT'S UNDERCOOKED! ADD SOME LOGS!
BOSS, LOOK!
HEY! WE'VE GOT A RAT IN THE KITCHEN!
SO, KIDDO, HOW ARE MY COOKIES?
MMM... GOOD. BUT MY MOM'S ARE BETTER!
REALLY?
YEAH, MY MOM'S A COOK LIKE YOU.
HA!
SOUNDS INTERESTING, KIDDO...

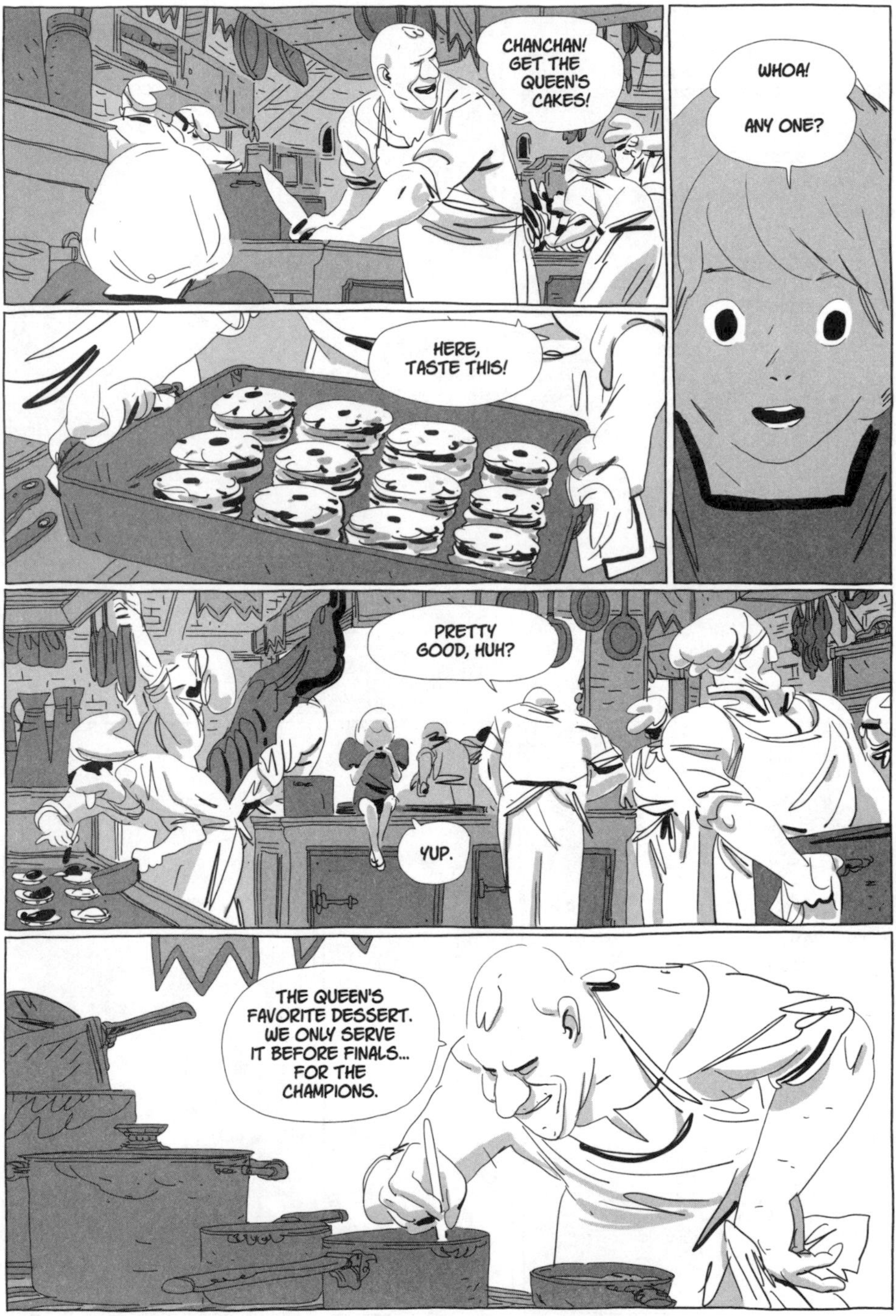
CHANCHAN! GET THE QUEEN'S CAKES!
HERE, TASTE THIS!
WHOA!
ANY ONE?
PRETTY GOOD, HUH?
YUP.
THE QUEEN'S FAVORITE DESSERT. WE ONLY SERVE IT BEFORE FINALS... FOR THE CHAMPIONS.

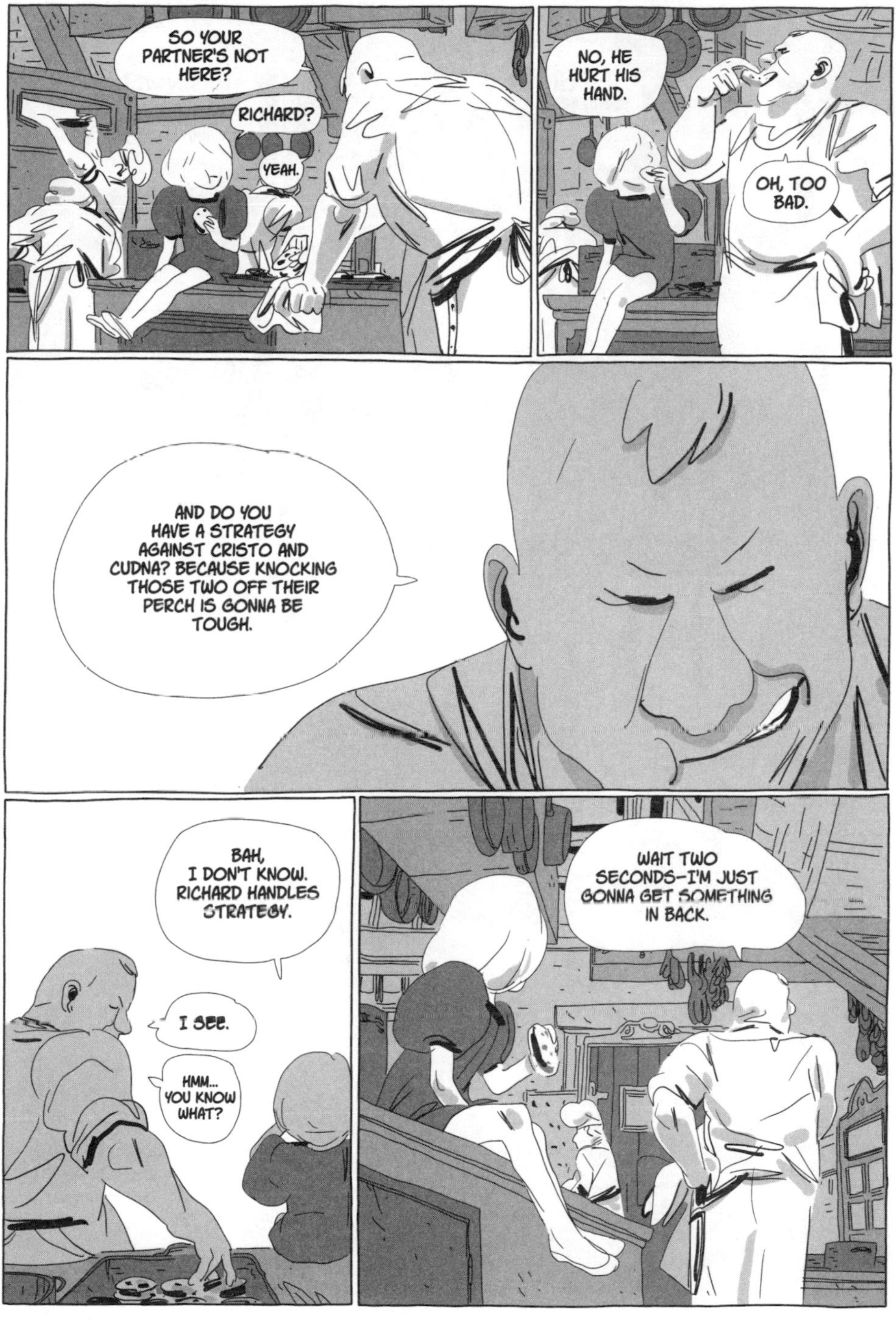
SO YOUR PARTNER'S NOT HERE?
RICHARD?
YEAH.
NO, HE HURT HIS HAND.
OH, TOO BAD.
AND DO YOU HAVE A STRATEGY AGAINST CRISTO AND CUDNA? BECAUSE KNOCKING THOSE TWO OFF THEIR PERCH IS GONNA BE TOUGH.
BAH, I DON'T KNOW. RICHARD HANDLES STRATEGY.
I SEE.
HMM... YOU KNOW WHAT?
WAIT TWO SECONDS—I'M JUST GONNA GET SOMETHING IN BACK.

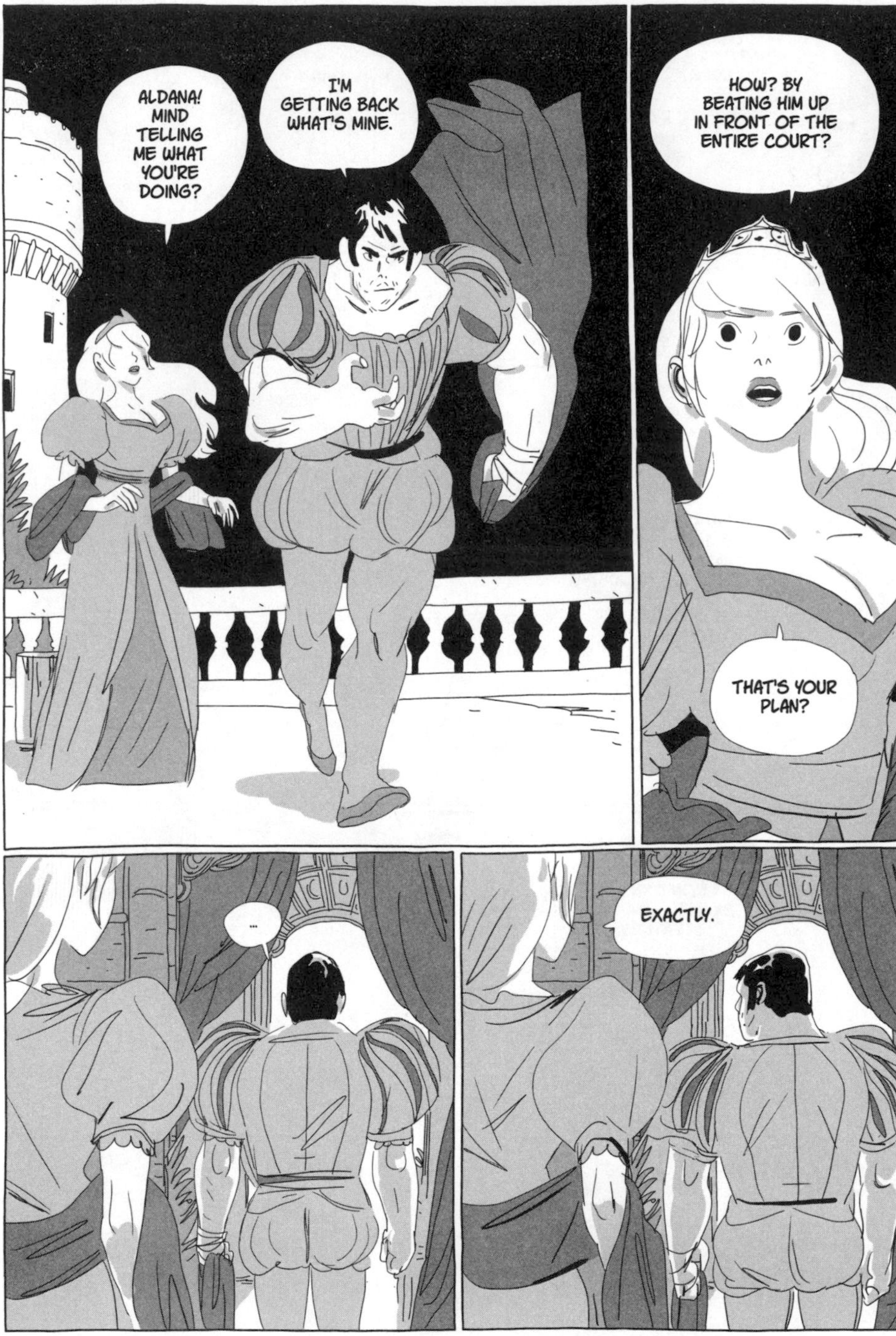
ALDANA! MIND TELLING ME WHAT YOU'RE DOING?
I'M GETTING BACK WHAT'S MINE.
HOW? BY BEATING HIM UP IN FRONT OF THE ENTIRE COURT?
THAT'S YOUR PLAN?
...
EXACTLY.

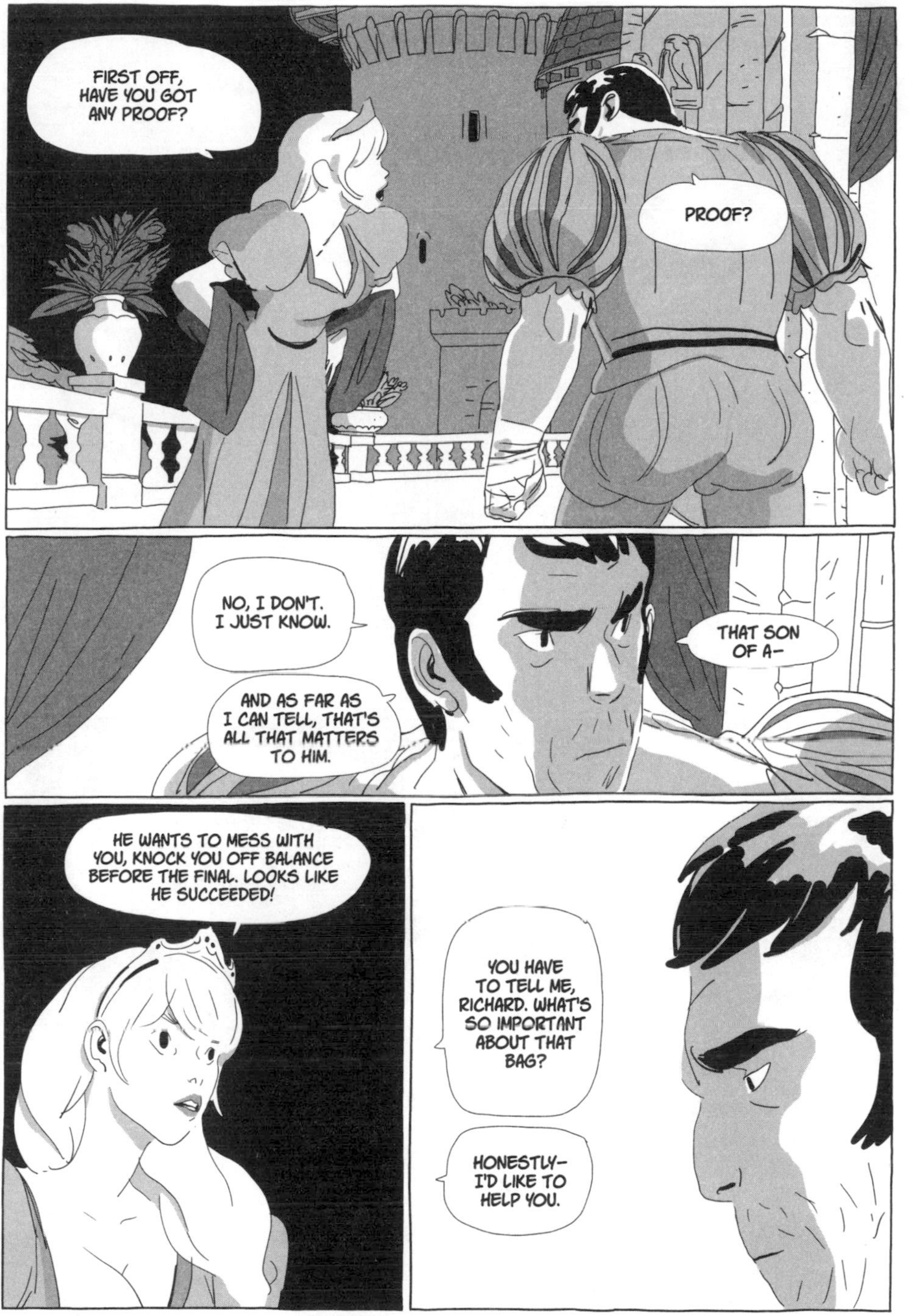
FIRST OFF, HAVE YOU GOT ANY PROOF?
PROOF?
NO, I DON'T. I JUST KNOW.
AND AS FAR AS I CAN TELL, THAT'S ALL THAT MATTERS TO HIM.
THAT SON OF A-
HE WANTS TO MESS WITH YOU, KNOCK YOU OFF BALANCE BEFORE THE FINAL. LOOKS LIKE HE SUCCEEDED!
YOU HAVE TO TELL ME, RICHARD. WHAT'S SO IMPORTANT ABOUT THAT BAG?
HONESTLY- I'D LIKE TO HELP YOU.

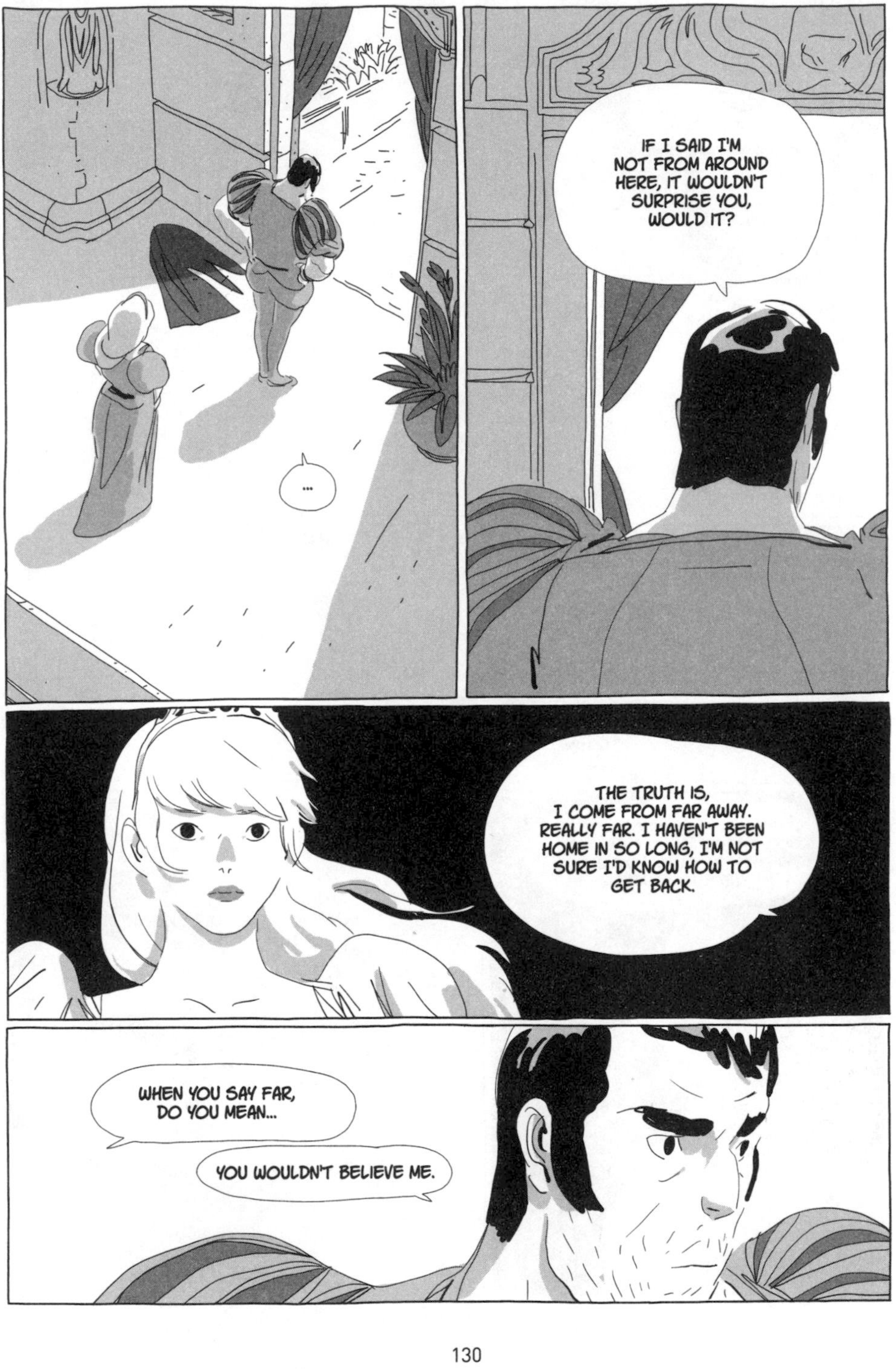
...
IF I SAID I'M NOT FROM AROUND HERE, IT WOULDN'T SURPRISE YOU, WOULD IT?
THE TRUTH IS, I COME FROM FAR AWAY. REALLY FAR. I HAVEN'T BEEN HOME IN SO LONG, I'M NOT SURE I'D KNOW HOW TO GET BACK.
WHEN YOU SAY FAR, DO YOU MEAN...
YOU WOULDN'T BELIEVE ME.

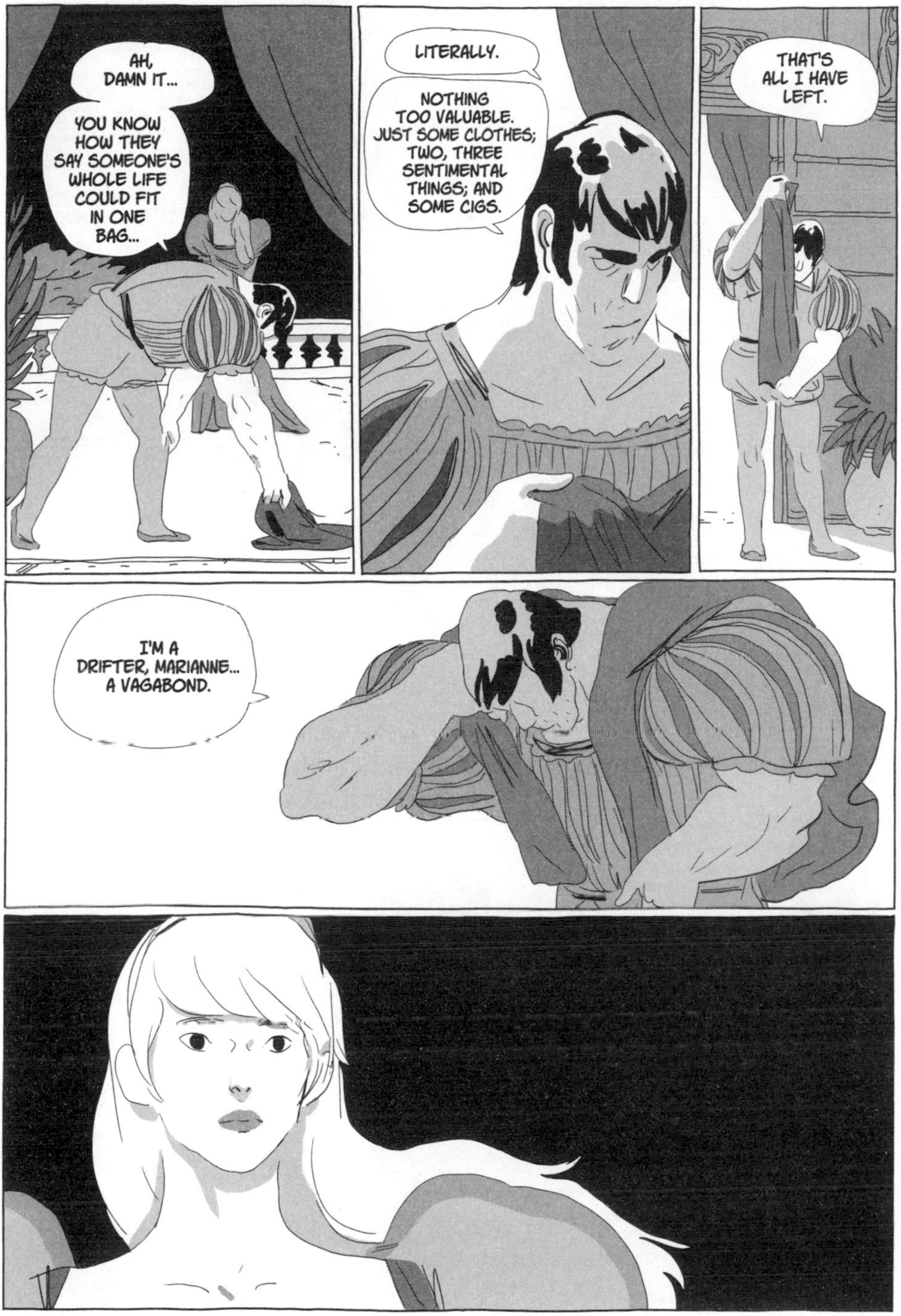
AH, DAMN IT...
YOU KNOW HOW THEY SAY SOMEONE'S WHOLE LIFE COULD FIT IN ONE BAG...
LITERALLY.
NOTHING TOO VALUABLE. JUST SOME CLOTHES; TWO, THREE SENTIMENTAL THINGS; AND SOME CIGS.
THAT'S ALL I HAVE LEFT.
I'M A DRIFTER, MARIANNE... A VAGABOND.

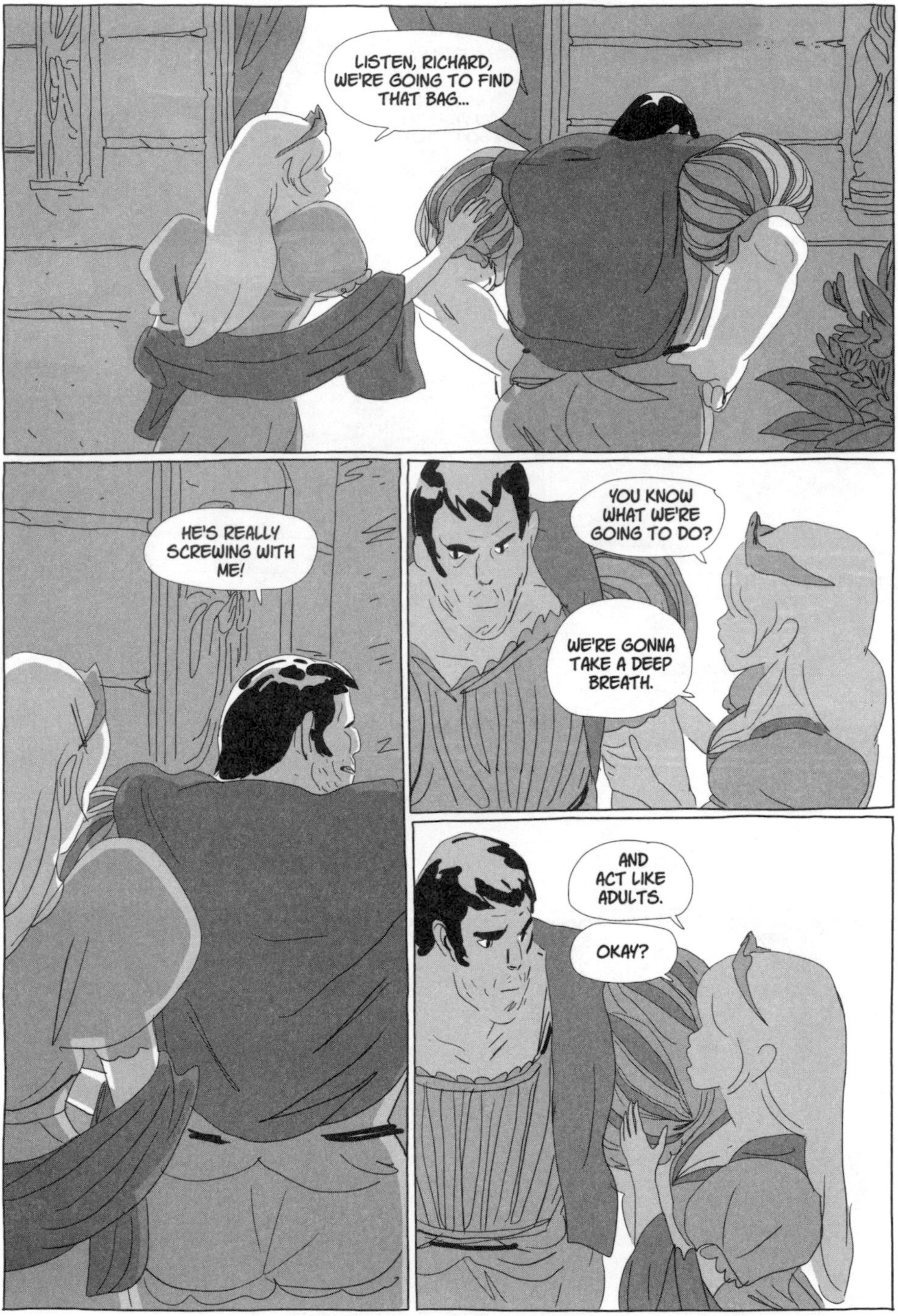
LISTEN, RICHARD, WE'RE GOING TO FIND THAT BAG...
HE'S REALLY SCREWING WITH ME!
YOU KNOW WHAT WE'RE GOING TO DO?
WE'RE GONNA TAKE A DEEP BREATH.
AND ACT LIKE ADULTS.
OKAY?

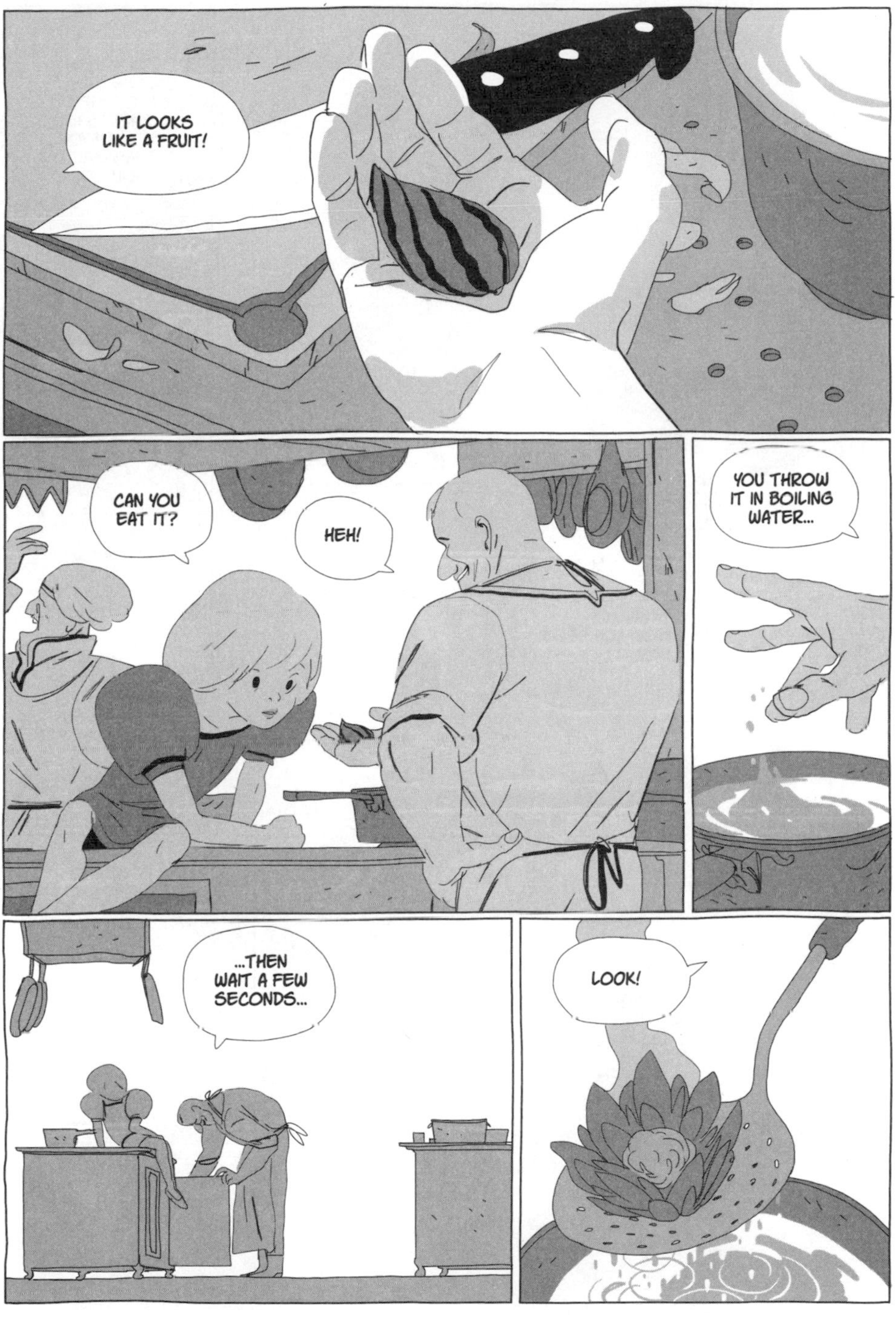
IT LOOKS LIKE A FRUIT!
CAN YOU EAT IT?
HEH!
YOU THROW IT IN BOILING WATER...
...THEN WAIT A FEW SECONDS...
LOOK!

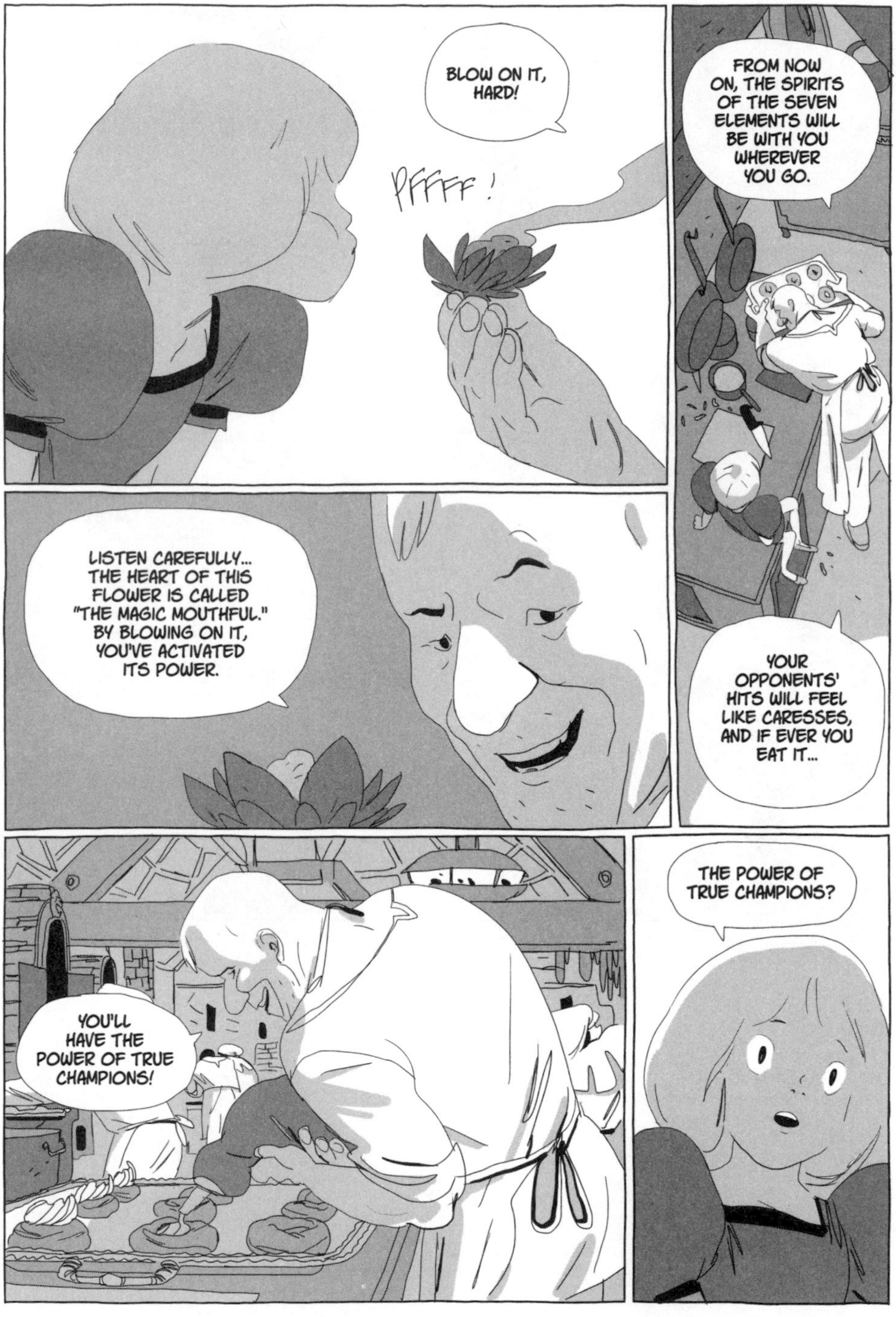
BLOW ON IT, HARD!
PFFFF!
FROM NOW ON, THE SPIRITS OF THE SEVEN ELEMENTS WILL BE WITH YOU WHEREVER YOU GO.
LISTEN CAREFULLY... THE HEART OF THIS FLOWER IS CALLED "THE MAGIC MOUTHFUL." BY BLOWING ON IT, YOU'VE ACTIVATED ITS POWER.
YOUR OPPONENTS' HITS WILL FEEL LIKE CARESSES, AND IF EVER YOU EAT IT...
YOU'LL HAVE THE POWER OF TRUE CHAMPIONS!
THE POWER OF TRUE CHAMPIONS?

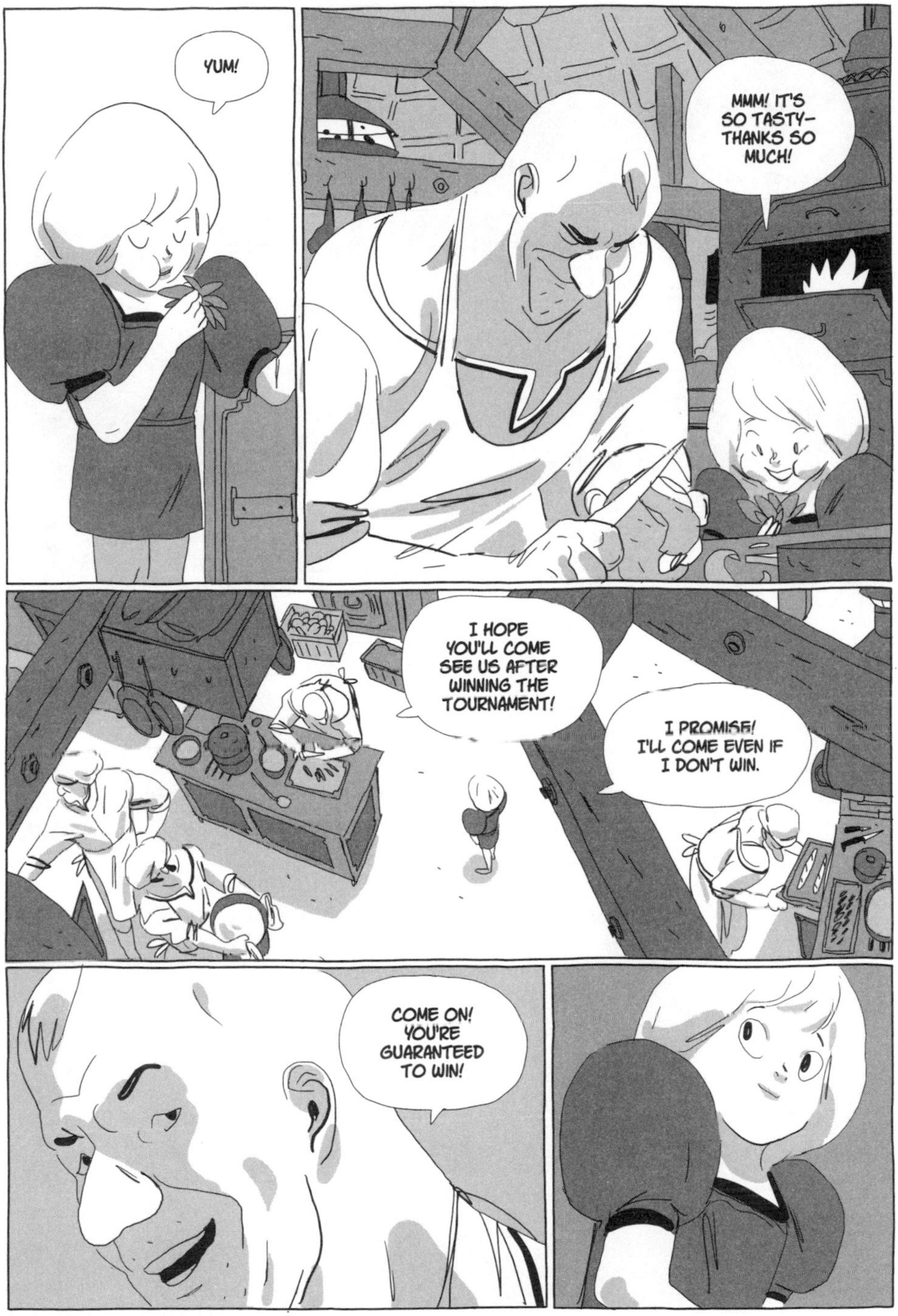
YUM!
MMM! IT'S SO TASTY-THANKS SO MUCH!
I HOPE YOU'LL COME SEE US AFTER WINNING THE TOURNAMENT!
I PROMISE! I'LL COME EVEN IF I DON'T WIN.
COME ON! YOU'RE GUARANTEED TO WIN!

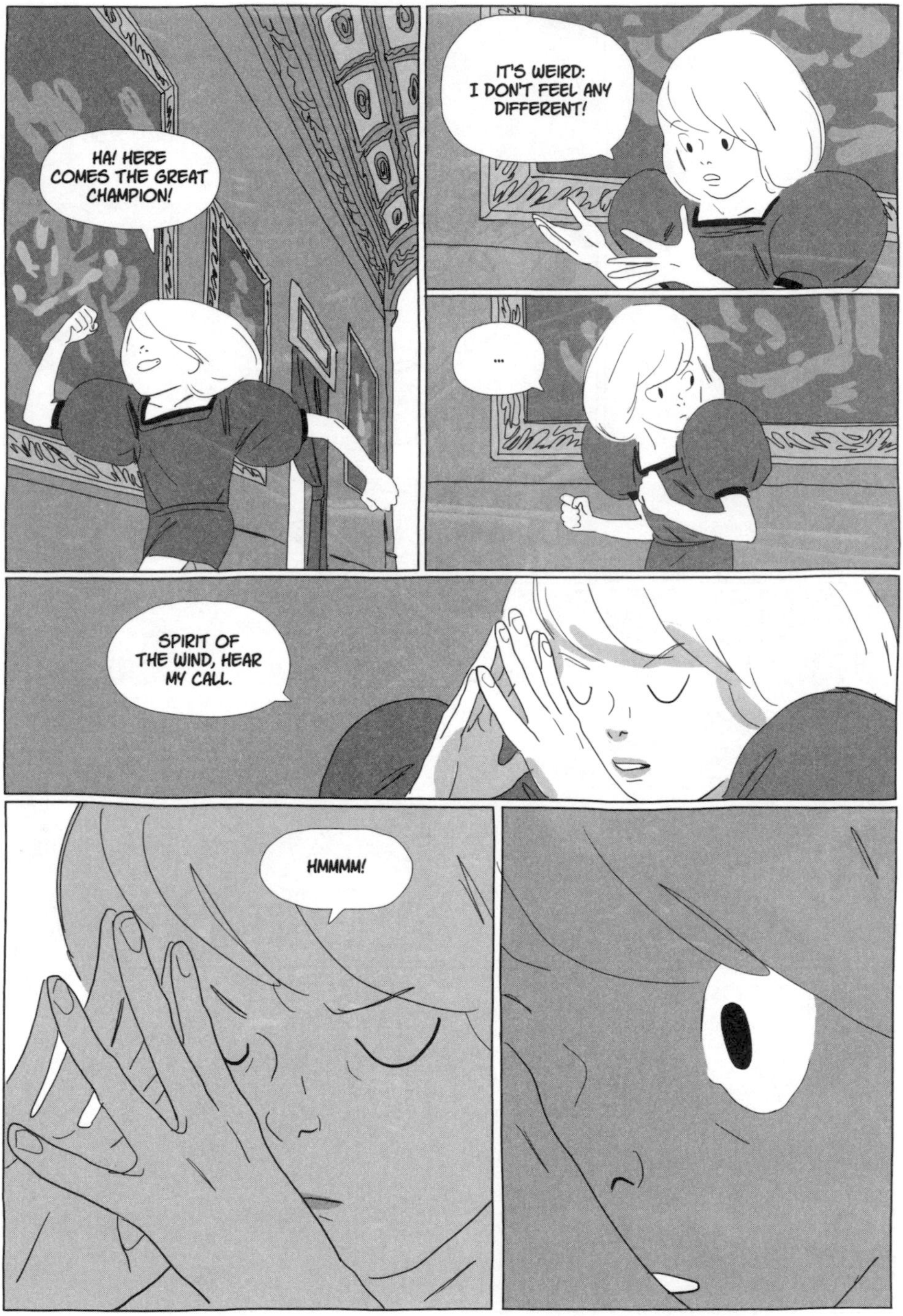
HA! HERE COMES THE GREAT CHAMPION!
IT'S WEIRD: I DON'T FEEL ANY DIFFERENT!
...
SPIRIT OF THE WIND, HEAR MY CALL.
HMMMM!

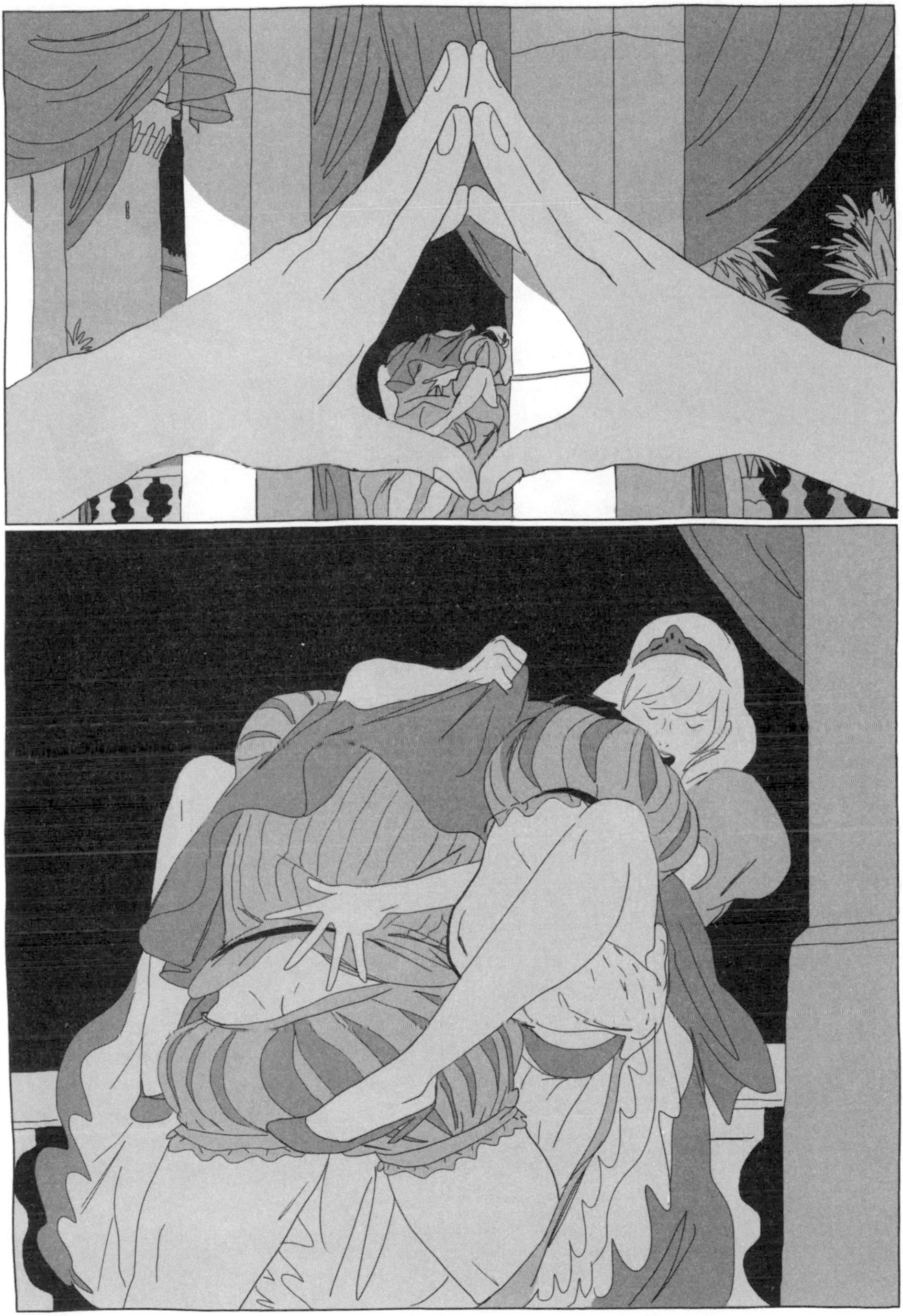

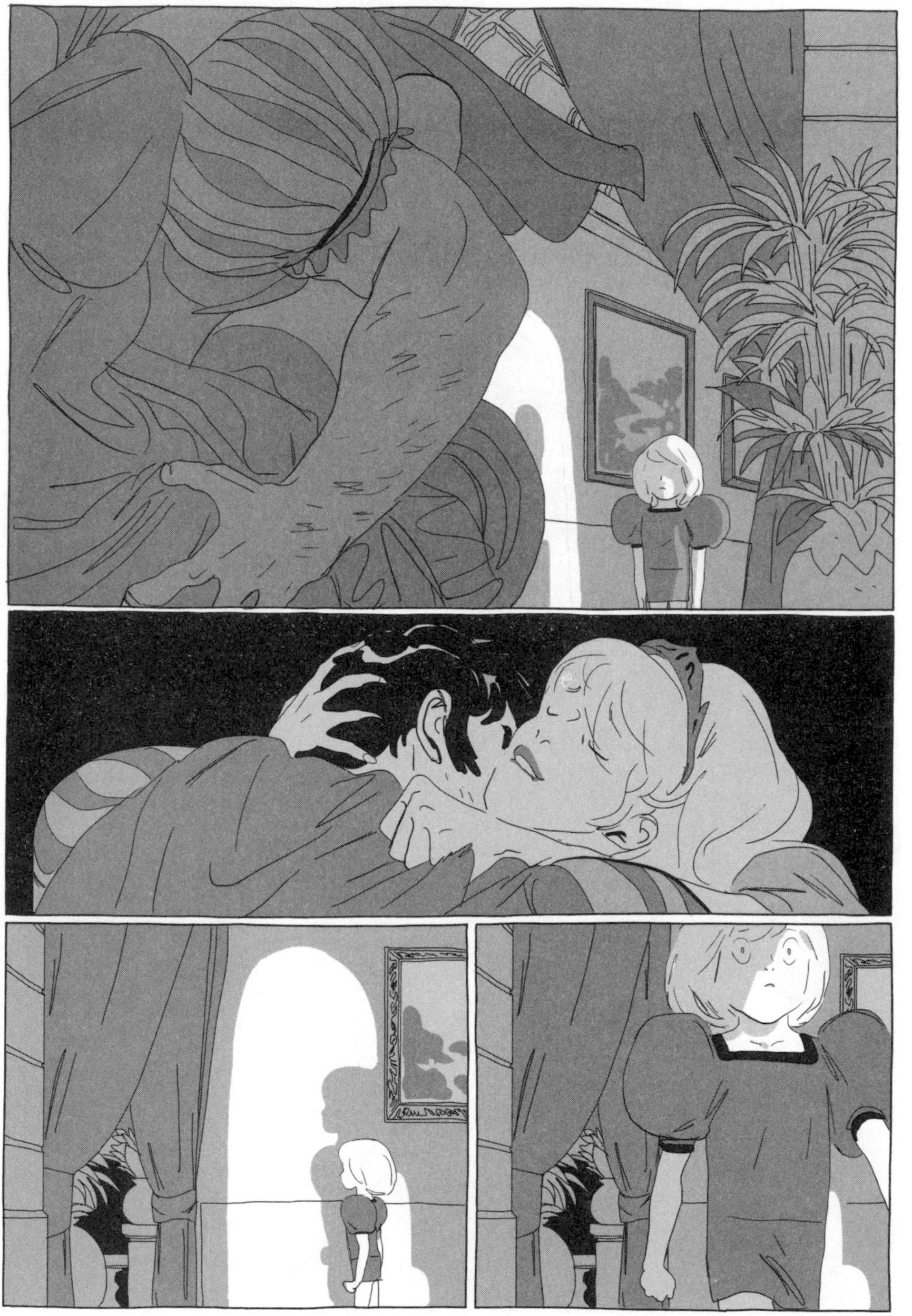

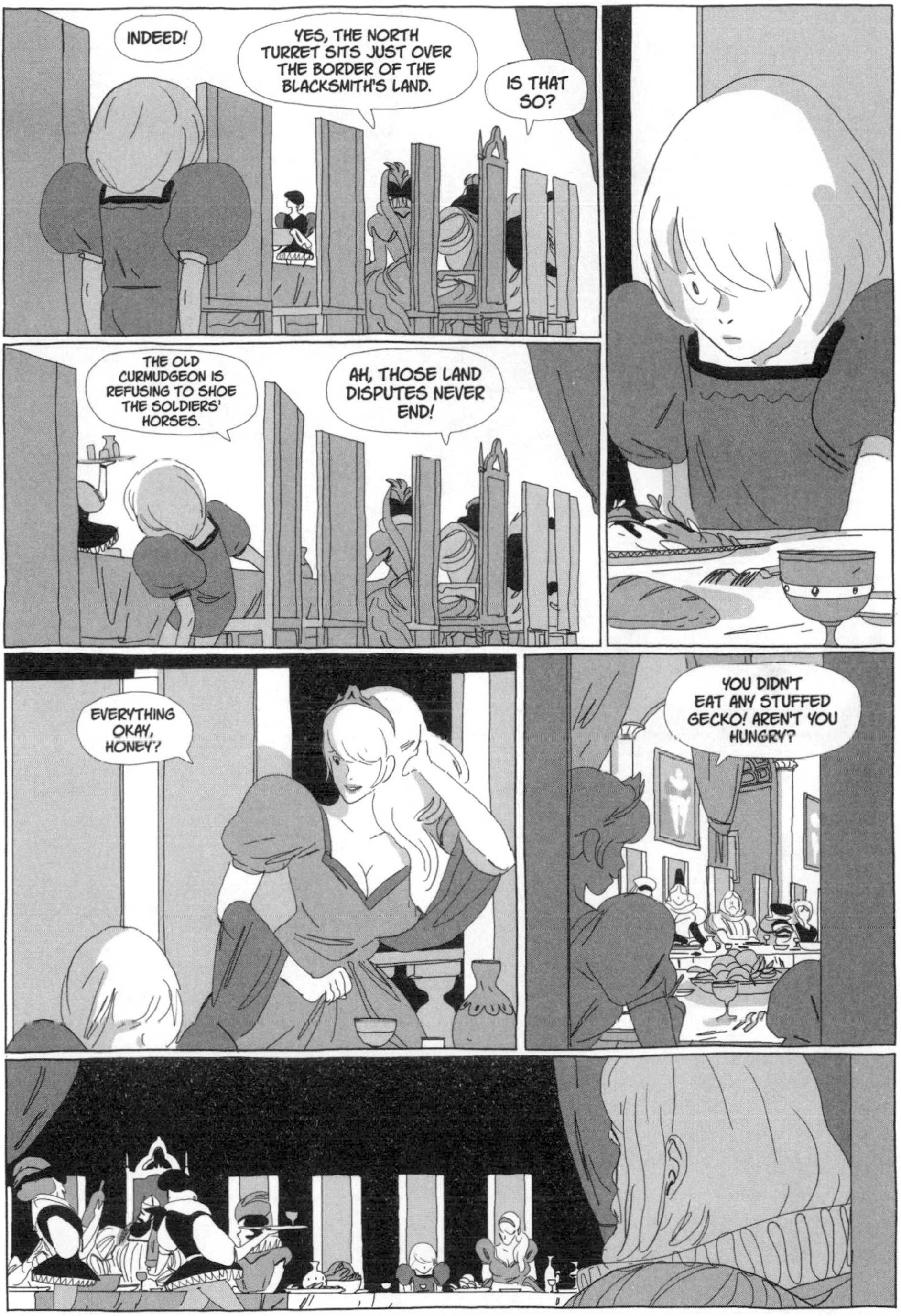
INDEED!
YES, THE NORTH TURRET SITS JUST OVER THE BORDER OF THE BLACKSMITH'S LAND.
IS THAT SO?
THE OLD CURMUDGEON IS REFUSING TO SHOE THE SOLDIERS' HORSES.
AH, THOSE LAND DISPUTES NEVER END!
EVERYTHING OKAY, HONEY?
YOU DIDN'T EAT ANY STUFFED GECKO! AREN'T YOU HUNGRY?

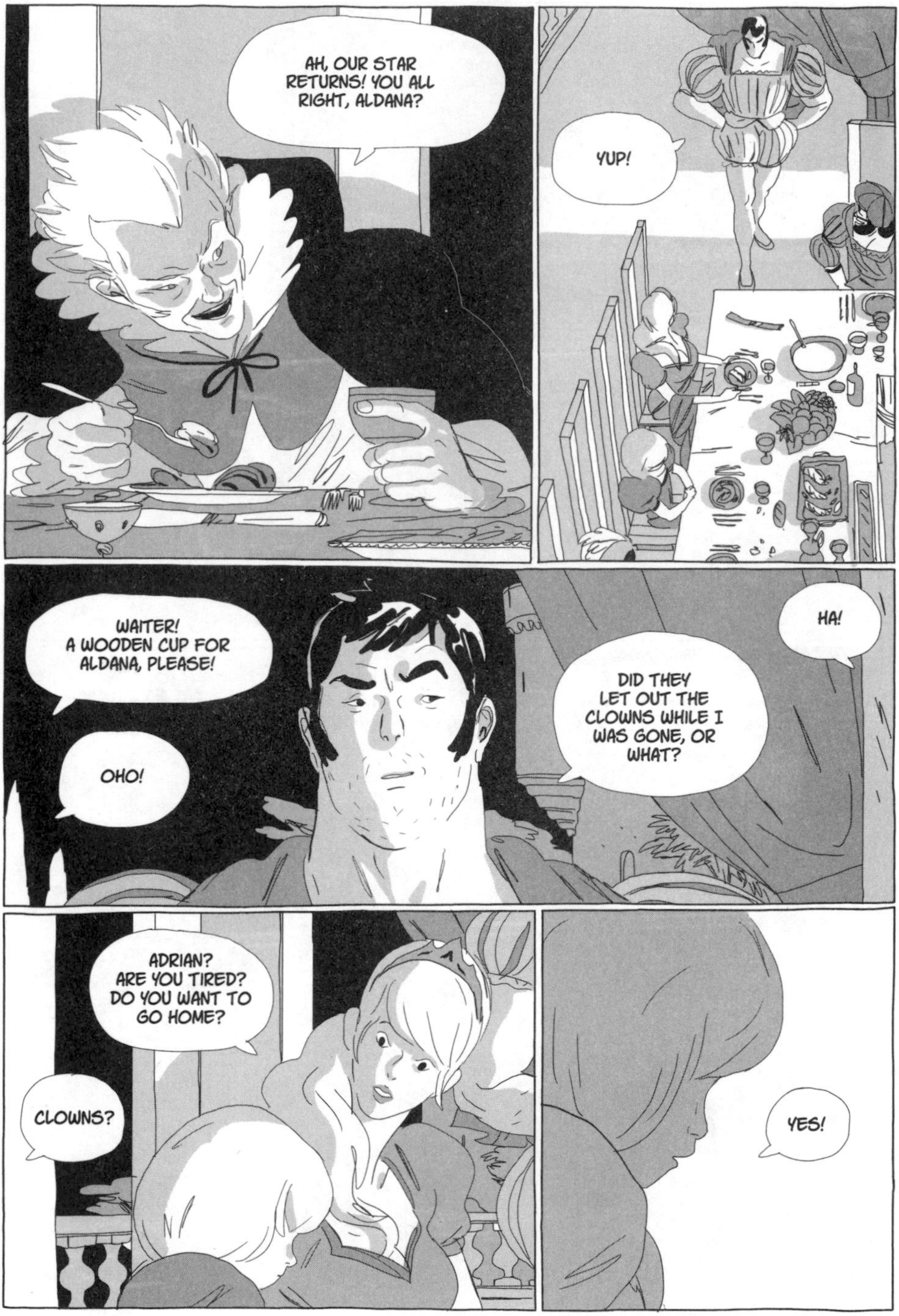
AH, OUR STAR RETURNS! YOU ALL RIGHT, ALDANA?
YUP!
WAITER! A WOODEN CUP FOR ALDANA, PLEASE!
OHO!
DID THEY LET OUT THE CLOWNS WHILE I WAS GONE, OR WHAT?
HA!
ADRIAN? ARE YOU TIRED? DO YOU WANT TO GO HOME?
CLOWNS?
YES!

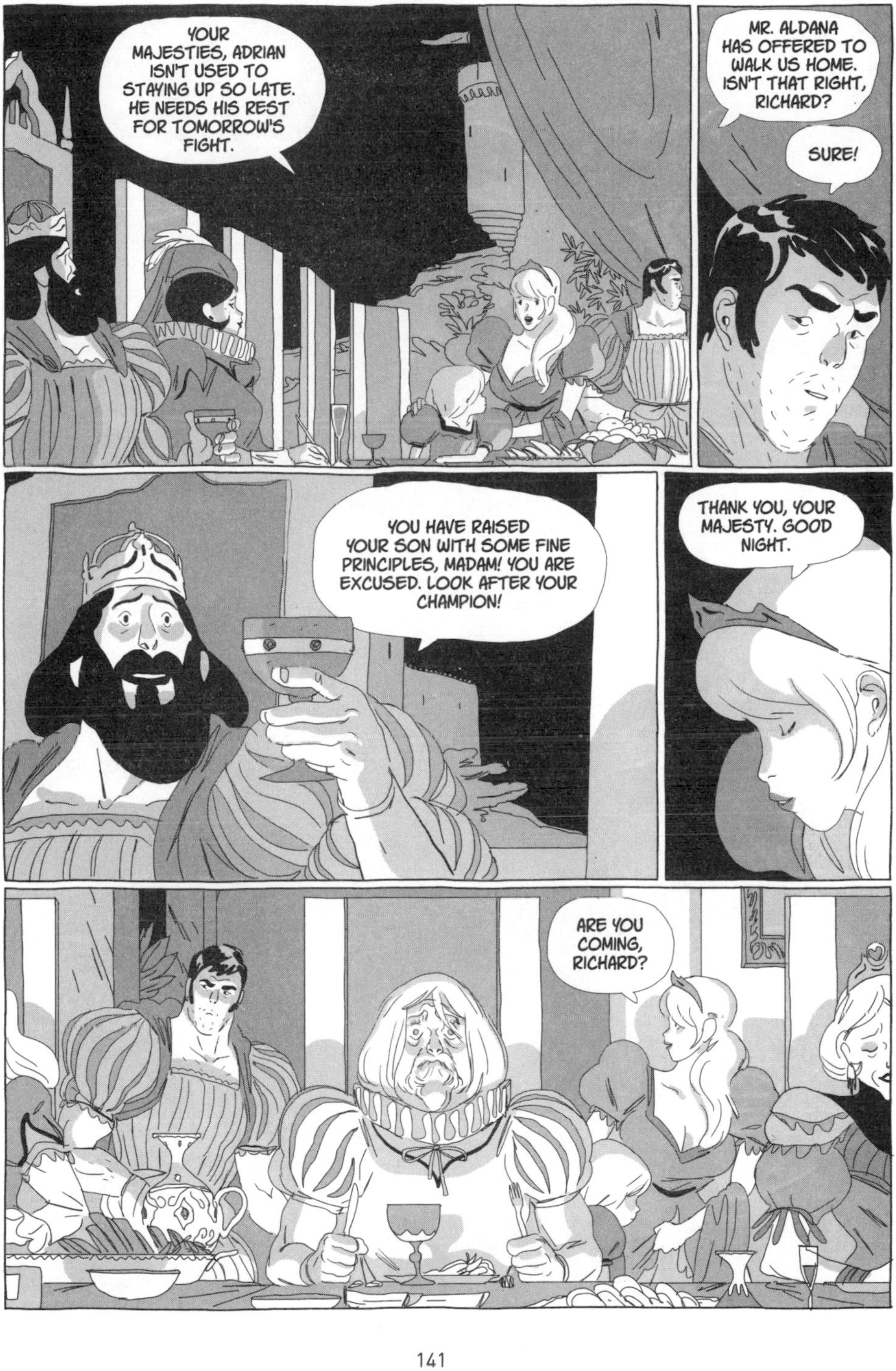
YOUR MAJESTIES, ADRIAN ISN'T USED TO STAYING UP SO LATE. HE NEEDS HIS REST FOR TOMORROW'S FIGHT.
MR. ALDANA HAS OFFERED TO WALK US HOME. ISN'T THAT RIGHT, RICHARD?
SURE!
YOU HAVE RAISED YOUR SON WITH SOME FINE PRINCIPLES, MADAM! YOU ARE EXCUSED. LOOK AFTER YOUR CHAMPION!
THANK YOU, YOUR MAJESTY. GOOD NIGHT.
ARE YOU COMING, RICHARD?

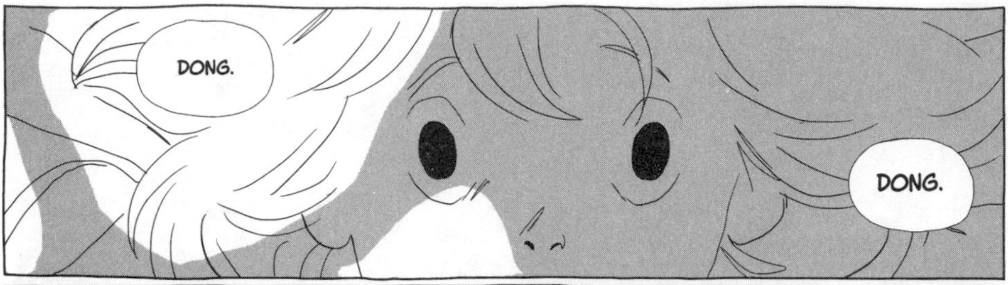
DONG.
DONG.
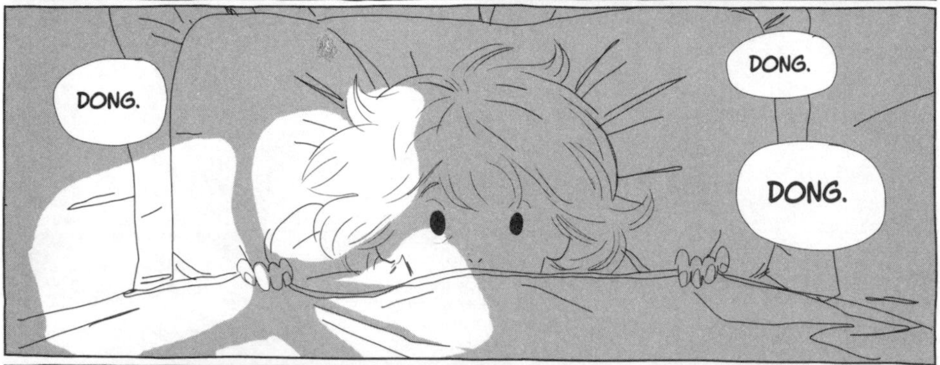
DONG.
DONG.
DONG.
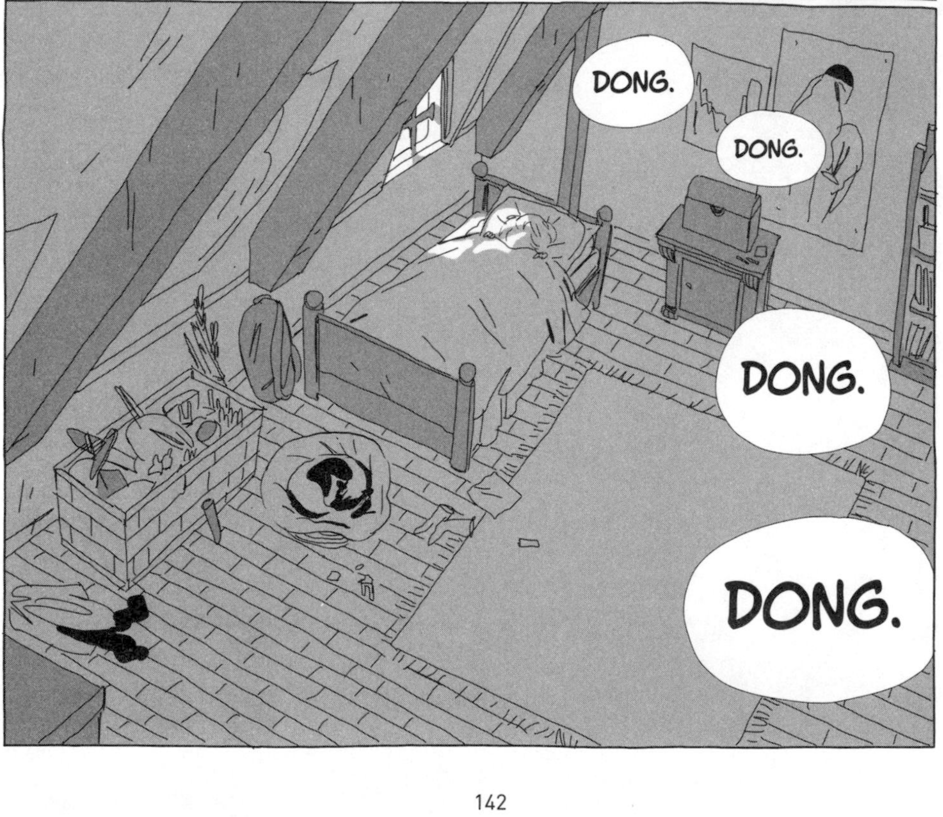
DONG.
DONG.
DONG.
DONG.

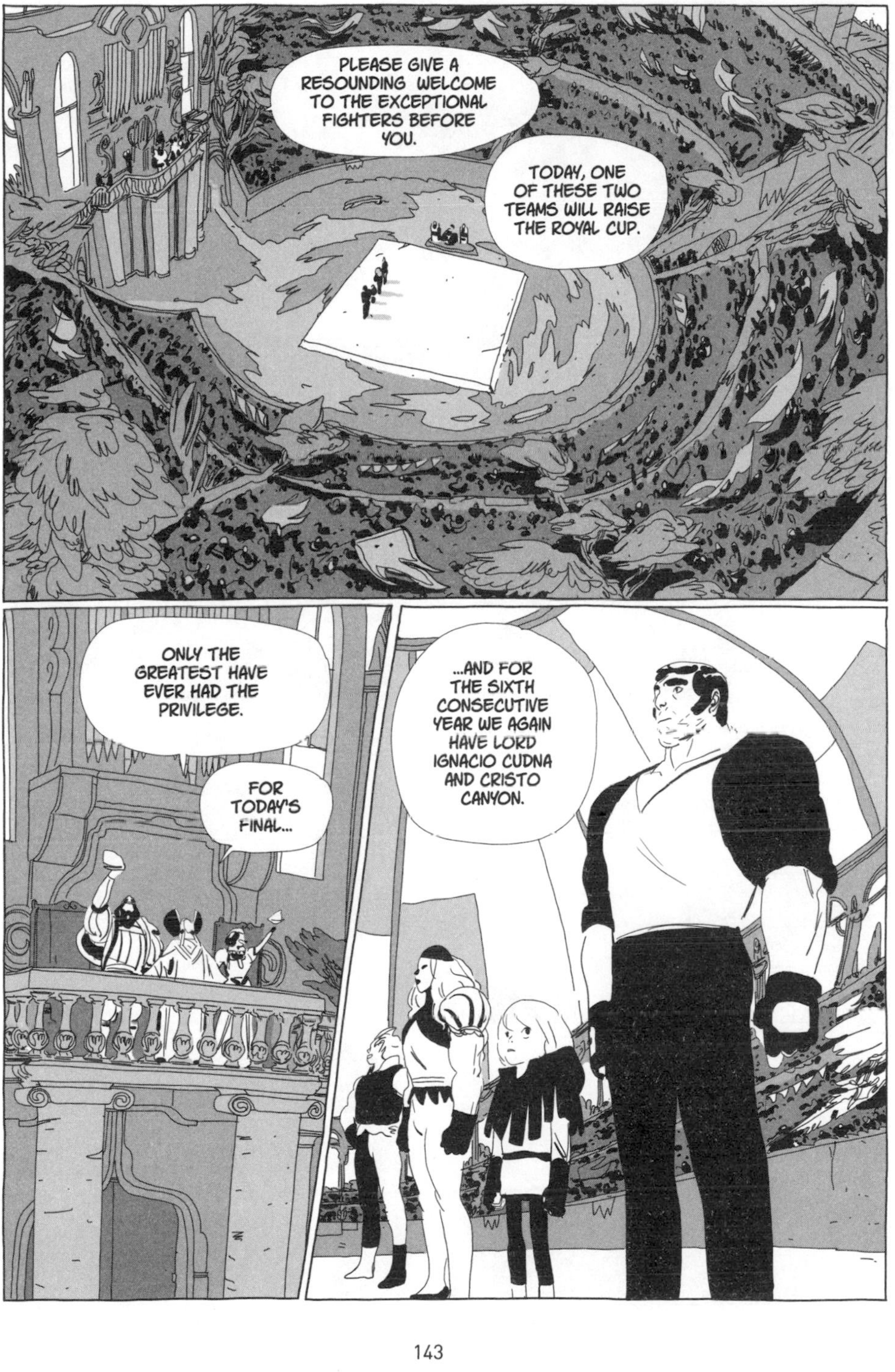
PLEASE GIVE A RESOUNDING WELCOME TO THE EXCEPTIONAL FIGHTERS BEFORE YOU.
TODAY, ONE OF THESE TWO TEAMS WILL RAISE THE ROYAL CUP.
ONLY THE GREATEST HAVE EVER HAD THE PRIVILEGE.
FOR TODAY'S FINAL...
...AND FOR THE SIXTH CONSECUTIVE YEAR WE AGAIN HAVE LORD IGNACIO CUDNA AND CRISTO CANYON.

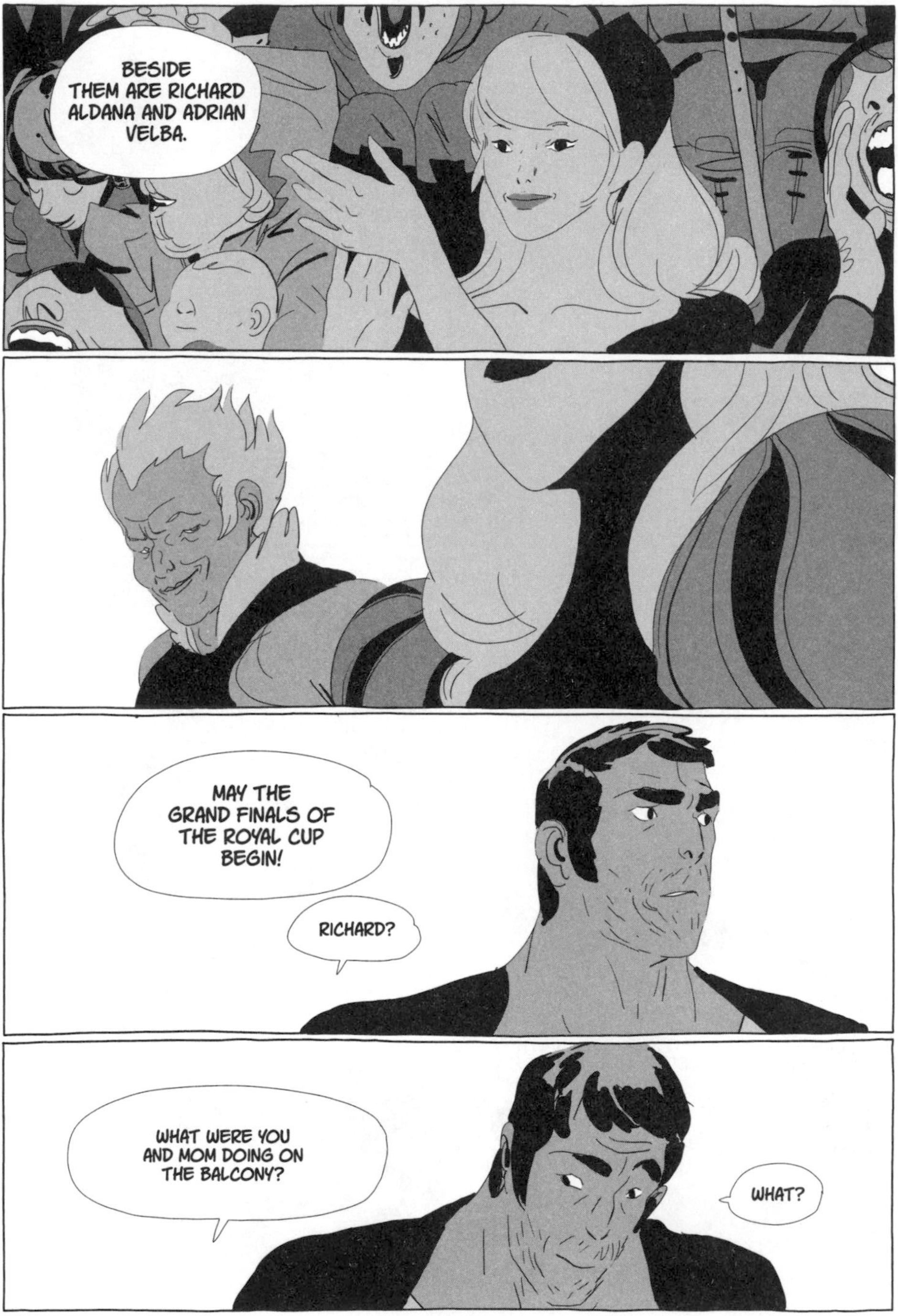
BESIDE THEM ARE RICHARD ALDANA AND ADRIAN VELBA.
MAY THE GRAND FINALS OF THE ROYAL CUP BEGIN!
RICHARD?
WHAT WERE YOU AND MOM DOING ON THE BALCONY?
WHAT?

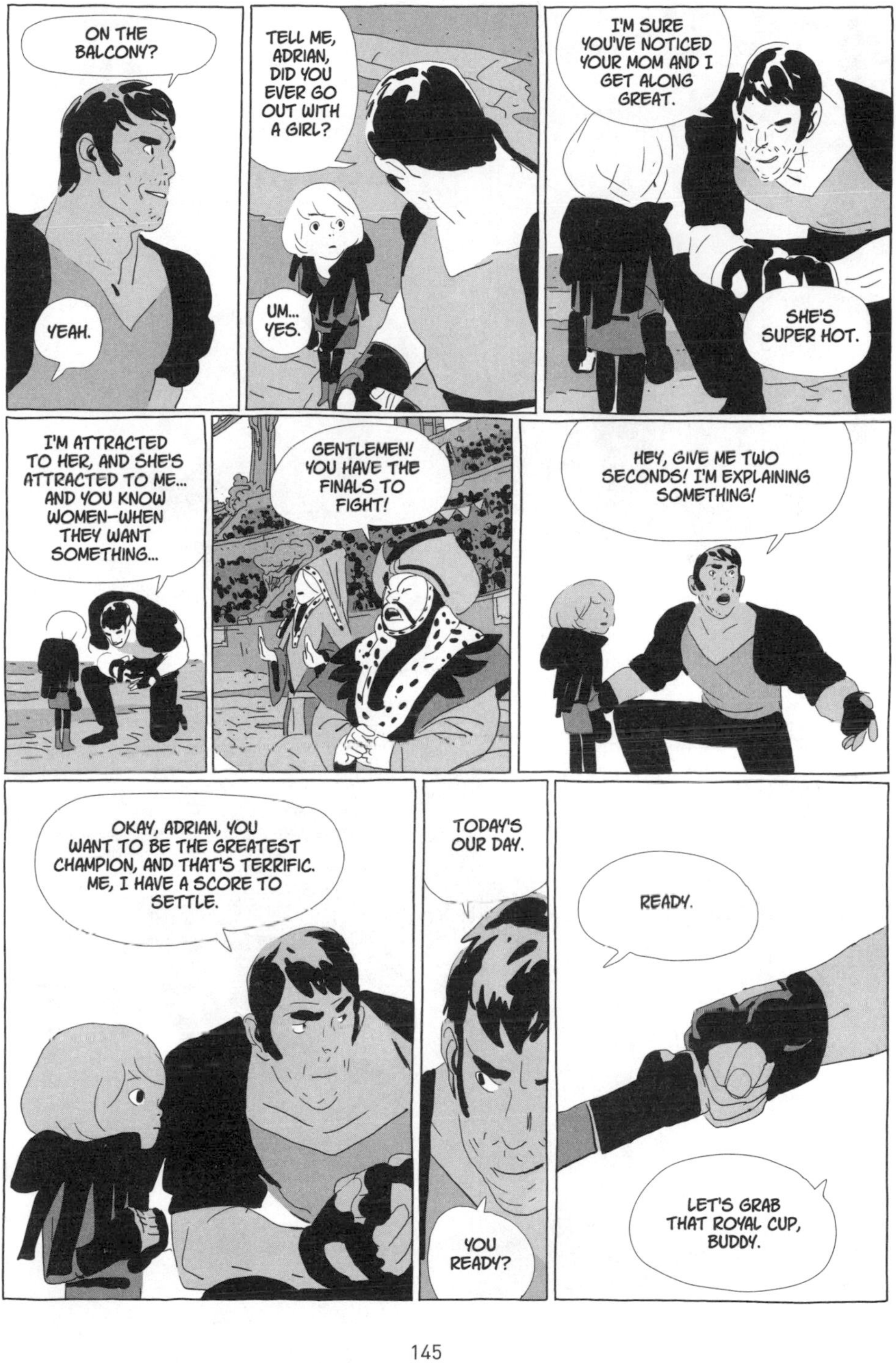
ON THE BALCONY?
YEAH.
TELL ME, ADRIAN, DID YOU EVER GO OUT WITH A GIRL?
UM... YES.
I'M SURE YOU'VE NOTICED YOUR MOM AND I GET ALONG GREAT.
SHE'S SUPER HOT.
I'M ATTRACTED TO HER, AND SHE'S ATTRACTED TO ME... AND YOU KNOW WOMEN—WHEN THEY WANT SOMETHING...
GENTLEMEN! YOU HAVE THE FINALS TO FIGHT!
HEY, GIVE ME TWO SECONDS! I'M EXPLAINING SOMETHING!
OKAY, ADRIAN, YOU WANT TO BE THE GREATEST CHAMPION, AND THAT'S TERRIFIC. ME, I HAVE A SCORE TO SETTLE.
TODAY'S OUR DAY.
YOU READY?
READY.
LET'S GRAB THAT ROYAL CUP, BUDDY.

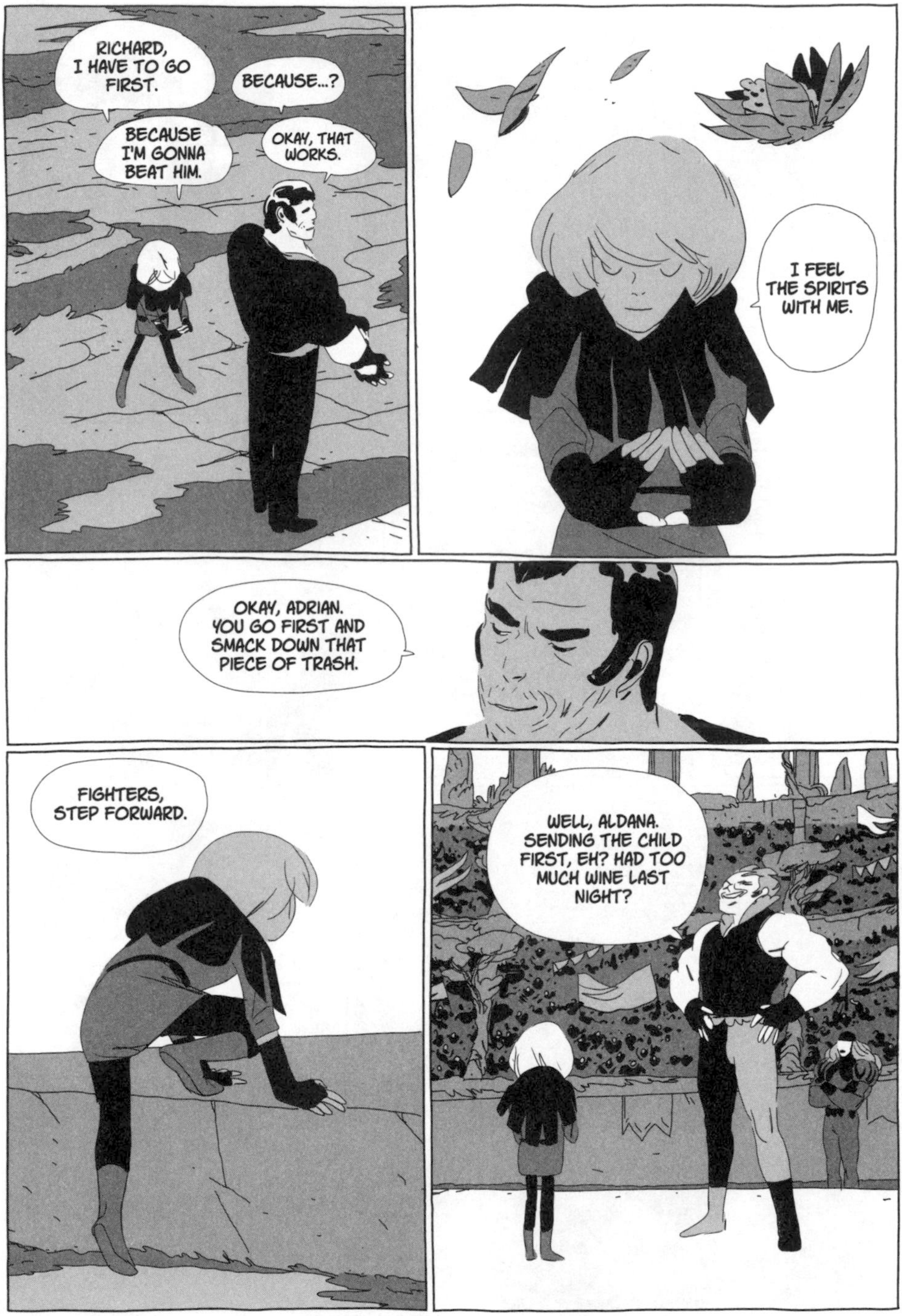
RICHARD, I HAVE TO GO FIRST.
BECAUSE...?
BECAUSE I'M GONNA BEAT HIM.
OKAY, THAT WORKS.
I FEEL THE SPIRITS WITH ME.
OKAY, ADRIAN. YOU GO FIRST AND SMACK DOWN THAT PIECE OF TRASH.
FIGHTERS, STEP FORWARD.
WELL, ALDANA. SENDING THE CHILD FIRST, EH? HAD TOO MUCH WINE LAST NIGHT?

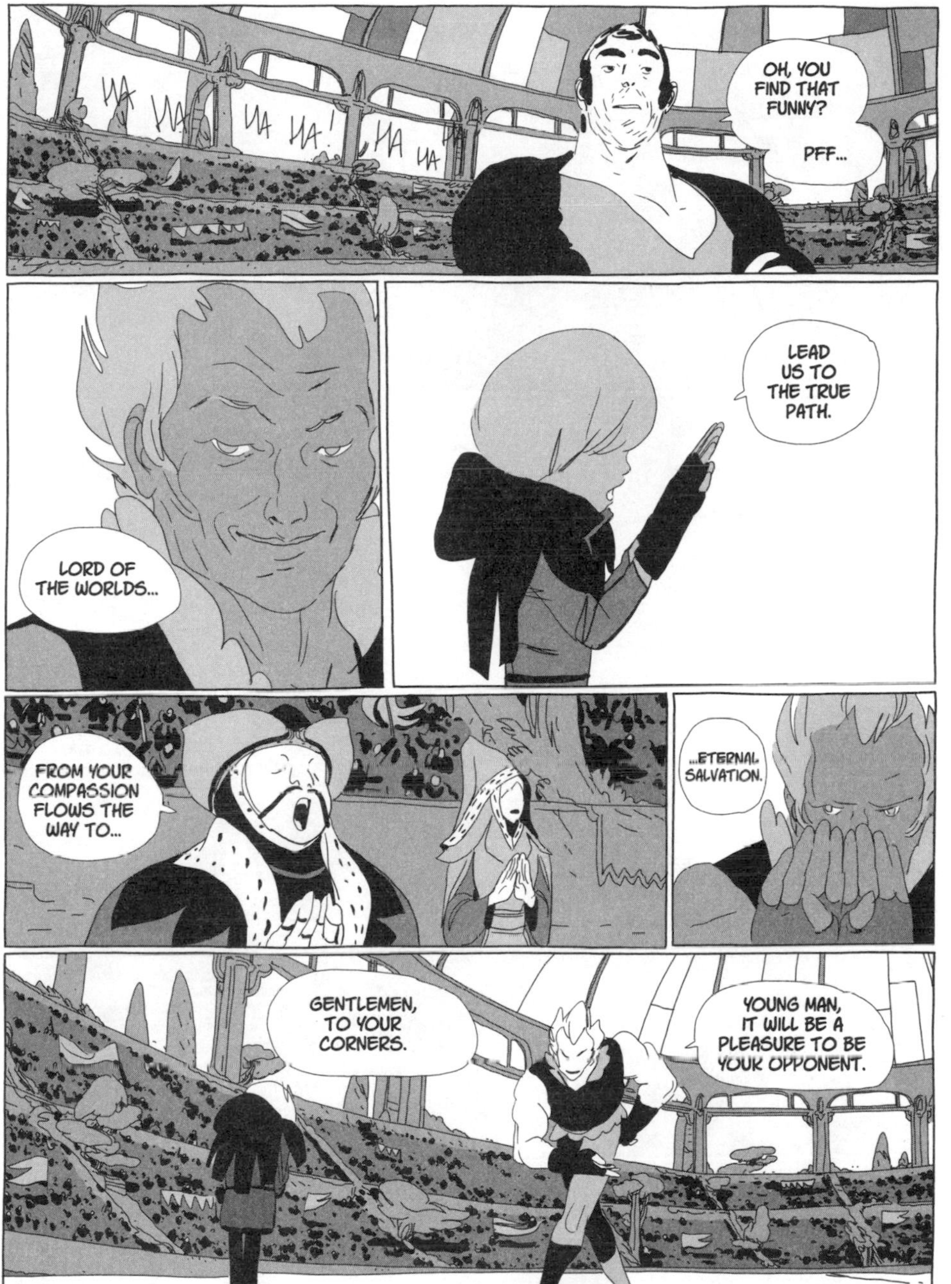
HA HA! HA HA! HA HA HA
OH, YOU FIND THAT FUNNY?
PFF...
LORD OF THE WORLDS...
LEAD US TO THE TRUE PATH.
FROM YOUR COMPASSION FLOWS THE WAY TO...
...ETERNAL SALVATION.
GENTLEMEN, TO YOUR CORNERS.
YOUNG MAN, IT WILL BE A PLEASURE TO BE YOUR OPPONENT.

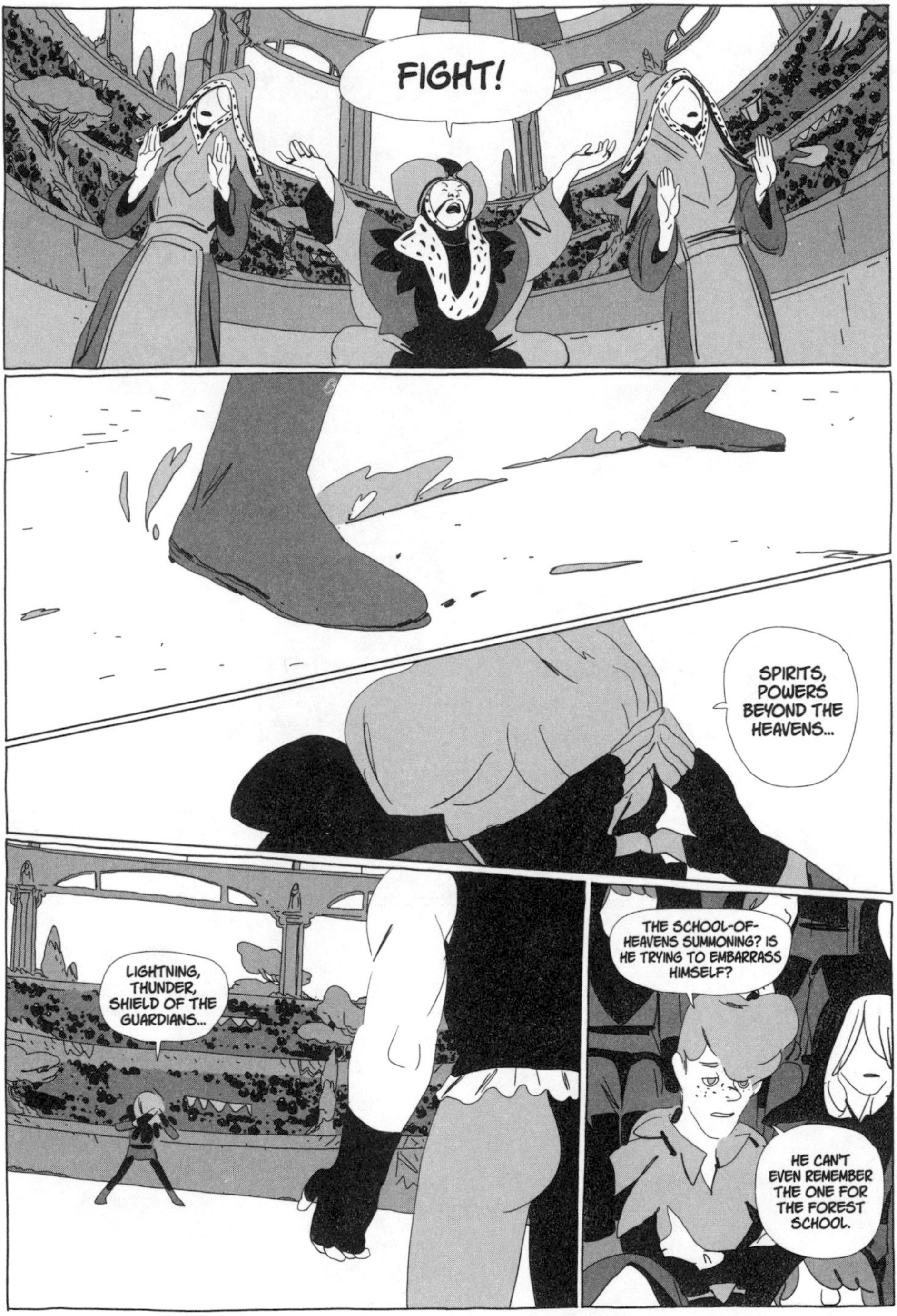
FIGHT!
SPIRITS, POWERS BEYOND THE HEAVENS...
LIGHTNING, THUNDER, SHIELD OF THE GUARDIANS...
THE SCHOOL-OF-HEAVENS SUMMONING? IS HE TRYING TO EMBARRASS HIMSELF?
HE CAN'T EVEN REMEMBER THE ONE FOR THE FOREST SCHOOL.

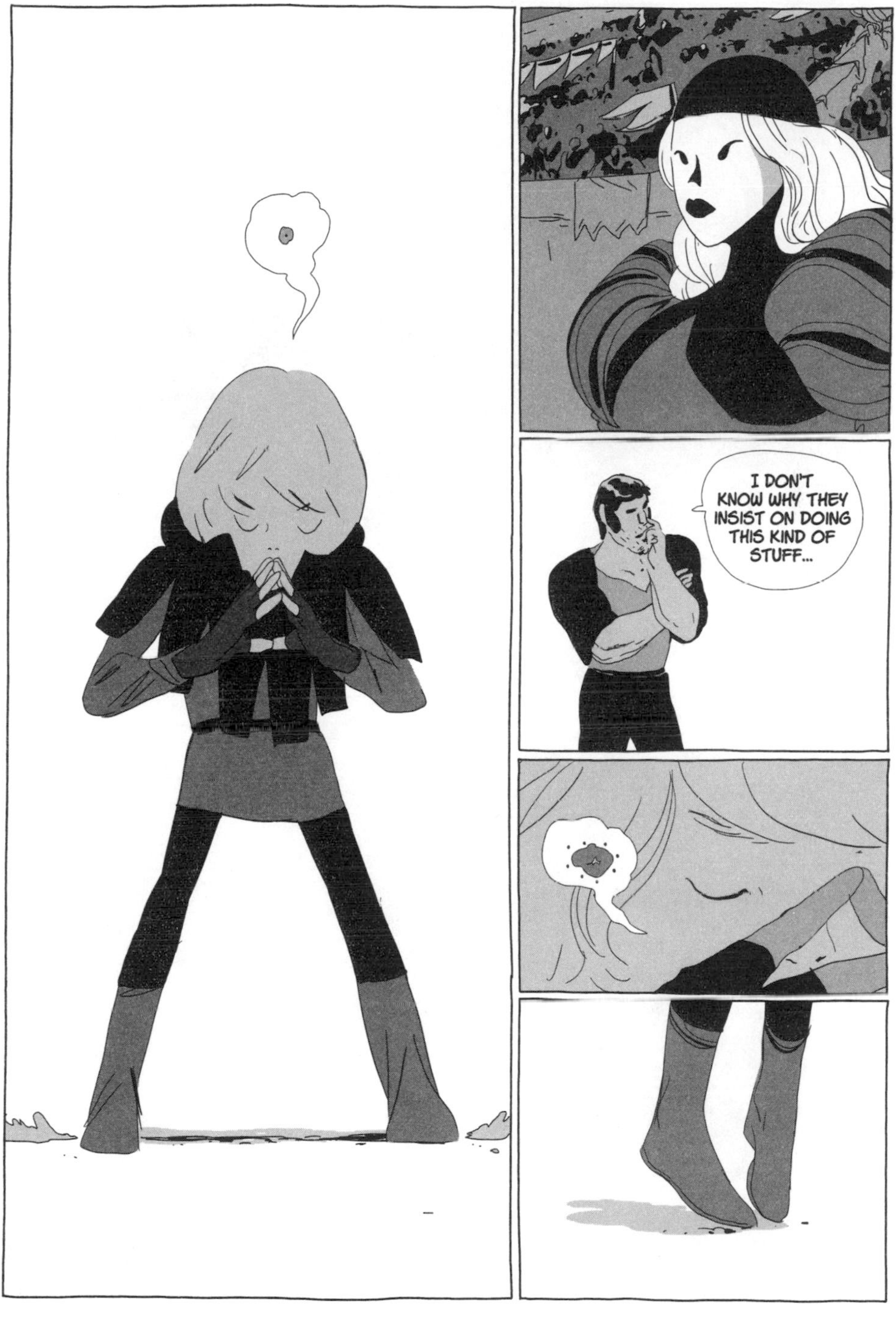
I DON'T KNOW WHY THEY INSIST ON DOING THIS KIND OF STUFF...

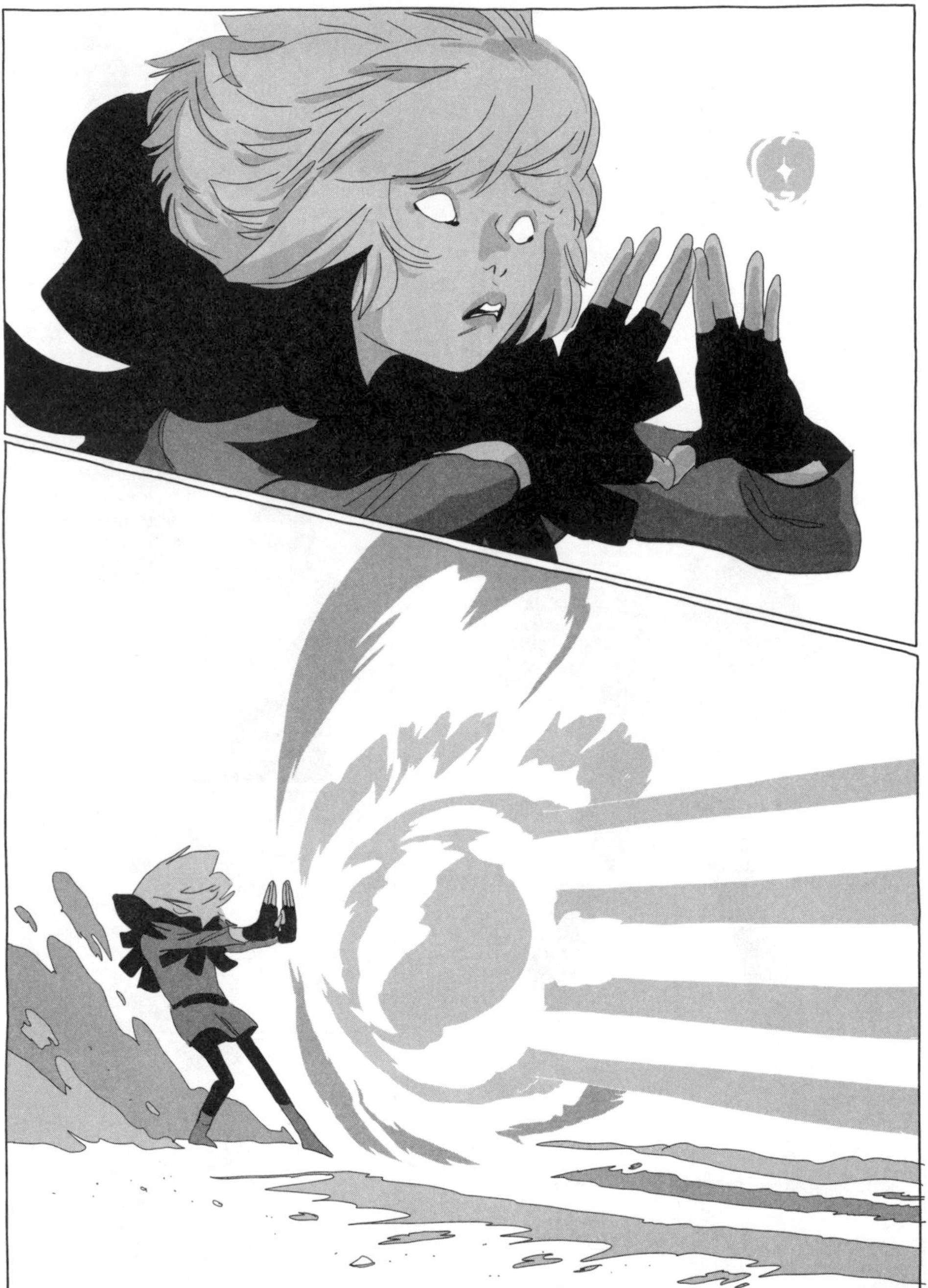

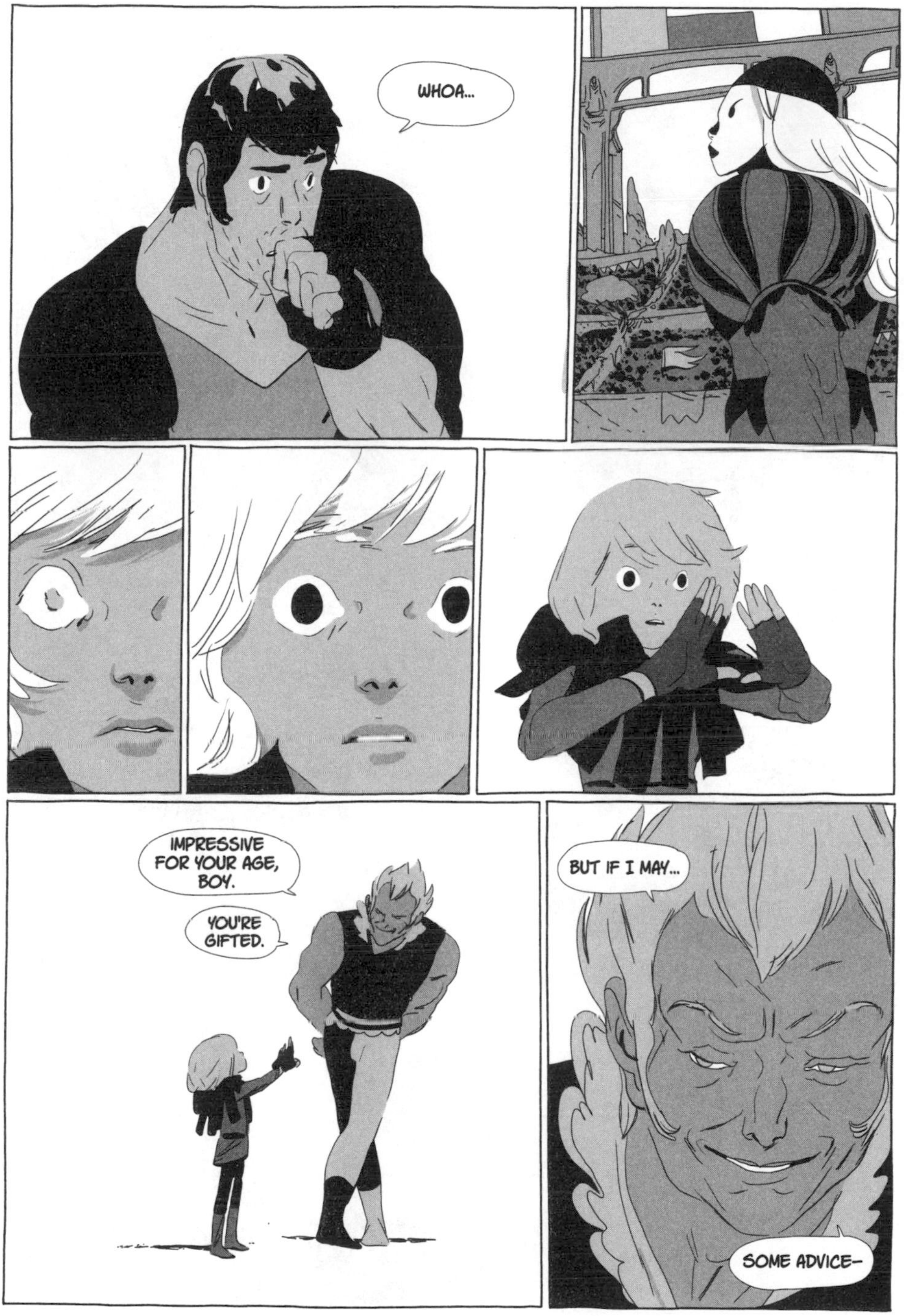
WHOA...
IMPRESSIVE FOR YOUR AGE, BOY.
YOU'RE GIFTED.
BUT IF I MAY...
SOME ADVICE-

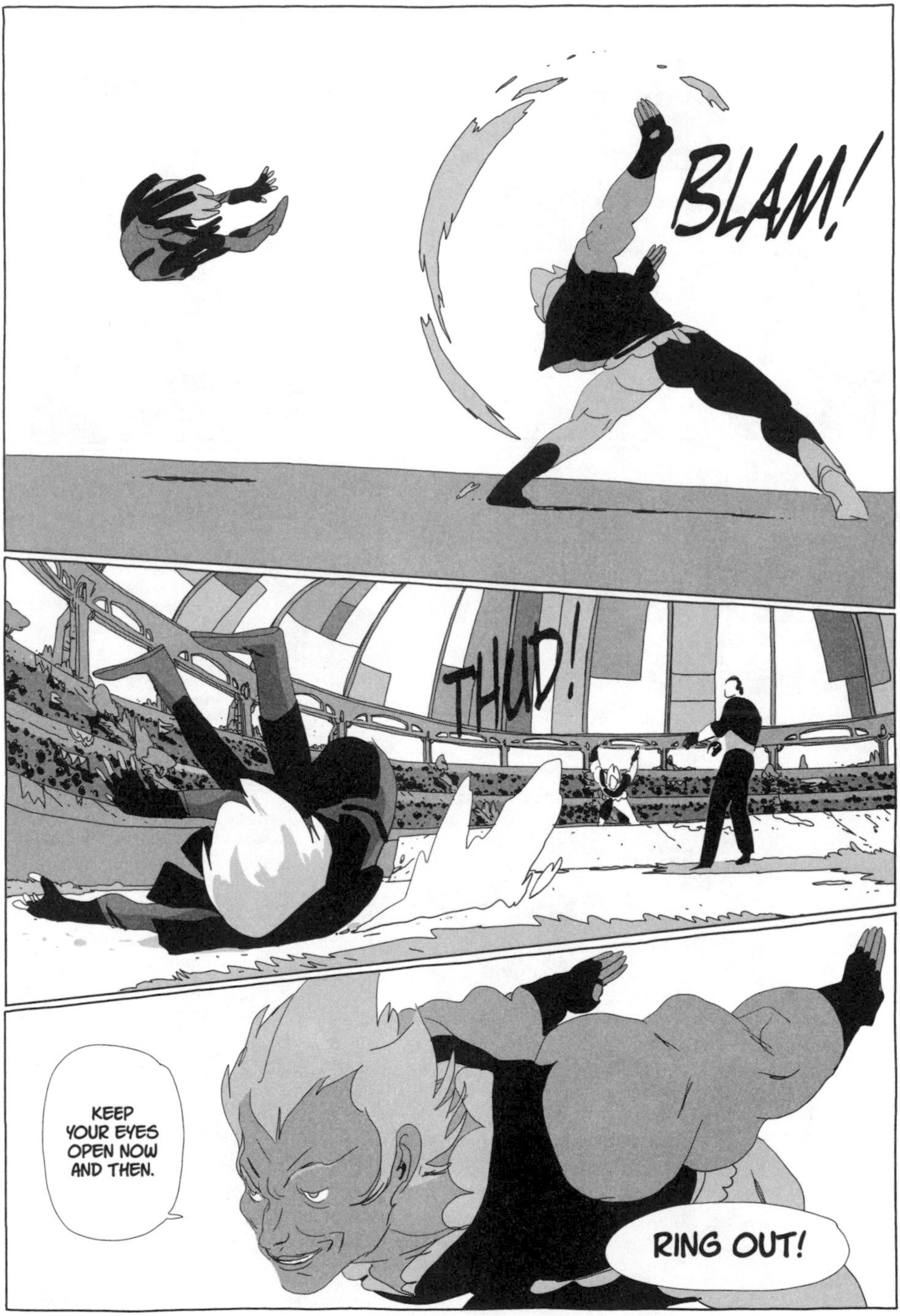
BLAM!
THUD!
KEEP YOUR EYES OPEN NOW AND THEN.
RING OUT!

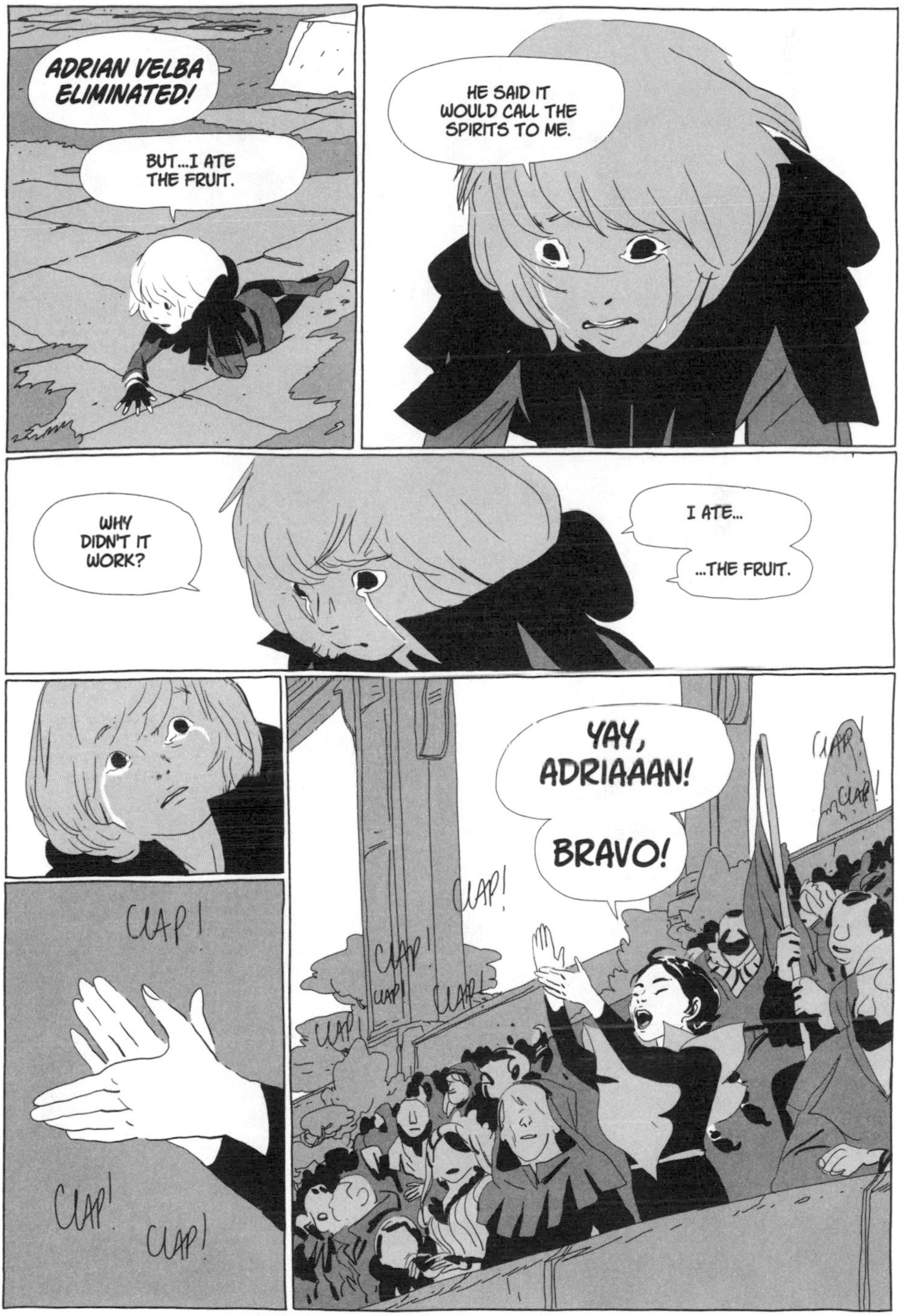
ADRIAN VELBA ELIMINATED!
BUT...I ATE THE FRUIT.
HE SAID IT WOULD CALL THE SPIRITS TO ME.
WHY DIDN'T IT WORK?
I ATE...
...THE FRUIT.
CLAP!
CLAP!
CLAP!
YAY, ADRIAAAN!
BRAVO!
CLAP!
CLAP!
CLAP!
CLAP!
CLAP!
CLAP!
CLAP!

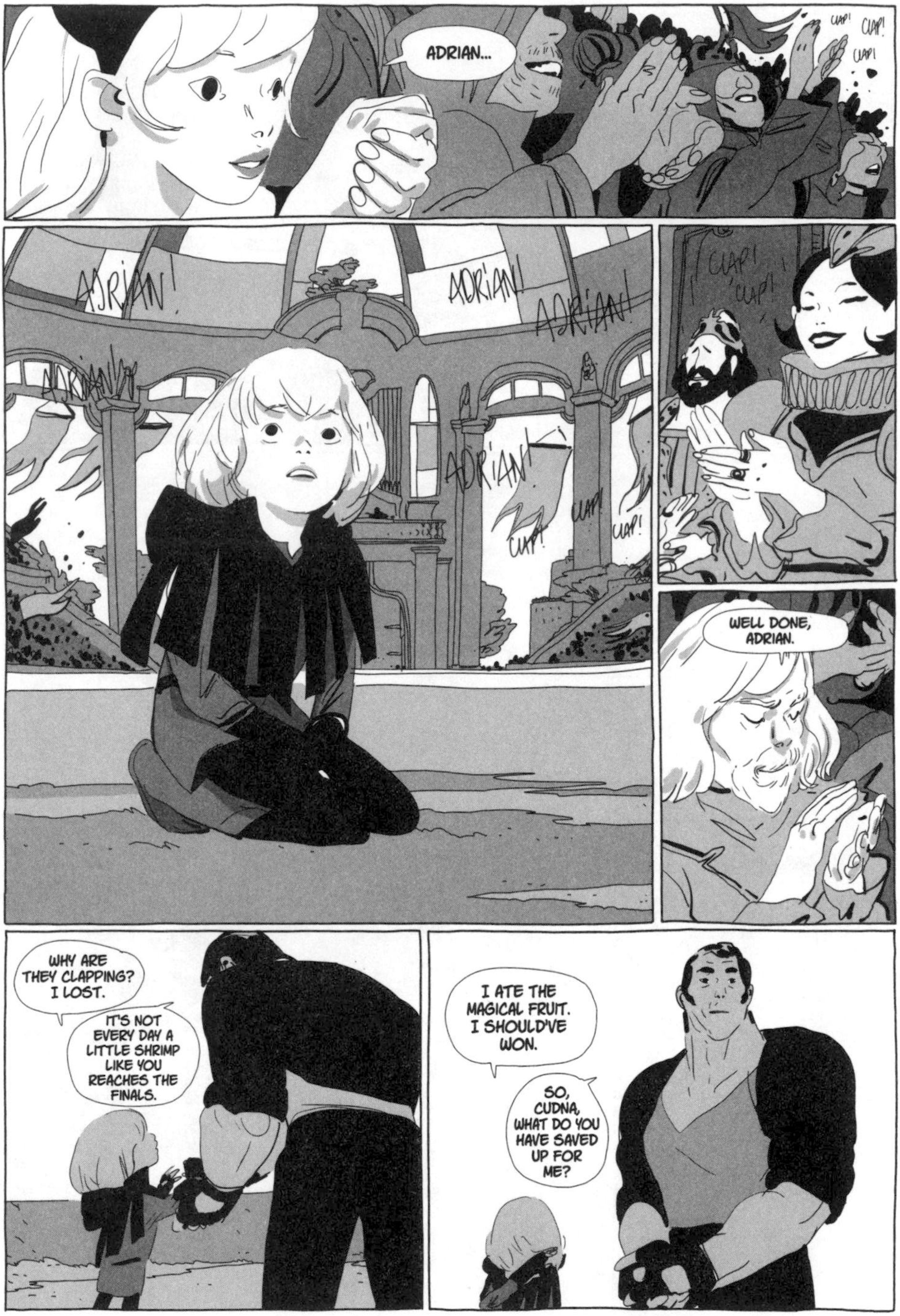
ADRIAN...
CLAP! CLAP! CLAP!
ADRIAN! ADRIAN! ADRIAN! ADRIAN! ADRIAN!
CLAP! CLAP! CLAP!
CLAP! CLAP!
WELL DONE, ADRIAN.
WHY ARE THEY CLAPPING? I LOST.
IT'S NOT EVERY DAY A LITTLE SHRIMP LIKE YOU REACHES THE FINALS.
I ATE THE MAGICAL FRUIT. I SHOULD'VE WON.
SO, CUDNA, WHAT DO YOU HAVE SAVED UP FOR ME?

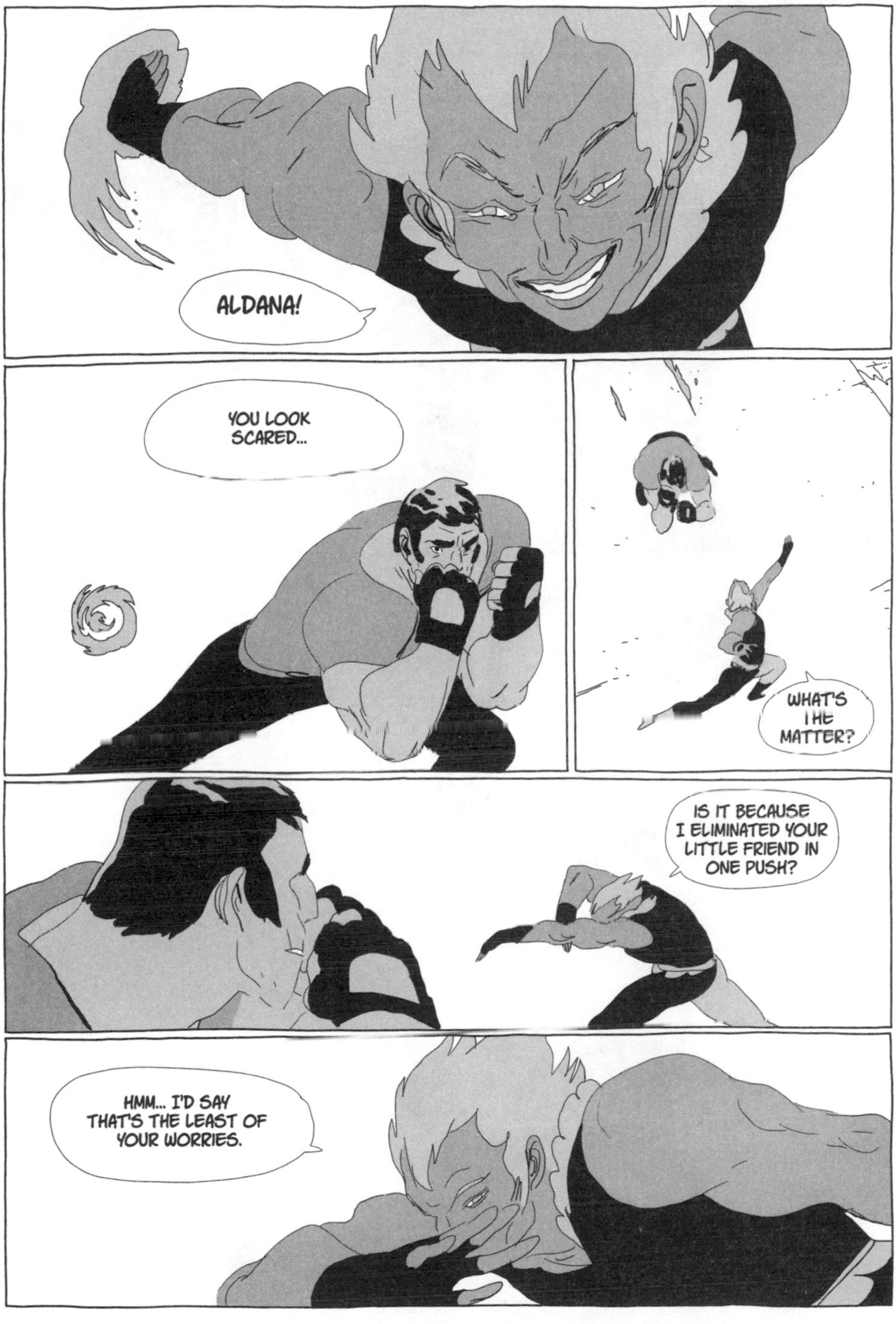
ALDANA!
YOU LOOK SCARED...
WHAT'S THE MATTER?
IS IT BECAUSE I ELIMINATED YOUR LITTLE FRIEND IN ONE PUSH?
HMM... I'D SAY THAT'S THE LEAST OF YOUR WORRIES.

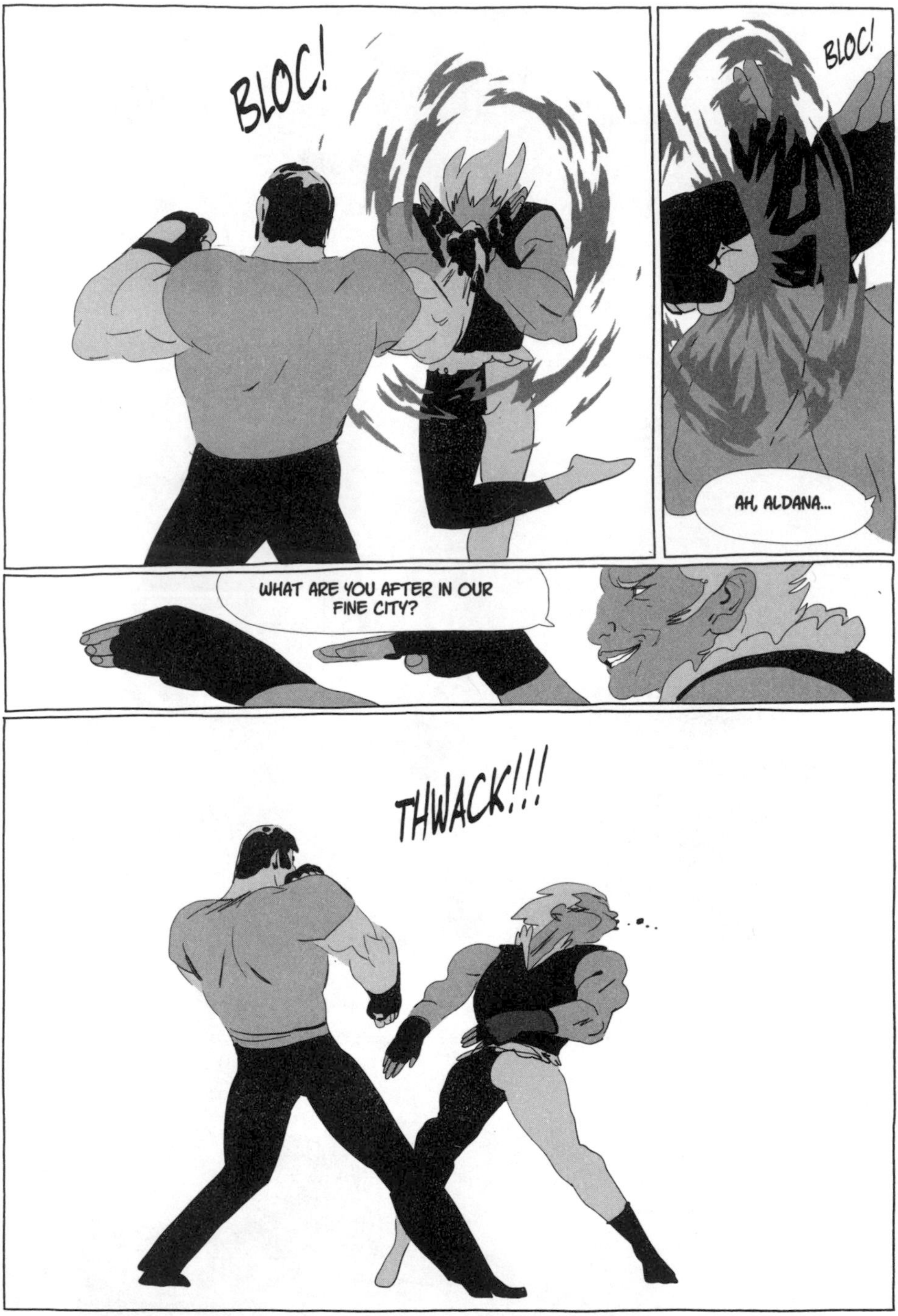
BLOC!
BLOC!
AH, ALDANA...
WHAT ARE YOU AFTER IN OUR FINE CITY?
THWACK!!!

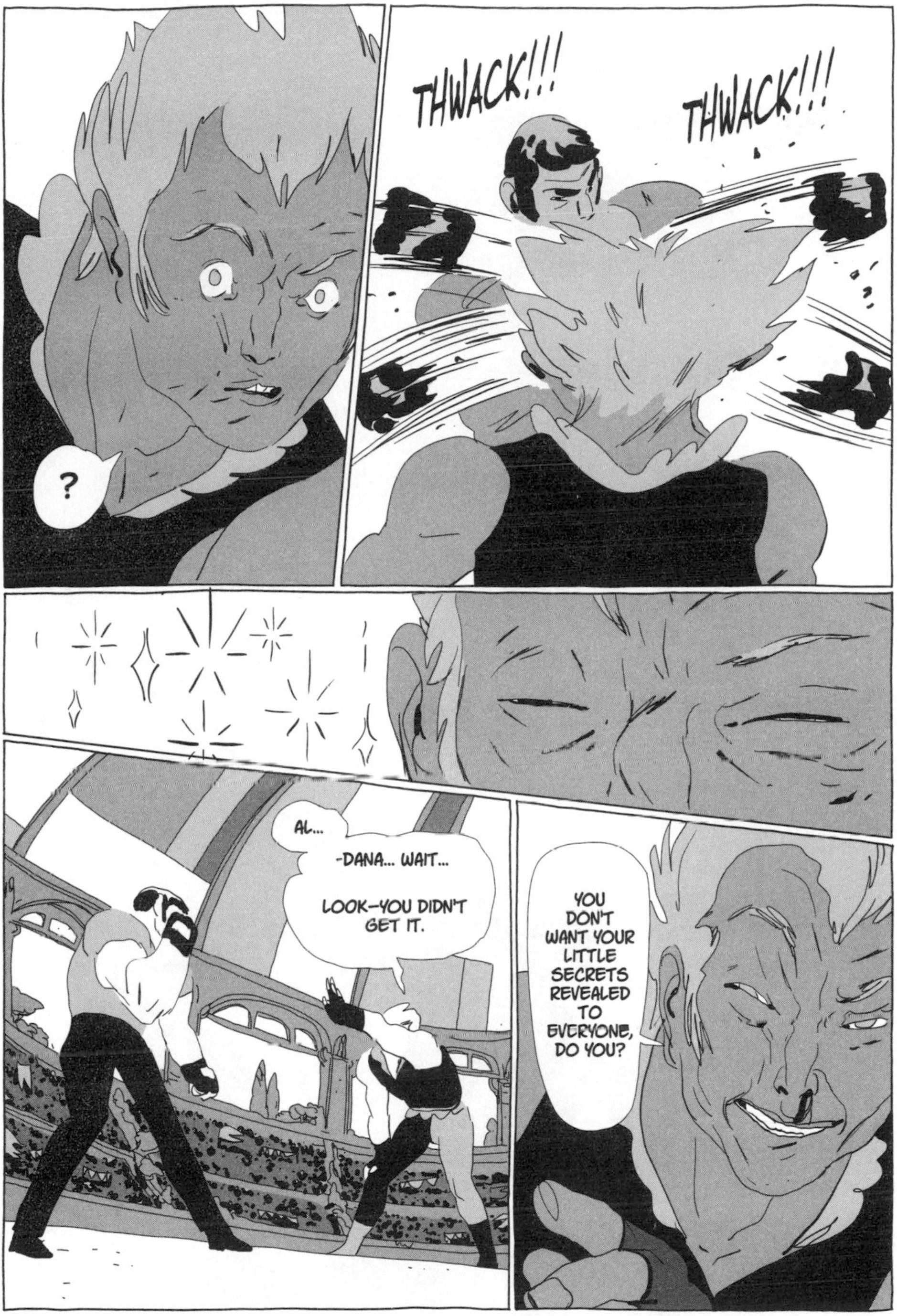
?
THWACK!!!
THWACK!!!
AL...
-DANA... WAIT...
LOOK—YOU DIDN'T GET IT.
YOU DON'T WANT YOUR LITTLE SECRETS REVEALED TO EVERYONE, DO YOU?

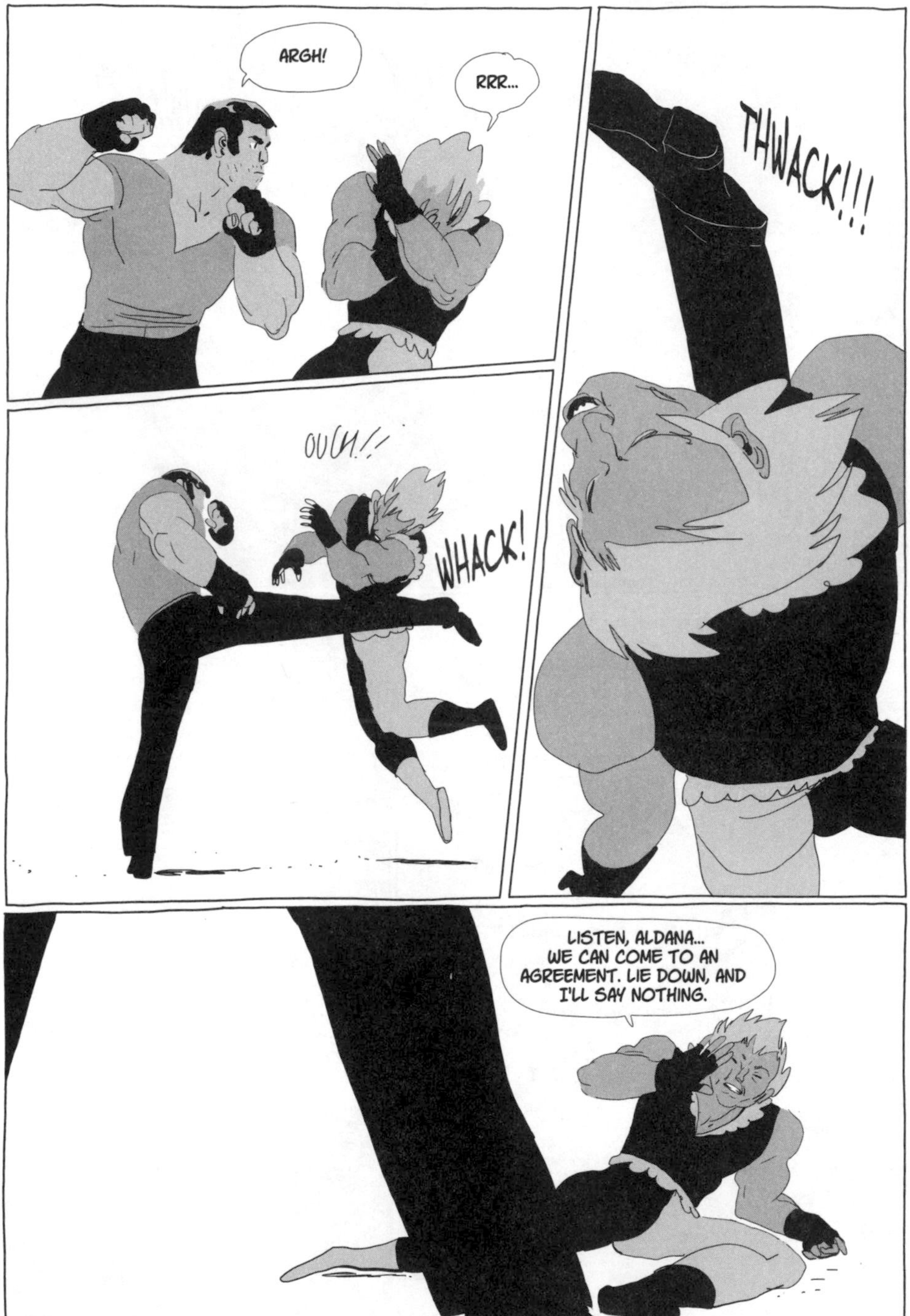
ARGH!
RRR...
THWACK!!!
OUCH!!
WHACK!
LISTEN, ALDANA... WE CAN COME TO AN AGREEMENT. LIE DOWN, AND I'LL SAY NOTHING.

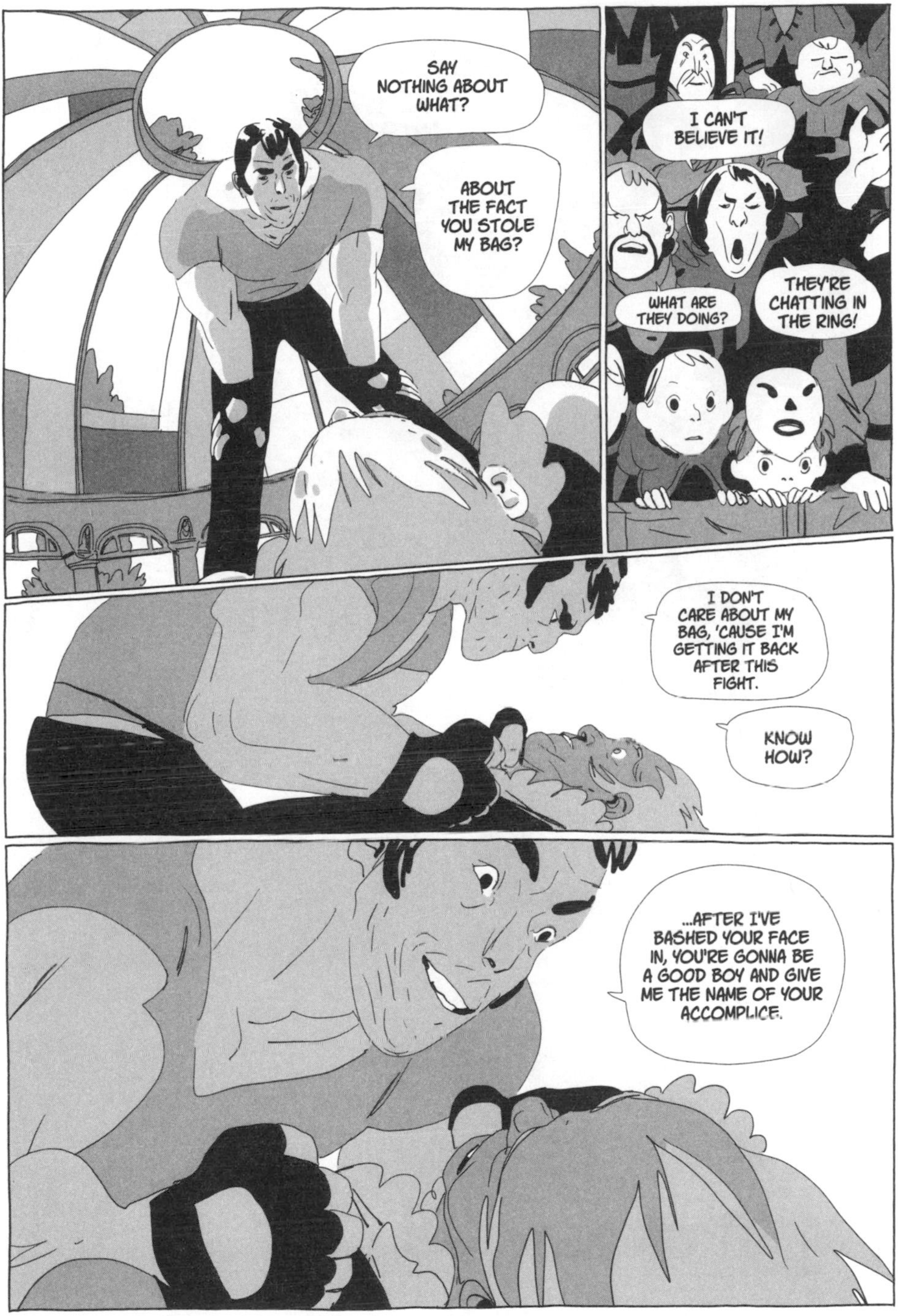
SAY NOTHING ABOUT WHAT?
ABOUT THE FACT YOU STOLE MY BAG?
I CAN'T BELIEVE IT!
WHAT ARE THEY DOING?
THEY'RE CHATTING IN THE RING!
I DON'T CARE ABOUT MY BAG, 'CAUSE I'M GETTING IT BACK AFTER THIS FIGHT.
KNOW HOW?
...AFTER I'VE BASHED YOUR FACE IN, YOU'RE GONNA BE A GOOD BOY AND GIVE ME THE NAME OF YOUR ACCOMPLICE.

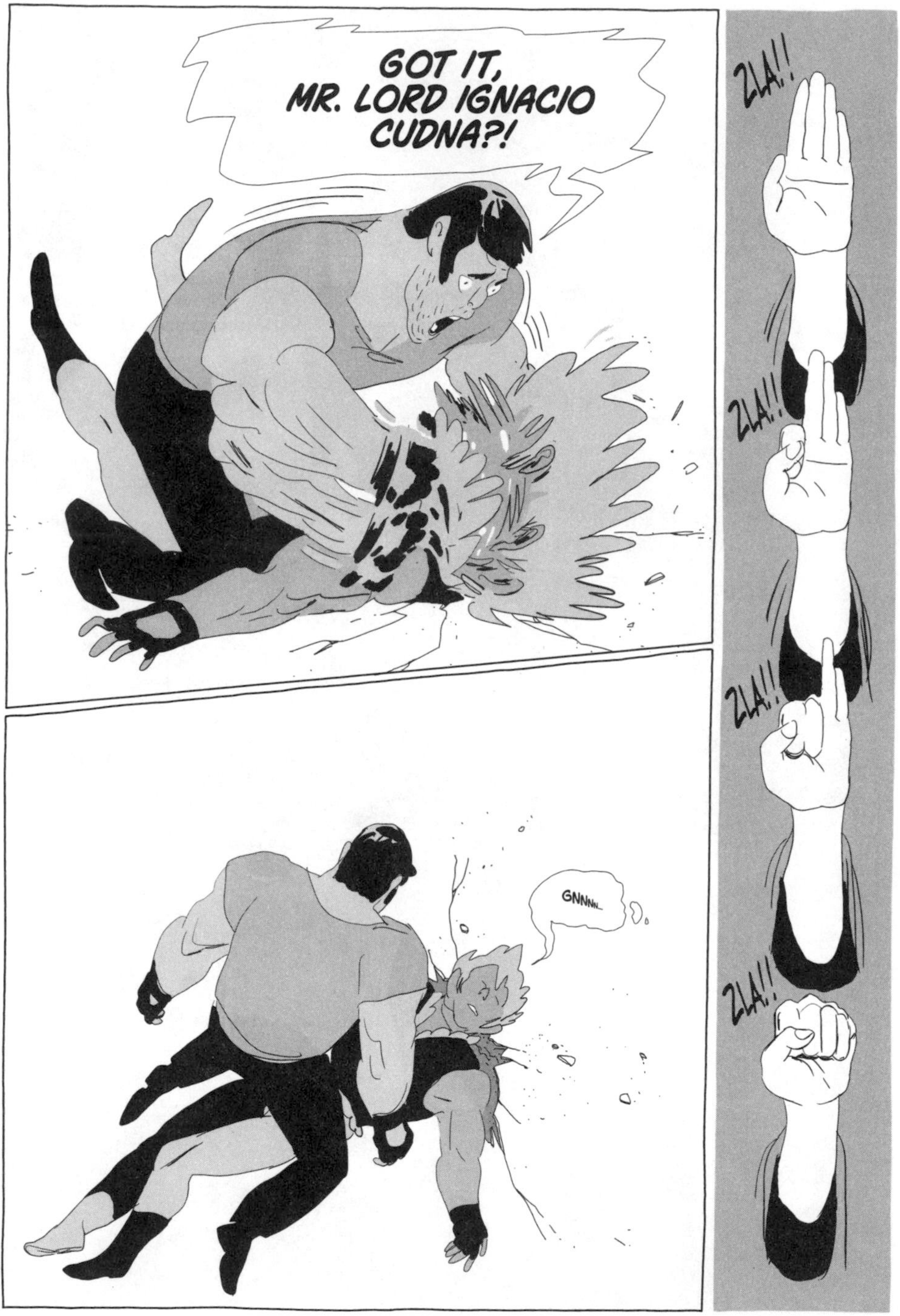
GOT IT, MR. LORD IGNACIO CUDNA?!
ZLA!!
ZLA!!
ZLA!!
ZLA!!
GNNNN...

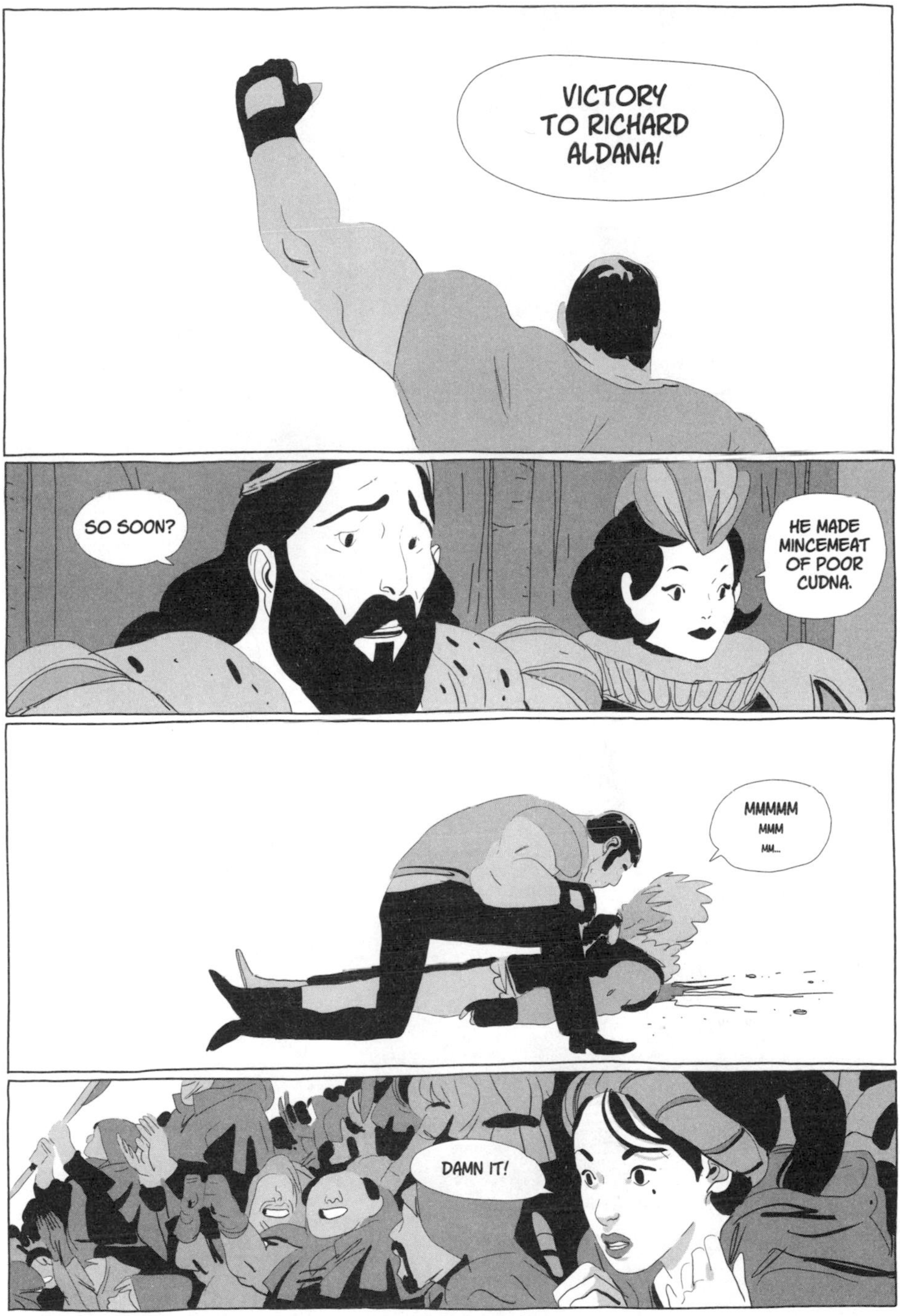
VICTORY TO RICHARD ALDANA!
SO SOON?
HE MADE MINCEMEAT OF POOR CUDNA.
MMMMM MMM MM...
DAMN IT!

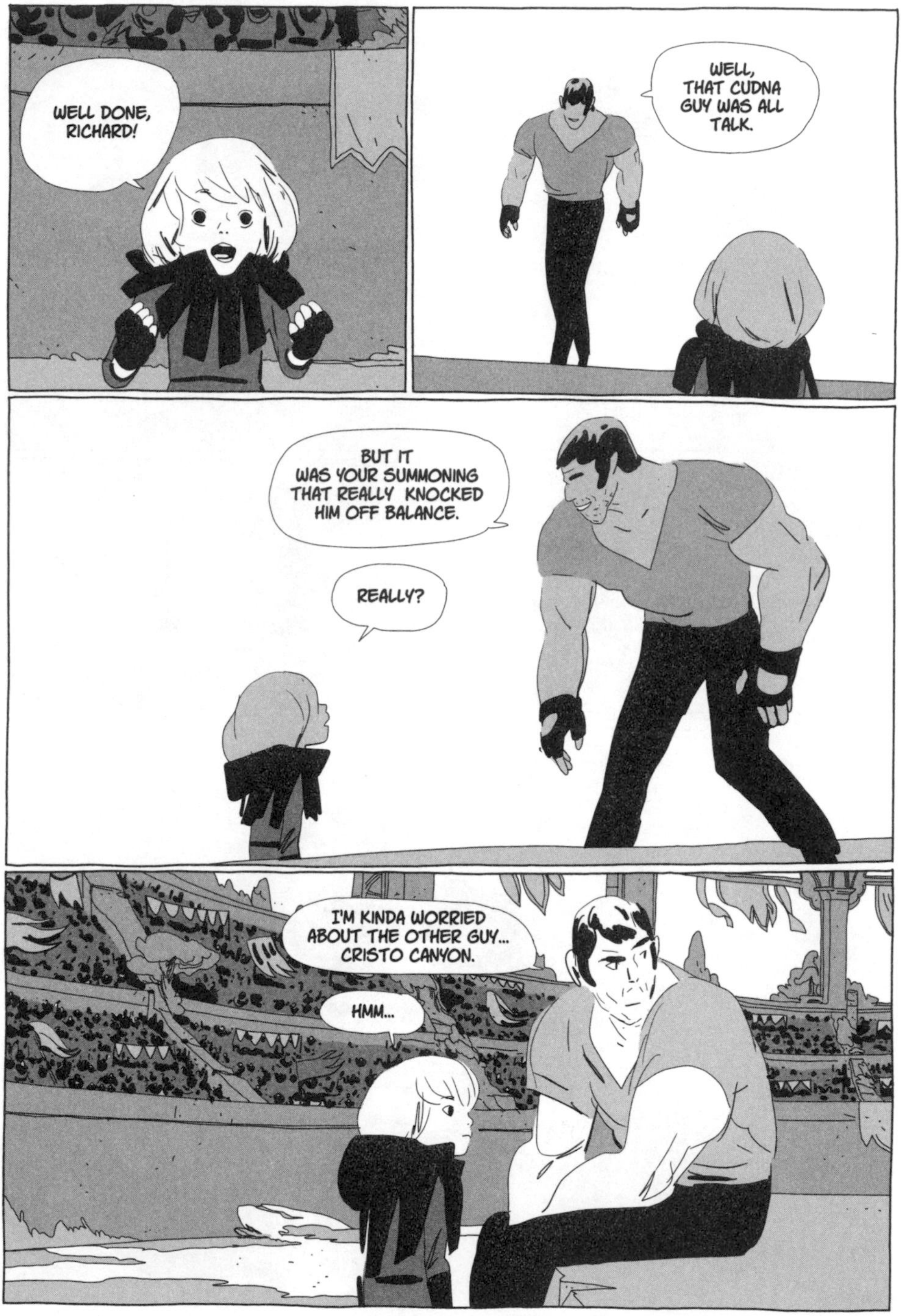
WELL DONE, RICHARD!
WELL, THAT CUDNA GUY WAS ALL TALK.
BUT IT WAS YOUR SUMMONING THAT REALLY KNOCKED HIM OFF BALANCE.
REALLY?
I'M KINDA WORRIED ABOUT THE OTHER GUY... CRISTO CANYON.
HMM...

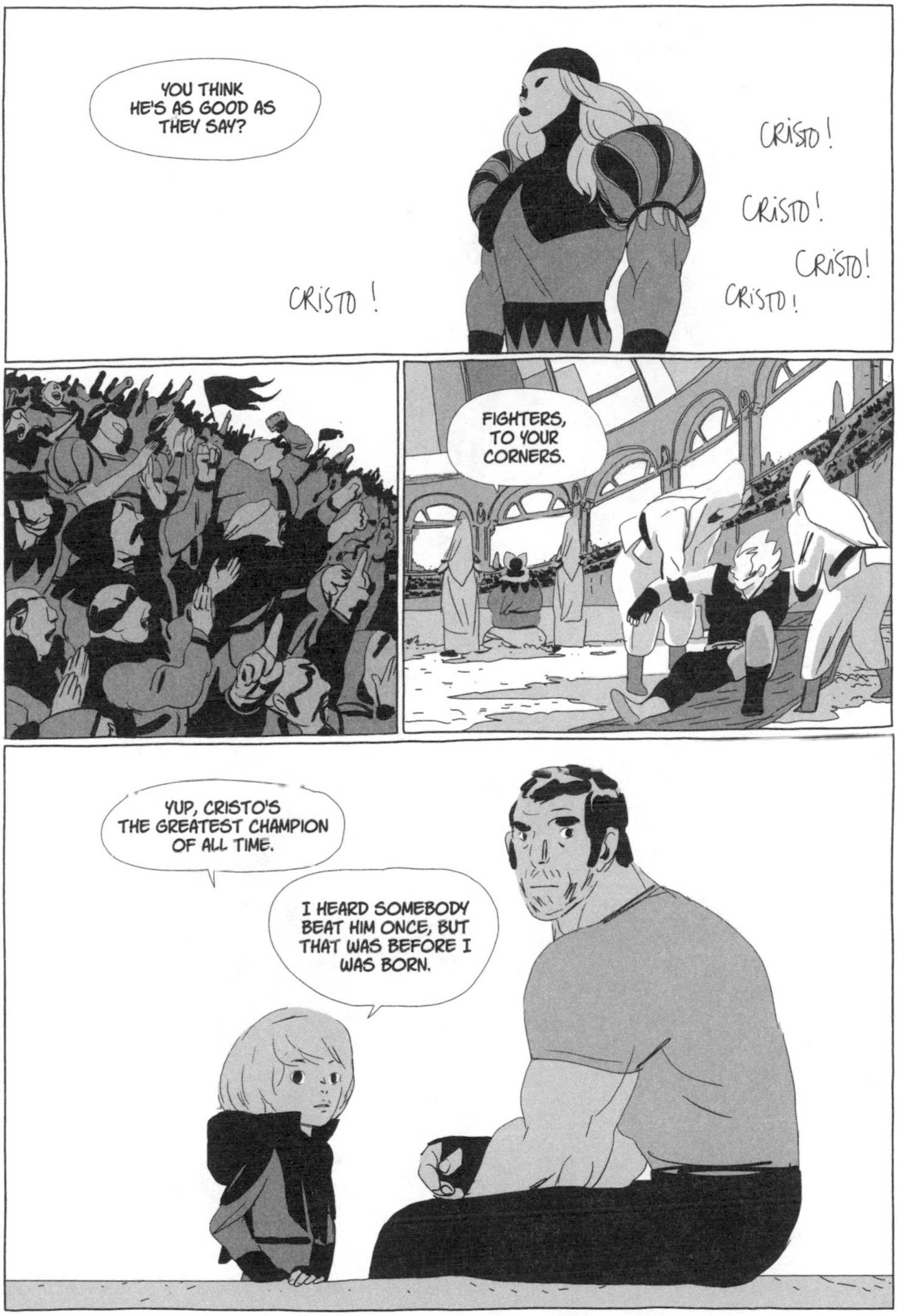
YOU THINK HE'S AS GOOD AS THEY SAY?
CRISTO!
CRISTO!
CRISTO!
CRISTO!
CRISTO!
FIGHTERS, TO YOUR CORNERS.
YUP, CRISTO'S THE GREATEST CHAMPION OF ALL TIME.
I HEARD SOMEBODY BEAT HIM ONCE, BUT THAT WAS BEFORE I WAS BORN.

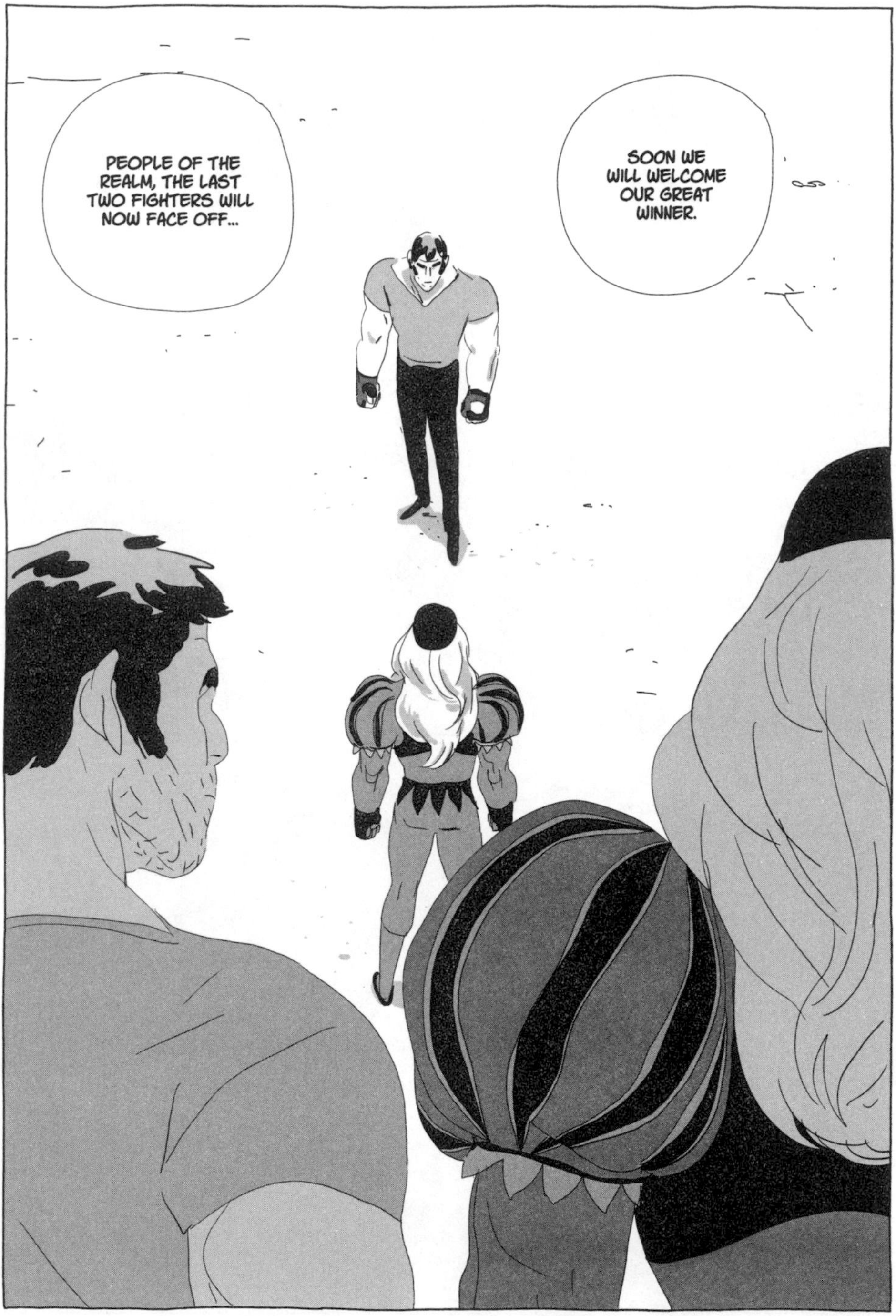
PEOPLE OF THE REALM, THE LAST TWO FIGHTERS WILL NOW FACE OFF...
SOON WE WILL WELCOME OUR GREAT WINNER.

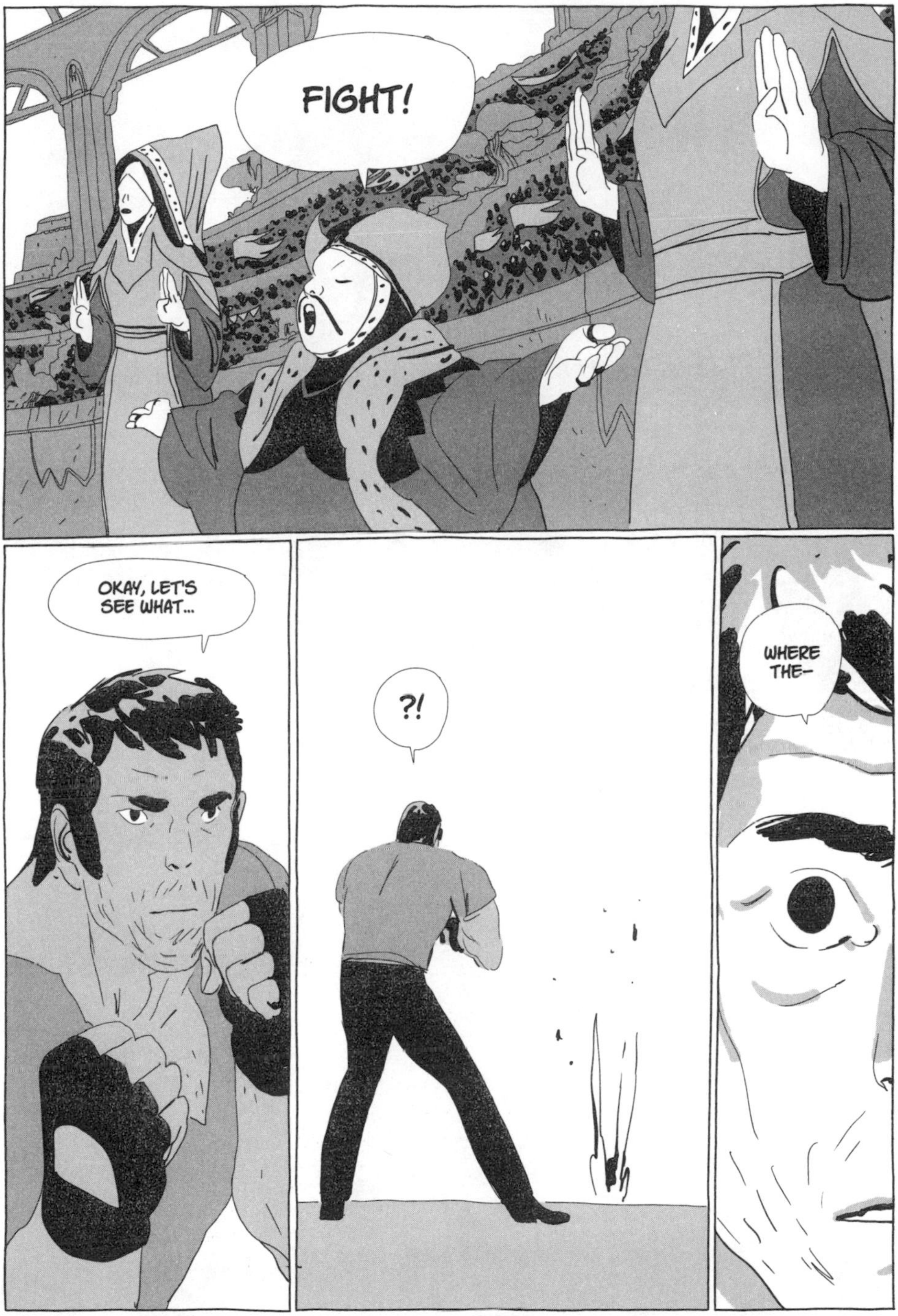
FIGHT!
OKAY, LET'S SEE WHAT...
?!
WHERE THE-

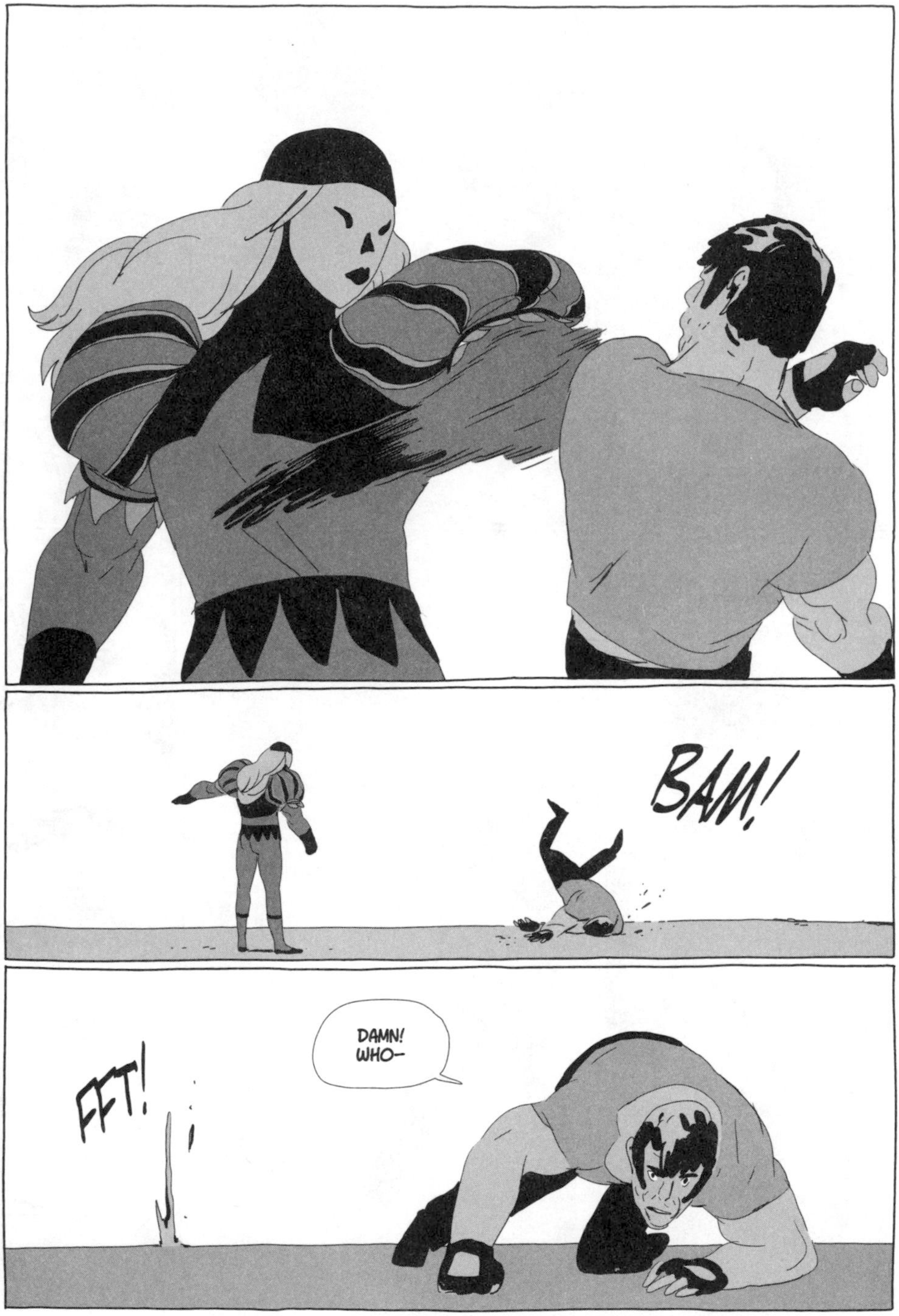
BAM!
FFT!
DAMN! WHO-

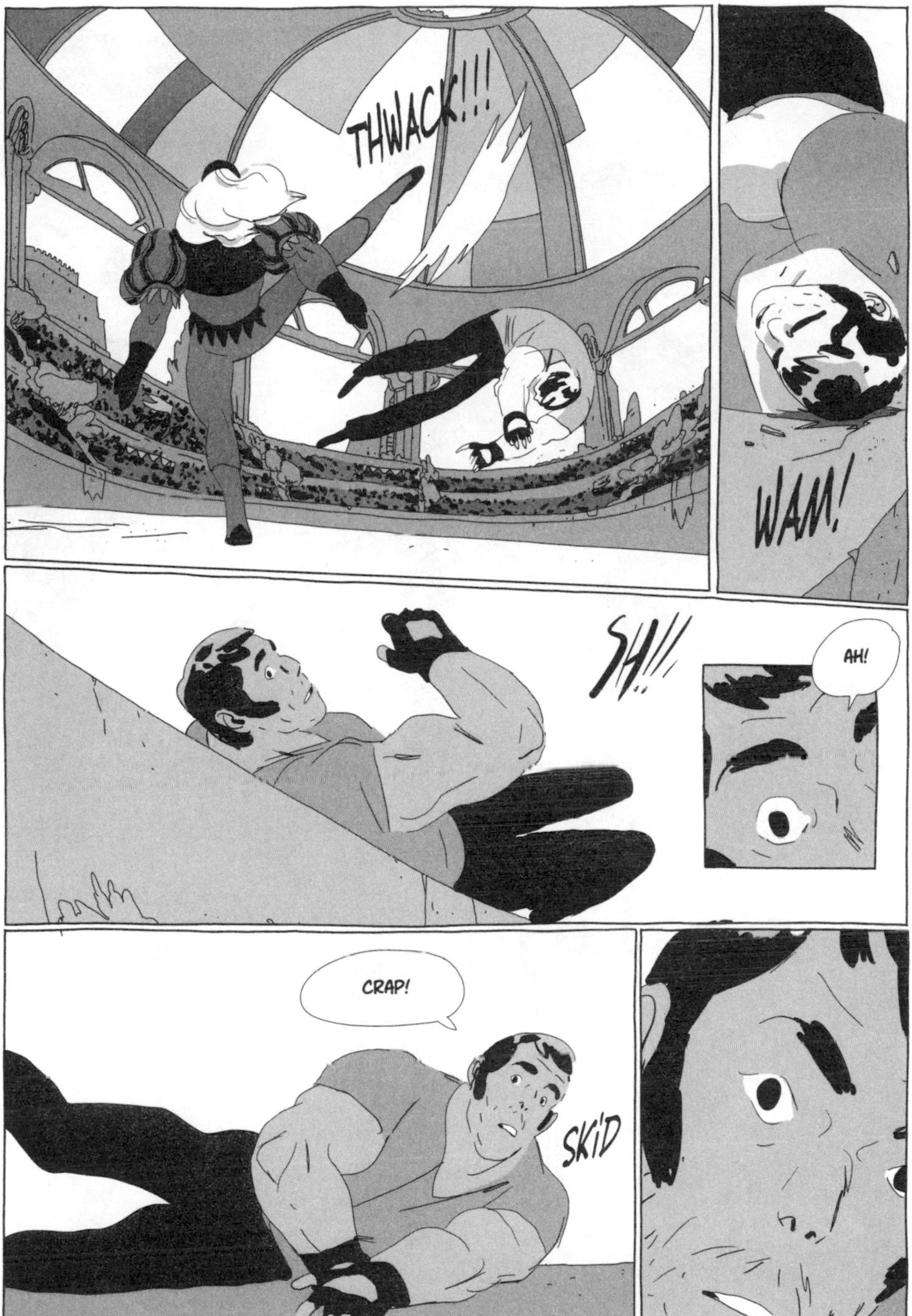
THWACK!!!
WAM!
SH!!
AH!
CRAP!
SKID

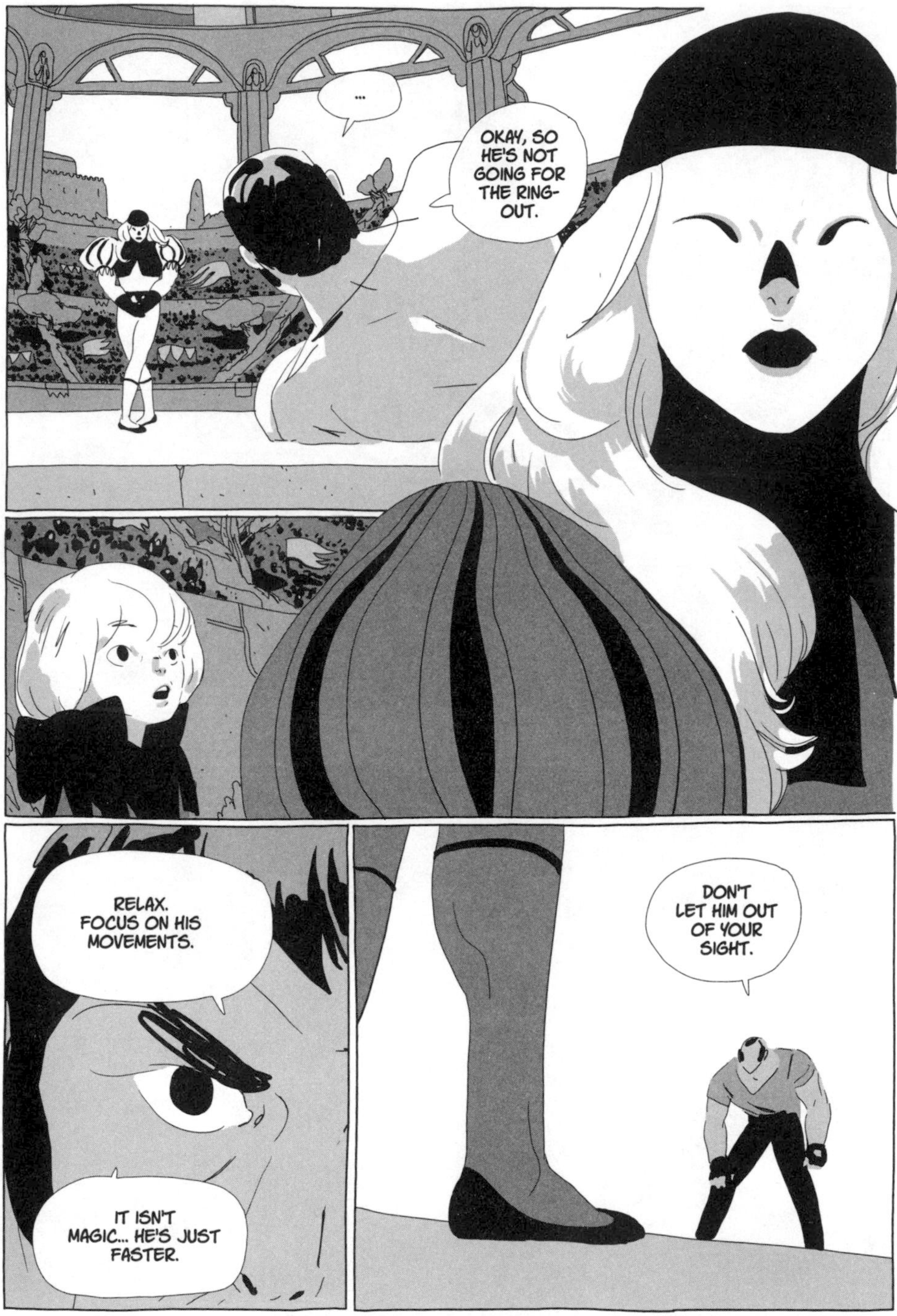
...
OKAY, SO HE'S NOT GOING FOR THE RING-OUT.
RELAX. FOCUS ON HIS MOVEMENTS.
IT ISN'T MAGIC... HE'S JUST FASTER.
DON'T LET HIM OUT OF YOUR SIGHT.

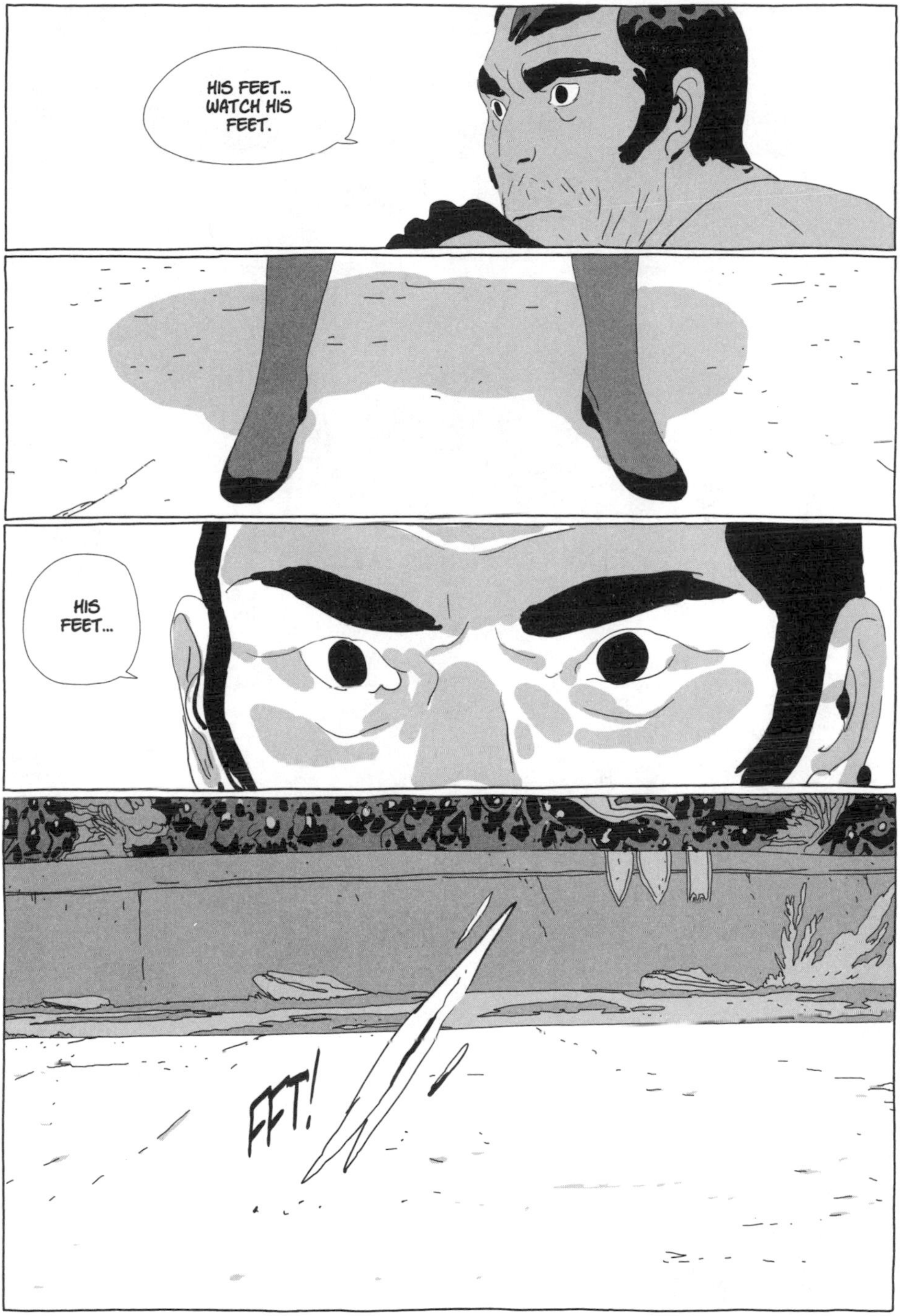
HIS FEET... WATCH HIS FEET.
HIS FEET...
FFT!

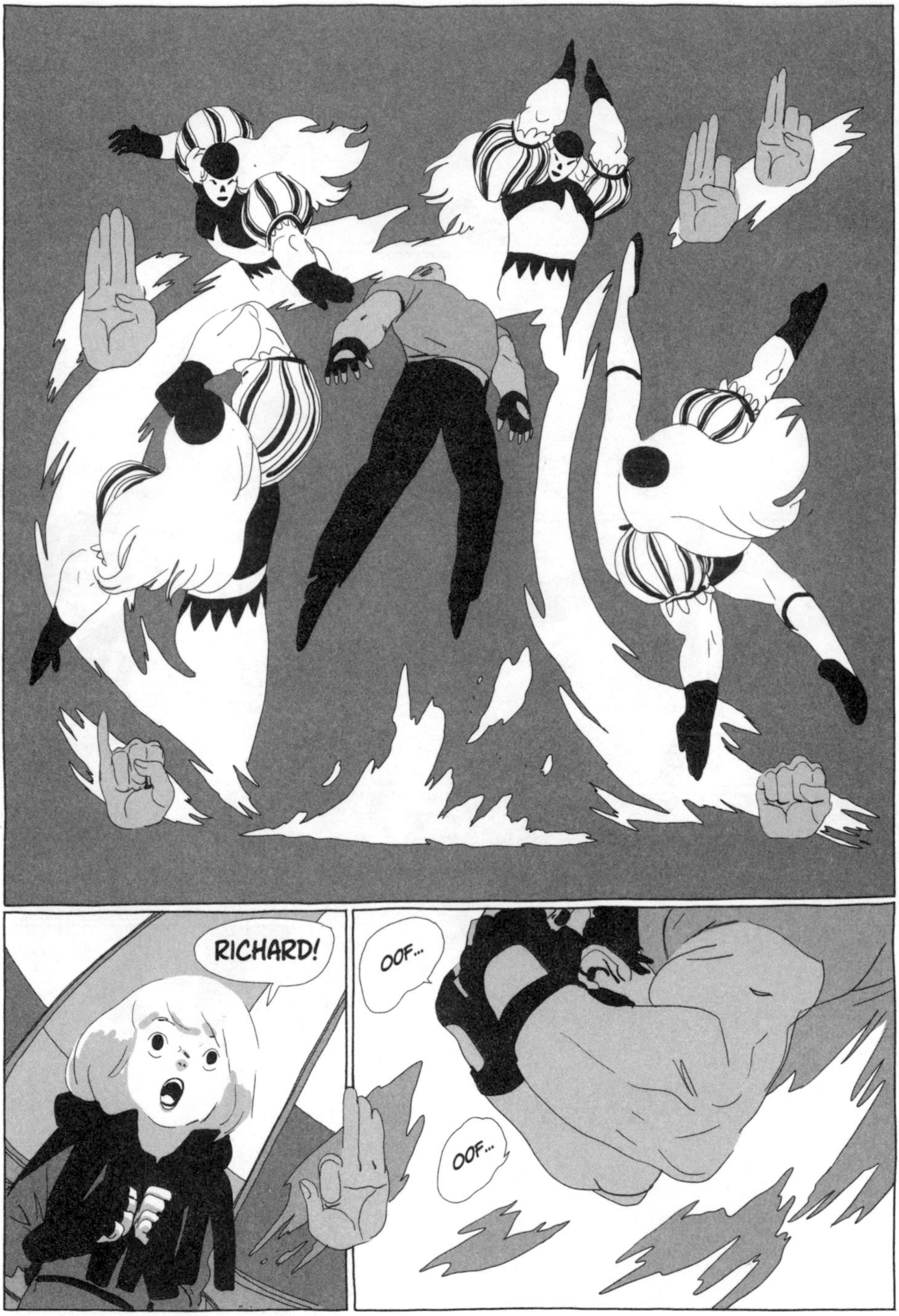
RICHARD!
OOF...
OOF...

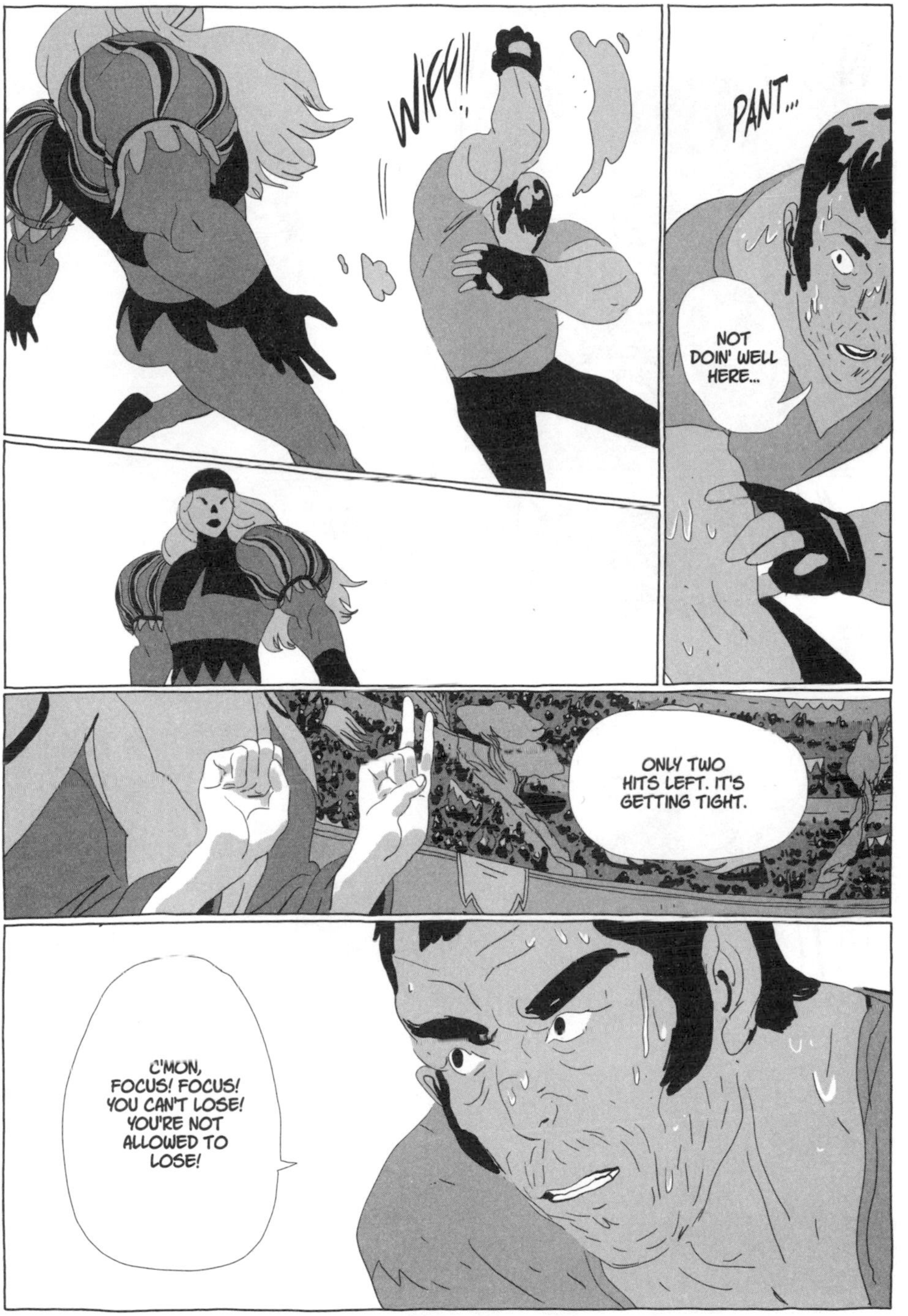
WIFF!!
PANT...
NOT DOIN' WELL HERE...
ONLY TWO HITS LEFT. IT'S GETTING TIGHT.
C'MON, FOCUS! FOCUS! YOU CAN'T LOSE! YOU'RE NOT ALLOWED TO LOSE!

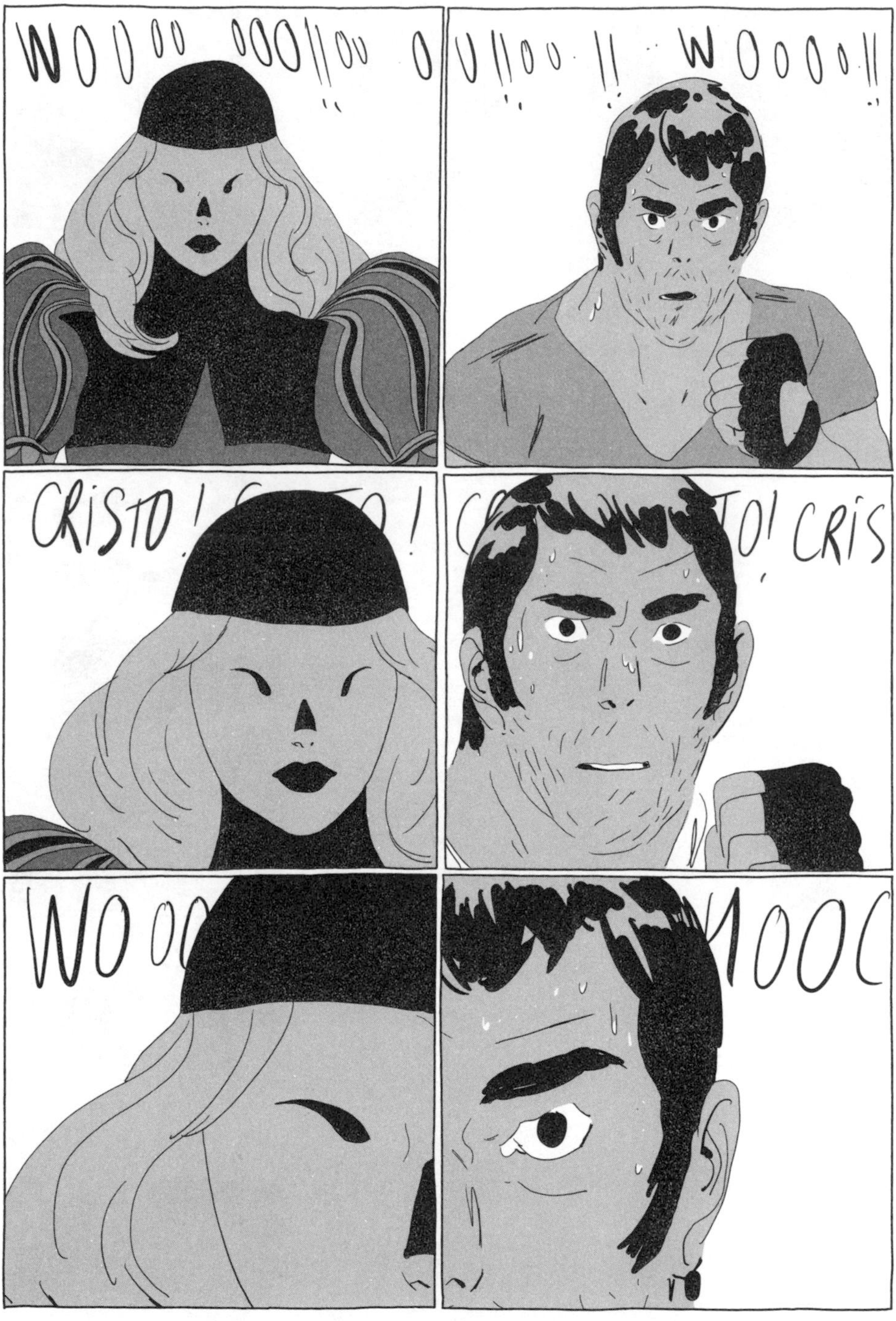
WOOOO OOO!!OO O
O!!OO!! WOOOO!!
CRISTO! CRISTO!
CRISTO! CRIS
WOOO
WOOO

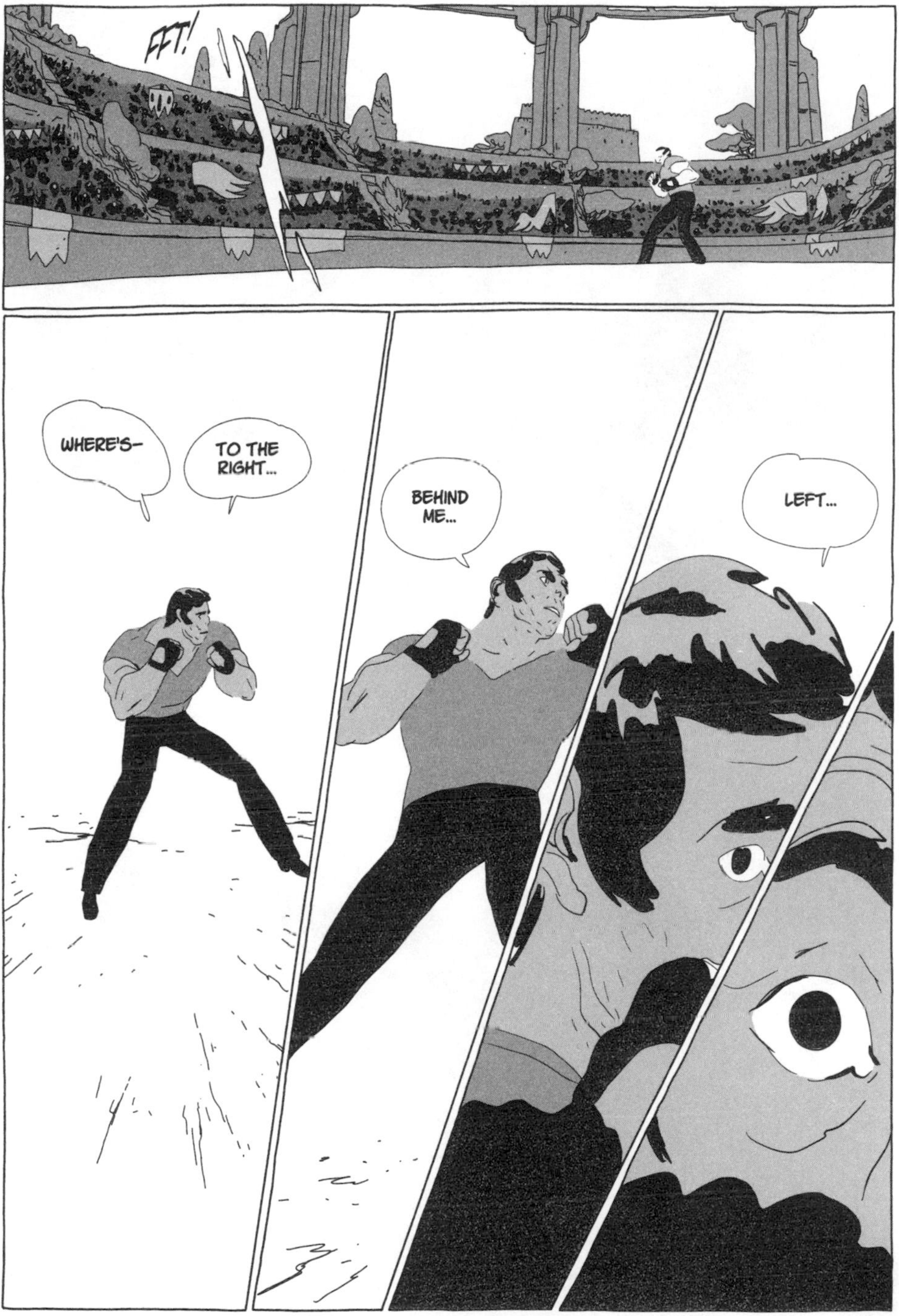
FFT!
WHERE'S-
TO THE RIGHT...
BEHIND ME...
LEFT...

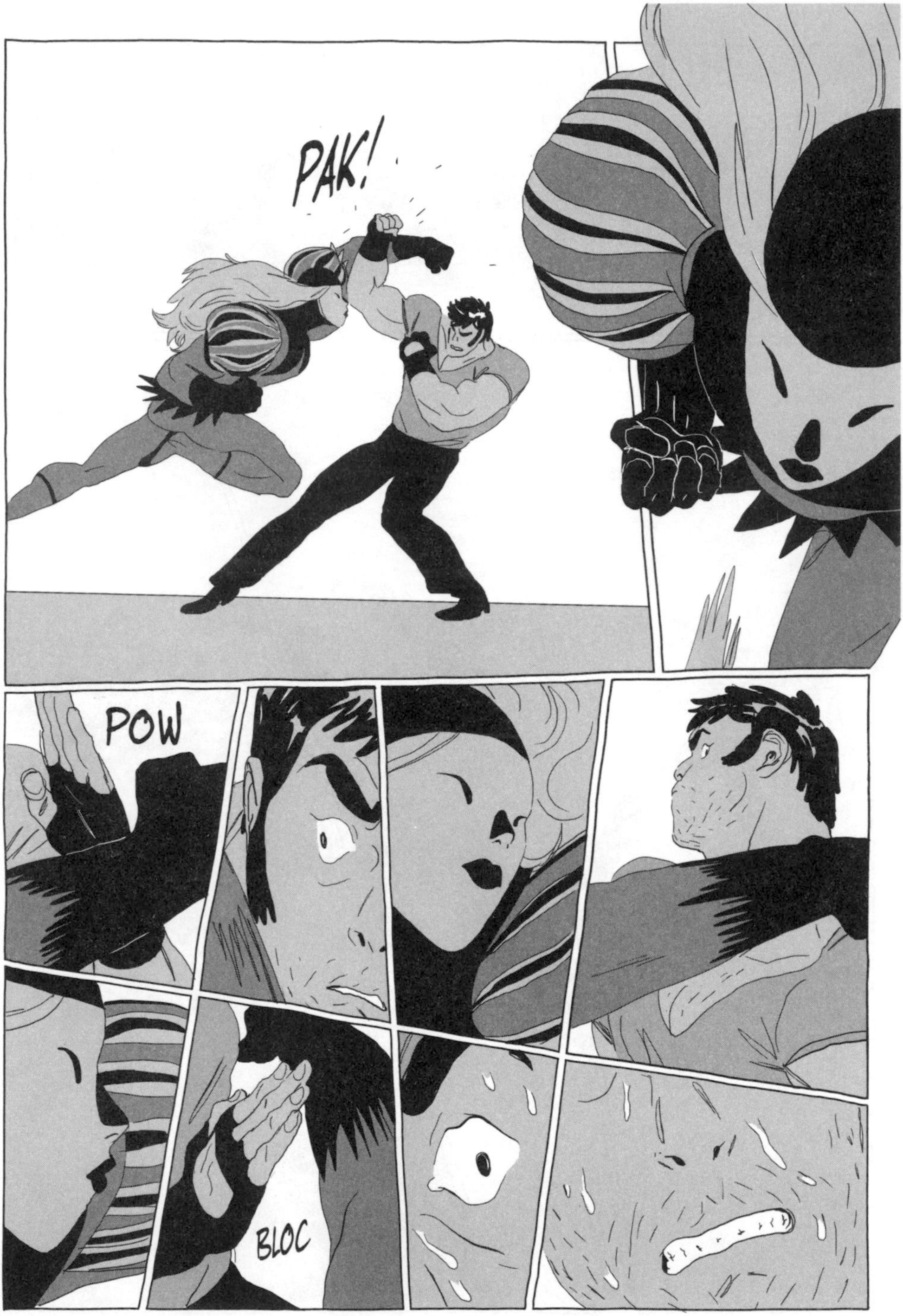
PAK!
POW
BLOC

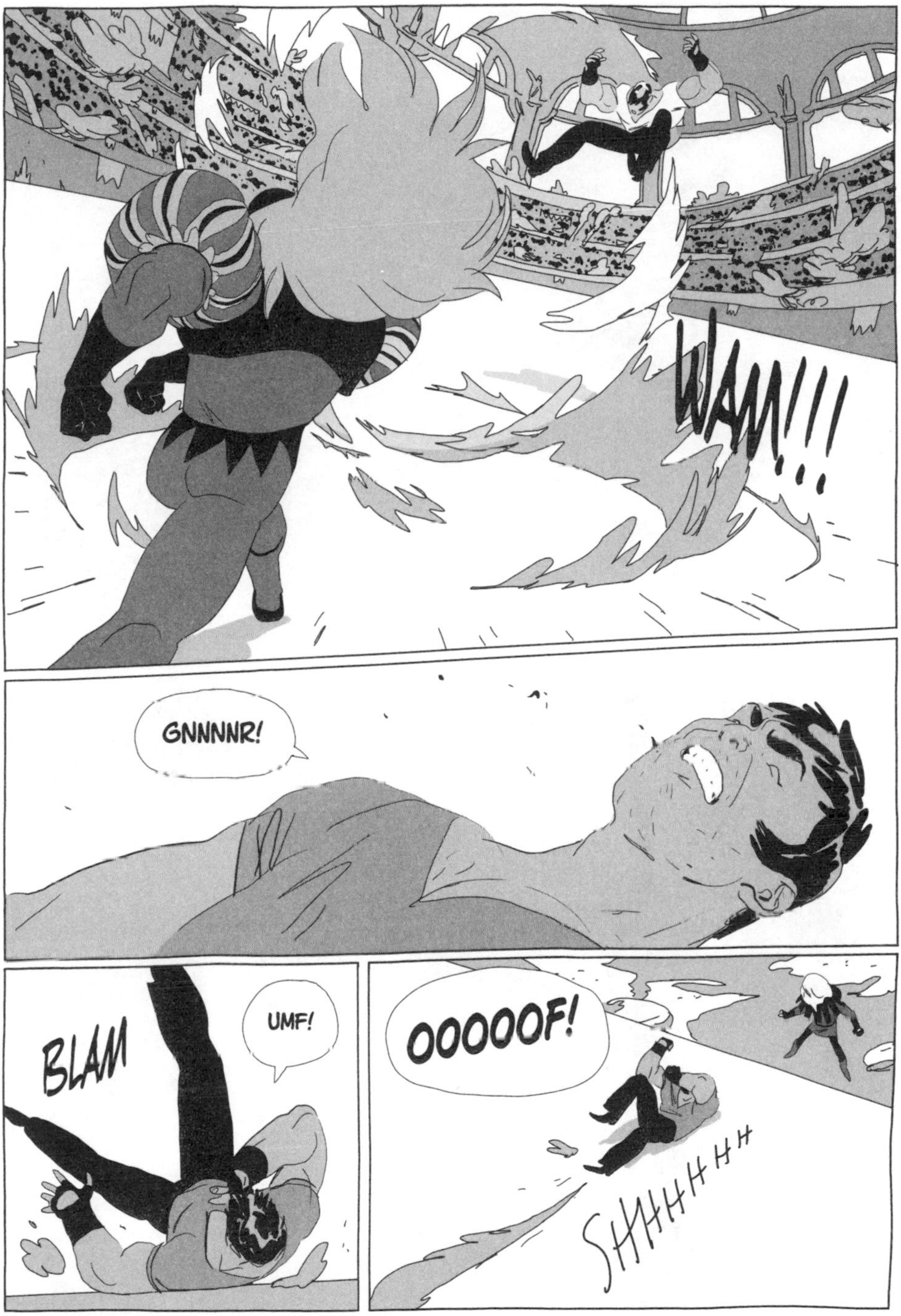

WAM!!!
GNNNNR!
BLAM
UMF!
OOOOOF!
SHHHHHHH

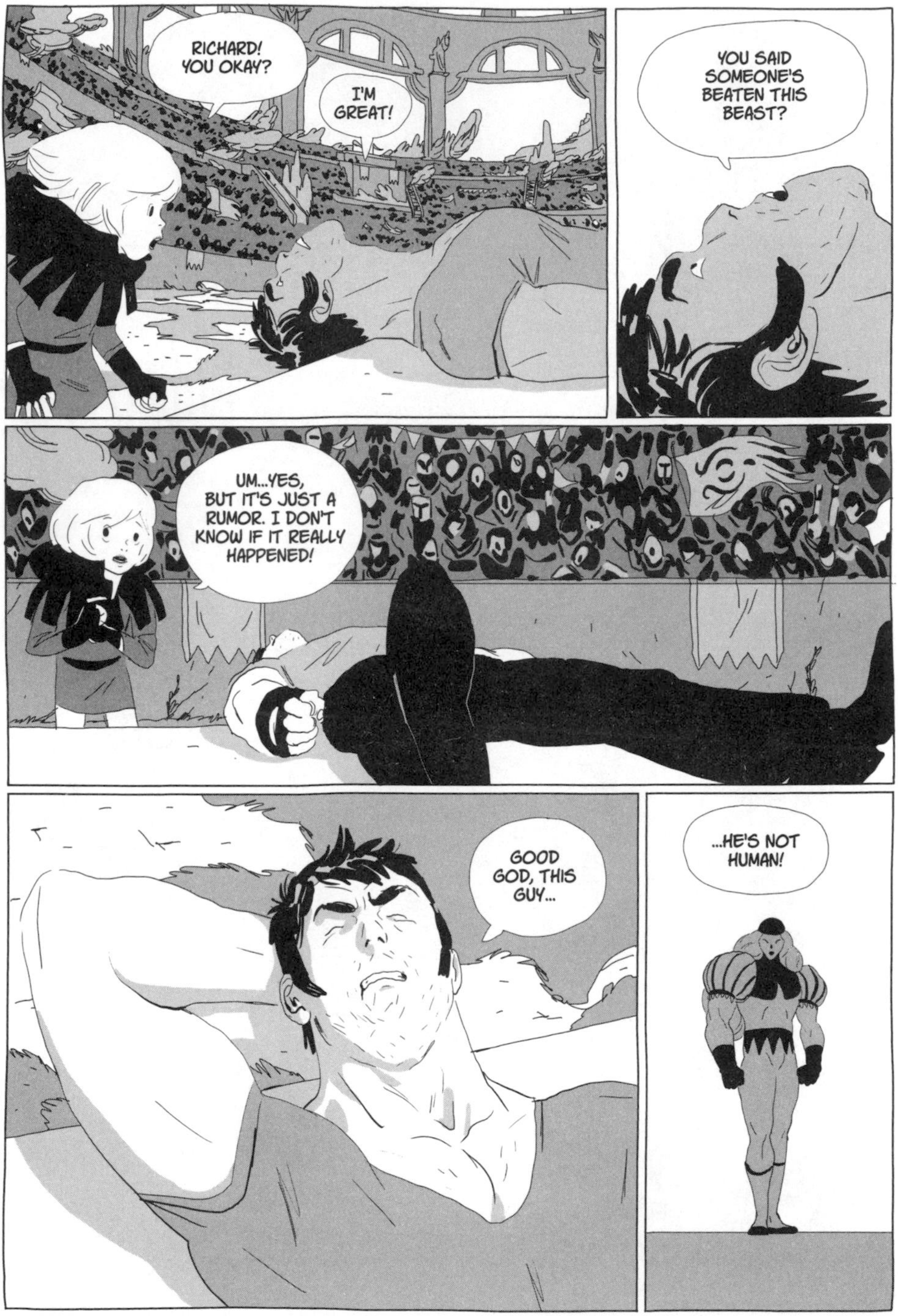
RICHARD! YOU OKAY?
I'M GREAT!
YOU SAID SOMEONE'S BEATEN THIS BEAST?
UM...YES, BUT IT'S JUST A RUMOR. I DON'T KNOW IF IT REALLY HAPPENED!
GOOD GOD, THIS GUY...
...HE'S NOT HUMAN!

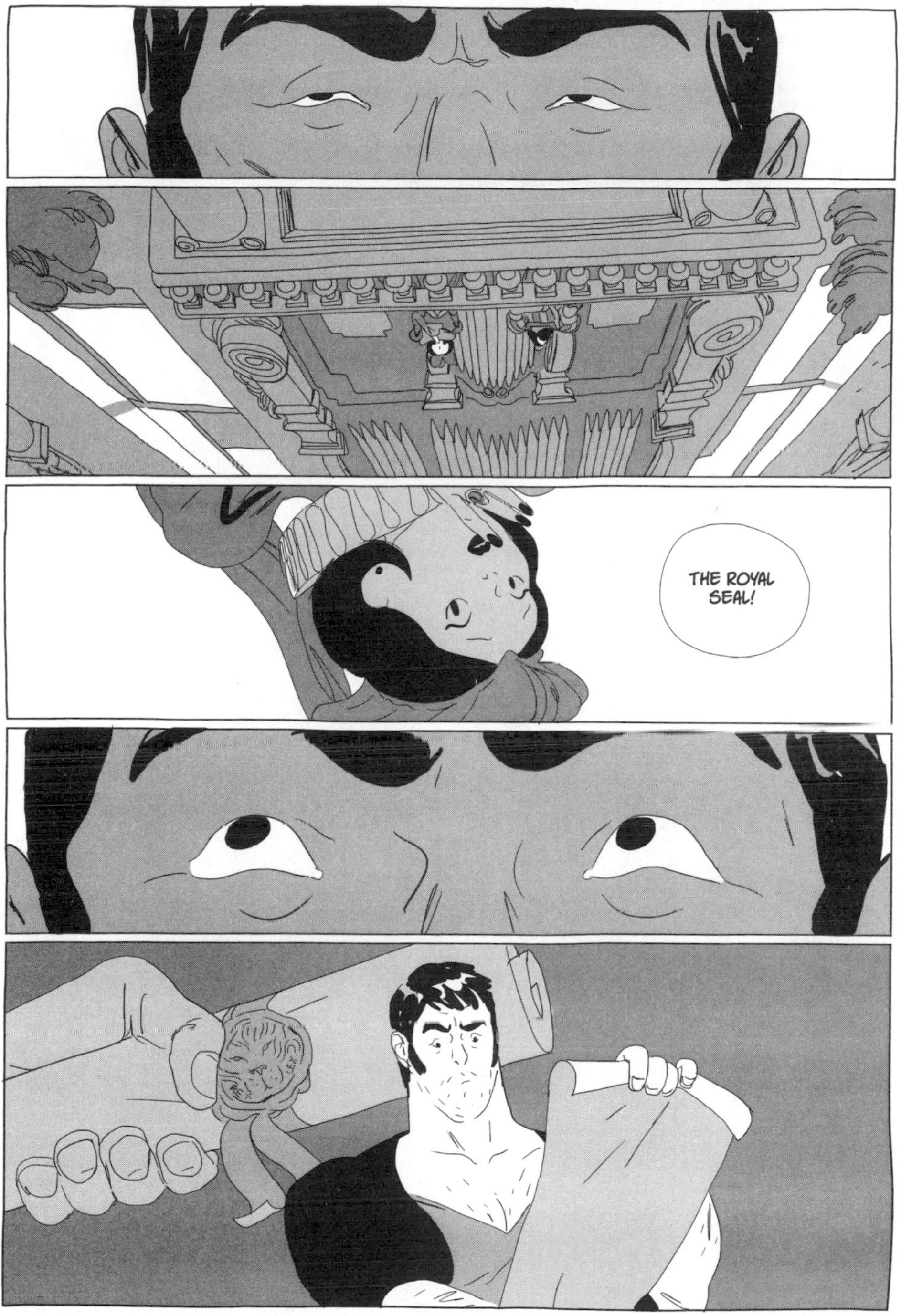
THE ROYAL SEAL!

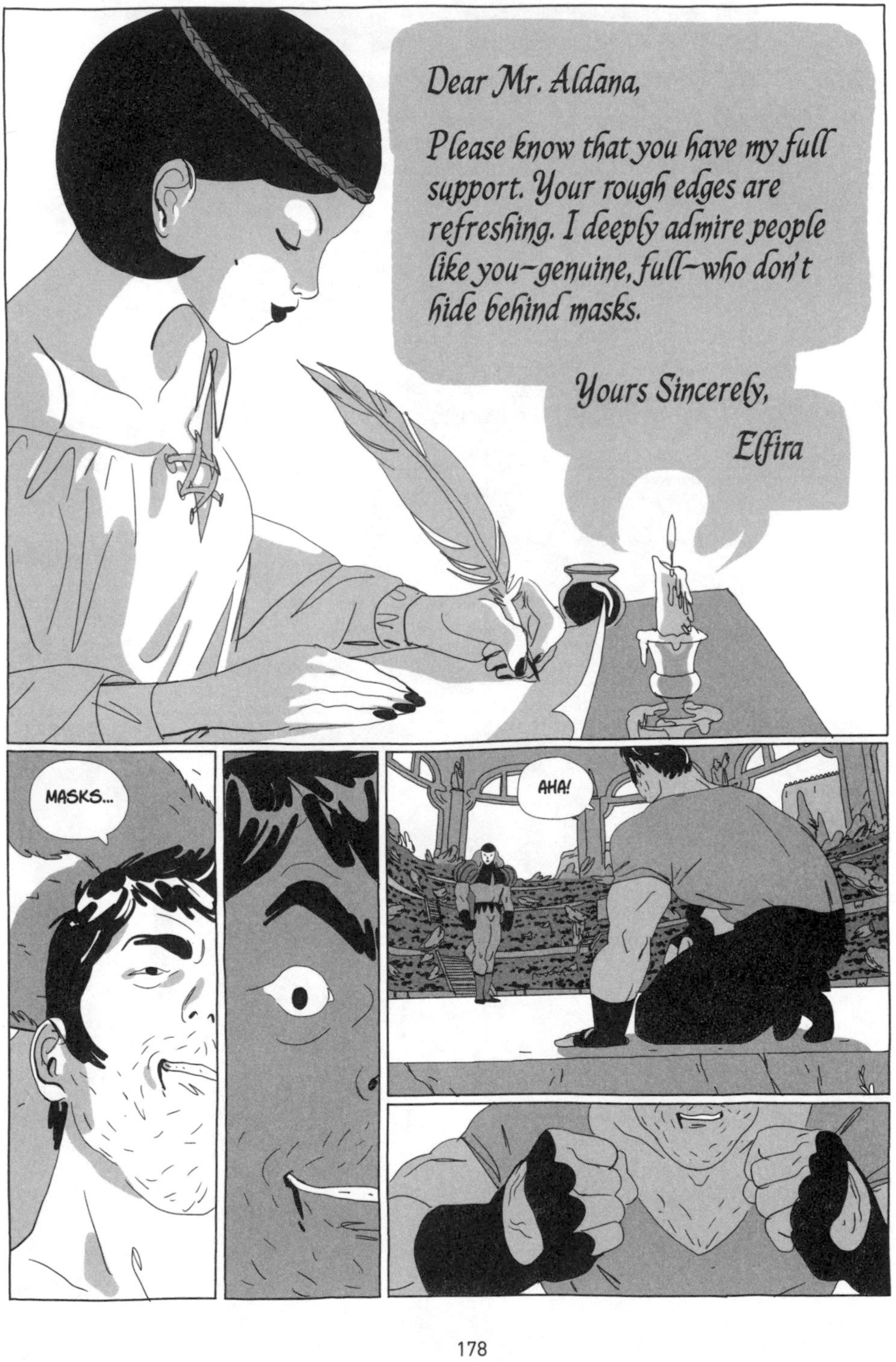
Dear Mr. Aldana,
Please know that you have my full support. Your rough edges are refreshing. I deeply admire people like you–genuine, full–who don't hide behind masks.
Yours Sincerely,
Elfira
MASKS...
AHA!

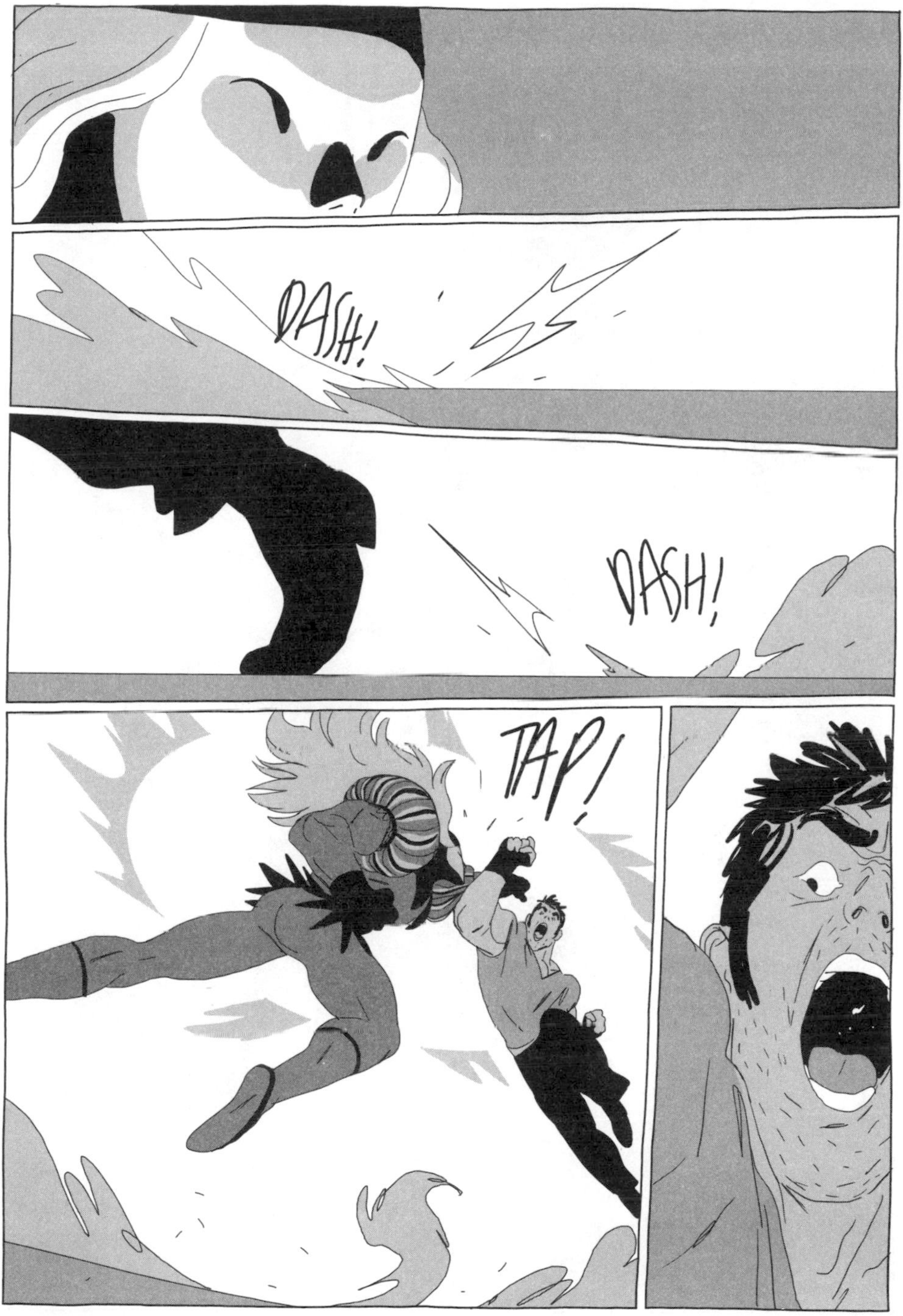
DASH!
DASH!
TAP!

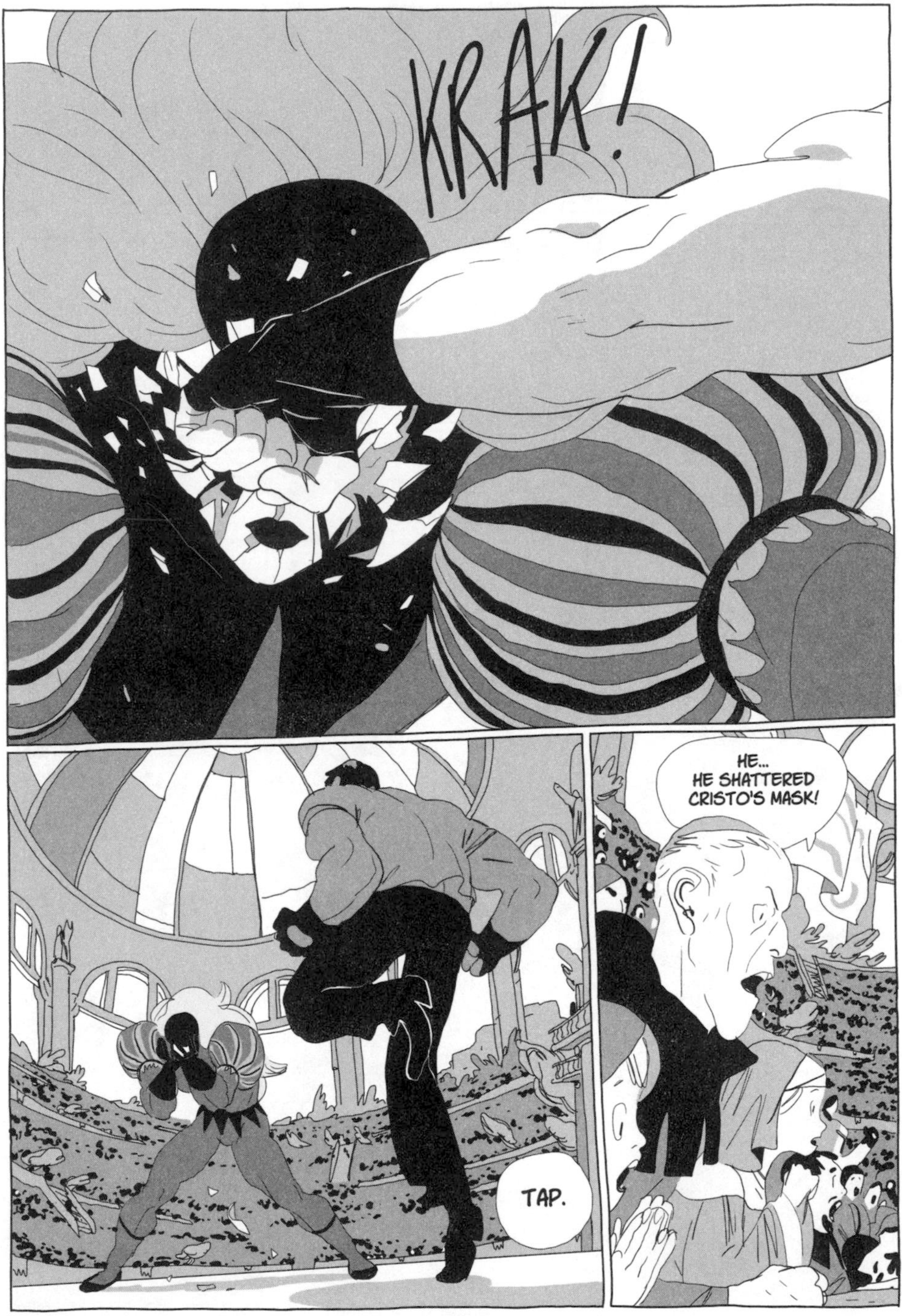
KRAK!
TAP.
HE... HE SHATTERED CRISTO'S MASK!

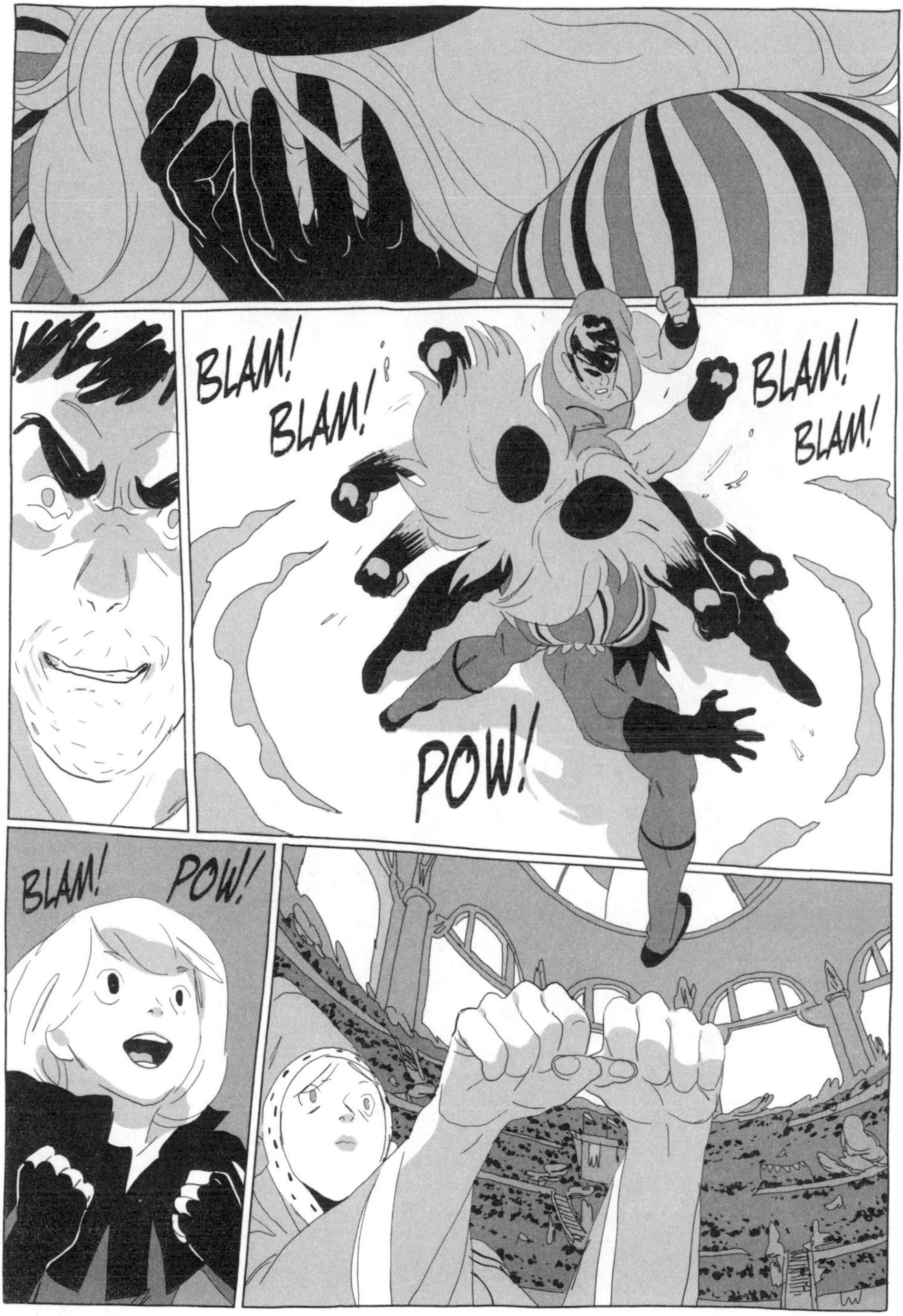
BLAM!
BLAM!
BLAM!
BLAM!
POW!
BLAM!
POW!

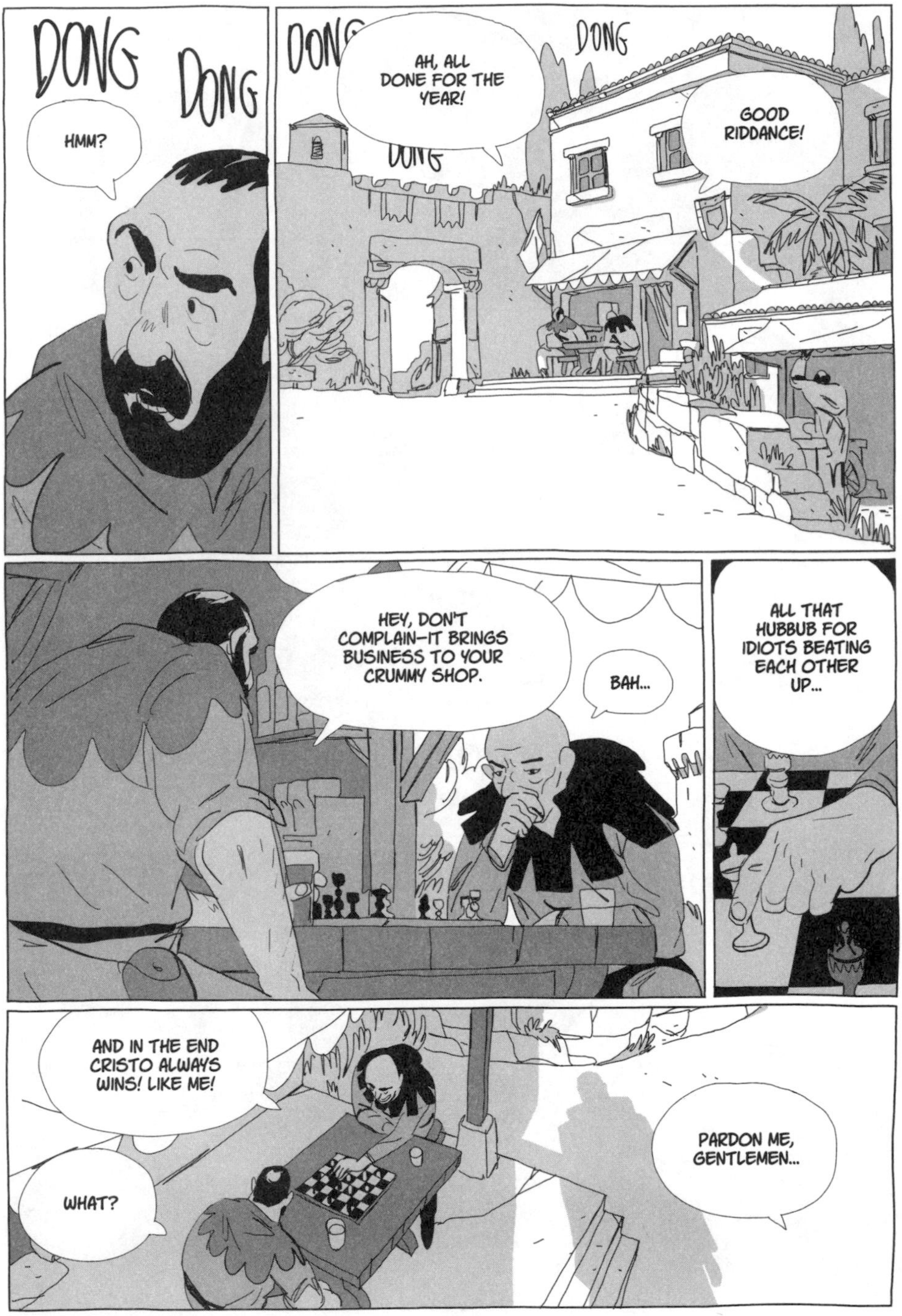
DONG
DONG
HMM?
DONG
AH, ALL DONE FOR THE YEAR!
DONG
DONG
GOOD RIDDANCE!
HEY, DON'T COMPLAIN—IT BRINGS BUSINESS TO YOUR CRUMMY SHOP.
BAH...
ALL THAT HUBBUB FOR IDIOTS BEATING EACH OTHER UP...
AND IN THE END CRISTO ALWAYS WINS! LIKE ME!
WHAT?
PARDON ME, GENTLEMEN...

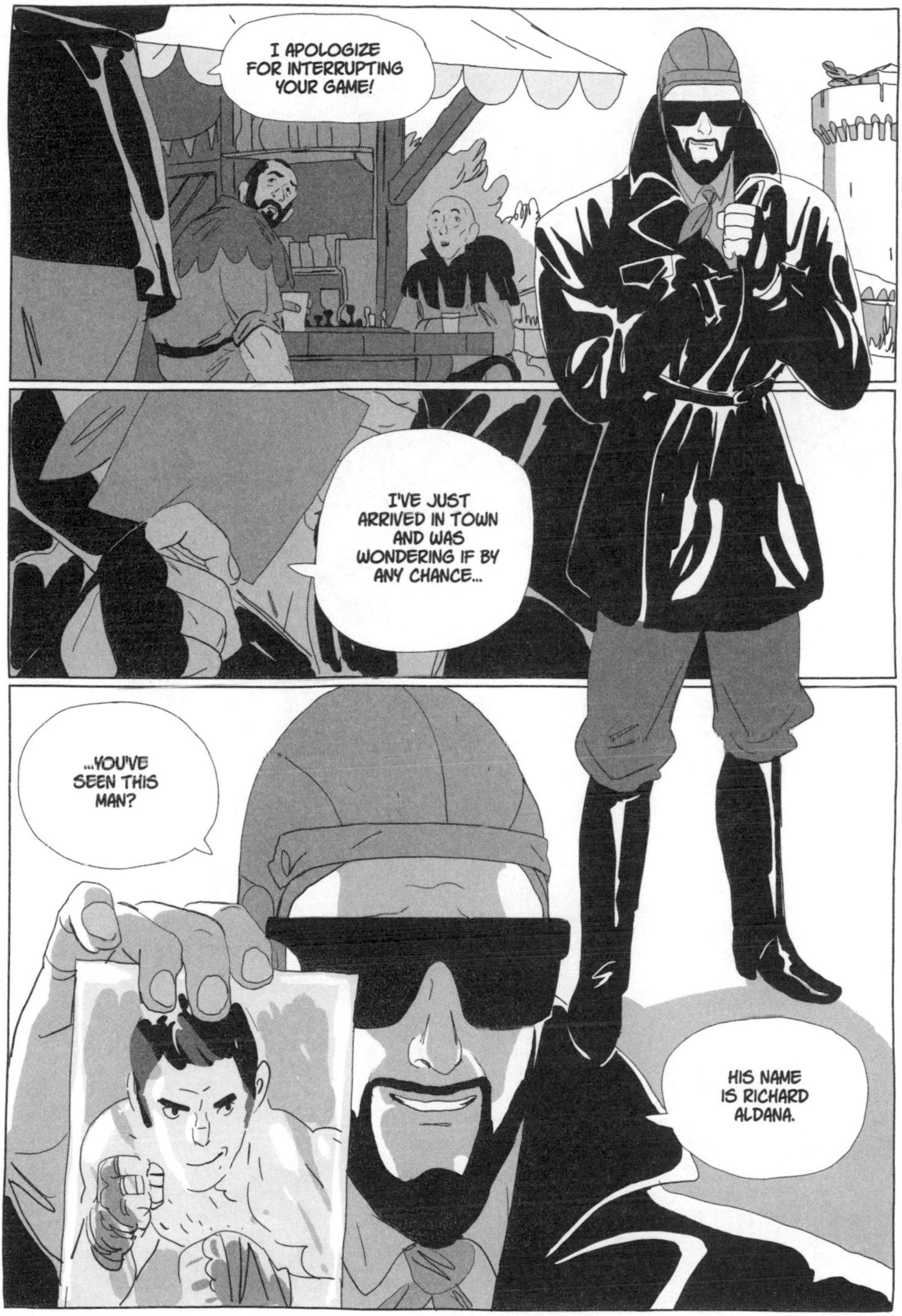
I APOLOGIZE FOR INTERRUPTING YOUR GAME!
I'VE JUST ARRIVED IN TOWN AND WAS WONDERING IF BY ANY CHANCE...
...YOU'VE SEEN THIS MAN?
HIS NAME IS RICHARD ALDANA.

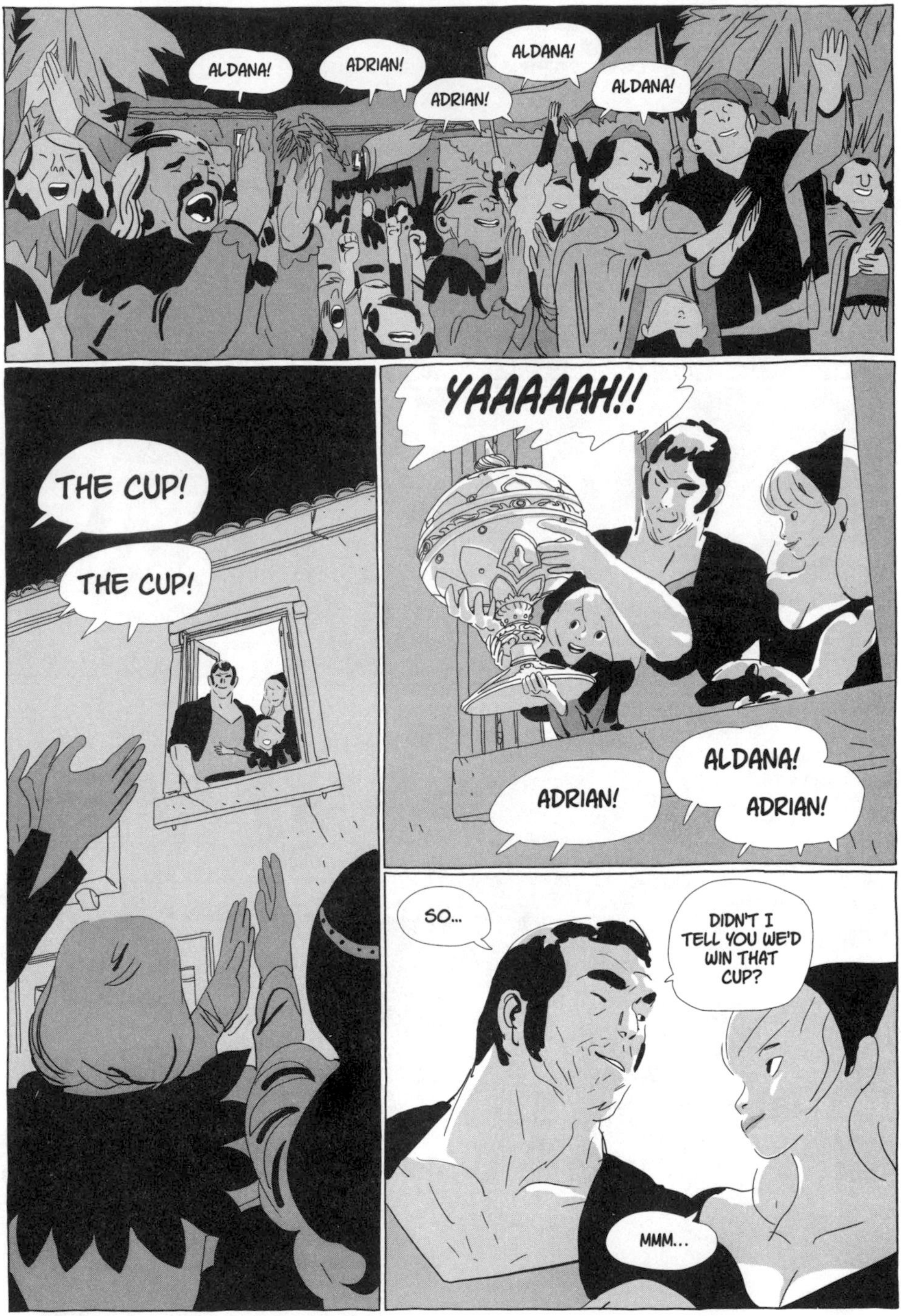

ALDANA!
ADRIAN!
ADRIAN!
ALDANA!
ALDANA!
THE CUP!
THE CUP!
YAAAAAH!!
ADRIAN!
ALDANA!
ADRIAN!
SO...
DIDN'T I TELL YOU WE'D WIN THAT CUP?
MMM...

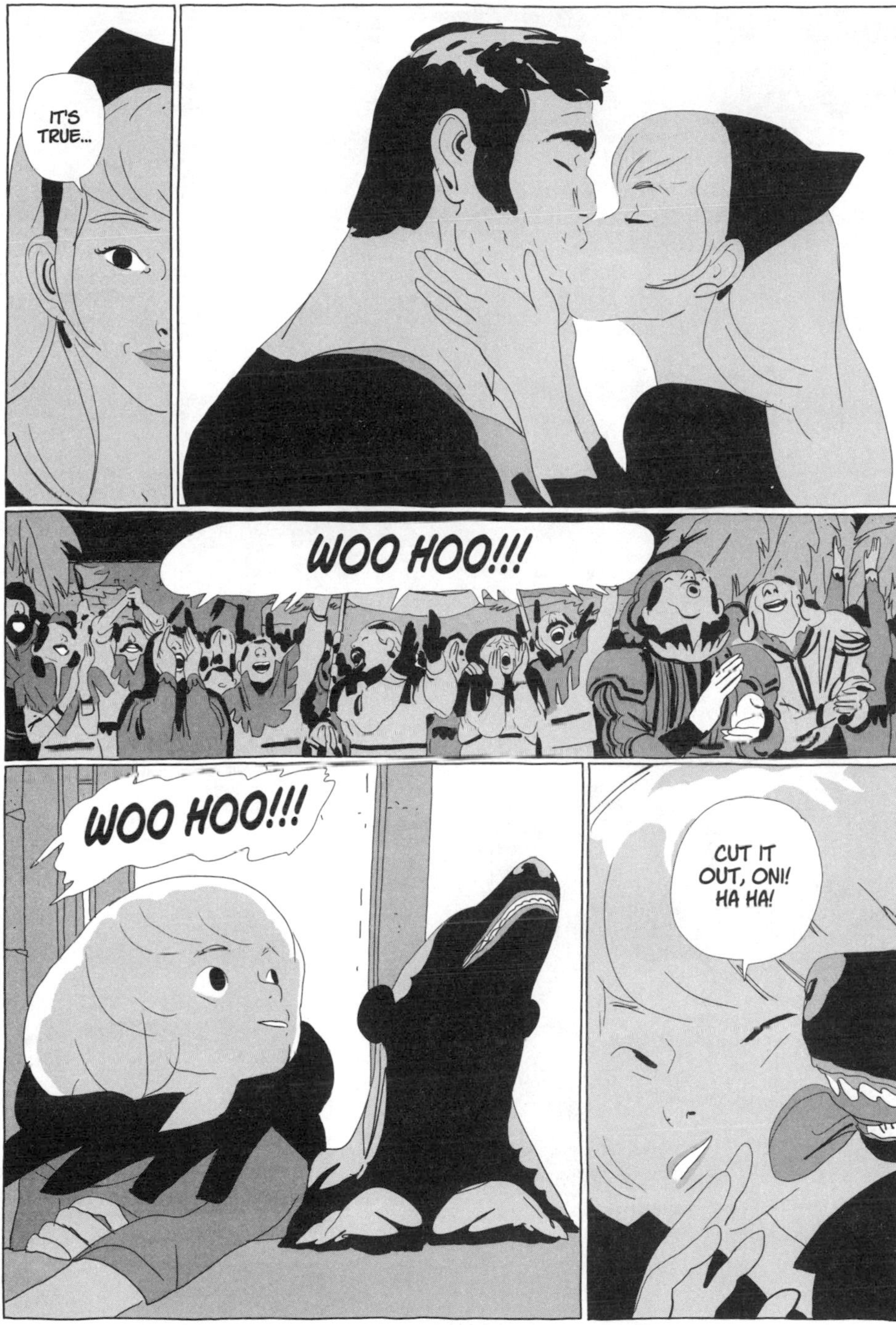
IT'S TRUE...
WOO HOO!!!
WOO HOO!!!
CUT IT OUT, ONI! HA HA!

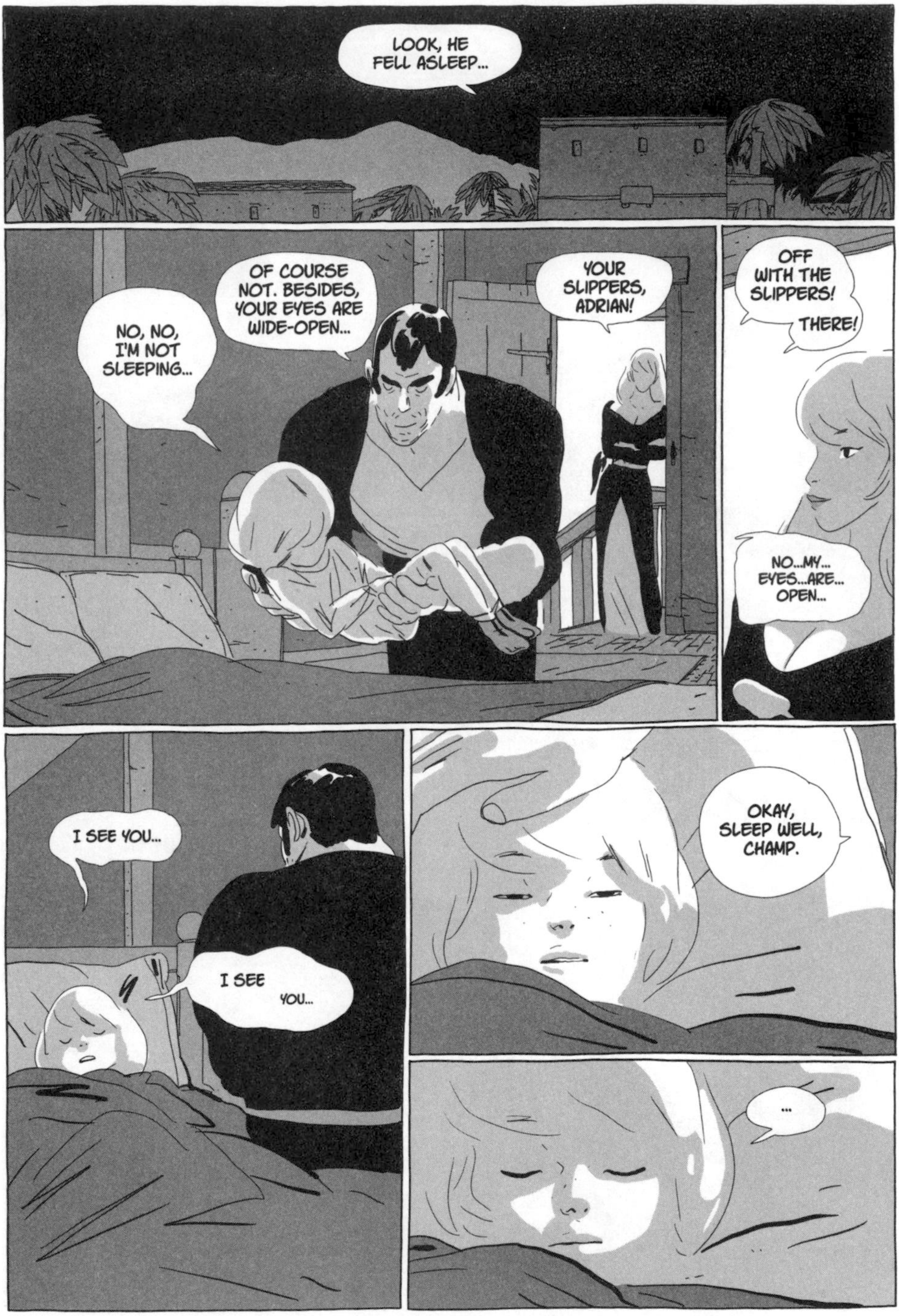
LOOK, HE FELL ASLEEP...
NO, NO, I'M NOT SLEEPING...
OF COURSE NOT. BESIDES, YOUR EYES ARE WIDE-OPEN...
YOUR SLIPPERS, ADRIAN!
OFF WITH THE SLIPPERS!
THERE!
NO...MY... EYES...ARE... OPEN...
I SEE YOU...
I SEE YOU...
OKAY, SLEEP WELL, CHAMP.
...

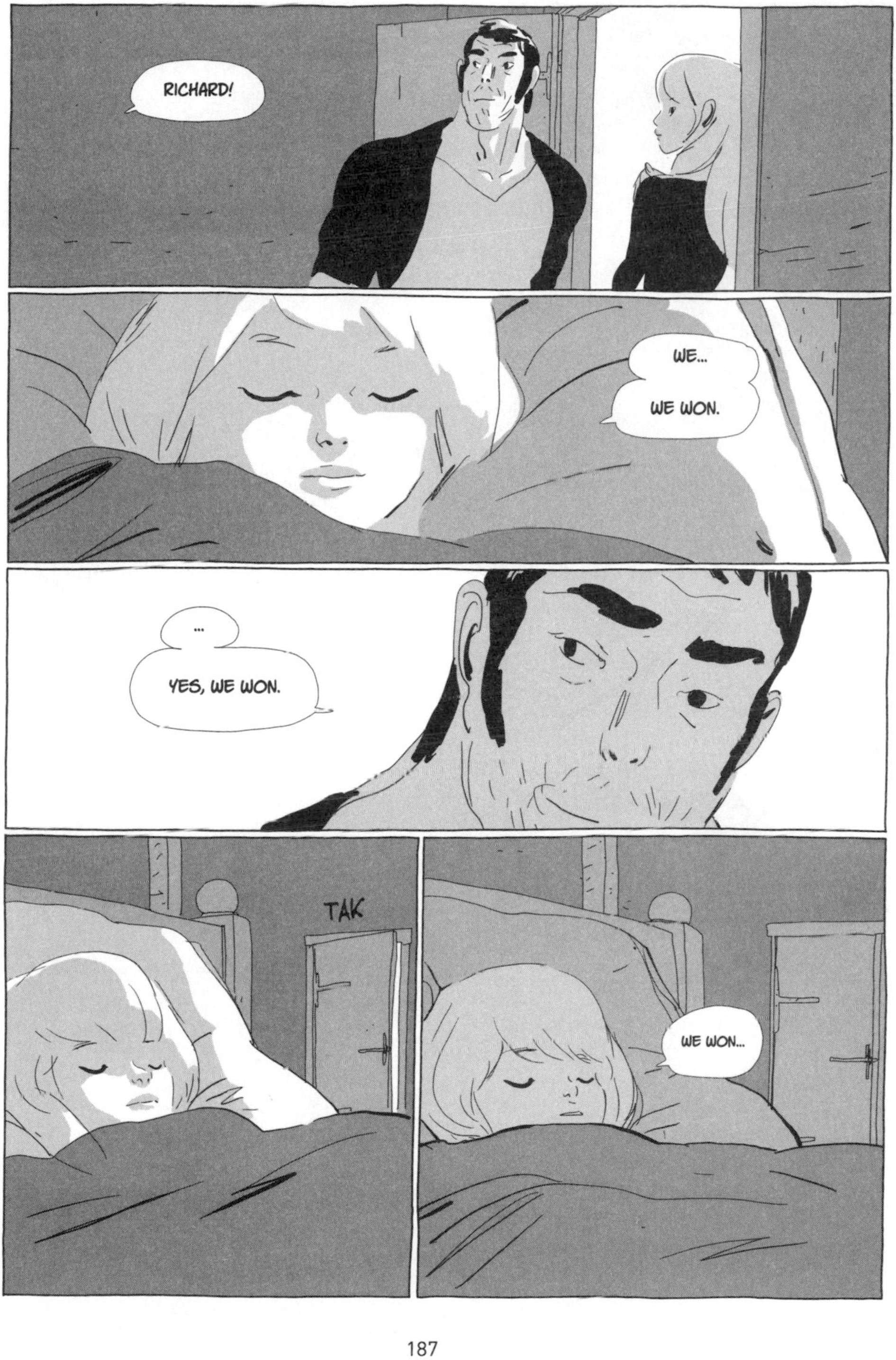
RICHARD!
WE...
WE WON.
...
YES, WE WON.
TAK
WE WON...

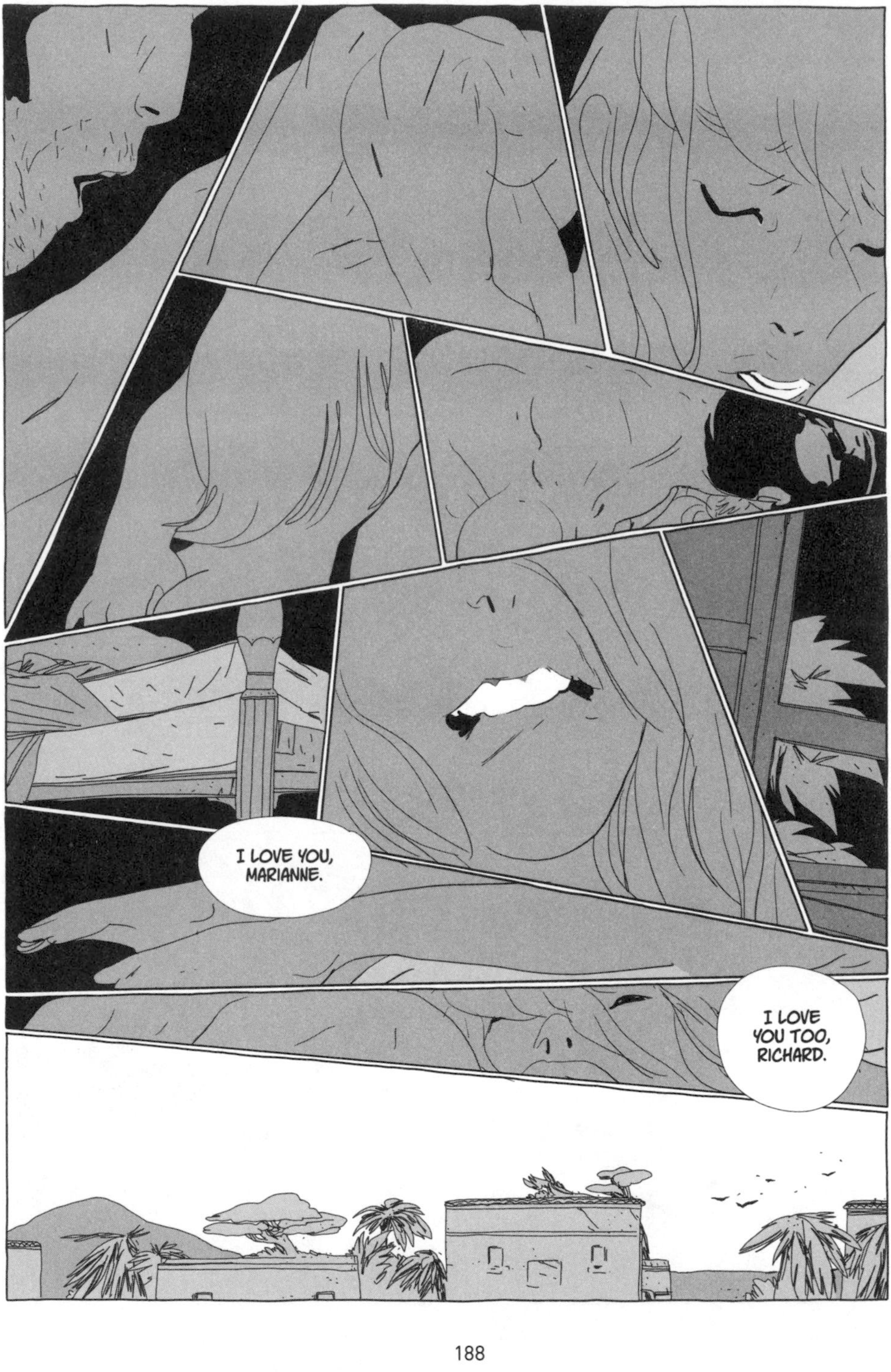
I LOVE YOU, MARIANNE.
I LOVE YOU TOO, RICHARD.

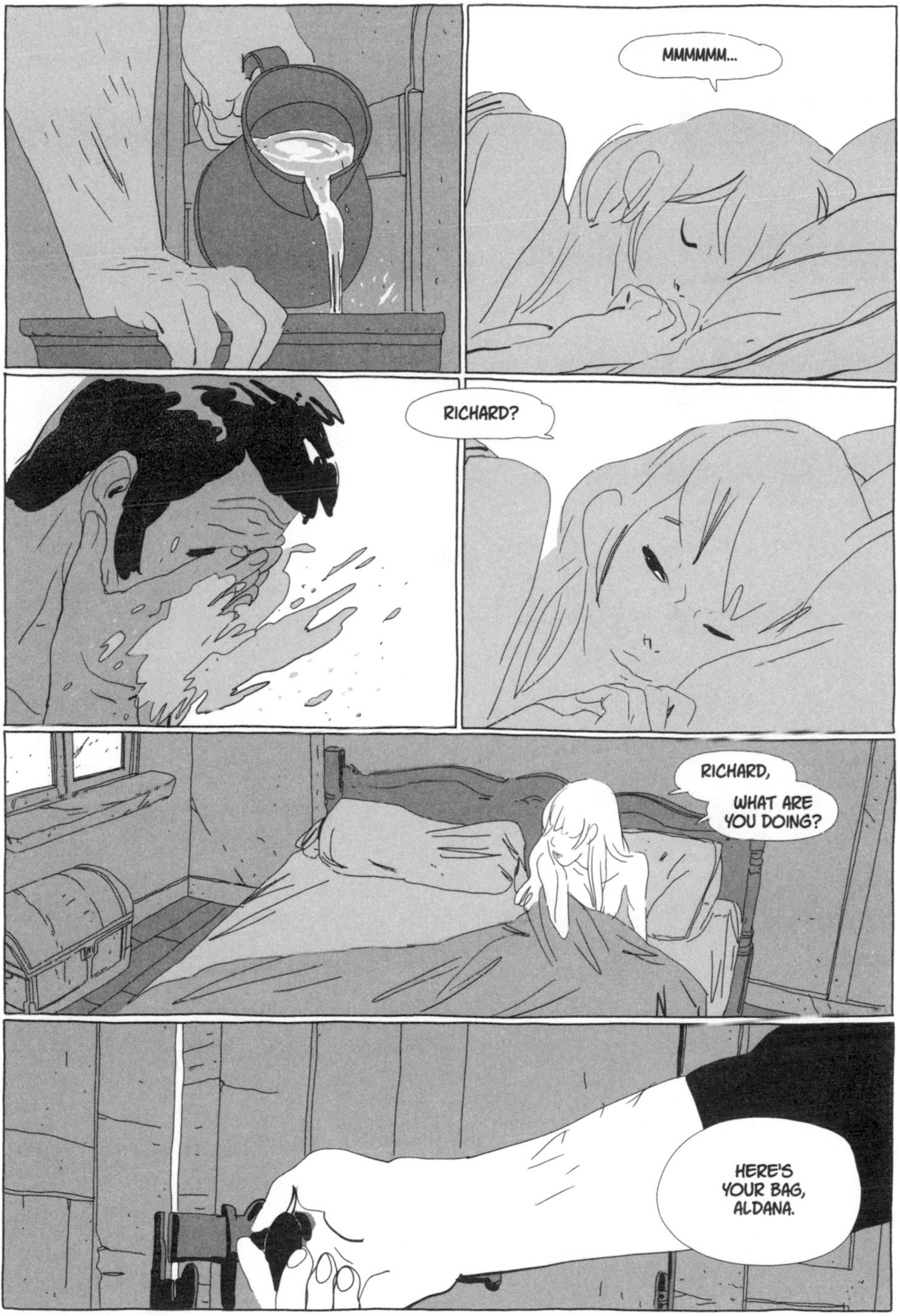
MMMMMM...
RICHARD?
RICHARD,
WHAT ARE YOU DOING?
HERE'S YOUR BAG, ALDANA.

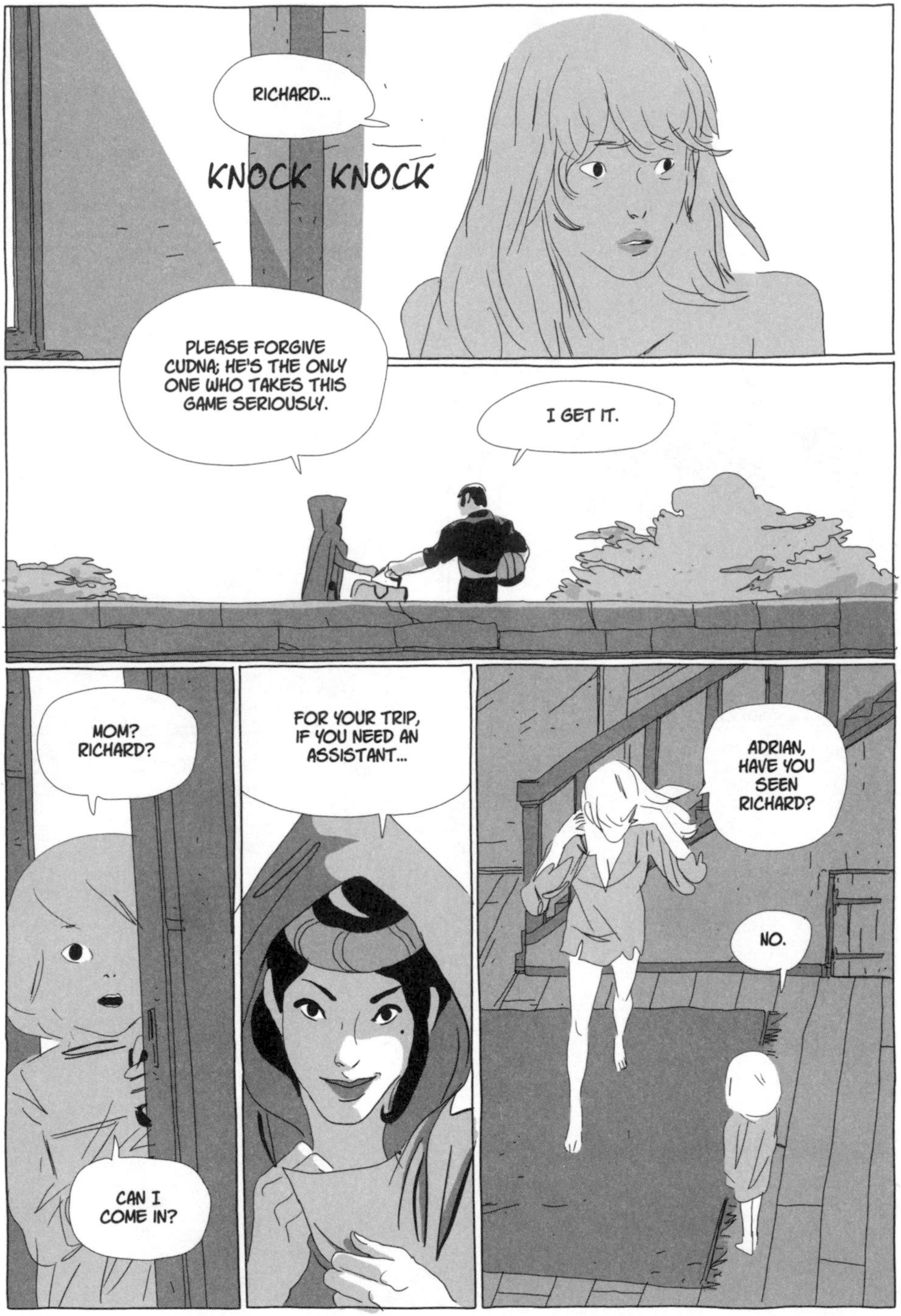
RICHARD...
KNOCK KNOCK
PLEASE FORGIVE CUDNA; HE'S THE ONLY ONE WHO TAKES THIS GAME SERIOUSLY.
I GET IT.
MOM? RICHARD?
CAN I COME IN?
FOR YOUR TRIP, IF YOU NEED AN ASSISTANT...
ADRIAN, HAVE YOU SEEN RICHARD?
NO.

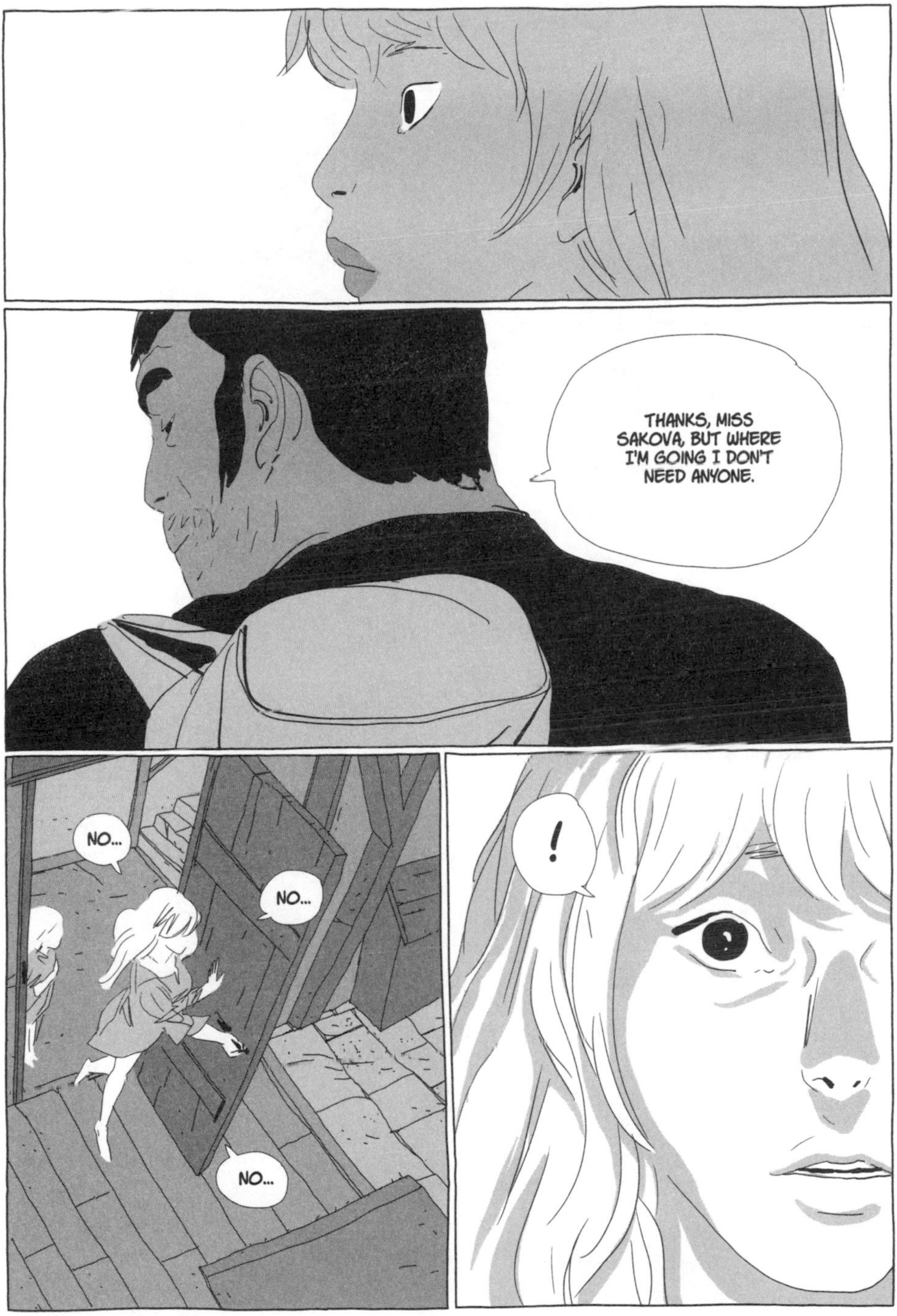
THANKS, MISS SAKOVA, BUT WHERE I'M GOING I DON'T NEED ANYONE.
NO...
NO...
NO...
!

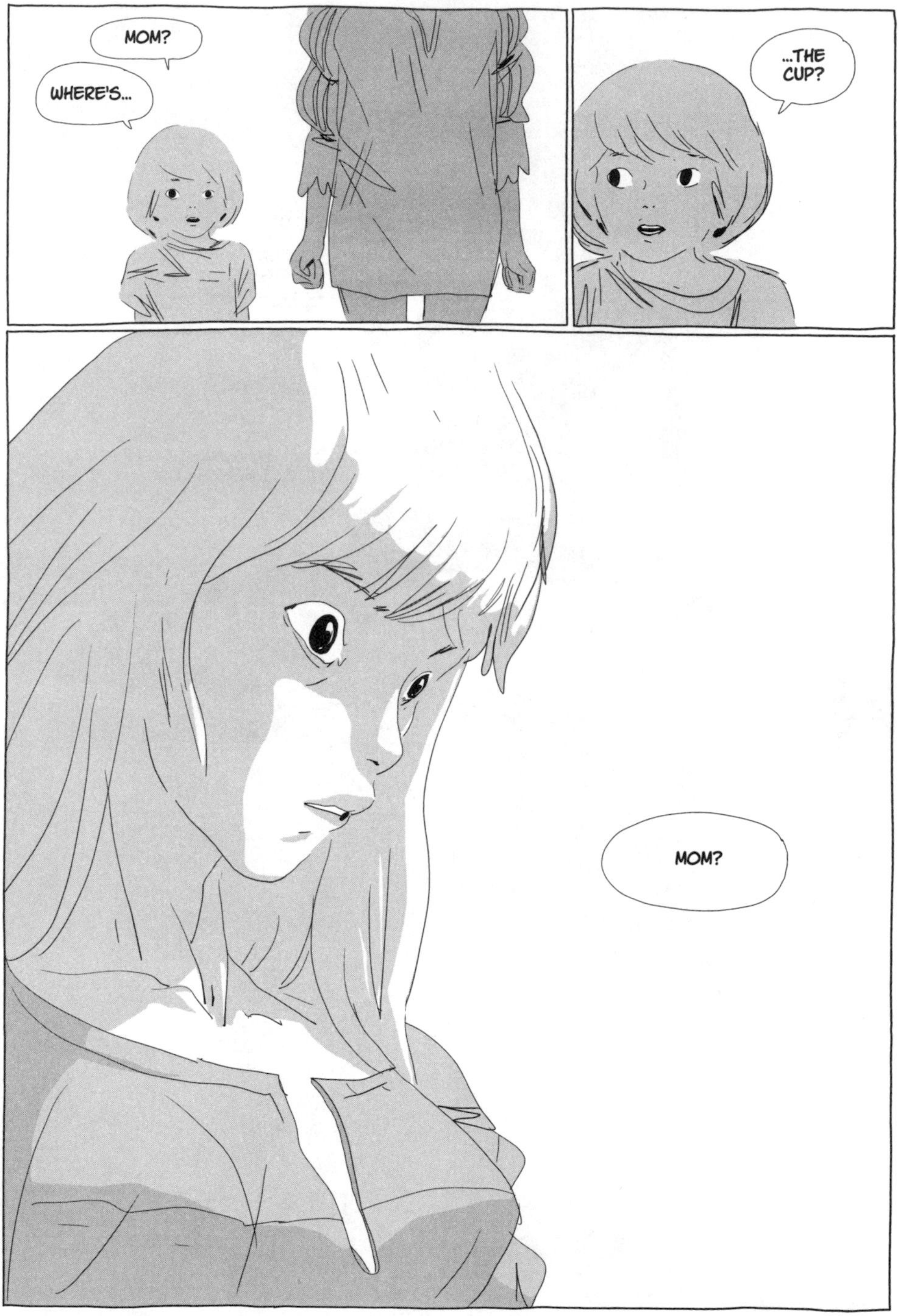
MOM?
WHERE'S...
...THE CUP?
MOM?

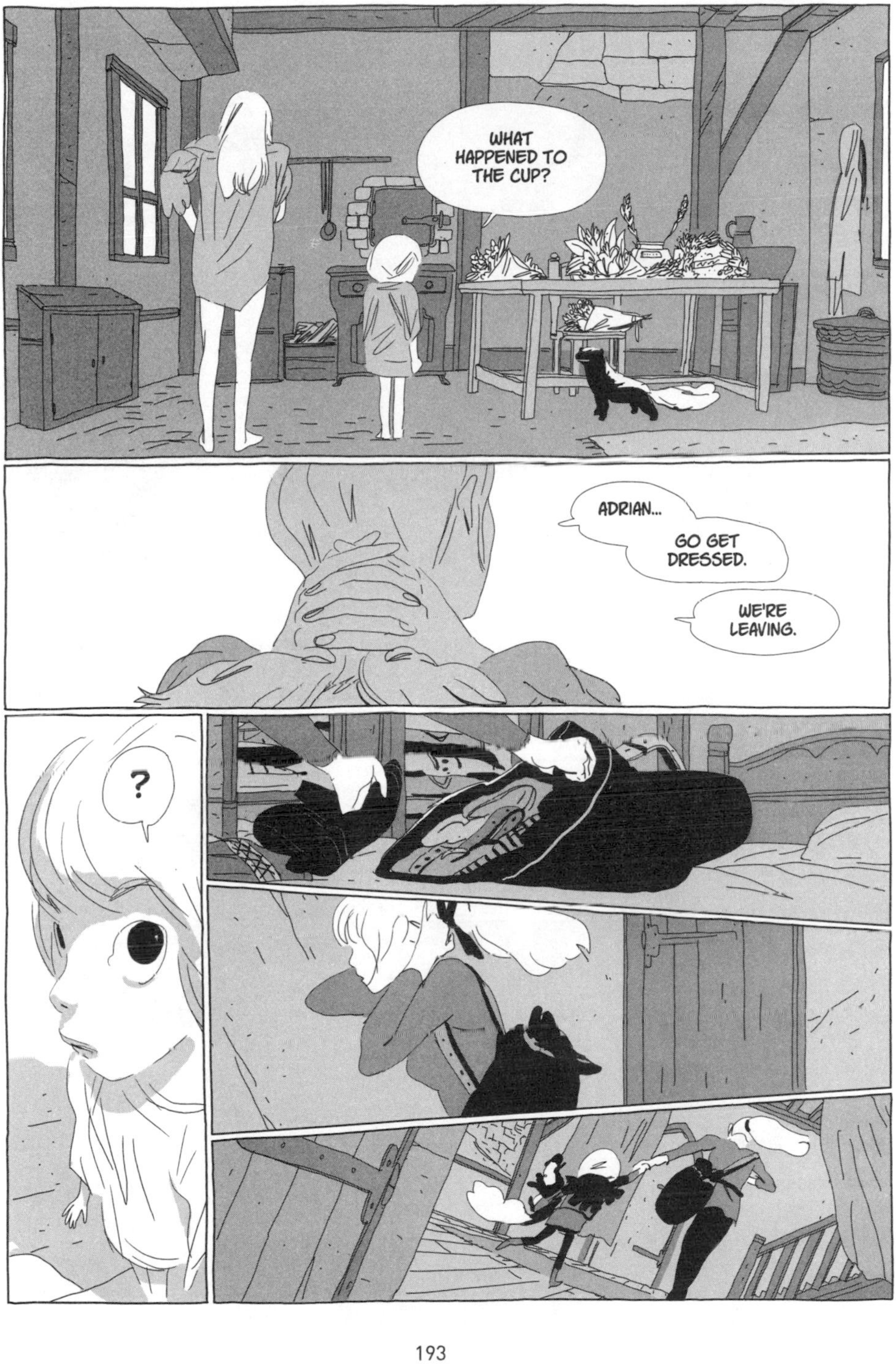
WHAT HAPPENED TO THE CUP?
ADRIAN...
GO GET DRESSED.
WE'RE LEAVING.
?

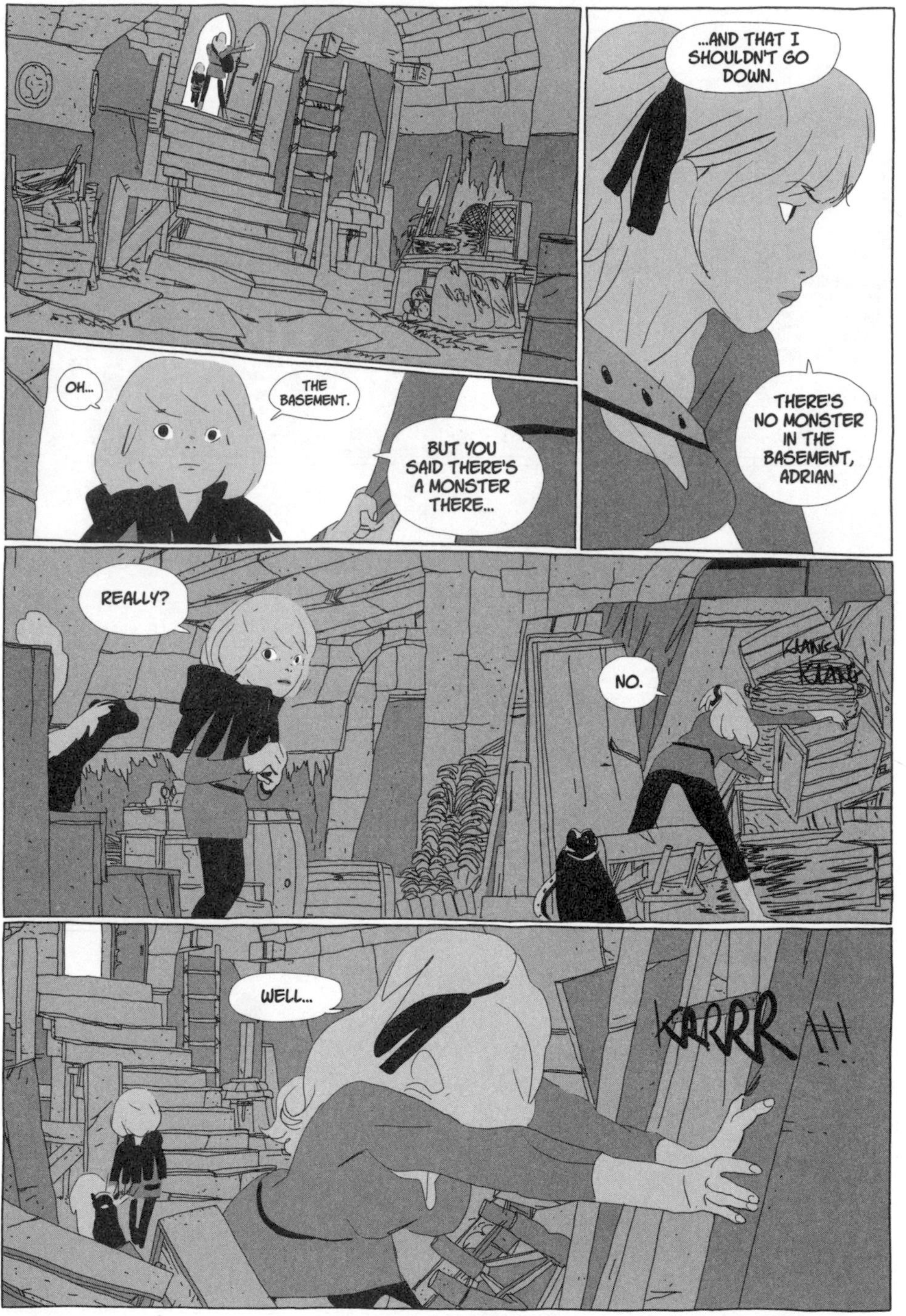
...AND THAT I SHOULDN'T GO DOWN.
OH...
THE BASEMENT.
BUT YOU SAID THERE'S A MONSTER THERE...
THERE'S NO MONSTER IN THE BASEMENT, ADRIAN.
REALLY?
NO.
KLANG KLANG
WELL...
KARRR !!!

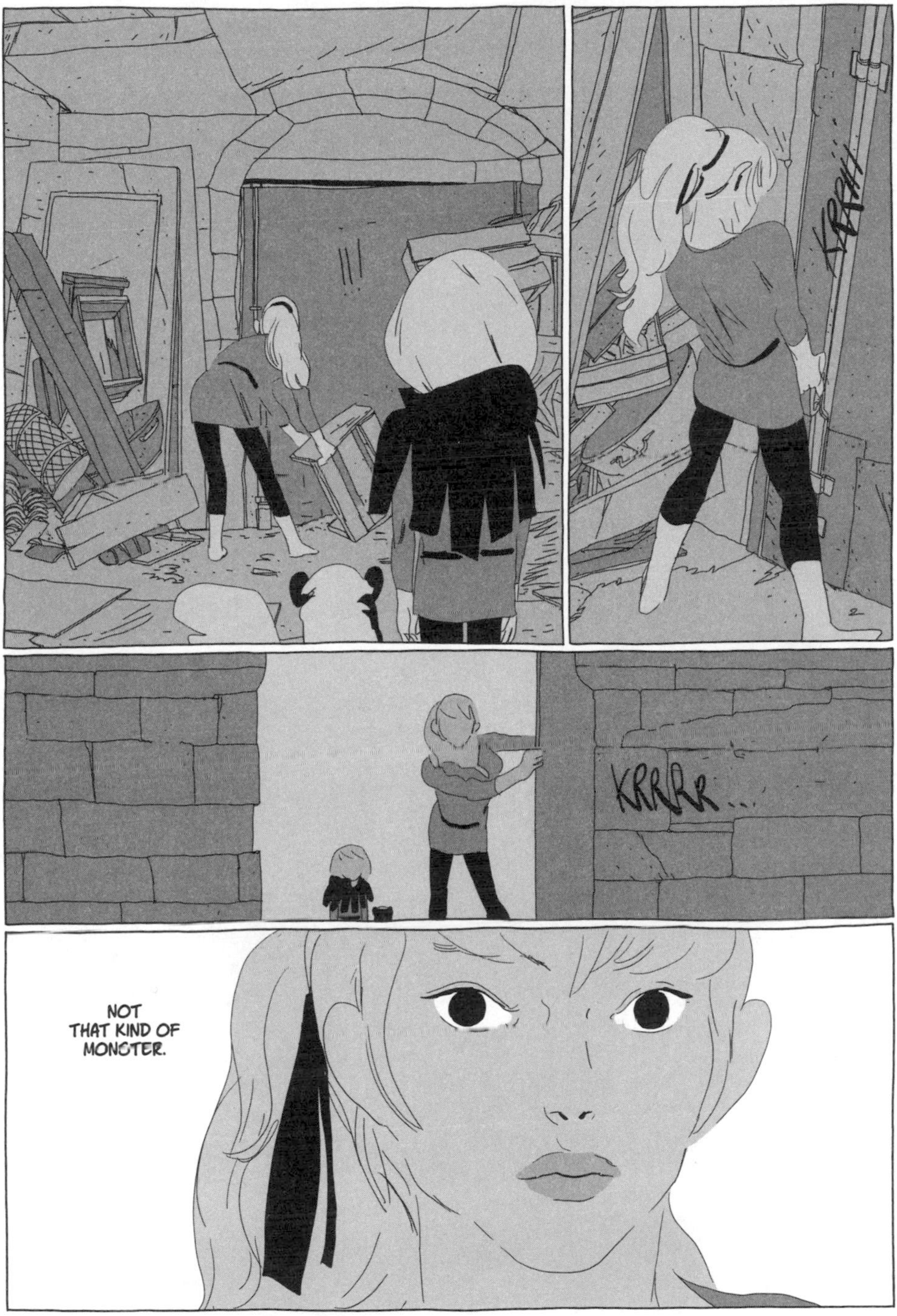
KRRH...
KRRRR...
NOT THAT KIND OF MONSTER.

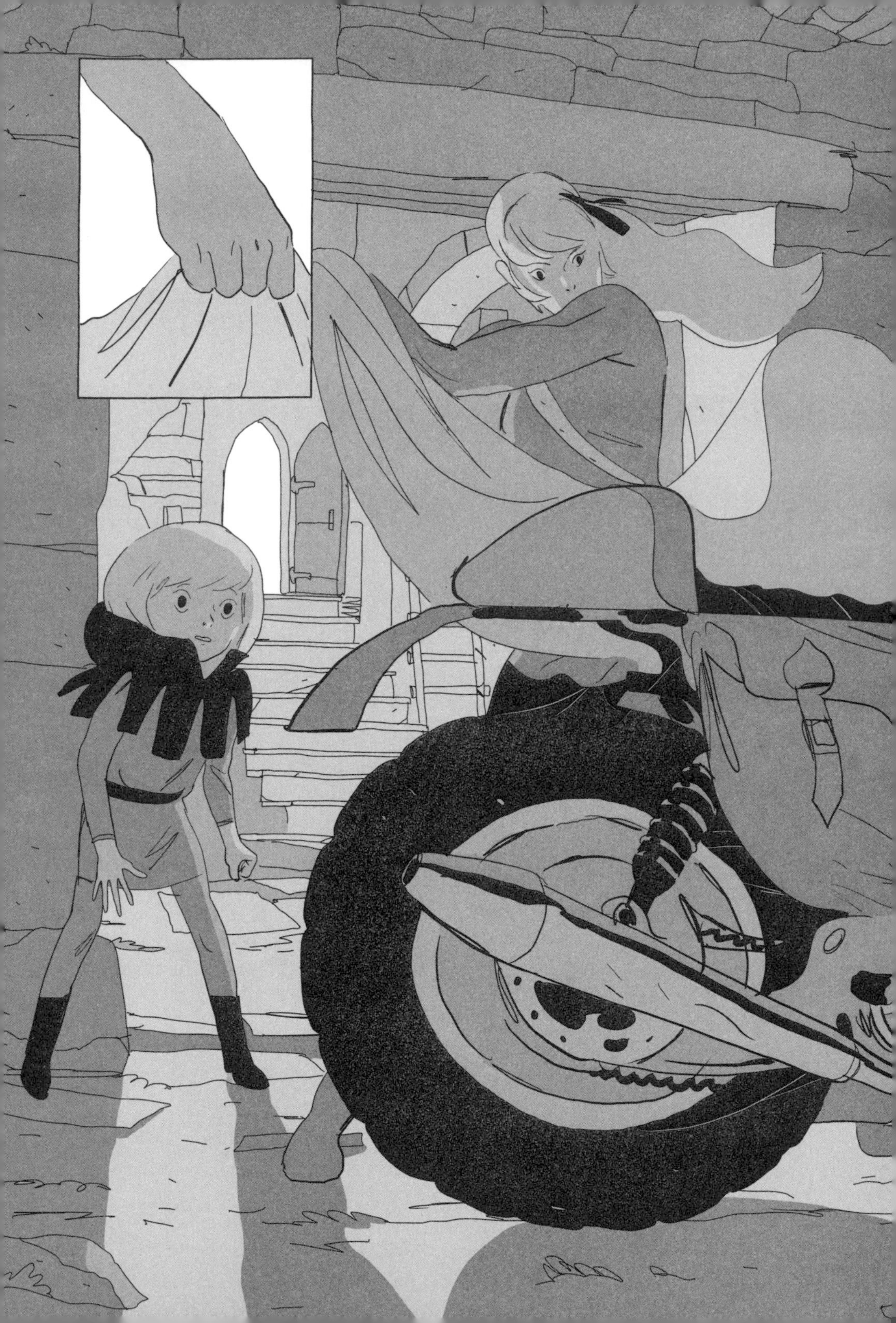

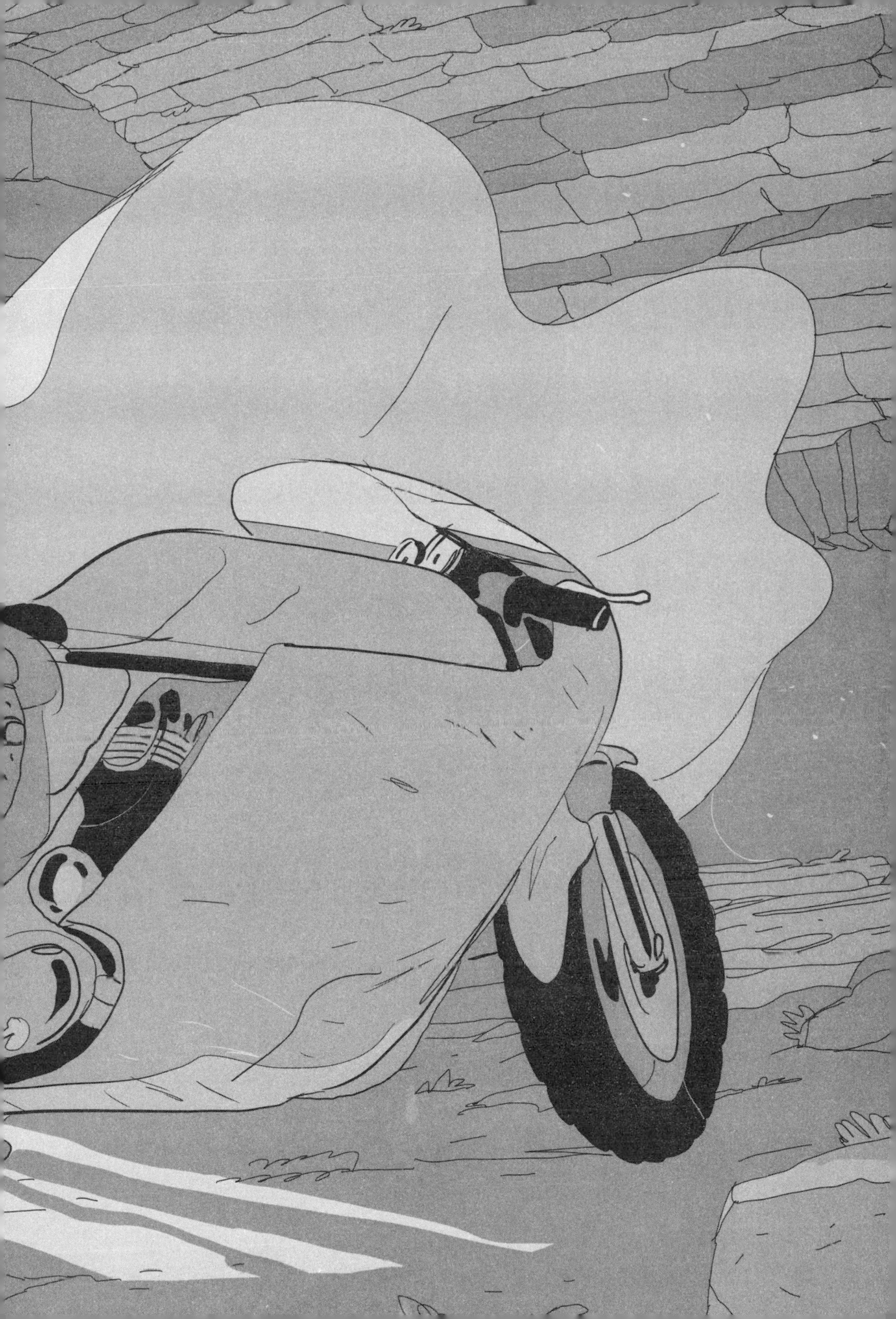

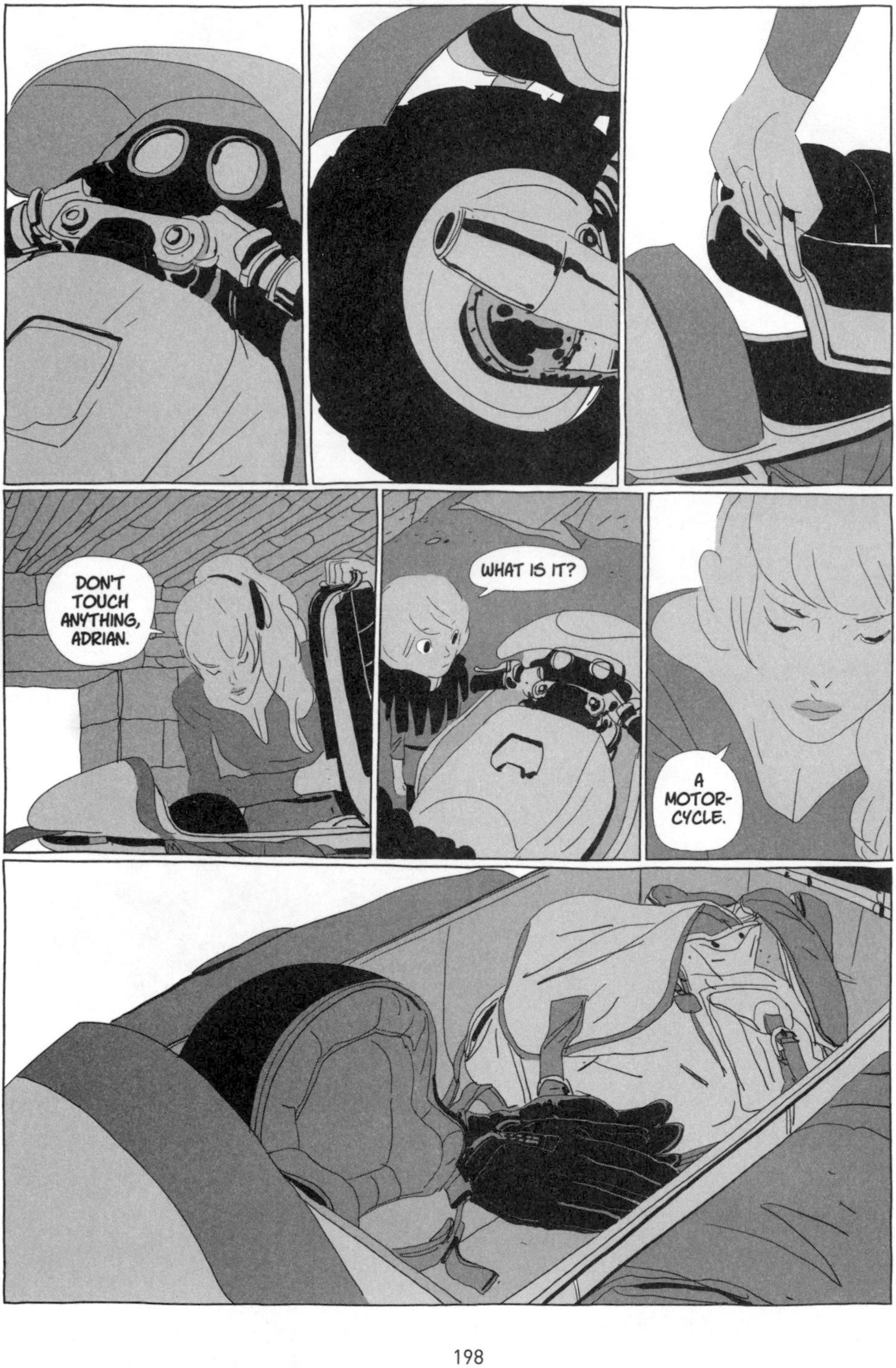
DON'T TOUCH ANYTHING, ADRIAN.
WHAT IS IT?
A MOTOR-CYCLE.

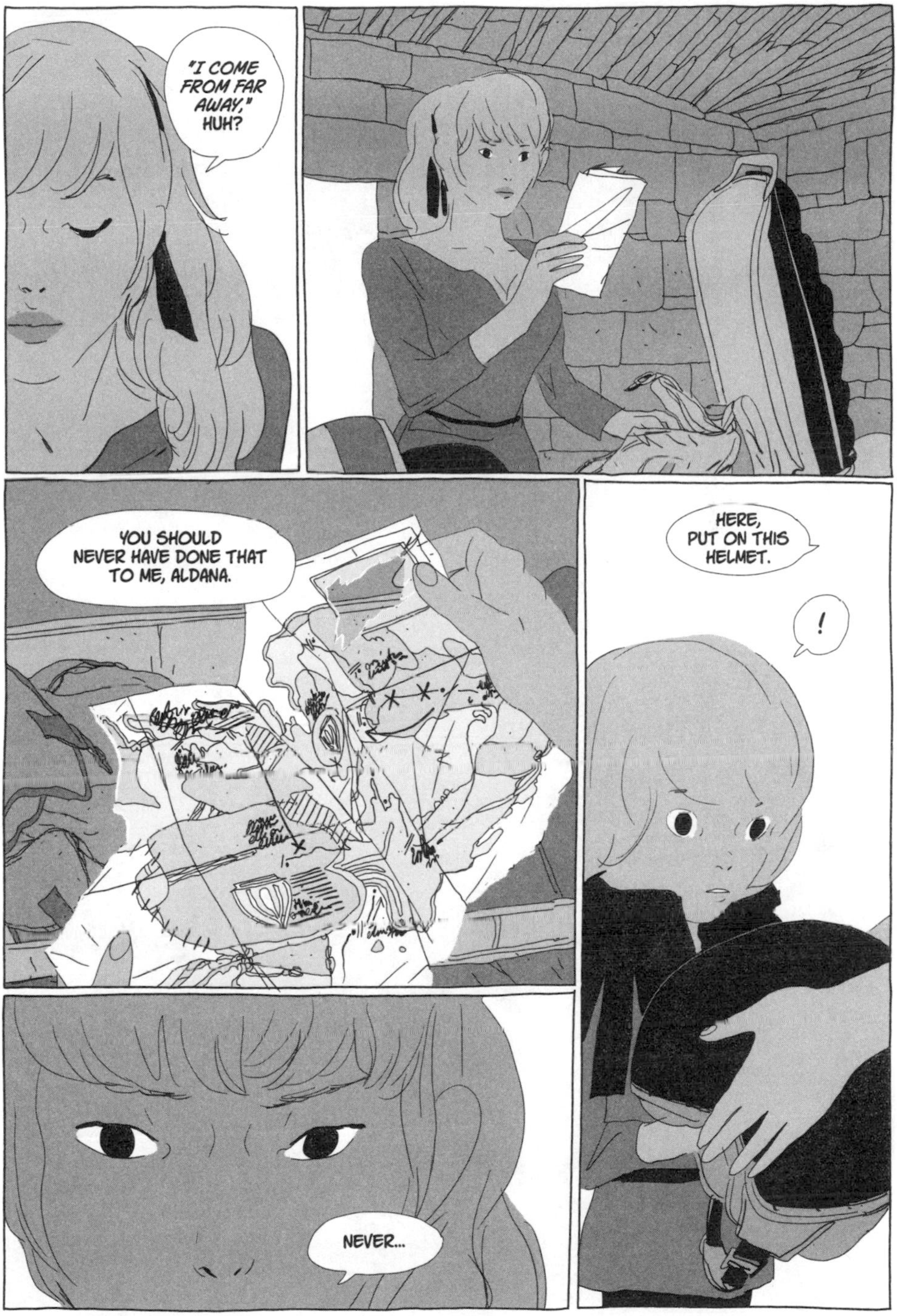
"I COME FROM FAR AWAY," HUH?
YOU SHOULD NEVER HAVE DONE THAT TO ME, ALDANA.
NEVER...
HERE, PUT ON THIS HELMET.
!

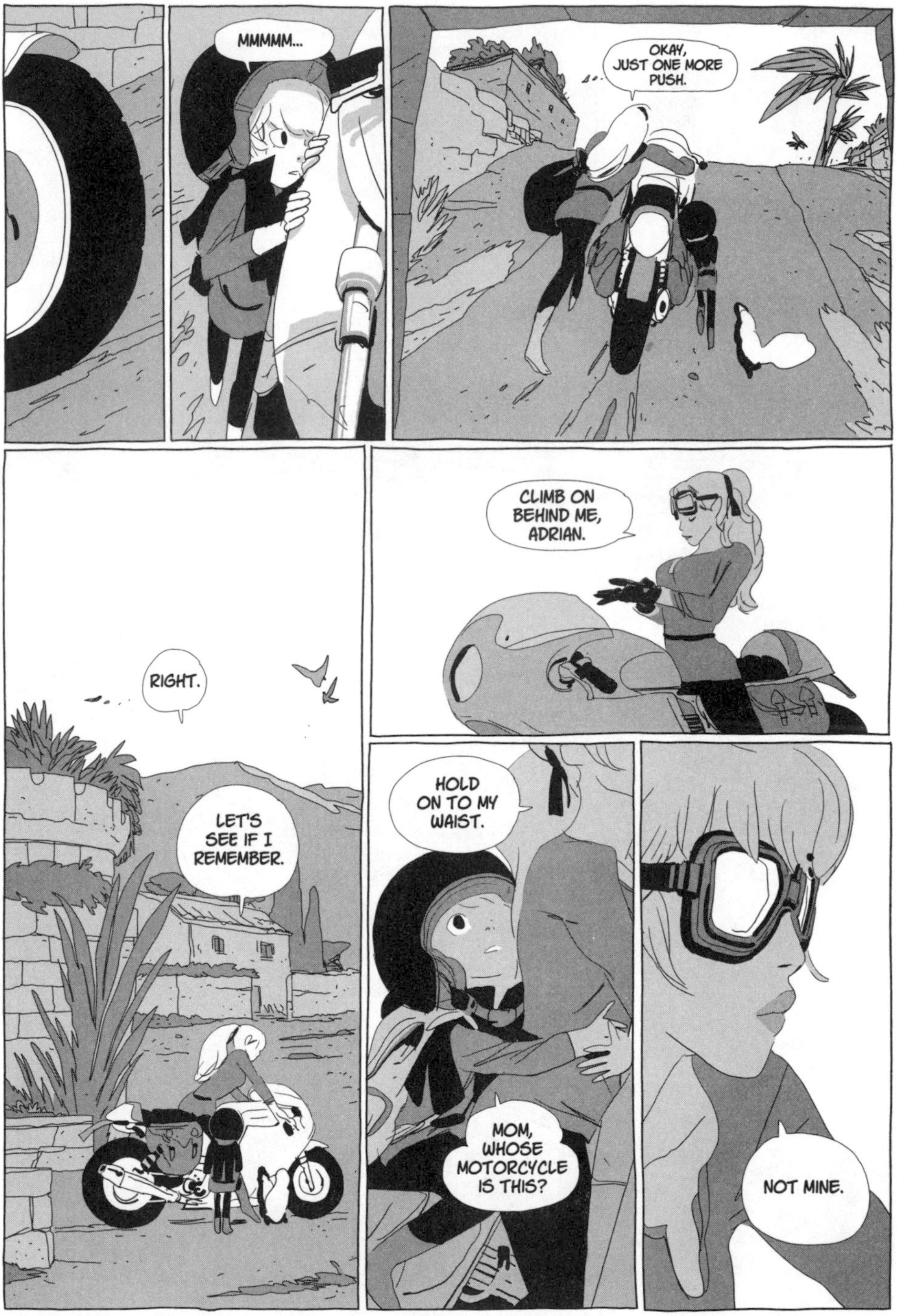
MMMMM...
OKAY, JUST ONE MORE PUSH.
RIGHT.
LET'S SEE IF I REMEMBER.
CLIMB ON BEHIND ME, ADRIAN.
HOLD ON TO MY WAIST.
MOM, WHOSE MOTORCYCLE IS THIS?
NOT MINE.

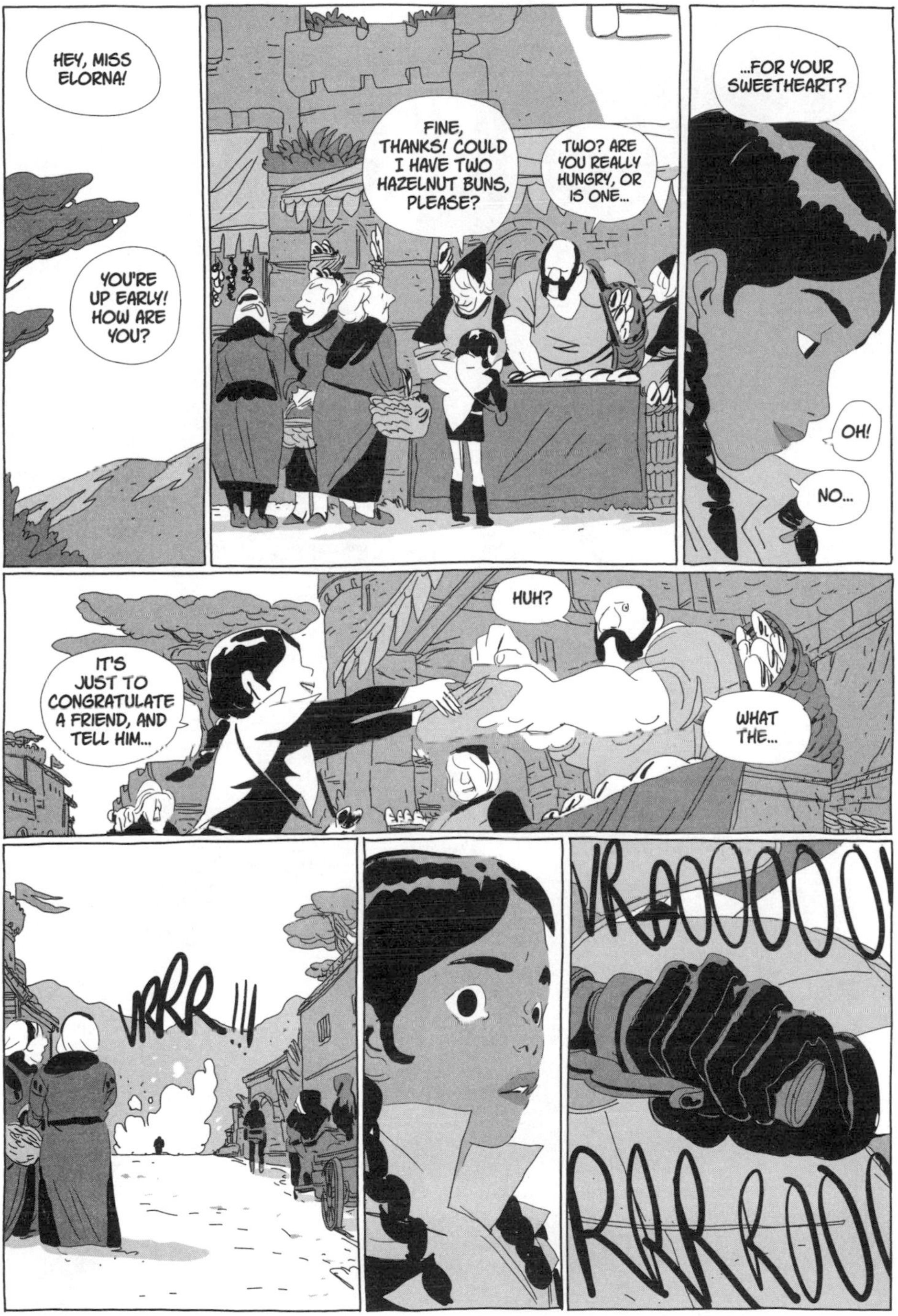

HEY, MISS ELORNA!
YOU'RE UP EARLY! HOW ARE YOU?
FINE, THANKS! COULD I HAVE TWO HAZELNUT BUNS, PLEASE?
TWO? ARE YOU REALLY HUNGRY, OR IS ONE...
...FOR YOUR SWEETHEART?
OH!
NO...
IT'S JUST TO CONGRATULATE A FRIEND, AND TELL HIM...
HUH?
WHAT THE...
VRRR !!!
VROOOOOO
RRR ROO

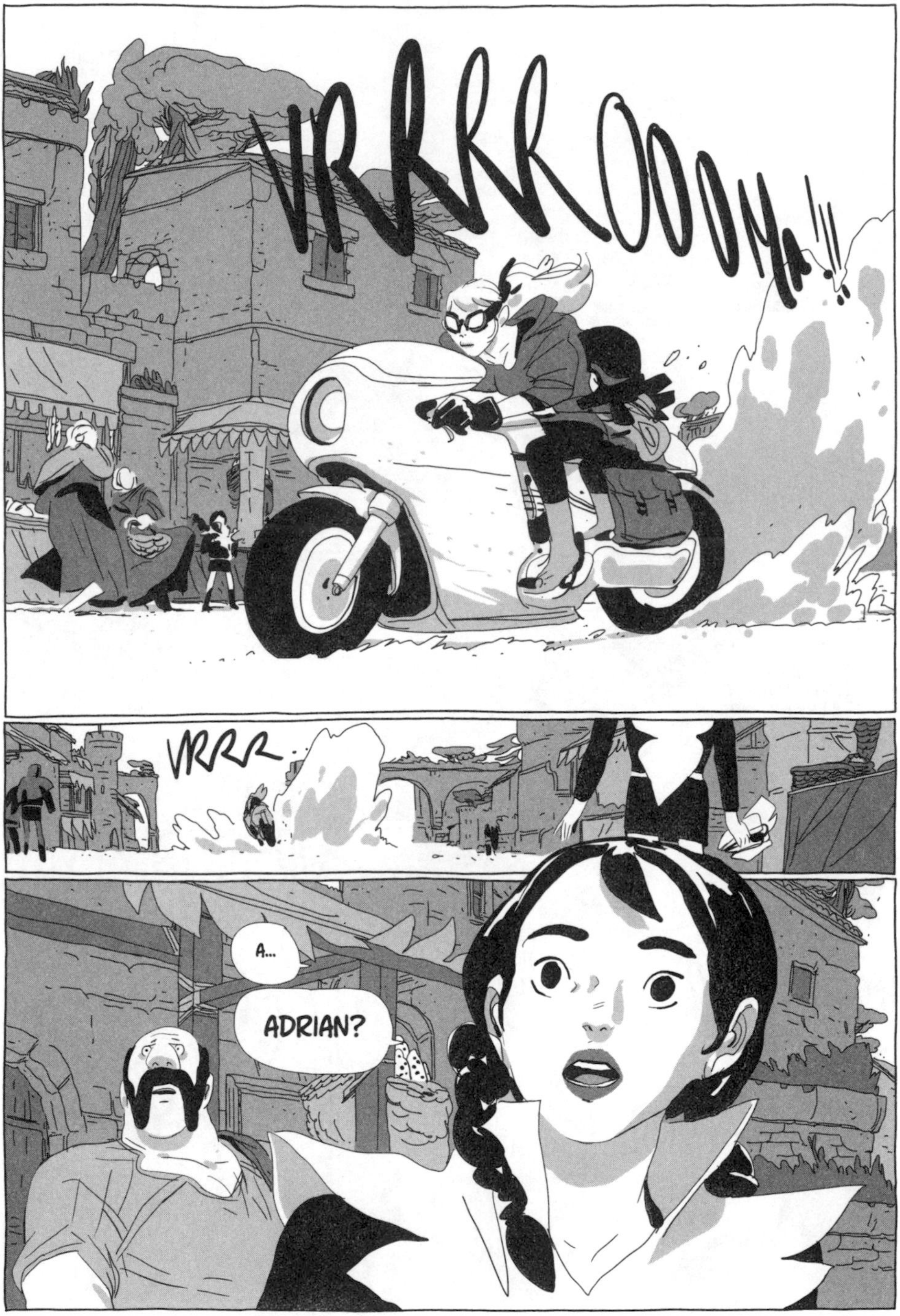
VRRRROOOOM!!!
VRRR
A...
ADRIAN?

Read on for a preview of

LAST man

3

The Chase

Balak + Sanlaville + Vivès

Available in October 2015 by First Second Books

First Second

ISBN 978-1-62672-048-0

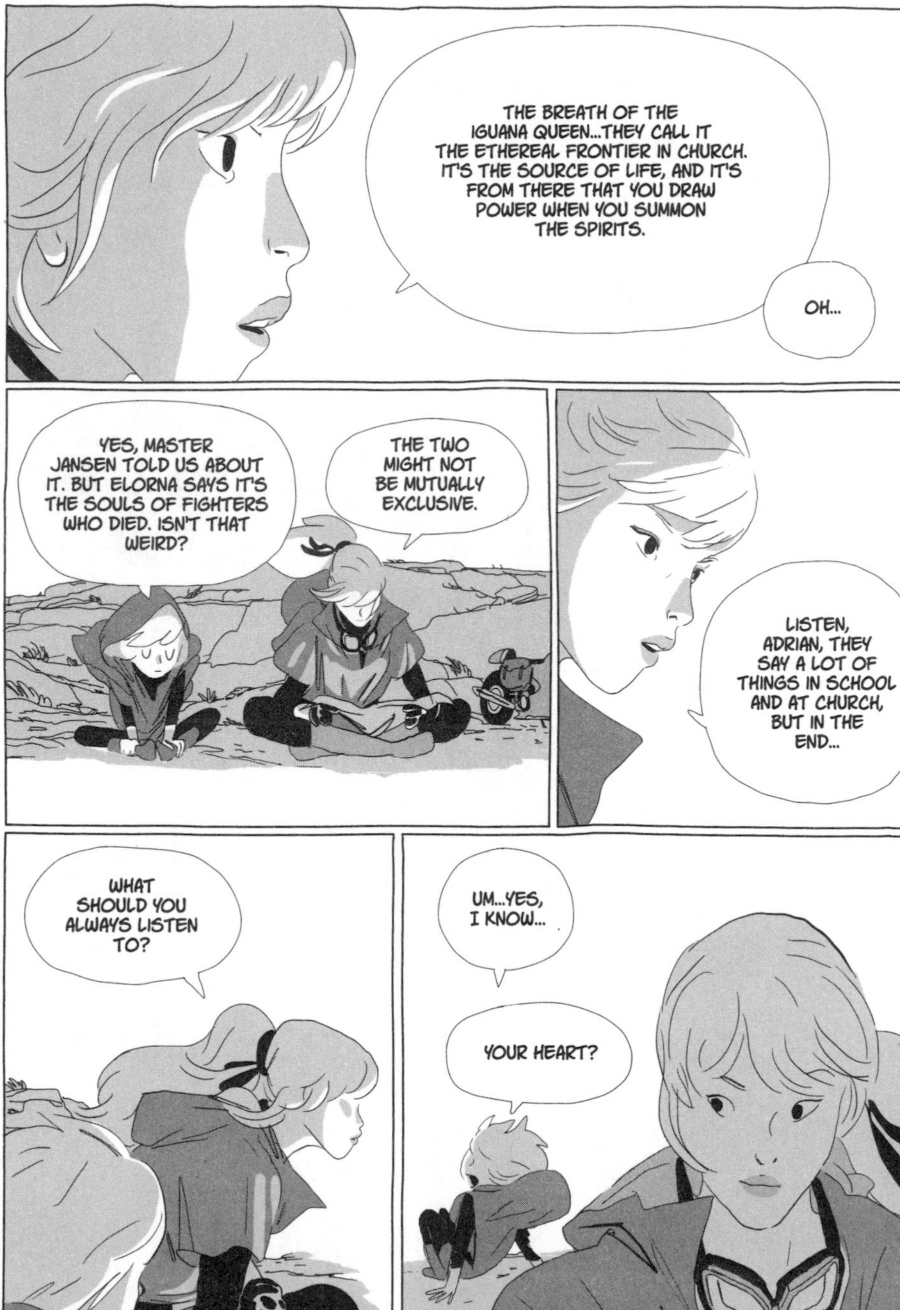
THE BREATH OF THE IGUANA QUEEN...THEY CALL IT THE ETHEREAL FRONTIER IN CHURCH. IT'S THE SOURCE OF LIFE, AND IT'S FROM THERE THAT YOU DRAW POWER WHEN YOU SUMMON THE SPIRITS.
OH...
YES, MASTER JANSEN TOLD US ABOUT IT. BUT ELORNA SAYS IT'S THE SOULS OF FIGHTERS WHO DIED. ISN'T THAT WEIRD?
THE TWO MIGHT NOT BE MUTUALLY EXCLUSIVE.
LISTEN, ADRIAN, THEY SAY A LOT OF THINGS IN SCHOOL AND AT CHURCH, BUT IN THE END...
WHAT SHOULD YOU ALWAYS LISTEN TO?
UM...YES, I KNOW...
YOUR HEART?

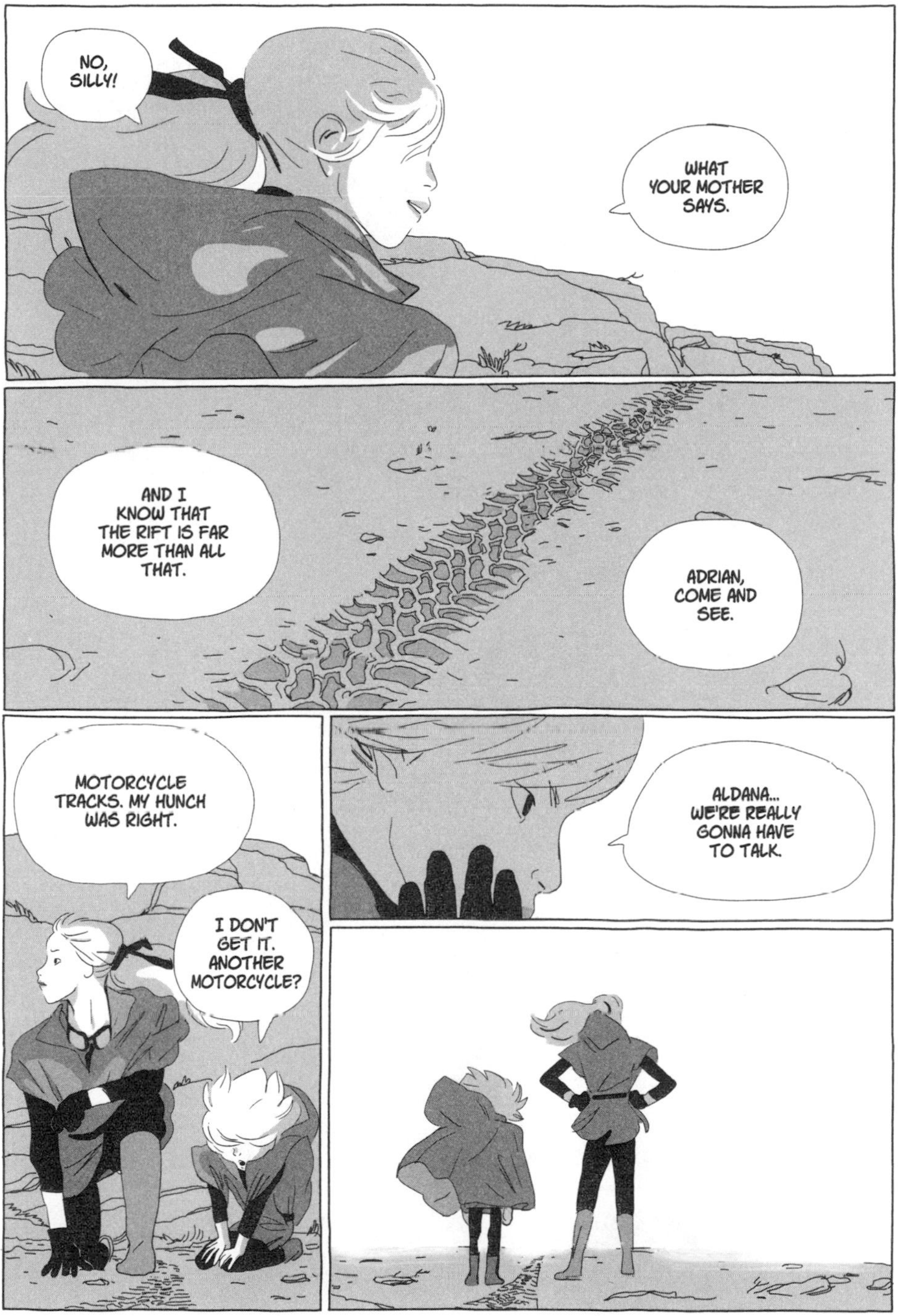
NO, SILLY!
WHAT YOUR MOTHER SAYS.
AND I KNOW THAT THE RIFT IS FAR MORE THAN ALL THAT.
ADRIAN, COME AND SEE.
MOTORCYCLE TRACKS. MY HUNCH WAS RIGHT.
I DON'T GET IT. ANOTHER MOTORCYCLE?
ALDANA... WE'RE REALLY GONNA HAVE TO TALK.

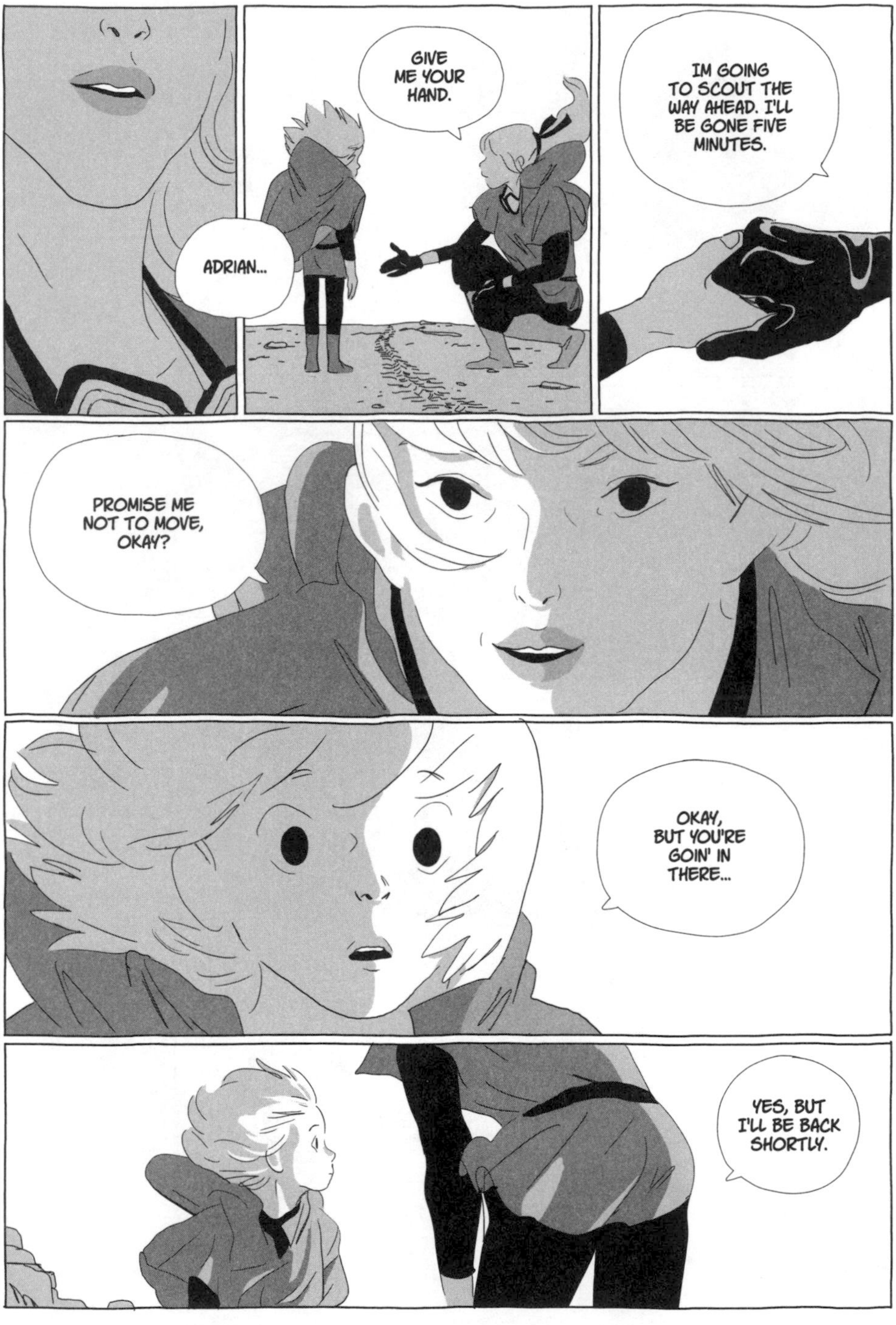
ADRIAN...
GIVE ME YOUR HAND.
IM GOING TO SCOUT THE WAY AHEAD. I'LL BE GONE FIVE MINUTES.
PROMISE ME NOT TO MOVE, OKAY?
OKAY, BUT YOU'RE GOIN' IN THERE...
YES, BUT I'LL BE BACK SHORTLY.

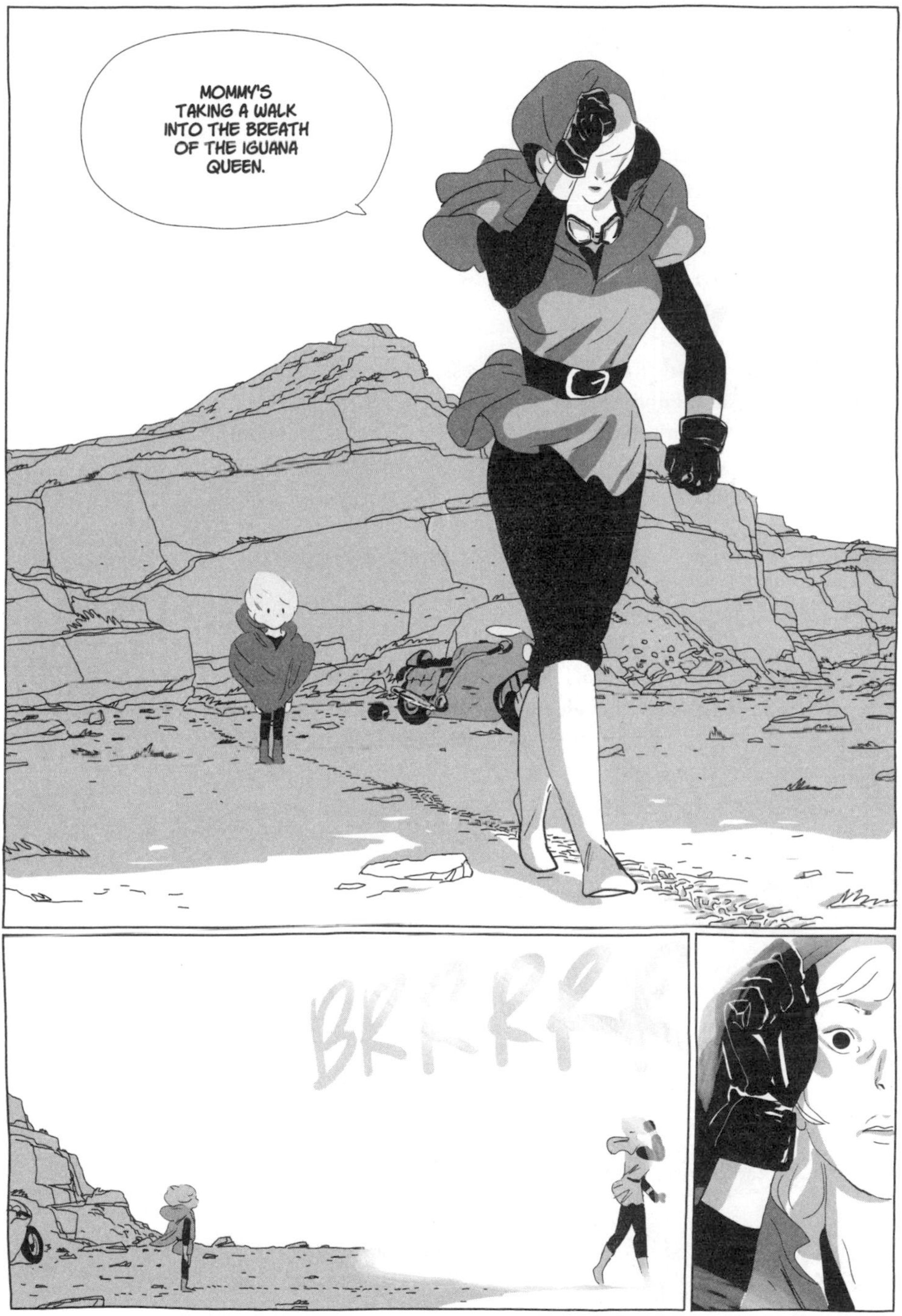
MOMMY'S TAKING A WALK INTO THE BREATH OF THE IGUANA QUEEN.

First Second

New York

Lastman tome 2 copyright © 2013 Casterman
English translation by Alexis Siegel
English translation copyright © 2015 by First Second

Published by First Second
First Second is an imprint of Roaring Brook Press,
a division of Holtzbrinck Publishing Holdings Limited Partnership
175 Fifth Avenue, New York, New York 10010

Cataloging-in-Publication Data is on file at the Library of Congress

ISBN: 978-1-62672-047-3

First Second books may be purchased for business or promotional use.
For information on bulk purchases please contact Macmillan Corporate
and Premium Sales Department at (800) 221-7945 x5442 or by email at
specialmarkets@macmillan.com.

Originally published in France by Casterman as *Lastman tome 2.*

First American edition 2015

Book design by Rob Steen

Printed in the United States of America

10 9 8 7 6 5 4 3 2 1